T0306020

Market Investigations

In many economic sectors – the digital industries being first and foremost – the market power of dominant firms has been steadily increasing and is rarely challenged by competitors. Existing competition laws and regulations have been unable to make markets more contestable. This book argues that a new competition tool is needed: market investigations. This tool allows authorities to intervene in markets which do not function as they should, due to market features such as network effects, scale economies, switching costs, and behavioural biases. The book explains the role of market investigations, assesses their use in the few jurisdictions where they exist, and discusses how they should be designed. In so doing, it provides an invaluable and timely instrument to both practitioners and academics.

MASSIMO MOTTA is the author of *Competition Policy: Theory and Practice* (Cambridge University Press, 2004), and the co-author of *Exclusionary Practices. The Economics of Monopolisation and Abuse of Dominance* (Cambridge University Press, 2018). He was the chief competition economist of the European Commission from 2013 to 2016.

MARTIN PEITZ is the co-author of *Industrial Organization: Markets and Strategies* (Cambridge University Press, 2nd ed., 2015) and *The Economics of Platforms: Concepts and Strategy* (Cambridge University Press, 2021). He is co-director of the Mannheim Centre for Competition and Innovation (MaCCI).

HEIKE SCHWEITZER was one of three special advisors to Commissioner Vestager on future challenges of digitisation for competition policy and co-authored the report on *Competition policy for the digital era*. She co-chaired the German governmental Commission *Competition Law 4.0* and advised the German Economic Ministry on the reform of the regime of abuse control in the context of the 10th amendment to the German Competition Law.

Market Investigations

A New Competition Tool for Europe?

Edited by

MASSIMO MOTTA
Pompeu Fabra University

MARTIN PEITZ
University of Mannheim

HEIKE SCHWEITZER
Humboldt University of Berlin

CAMBRIDGE
UNIVERSITY PRESS

CAMBRIDGE
UNIVERSITY PRESS

University Printing House, Cambridge CB2 8BS, United Kingdom

One Liberty Plaza, 20th Floor, New York, NY 10006, USA

477 Williamstown Road, Port Melbourne, VIC 3207, Australia

314–321, 3rd Floor, Plot 3, Splendor Forum, Jasola District Centre,
New Delhi – 110025, India

103 Penang Road, #05-06/07, Visioncrest Commercial, Singapore 238467

Cambridge University Press is part of the University of Cambridge.

It furthers the University's mission by disseminating knowledge in the pursuit of
education, learning, and research at the highest international levels of excellence.

www.cambridge.org
Information on this title: www.cambridge.org/9781316513163
DOI: 10.1017/9781009072007

First published 2022

A catalogue record for this publication is available from the British Library.

Library of Congress Cataloging-in-Publication Data
Names: Motta, Massimo, editor. | Peitz, Martin, editor. | Schweitzer, Heike, editor.
Title: Market investigations : a new competition tool for Europe? / edited by Massimo
   Motta, Pompeu Fabra University, Martin Peitz, University of Mannheim, Heike
   Schweitzer, Humboldt University of Berlin.
Description: Cambridge, United Kingdom ; New York, NY : Cambridge University Press,
   2022. | Includes bibliographical references and index.
Identifiers: LCCN 2021037866 (print) | LCCN 2021037867 (ebook) |
   ISBN 9781316513163 (hardback) | ISBN 9781009073189 (paperback) |
   ISBN 9781009072007 (epub)
Subjects: LCSH: Competition. | Competition, Unfair. | Information technology. |
   Business–Data processing. | BISAC: BUSINESS & ECONOMICS / Labor / General
Classification: LCC HF1414 .M366 2022 (print) | LCC HF1414 (ebook) |
   DDC 338.6/048–dc23
LC record available at https://lccn.loc.gov/2021037866
LC ebook record available at https://lccn.loc.gov/2021037867

ISBN 978-1-316-51316-3 Hardback

Contents

Figures

Tables

Contributors

TEMBINKOSI BONAKELE
The Competition Commission of South Africa

GREGORY S. CRAWFORD
University of Zurich and Center for Economic Policy Research

AMELIA FLETCHER
University of East Anglia

PIERRE LAROUCHE
University of Montreal

MASSIMO MOTTA
Pompeu Fabra University

REENA DAS NAIR
University of Johannesburg

MARTIN PEITZ
University of Mannheim

PATRICK REY
University Toulouse Capitole

SIMON ROBERTS
University of Johannesburg

MONIKA SCHNITZER
Ludwig Maximilian University of Munich

HEIKE SCHWEITZER
Humboldt University of Berlin

ALEXANDRE DE STREEL
University of Namur and College of Europe

RICHARD WHISH
Kings College London

1 | Market Investigations in the EU
A Road Map

MASSIMO MOTTA, MARTIN PEITZ,
AND HEIKE SCHWEITZER

1.1 The European Commission and the Quest for a New Competition Tool

Policy makers around the world are increasingly worried about developments in some digital markets and, in particular, digital platforms that use business practices to obtain an advantage vis-à-vis competitors in vertically related activities (e.g., self-preferencing) or that use their advantages, for example, in data collection and analytics to gain the upper hand over competitors in adjacent markets. Network effects and economies of scale and scope are seen as drivers of market tipping, possibly leading to an entrenched position of the most successful or lucky firm to the detriment of consumers in the long run. This is reflected by the thinking of the European Commission. As European Commission Vice President Margrethe Vestager put it,

digitisation is making it harder to keep competition working the way that it should .... There can be a constant risk that by abusing their power, big companies will push a market to the tipping point, where competition is gone forever. That the spring will be stretched so far that it no longer snaps back – that just ordering companies to stop their harmful behaviour is no longer enough, to bring competition back to these markets.[1]

In her mission letter from December 2019, European Commission President von der Leyen gave Executive Vice-President Vestager the task to make sure that "competition policy and rules are fit for the modern economy" as well as to "strengthening competition enforcement in all sectors."[2] The European Commission then identified

---

[1] Vestager, Competition in a Digital Age: Changing Enforcement for Changing Times, speech delivered at ASCOLA Annual Conference, June 26, 2020
[2] See https://ec.europa.eu/commission/commissioners/sites/comm-cwt2019/files/commissioner_mission_letters/mission-letter-margrethe-vestager_2019_en.pdf.

1

situations where the existing legal framework would not be sufficient to deal with this task:

The enforcement experience of the Commission and national competition authorities, and the reflection process on the fitness of the existing competition rules have helped identify certain structural competition problems that these rules cannot tackle (e.g. monopolisation strategies by non-dominant companies with market power) or cannot address in the most effective manner (e.g. parallel leveraging strategies by dominant companies into multiple adjacent markets).[3]

As a result, Vice-President Vestager proposed to introduce market investigations as a "New Competition Tool" (NCT) aimed at complementing existing legal instruments[4] and whose goal and scope was summarized thus:

This new tool would let us deal with structural problems with competition, when we can't do that with the powers that we already have – or when those existing powers would be much less effective. It would let us investigate markets, in the same rigorous way that we already look into individual cases .... And if we did find problems, we could intervene. Not by fining companies, or finding them guilty of breaking the rules – but by imposing obligations that would protect competition. That could involve duties to behave in a certain way .... As a last resort, it could even mean breaking up companies, to protect competition.[5]

What are the competition problems that existing competition tools fail to catch, which lead to harm to consumers and society? Among others, it is about firm behavior in a gray zone of competition law; that is, firm behavior that harms consumers but is not explicitly prohibited under competition law. One such example is *tacit collusion*. Again, quoting from the Vestager speech,

it would mean we could deal with concentrated markets where companies keep their prices in line, not by agreeing to form a cartel, but just by

---

[3] European Commission, Incept Impact Assessment "New Competition Tool," 2 June 2020, Ref. Ares(2020)2836004–02/06/2020.

[4] "This tool wouldn't replace the powers we already have. We'd still primarily investigate cartels, agreements that harm competition, and abuses of power under those existing rules. But the new tool would also allow us to act when those rules aren't enough to keep markets competitive." Vestager (fn. 1)

[5] Ibid.

taking care not to undercut each other. That tacit collusion can be especially easy in a transparent digital world like ours, where companies can constantly watch each other's prices, and change their own very quickly in response. When there's no agreement, that's not illegal under the rules as they are now – even though it means that consumers end up paying more than they should. But with this new tool, we could tackle this problem.[6]

There are markets with lack of competition because of institutional features or industry-wide business practices in which interventions may lead to more competitive outcomes to the benefit of consumers and society. While interventions to rule out certain opaque business practices may be considered to be the realm of consumer protection policy, some of these practices harm consumers because of the associated market power they give to firms. If none of these firms is deemed to have significant market power, existing competition law will find it difficult to deal with their practices. What is more, some institutional features are largely outside the control of individual firms; interventions that remove obstacles to competition could then be part of the remedies of a market investigation.

A more recent concern is the winner-takes-all feature of some markets and the tendency of tipping with one firm obtaining an entrenched position – that is, that it becomes difficult to be replaced. This mostly applies to "digital" markets when economies of scale and scope or network effects are pronounced. As Vestager mentions in her speech:

We could also deal better with markets that are prone to tip. We could move a lot faster to prevent this from happening, by stepping in as soon as a company starts to misuse its power to drive out competition – even if it isn't yet big enough to have broken the competition rules as they stand. And with just one investigation, we could deal with a situation where a gatekeeper platform is using its power to drive out competition in a whole series of markets.[7]

In light of the challenges in some markets called digital, one possible path was to restrict market investigations to such markets. In her speech, Vestager discussed this possibility:

---

[6] Ibid.   [7] Ibid.

Many of the biggest issues that this tool could help us resolve are linked to digital markets. But I doubt that it would make sense to apply it only to these markets – instead of covering the whole economy, as our existing competition powers do.[8]

Vestager gives two reasons not to follow such a narrow approach. The first is conceptual: "The sort of issues I've discussed come up in many other markets as well. In fact, the Greek, Icelandic and British competition authorities have so far only used this type of power in markets that aren't digital." The other reason is that it is difficult to draw a meaningful dividing line between "digital" and "non-digital." As Vestager pointed out, "the digital transition is affecting pretty much every industry there is. So it's hard to draw the line between what's digital and what isn't – especially when you consider that the rules we come up with now should be ready for the future, when that line may get even more blurred."[9]

As we put this book together, looking across the Channel, a recent market investigation in the UK is about funeral services.[10] Do they belong to the "digital" market in times of the COVID-19 pandemic?

Thus, the stage had been well prepared. A new competition tool for Europe: market investigations that allow the European Commission to address structural competition problems in an effective and efficient way. Why do we need a book on this new competition tool even before the tool has been implemented? Well, one way of reading the course of events is that legislative efforts have come to a halt. Another reading is that they have been redirected in a very specific way. Either way, market investigations as a horizontal competition tool appear not to be politically viable at the moment,[11] with recent legislative proposals aiming at limiting the use of such a tool exclusively to the digital industry (however defined).

---

[8] Ibid.   [9] Ibid.
[10] For details, see https://www.gov.uk/cma-cases/funerals-market-study. See also the Annex (Section 5.9) of Whish, Chapter 5.
[11] "The Commission's decision to drop the idea of a wide-ranging instrument to target only tech companies is likely to please the NCT's powerful enemies. Germany's Federation of German Industries (BDI) and France's Movement of the Enterprises of France (MEDEF) both strongly pushed back against an instrument that would apply to the whole economy." Kayali, Brussels eyes bigger stick to take on Big Tech, politico.eu, October 12, 2020.

However, we do believe that market investigations merit a full academic discussion as a new horizontal competition tool. Our aim is to revive this discussion.[12]

1.2 The New Competition Tool's Place in the European Competition Policy: The Legal Context

A core reason for the failure to introduce a general market investigation regime at the European level has apparently been the difficulty to find a workable legal basis for its introduction – a question directly linked to the relation between the NCT and EU competition law. Article 103 TFEU empowers the Council to pass appropriate regulations or directives giving effect to the principles set out in Articles 101 and 102 TFEU, on a proposal from the Commission and after consultations with the European Parliament. A European market investigation regime would, however, reach beyond Articles 101 and 102 TFEU. The fact that market investigations are not broadly used in the Member States so far stands in the way of using Article 114 TFEU as a legal basis for a European market investigation regime. The recent debates and studies on the NCT would appear to back up an argument that a European market investigation can be considered a necessary instrument to effectively ensure undistorted competition in the internal market, such that Article 352 TFEU would provide a viable legal basis. But Article 352 TFEU would require the Council to act unanimously.

Strong arguments are required, therefore, to complement the existing competition rules by a novel market investigation regime. The economic considerations are summarized below and further explored in Chapter 2 of this volume. On the legal side, the interaction

---

[12] This discussion may take place not only at the EU level but also in its Member States (or countries outside the EU). This discussion has at least started in Sweden. In 2021, the Swedish Competition Authority (SCA) released the report "The competition on digital platform markets in Sweden." In the English summary, it says that the "SCA proposes that work be initiated to investigate the need for and design of a flexible legal framework that can be used to investigate and remedy competition concerns that cannot, or cannot in an effective manner, be remedied under the current competition law prohibitions. One legal framework that may be able to fulfil these needs is that of market investigations that the British competition authority CMA has the possibility to conduct. A similar proposal was also presented by the European Commission ('New Competition Tool,' NCT), but this proposal has only in part been integrated within the DMA proposal."

between the long-established legal framework and a novel empowerment of the Commission to intervene ex ante and on a significantly
broader basis must be explored. So far, Articles 101 and 102 TFEU
have not only served as a basis for the Commission, national competition authorities, and courts to intervene to protect competition, but
they have likewise defined the limits of intervention. A European
market investigation instrument would provide the Commission
with a much wider discretion to meddle in the functioning of markets
and to engage in pro-active market design. Ongoing debates about
an increased politization of competition policy – be it with a view
to industrial policy or to sustainability goals – illustrate the risks
associated with such an empowerment.

Furthermore, the interaction between a European market investigation regime and Articles 101 and 102 TFEU needs further exploration. This is so, in particular, because market investigations might
have some overlaps with the existing competition rules, rather than
purely complementing them. Apart from addressing certain gaps of
competition law, this new tool should enable the Commission to
engage in a more holistic analysis of possible market failures and to
more effectively address certain market features that tend to produce
anti-competitive outcomes in the longer run but will typically go
beyond the reach of remedial action in infringement proceedings:
Article 7 Regulation 1/2003 remedies are focused on putting an end
to an infringement, not on addressing the features of the market that
hamper competition. A future market investigation regime, on the
other hand, would be justified by its ambition to preserve or restore
the possibility for competition in reaction to the special features of the
market identified that may hamper competition. Given the vaster
remedial powers of the Commission in the context of a market investigation regime, concerns could arise that it would tend to displace
traditional competition law enforcement and induce the Commission
to engage in potentially far-reaching "market engineering," bypassing
some of the procedural and judicial checks that come with Articles
101 and 102 TFEU.

Where a new market investigation instrument would come with pros
and cons from a legal and institutional perspective, much turns on an
economic analysis: Which forms of malfunctioning of competition are
currently not, or not effectively, addressed by competition law rules,
and how could market investigations contribute to closing these gaps?

1.3 Economic Rationales for a Market Investigation Tool in the EU

In some sectors, market mechanisms do not function as well as they should, for at least two reasons. First, they may be characterized by market features that are not necessarily caused by the firms' behavior (although they may be reinforced by it) – such as scale or scope economies, (direct or indirect) network effects, switching costs and lock-in effects, asymmetric information, and behavioral biases by consumers. Second, they may be adversely affected by the conduct of the firms themselves – such as (tacit or explicit) collusion, other (horizontal or vertical) agreements, contractual clauses imposed on consumers, and business practices that may be deemed abusive. Note also that these two reasons may coexist within the same sector.

"Traditional" competition law tools in the EU would not allow to restore effective competition in markets that do not function properly due to the market features mentioned above, because such features are not, or not entirely, the product of firms' actions. Further, competition law provisions might not allow to take care of firms' conduct that may nonetheless have anti-competitive effects. For instance, competition law does not preclude firms from tacitly colluding (and for good reasons); and as things stand, there are few obstacles for rivals to have minority shareholding in each other, or to have common owners, although this may dampen market competition and/or possibly promote collusive outcomes. Arguably, there may also exist business practices that may be anti-competitive but for which the intervention threshold is for various reasons very high or the timing of intervention very long, thereby making it difficult to use competition law in a timely and effective way. This implies that only a subset of the potentially anti-competitive conduct of firms may be covered by the competition law provisions contained in Articles 101 and 102 TFEU and the Merger Regulation.

For these reasons, an economic argument can be made that it would be desirable to integrate the existing competition tools with a new instrument consisting of market investigations, which may help promote effective competition in situations where markets do not work properly.

Furthermore, there may exist markets that are not currently experiencing problems but that for different reasons (whether conduct by the incumbent or other market features, or both) may be at risk in the near future. In such cases, it is conceivable that market investigations might provide a *preventive* tool of intervention that is currently not available under EU competition law.

A market investigation should identify the mechanisms that lock competition in the market and hence the interventions that should possibly neutralize those mechanisms and unlock competition. Whatever the theory of harm that may justify such an investigation, in order to address consumer harm in a meaningful way, the European Commission must have the power to implement suitable remedies, including structural ones.

This does not mean, however, that market investigations are the panacea of markets or that they should replace the central role of Articles 101 and 102. Markets are complex, and different market features and firms' conduct interact to determine market outcomes in ways that are not always easy to foresee. In other words, considerable uncertainty may exist about the impact of a concrete intervention. In particular, while some remedies have virtually no likely "side-effects" and hence could be imposed relatively safely, others may have adverse consequences, not only on the firms at issue but also on consumers – and hence trade-offs should be carefully considered before remedies are imposed.

More generally, a market investigation will employ the scarce resources of an antitrust authority and may have significant costs (for instance, in terms of uncertainty) for the firms operating in the sector. A necessary condition for opening a market investigation should therefore be that the potential consumer harm is sufficiently large (due to long-run effects or to immediate serious harm), and one could foresee that there may be feasible and appropriate remedies. Furthermore, in each specific case, the European Commission will also have to consider whether a market investigation is the preferred instrument to solve the problem and is superior to traditional competition law tools such as Articles 101 or 102 or even sectoral regulation (to the extent that they are applicable).

1.4 "Market Investigations" in the Digital Markets Act

The Commission's consultation on the NCT revealed some support in favor of the introduction of a general, cross-sectoral market investigation regime "UK style." However, with its proposed legislative package of December 15, 2020, the Commission has opted for a narrow scope of the market investigation. The proposed Digital Markets Act (DMA), which has a quasi-regulatory approach and comprises a list of "dos" and "don'ts" for the digital platforms with "gatekeeping power," foresees the use of a market investigation tool in various respects. But its scope is tied to the scope of the DMA itself: market investigations shall be used as an instrument to make the DMA future proof, namely, to expand the list of "core platform services" as set out in Article 2(2) of the draft DMA; to designate gatekeepers that meet the requirements of Article 3(1) of the draft DMA, but do not satisfy the quantitative thresholds of Article 3(2) of the draft DMA; or to update the list of obligations for gatekeepers as laid down in Articles 5 and 6 of the draft DMA (see Article 10 DMA).

The draft DMA is conceived as an ex ante regulation of the provision of core platform services offered by entities that qualify as "gatekeepers" within the meaning of Article 3 of the draft DMA. "Core platform services," as defined in Article 2(2) of the draft DMA, shall encompass online intermediation services, online search engines, online social networking services, video-sharing platform services, messenger services, operating systems, cloud computing services, and advertising services provided by a provider of any of the prementioned core platform services. A provider of such services shall be designated as a "gatekeeper" if it has a significant impact on the internal market, serves as an important gateway for business users to reach end users, and enjoys an entrenched and durable position in its operations or will foreseeably enjoy such a position in the near future (Article 3(1) of the draft DMA).

These preconditions shall be presumed to be satisfied if the core platform services are provided in at least three Member States and certain quantitative thresholds are met, namely, if the undertaking to which the provider of core platform services belongs achieves an annual EEA turnover of no less than 6.5 billion Euros or where the average market capitalization or fair market value amounted to at least 65 billion in the last financial year, if the core platform service has more than 45 million monthly active end users established or is located in the Union and has more than 10,000 yearly active business users established in the Union in the last financial year, and if these thresholds were met in each of the last three financial years (Article 3(2) of

the draft DMA). According to Commissioner Thierry Breton, an estimated 10–15 platforms may meet these criteria.

But a provider of core platform services may qualify as a "gatekeeper" even if it fails these thresholds, provided that it meets the
criteria set out in Article 3(1) of the draft DMA (see Article 3(6) of
the draft DMA). In order to designate a gatekeeper in such cases,
the Commission must conduct a "market investigation." Relevant
criteria for the gatekeeper qualification include the size of the platform
services provider; the number of business users depending on the core
platform service to reach end users and the number of end users;
the entry barriers deriving from network effects and data driven
advantages, economies of scale and scope, including, with regard to
data, a business user or end user lock-in; and other structural market
characteristics.

In the provision of core platform services that serve as an important
gateway to business users to reach end users, all gatekeepers will then
be required to comply with the rules of conduct listed in Articles 5 and
6, where Article 5 contains those obligations that the Commission
considers to be self-explanatory, and Article 6 lists those obligations
that may need further specification. In essence, the obligations set out
in Articles 5 and 6 of the draft DMA are a collection of the remedies
that have been imposed upon dominant digital platforms in various
competition law proceedings at the EU or at the Member States level
over the last couple of years or are currently being considered for
imposition. Following a "one size fits all" approach, this code of
conduct shall apply to the provision of all core platform services that
serve as an important gateway for business users to reach end users and
are provided by designated gatekeepers, and both Article 5 and Article
6 are designed as per se rules: with one exception – namely, designated
gatekeepers that do not yet enjoy an entrenched and durable position
but will foreseeably do so in the near future (see Article 15(4)) – the
draft DMA does not foresee a tailoring of the rules of conduct to the
individual gatekeepers, the possibility of an objective justification, or
an efficiency defense. According to Article 10 of the draft DMA, the
Commission shall be empowered to adopt delegated acts to update the
lists of obligations where, based on a market investigation, it has
identified a need for doing so to address practices that limit the contestability of core platform services or that are "unfair" in the same way as
the practices currently addressed in Article 5 and 6.

The envisioned market investigation procedure is further specified in Chapter IV of the draft DMA. Any market investigation shall start with an opening decision that, inter alia, specifies the purpose of the investigation. The draft DMA distinguishes between a market investigation for designating gatekeepers (Article 15), market investigations into new services and new practices (Article 17), and market investigations into systematic non-compliance (Article 16). Different time lines shall apply in the different settings – for example, a market investigation for designating gatekeepers that do not meet the thresholds set out in Article 3(2) shall be concluded within twelve months from the opening decision, with preliminary findings being communicated within six months, whereas a market investigation following an alleged gatekeeper's claim that it does not fulfill the requirements of Article 3(1) despite meeting the Article 3 (2) thresholds shall be concluded within five months from the opening decision, with preliminary findings being communicated within three months (see Article 15). A market investigation into new services potentially to be added to the list of core platform services or to detect types of practices that may limit the contestability of core platform services or may be unfair and are not effectively addressed by the DMA shall result into the issuing of a public report within 24 months from the opening decision. Where appropriate, the report shall be accompanied by a proposal to amend the DMA to include additional core platform services or by a delegated act amending the rules of conduct in Articles 5 and 6 DMA (see Article 16). A market investigation into a gatekeeper's systematic non-compliance with the obligations set out in Articles 5 and 6 shall be concluded within twelve months from the opening decision, with a statement of objections being communicated to the gatekeeper concerned within six months, but with a possibility for extension of no more than six months. The non-compliance market investigation shall establish whether a designated gatekeeper has systematically infringed the rules laid down in Articles 5 and 6 and has further strengthened or extended its gatekeeper position thereby. If this is so, the Commission can impose behavioral or structural remedies that are proportionate to the infringements and necessary to ensure compliance with the DMA. A systematic infringement is presumed where at least three non-compliance or fining decisions have been issued within the last five years (see Article 16).

As this brief overview shows, market investigations of some sort are an important element of the proposed DMA: it partially adopts the core idea of the market investigation instrument to identify structural features of the market that create particular risks to competition and to react to such risks by imposing rules of conduct, regardless of an initial finding of a position of dominance and an infringement of Article 102 TFEU. But the DMA market investigations are very much part of the regulatory regime that the DMA proposes to establish in the first place, rather than a flexible instrument to identify and remedy competition problems that are currently not effectively addressed by EU competition law. And they are of course limited to the digital sector only.

1.5 Outline of the Book

Given these limitations of the market investigation mechanism in the Digital Markets Act, the debate whether such an instrument will be needed to complement EU competition law in the future remains open. The following chapters provide context and shed light on important issues in this debate.

Chapter 2, by Massimo Motta and Martin Peitz, assesses the possible role of a market investigation tool endowed with broad remedies, when a market suffers from competition problems and infringement cases under 101 TFEU and 102 TFEU would be infeasible or ineffective. The chapter lays out a number of theories of harm, that is, reasons why certain market features or behavior by market participants may lead to consumer harm compared to a relevant counterfactual. The report identifies theories of harm (i) in markets in which none of the firms is dominant and (ii) in markets with a dominant firm but Article 102 TFEU is not effective or applicable or there may be a dominant firm in the future. It also argues that the European Commission should look for simple measures as "intervention triggers" for a market investigation and identifies some possible triggers. While some of the identified harms are more likely or more pronounced in digital markets, the authors argue that a presumption that narrowing the tool to primarily address competition problems in digital markets would be misguided. Finally, when sector regulation is, in principle, applicable, the authors see the market investigation tool as filling a gap between standard competition tools and sector regulation.

Chapter 3, by Heike Schweitzer, discusses the institutional set-up and procedural design of a possible future European market investigation regime. The institutional framework and procedural rules must be tailored to promote the core goals of the new instrument, namely, to address competition problems that do not primarily follow from conduct but from "features of the market," such that a European market investigation – contrary to traditional infringement proceedings – will not be of a quasi-criminal nature but a purely administrative proceedings and will allow for a particular timely intervention. Against this background, the following questions are raised: How does the market investigation regime interact with Article 101 and 102 TFEU enforcement and sector inquiries at the EU level and at the national level? How can the procedure be structured such as to allow for a timely and effective intervention? What can be done to allow for a less adversarial and more participative interaction between the Commission and market actors? Furthermore, the remedial regime, voluntary commitments, the possibility for interim measures, and judicial review are discussed.

Chapter 4, by Pierre Larouche and Alexandre de Streel, reviews the relationship among competition law and the various sectoral regulatory regimes making up EU economic law and, on that basis, make recommendations regarding how a wide and a narrow version of a market investigation could be integrated in EU economic law. The authors consider the integration of the broad market investigation to be easy. At the systemic level, this broad version could usefully close regulatory gaps. At the substantive level, it should rest on economic analysis, yet without being straitjacketed within specific competition law analysis. At the institutional level, a close transversal cooperation between the authority in charge of the market investigation and the relevant NRA(s) is deemed necessary. However, with the European Commission's draft DMA, a narrow version of the market investigation is on the table that could also easily be integrated in EU economic law. At the systemic level, the DMA complements competition law where practice has shown that competition law is ineffective in solving competitive problems. At the substantive level, the standards, the criteria, and the indicators used to implement the three types of DMA market investigations are not straightjacketed within competition methodologies but should be applied and interpreted with sound economic analysis. At the institutional level, the Commission would acquire concurrent regulatory and competition powers and it should explain the criteria it will use to choose between those different powers when addressing the conducts of the digital gatekeepers. Moreover,

given the possible parallel application of the DMA by the Commission
and national competition law by the NCAs, Larouche and de Streel
consider it key that the cooperation between the Commission and the
NCAs is ensured.

Chapter 5, by Richard Whish, provides an account of the market
investigation provisions on the UK Enterprise Act of 2002, which
enables the Competition and Markets Authority (CMA) to investigate
markets and to determine whether any "features" of a market prevent,
restrict, or distort competition. If the CMA discovers "adverse effects on
competition," powers are available to achieve as "comprehensive a
solution as is reasonable and practicable" through the imposition of
remedies, up to and including mandatory divestiture. This chapter
describes these powers, explains the institutional regime within which
decisions are made, and the procedure that the CMA follows in market
investigation cases. Some other jurisdictions possess similar powers to
those contained in the Enterprise Act. In particular, the chapter describes
the powers available to the competition authorities in Greece, Iceland,
Mexico, and South Africa.

Chapter 6, by Tembinkosi Bonakele, Reena das Nair, and Simon
Roberts, assesses the South African record with market inquiries,
which are the equivalent of market investigations in other jurisdictions.
The authors find that market inquiries have been an important tool for
the Competition Commission of South Africa to address competition
problems reflecting entrenched positions of firms with market power in
key sectors. Inquiries have been completed into banking, private
healthcare, liquefied petroleum gas, grocery retail, and data services,
with inquires in passenger transport and online intermediation platforms underway. In a comparative review of the inquiries, the authors
find that the inquisitorial process has been very valuable in identifying
and remedying competition issues more expeditiously than the adversarial process in enforcement investigations. This has been the case
where independent panels were used to conduct the inquiries as well as
where the inquiries were undertaken by the Commission's own team.
Issues relating to competition policy questions such as barriers to entry
and the ability of smaller firms to compete have also been canvassed in
inquiries. Recommendations on these "competition-plus" issues have
tended to require improved regulation and/or related policy measures,
for which inquiries have played an important agenda-setting role.
Inquiries have also been used to address wider questions of public

policy, often at the request of government, and here, while important data and analysis have been brought into the public domain, the impacts are less clear.

Chapter 7, by Gregory Crawford, Patrick Rey, and Monika Schnitzer, provides an assessment of the economic merits of the NCT, as it was considered in Summer 2020 by the European Commission as a tool to address structural competition problems in a timely and effective manner. The NCT has strong analogies to the UK's "markets regime," which empowers the UK competition regulator, the CMA, to initiate market studies and investigations. The authors review the UK's markets regime and survey some of the competition concerns the regime is intended to address. This includes a selective review of UK market studies and investigations to illustrate some of the ways these concerns have been explored and a description of the remedies imposed or proposed (in the case of market studies or ongoing investigations). The authors conclude with a critical evaluation of the functioning of the UK's markets regime in light of this evidence and offer seven recommendations regarding the merits and design of market investigations as an NCT for the EU. In sum, they see a strong case for the introduction of an NCT to address factors that prevent effective competition in markets, and they see no benefit to limiting it to specific sectors and to dominant firms.

Chapter 8, by Amelia Fletcher, considers the pros and cons of market investigations in the context of the UK regime. The author sees them as a valuable addition to the standard competition law toolkit and concludes that this would likely be true also at EU level, both when applied to digital platforms and more widely. Since the tool is potentially so powerful and flexible, the author argues in favor of strong procedural checks and balances. These should guard against confirmation bias and politicization. While powerful and flexible, the tool also has important limitations and thus, as the author argues, should not be viewed as a full solution to the issues raised by digital platforms but rather as a valuable complementary tool alongside new ex ante regulation. Interoperability is discussed as one example where the tools could valuably be used alongside each other.

2 Intervention Triggers and Underlying Theories of Harm*

MASSIMO MOTTA AND MARTIN PEITZ

2.1 Introduction

In this chapter, we explain why market investigations would be a useful New Competition Tool (NCT) to complement existing competition law and sector regulation. We also identify the circumstances where this tool could be deployed and discuss the theories of harm that it could address.

In Section 2.2, we argue that some markets may not work as they should, either because of market features that do not necessarily depend on firms' conduct (although firms' strategies may reinforce such features) or because firms may engage in business practices that are beneficial to them but may be detrimental to society. In the former case, traditional competition law tools would not help because they are not applicable at all. In the latter, they may be of limited use because there may exist firm behavior that, for different reasons, might not be unlawful despite being harmful to consumers (think of tacit collusion, for instance) or because competition law might intervene on a particular firm's business practice but not address the more general underlying competition problem. We shall offer some examples of "theories of harm" that may motivate the use of a complementary legal instrument such as the NCT, but we should stress that the list of possible circumstances where an NCT may be deployed cannot be exhaustive. We also discuss the types of remedies that are appropriate.

In Section 2.3, we look for possible intervention triggers, that is, data or information that may signal that a market investigation may be

* This chapter is based on the expert report "Intervention triggers and underlying theories of harm," which was prepared in 2020 for the Directorate-General Competition of the European Commission. Massimo Motta gratefully acknowledges financial aid from the Spanish Agencia Estatal de Investigación (AEI) (Project PID2019–109377GB-I00/AEI/10.13039/501100011033) and from "Ayudas Fundación BBVA a Equipos de Investigación Científica 2019" (project on "Digital platforms: Effects and policy implications"). Martin Peitz gratefully acknowledges financial support from the Deutsche Forschungsgemeinschaft through CRC TR 224 (project B05).

worthwhile. We shall argue that these triggers should be intimately related to the theory of harm. In other words, when it has a suspicion that a market does not perform as it should, the European Commission (EC) – or any other competition agency – will likely have some initial hypothesis about the reasons why in the market environment at hand competition is preliminarily thought of not being effective, and it will be that initial hypothesis that should guide toward possible intervention triggers. If, say, it is thought that tacit collusion may be the source of the problem, then one should look for those variables that are typically associated with collusive outcomes. In that section, we shall also suggest looking for triggers that consist of simple indicators, since it is highly unlikely that before starting a market investigation the EC be in possession of rich datasets. Finally, we shall discuss a few concrete intervention triggers.

Section 2.4 will conclude the chapter. We stress that the EC should start thinking of remedies already at the very early stages of a market investigation. In particular, it should start thinking of remedies as soon as a theory of harm is formulated (the type of remedy will of course depend on the theory of harm) and even before starting a market investigation officially: if it is unlikely that a useful remedy may be found or implemented, then such an investigation would have little point. The EC should also assess whether, given the problem at hand, a market investigation is preferable to alternative instruments, such as starting an investigation under Articles 101 or 102 TFEU.

Finally, building on our analysis, we shall conclude that we believe that a NCT allowing the EC to conduct market investigations and impose remedies under them would be a very welcome tool that would complement the currently available competition law tools, which (as argued in Section 2.2) do not always allow to redress situations in which the market does not perform well, often for reasons that do not depend on firms' conduct. This NCT should be designed in as broad terms as possible, and the EC should have the possibility to deploy it in all sectors of the economy where it could be needed, not just in digital markets.

2.2 Reasons Why Markets Do Not Always Work as They Should (and Traditional Competition Law Tools May Not Help)

In this section, we explain why markets do not always work as they should and traditional competition law tools may not help, either because they are not applicable at all or because they are of limited use (e.g., apply only to dominant firms or can only address a particular business practice but do not address the more general underlying competition problem).

More specifically, in Section 2.2.1, we spell out the possible role of the market investigation tool and how it fits into an effective competition policy environment more broadly. In Section 2.2.2, we elaborate on the features that may hinder markets from working properly or because of which competition is at risk and require timely or preventive interventions. In Section 2.2.3, we investigate theories of harm resulting from firm behavior that – for different reasons – may not be addressed adequately by traditional competition law tools. We shall also discuss what interventions could unlock competition. In Section 2.2.4, we comment more specifically upon which remedies might address certain theories of harm. Section 2.2.5 contains the main takeaways of this section.

2.2.1 Market Investigations and Their Possible Role in Competition Policy

In this section, we shall explain why market investigations would be a useful NCT to deal with markets that do not function properly and in which traditional competition law tools – for various reasons – do not help.

The starting point of our analysis is the presumption that markets tend to work reasonably well, but in some circumstances, which may not necessarily be ascribed to the firms operating in the markets at issue, they do not – in the sense that they would not result in consumers benefiting from low enough prices and satisfactory products, in terms of quality, range, and service.

Of course, there exist some special sectors where one would not expect competition to be effective and even perhaps to be desirable, and which are designed to be subject to sectoral regulation or to a public monopoly. For instance, some activities entail such large investments that no more than a single firm could afford paying the associated fixed sunk costs; or the negative externalities for society of creating the necessary infrastructure may be so high (in terms of environment, disruption for citizens, public health, etc.) that it is optimal to have only one such infrastructure; due to informational problems or behavioral patterns, consumers would systematically be badly served; or there may be considerations related to social justice, equality, or public good provision that may lead a government not to let the supply of the products to free market forces.

But – as we shall argue in more detail in Sections 2.2.2 and 2.2.3 – even in other sectors in which a priori market forces might deliver an efficient outcome, there may be reasons why they do not work as they should. By and large, these reasons could consist of (i) market features that are not necessarily caused by the firms' behavior (although they may be reinforced by it) – such as scale or scope economies, (direct or indirect) network effects, switching costs and lock-in effects, and behavioral biases by consumers or (ii) the conduct of the firms themselves – such as (tacit or explicit) collusion, other (horizontal or vertical) agreements, contractual clauses imposed on consumers, and abusive practices. Note also that (i) and (ii) may coexist within the same sector.

We argue in Section 2.2.2 that current "traditional" competition law tools in the EU would not allow to restore effective competition in markets that do not function properly due to reasons other than firms' conduct. Further, as argued in Section 2.2.3, they would not allow to take care of some of the firms' conduct that may have anti-competitive effects. For instance, competition law does not preclude firms from tacitly colluding (and for good reasons); and as things stand, there are few obstacles for rivals to have minority shareholding in each other, or to have common owners, although this may dampen market competition and/or possibly promote collusive outcomes. Arguably, there may also exist conduct that may be anti-competitive but for which the intervention threshold is for various reasons very high or the timing of intervention very long, thereby making it difficult to use competition law in a timely and effective way. This implies that only a subset of the conduct category (ii) may be covered by the competition law provisions contained in Articles 101 and 102 and the Merger Regulation. Furthermore, the other features (i) that may make a market malfunction, and which are not (entirely) caused by firms, cannot be addressed by those provisions either.

For these reasons, we believe that it would be desirable to integrate the existing competition tools with this NCT, which may help promote effective competition in situations where markets do not work properly.[1]

Finally, we should add that there may be some markets that are not currently experiencing problems, but that for different reasons (whether conduct by the incumbent, or other market features, or both) may be at risk in the near future. In such cases, it is conceivable that market investigation might provide a *preventive* tool of intervention that is currently not available under EU competition law.

In Sections 2.2.2–2.2.5, we elaborate on the issues that we have briefly summarized in these introductory remarks.

2.2.2 Market Features That May Hinder Markets from Working Properly or Because of Which Competition Is at Risk (Need for Timely or Preventive Interventions)

One may expect that – absent "problematic" conduct by the incumbent firms in an industry – the market would work well. After all, economists have been teaching generation after generation of students that markets self-correct: if there exists market power and incumbent firms set prices above average costs, some potential entrants will spot the opportunity to make profits and will want to enter the industry, thereby increasing competition, lowering prices, and reducing market power. Unfortunately, though, this self-correcting mechanism is not always present or does not work properly. There are a number of circumstances that prevent this mechanism from operating as it should. In what follows, we mention five categories of such market features that might hinder the good functioning of markets: (i) scale (or scope) economies; (ii) (direct or indirect) network effects; (iii) switching costs; (iv) asymmetric information and limited information; and (v) behavioral biases by consumers.

---

[1] We do not address here the issue of whether it might be optimal in certain cases to resort to sectoral regulation. However, in Section 2.5 we shall indirectly touch upon this point: if one identifies features that make it unlikely that competition could be effective, but it is very difficult or impossible to design a proper remedy under a market investigation, then regulation may be more adequate. In other instances, it may also be a matter of judgment how to negotiate the trade-off between a market investigation remedy and continuous regulation.

It is important to stress that these market features are often not caused by the incumbent firms, although their conduct may possibly exacerbate those features or their effects, and as such would generally be difficult for "traditional" competition law provisions to deal with. Also, even to the extent that they are under their control, it may actually be desirable that firms invest, for example, in increasing firm-specific network effects. For instance, an improved matching algorithm of a matching platform increases gains from trade for market participants and increases indirect network effects. However, a market investigation may in some cases allow to intervene so as to correct or reduce the effects of such features.

We note that market features such as the degree of consumer switching costs and the scalability of economic activities may well be related to a market being "digital," but they are neither necessary nor sufficient for a market to be classified as a digital market. Therefore, market features serve as a better guide toward identifying potential or actual competition problems than the finding that a market is digital.

2.2.2.1 Scale Economies and Fixed Costs

The self-correcting mechanism we briefly mentioned above is based on the idea that high prices and incumbent firms' earnings signal profit opportunities for entrants. But this is true only to a certain extent: a potential entrant knows that the moment it enters the industry, the incumbents will react, and competition will push prices downwards. The prices the entrant will expect, therefore, and on which its entry decision will be based, are necessarily lower than the current ones.

A simple (and admittedly extreme) example will illustrate this point. Suppose that there is only one firm in the market and that it is setting monopoly prices and making supra-normal profits. Another firm, selling the same homogeneous good and producing at the same marginal costs as the incumbent monopolist, could enter the market by paying some fixed set up costs. Suppose that, if entry takes place, competition would be very fierce (technically, there is "Bertrand competition," with firms setting prices). Then, the potential entrant expects that, if it enters, competition will drive prices down to marginal costs, and it will make zero gross profits. As a result, it will prefer not to enter, because if it did it would not be able to recover its fixed entry costs, no matter how small they are. The incumbent firm will then continue to set monopoly prices.

This simple example illustrates how the self-correcting mechanism that will supposedly reduce market power might not necessarily take place whenever there exist entry costs, fixed costs, or scale economies.[2] Of course, under less extreme circumstances, some entry – and hence some market power correction – may take place.[3] However, markets may possess the "finiteness property":[4] if consumers value the quality of the products, and quality depends on investments in R&D or advertising, then market concentration will be bounded below even when market size becomes arbitrarily large.[5] Intuitively, firms want to invest in order to increase the attractiveness of their products.[6] With such investments in quality or advertising expenses, only a limited number of firms can profitably operate in the industry. As a result, even if there are no exogenous barriers to entry, few firms (and

[2] The well-known contestable market theory states that even a monopolist would set prices equal to average costs, resulting in efficient market outcomes. See Baumol, Contestable markets: An uprising in the theory of industry structure, (1982) 72 *American Economic Review*, 1; Baumol/Panzar/Willig, *Contestable Markets and the Theory of Industry Structure*, 1982. But the theory assumes that the fixed costs of entry are recoverable and that prices cannot be easily adjusted, even as an entrant decides to enter, starts production, sets up a distribution network and begins to sell. In most markets, both assumptions are unlikely to hold.

[3] For instance, if there was less fierce competition (say, Cournot rather than Bertrand competition), capacity constraints, limited information about the competitor's costs, search costs, or horizontal product differentiation, then entry may take place, as long as fixed set-up costs are not too large. See, e.g., Belleflamme/Peitz, *Industrial Organization: Markets and Strategies*, 2nd. ed., 2015, Chap. 5–7.

[4] See, in particular, Shaked/Sutton, Product differentiation and industrial structure, (1987) 36 *Journal of Industrial Economics*, 131; and Sutton, *Sunk Costs and Market Structure*, 1992.

[5] This finiteness property may even hold if quality can be chosen for free. For models with vertical product differentiation, which have this property, see Gabszewicz/Thisse, Entry and exit in a differentiated industry, (1980) 20 *Journal of Economic Theory*, 340; Shaked/Sutton, Price competition through product differentiation, (1982) 49 *Review of Economic Studies*, 3; and Shaked/Sutton, Natural oligopolies, (1983) 51 *Econometrica*, 1469.

[6] Such investment outlays are "endogenous sunk costs." They are sunk because typically they cannot be recovered (or only partially) if the firm exits the market; and they are endogenous because their level is determined by the firms' decisions.

possibly only one) will coexist in the market, as their investments lead to endogenous barriers to entry.[7]

2.2.2.2 Network Effects

Another reason why a monopoly might persist despite the absence of "legal" barriers to entry is due to network effects, which arise whenever the utility of a consumer or user increases with the number of other consumers using the same product.[8]

Network effects can be *direct* or *indirect*. For the former, think of communications or social networks: the more people one can reach by, say, telephone, email, or instant messaging, or one can be in contact with through some social networking apps, the more satisfying these services will be. For the latter, think of mutual cross-group network effects: the number of other people using the same credit card as I do does not affect my utility directly, but it increases the chance that merchants will adopt this credit card as a means of payment, which does increase my utility from the card. The same applies to video game consoles. Each gamer indirectly benefits from more people buying a particular console because this attracts more game developers who will provide games for this console.

Whatever the reason for their existence, whenever network effects exist, they tend to favor the incumbents, which have already an established customer base, and will hinder the market chances of the entrants, which need to build up a sufficient customer base in order to be desirable for consumers. Among other things, the larger the

---

[7] Of course, there may also be firms with negligible market shares, covering small or niche segments of the market. But they would largely be irrelevant for competitive dynamics. It is important to understand that what matters for competition is that there exist firms that are sufficiently well-placed to discipline the market power possessed by the incumbent(s). Small-scale entry does not limit market power, although it may be a preliminary step in that direction.

[8] There is a huge literature on network effects. Early contributions were Katz/Shapiro, Network externalities, competition, and compatibility, (1985) 75 *American Economic Review*, 424; and Farrell/Saloner, Standardization, compatibility, and innovation, (1985) 16 *Rand Journal of Economics*, 70. For a recent overview with links to the literature on network effects and two-sided platforms, see Belleflamme/Peitz, Platforms and network effects, in: Corchon/Marini (eds.), *Handbook of Game Theory and Industrial Organization*, vol. II, 2018, p. 286–317. Data give rise to network effects and competitive advantage in Hagiu/Wright, Data-enabled learning, network effects and competitive advantage, 2020 (unpublished manuscript).

incumbents' customer base, the more mature the market (that is, the lower the number of prospective new buyers around), the more likely that consumers are "single-homing" (that is, they do not use more than one network good), and the more difficult it is for the entrants to challenge the incumbents. Since consumers' utility depends on both the inherent quality of the good and on the number of (current and future) users, it is not sufficient for an entrant to have a superior product. Nor will aggressive initial price offers necessarily be able to overcome the disadvantage created by network effects, for at least two reasons.

The first one is that in many industries characterized by network effects, prices are often zero for consumers – for example, firms that monetize their services through advertising and/or access to consumer data (think of social networks such as Facebook or search engines). Therefore, the strategy of offering very low introductory prices to gain market share may not be available to entrants (offering complementary services or usage subsidies may sometimes be possible, but negative prices are often limited by adverse selection problems, i.e., they attract users who are more interested in receiving the subsidy than in using the product or service extensively).

The second one is that such markets are affected by coordination issues. Each consumer may be very keen on the entrant's product, provided a minimum number of other consumers will also use it. Therefore, beliefs about what the others will do matter. If, for some reason, there is a widespread expectation that the entrant will not gather a sufficient customer base, nobody will buy from it, and the expectation will be self-fulfilling.[9]

The incumbency advantage due to network effects implies that the incumbent firm would remain dominant after entry even if it offered lower quality for equally sized networks than the entrant. From the viewpoint of the incumbent platform, "[p]recisely because various

---

[9] On the role of expectations in determining the fate of network industries, see the description of the fight for the standard of music reproduction between DIVX and DVD in Dranove/Gandal, The DVD-vs.-DIVX standard war: Empirical evidence of network effects and preannouncement effects, (2003) 12 *Journal of Economics & Management Strategy*, 363. For a discussion of several mechanisms according to which network effects lead to an incumbency advantage, see Biglaiser/Calvano/Crémer, Incumbency advantage and its value, (2019) 28 *Journal of Economics & Management Strategy*, 41.

users find it so difficult to coordinate to switch to an incompatible technology, control over a large installed base of users can be the greatest asset you can have."[10]

Although the existence of network effects is typically determined by the kind of product at issue rather than the result of particular firm conduct, it should be stressed that *incumbents might engage in practices that contribute to entry deterrence* or make it difficult for new firms to expand and gather sufficient custom. Leaving aside the usual abusive practices that a dominant incumbent may resort to in all other industries, such as discriminatory offers, exclusive contracts, tying, and refusing access to a platform,[11] which might in principle be taken care of by traditional competition law instruments, there may exist other practices that are intimately related to network industries and that may be less easily deterred by Article 102.

For instance, incumbents may be able to affect customers' expectations by making strategic announcements, such as spreading rumors that the rival's product has problems, that it is not getting enough users, that the incumbent is about to launch a new version that will be superior to the entrant's one, or announcing that it will incorporate some features that users find particularly attractive in the entrant's product.[12]

By the very nature of network effects, any choice by an incumbent that makes the entrant's product or service less compatible with its own will lower the chances of success of the entrant. In some cases, refusal or degradation of interoperability may be dealt with by

---

[10] Shapiro/Varian, *Information Rules: A Strategic Guide to the Network Economy*, 1999, at p. 185.

[11] On tying, see, e.g., Carlton/Waldman, The strategic use of trying to preserve and create market power in evolving industries, (2002) 33 *Rand Journal of Economics*, 194. On discriminatory pricing, see Giardino-Karlinger/Motta, Exclusionary pricing when scale matters, (2012) 60 *Journal of Industrial Economics*, 75. On exclusive dealing, see Doganoglu/Wright, Exclusive dealing with network effects, (2010) 28 *International Journal of Industrial Organization*, 145.

[12] For formal analyses of product preannouncements as deterrence strategies, see Bayus/Jain/Rao, Truth or consequences: An analysis of vaporware and new product announcements, (2001) 38 *Journal of Marketing Research*, 3; and Haan, Vaporware as a means of entry deterrence, (2003) 51 *Journal of Industrial Economics*, 345.

resorting to Article 102.[13] It would be difficult to argue that compulsory interoperability is always the best course of action. Indeed, while it does facilitate entry, it is not a policy without drawbacks in general, among other things, because (i) it may discourage entrants from developing competing standards or technologies and (ii) it may deprive an incumbent of the fruits of its investment and effort (which has disincentivizing effects). Still, on point (i), a situation where entrants may successfully introduce competing standards may be a very unlikely counterfactual. And on point (ii), the success of the incumbent may not be due to innovations that are worth protecting at the cost of locking the market forever. Consider, for instance, the telecom incumbents' claim of ownership of the telephone number of their clients, which, at the beginning of the telecom liberalization program, greatly hindered the chances of new firms to attract clients (because everyone would like to keep one's number when changing telephone provider): it would be hard to claim that assigning phone numbers was an innovation worth protecting. Accordingly, the imposition of mobile number portability was certainly a good policy.

This is also a good example of a situation where – facing locked competition in the market – an intervention through Articles 101 and 102 may not solve the problem: first, because there may not be an agreement among incumbents not to offer portability, and there may not necessarily be a dominant position; second, because it is important that number portability applies to all the firms in the industry, so that consumers know they could experiment with a new provider but then move back to another without costs if they are not satisfied. A market investigation, instead, may allow to intervene and impose portability.[14]

Because network effects reward firms with a large customer base, they are subject to *market tipping*, a notion that captures the idea that once a firm has obtained a certain advantage over rivals in terms of

---

[13] Case T-201/04, *Microsoft Corp. v Commission of the European Communities*, EU:T:2007:289.

[14] See Fletcher, Chapter 8, who also points out that the UK telecom regulator imposed landline number portability in 1995, after a market investigation–like review. This also brings attention to the fact that in some cases an intervention of this type can be taken by a sectoral regulator. We would submit that a market investigation may be preferable when the problem appears to be temporary and the intervention is a one-off measure or does not require frequent monitoring. See Larouche/de Streel, Chapter 4, for the interplay between competition law and sector-specific regulation.

market share, its position may become unassailable and the market may tend to a situation of monopoly. Note, however, that tipping does not always occur, since there are situations in which consumers multi-home, and others where network effects may coexist with different tastes, so that more than one network good may well continue to receive a significant share of customers even beyond the short run. This extends to multi-sided platforms, which cater to multiple groups connected through cross-group network effects. For instance, Rochet and Tirole[15] and Armstrong[16] provide theoretical frameworks in which product differentiation is sufficiently strong so that markets do not tip despite indirect network effects resulting from mutual cross-group network effects.[17]

Competition among users on one side also affects the likelihood of tipping. For instance, Karle et al. (2020) show that more than one platform can be active despite the lack of product differentiation or other frictions because these platforms relax seller competition on the platform.[18] While market tipping is correctly seen as a competition problem, the mere fact that at a given moment in time one platform carries all the trade is, however, not necessarily a concern. It may simply suggest that there is competition for the market and interventions that enable competition in the market may lead to less competitive outcomes.

Motivated by recent developments in digital markets, but not limited to those, the issue of tipping markets and entrenchment deserves careful consideration. As pointed out above, some markets have features such that, if left unchecked, only a few and in the extreme only one firm can consistently make positive profits at any given moment in

[15] Rochet/Tirole, Platform competition in two-sided markets, (2003) 1 *Journal of the European Economic Association*, 990.

[16] Armstrong, Competition in two-sided markets, (2006) 37 *Rand Journal of Economics*, 668.

[17] The issue of single-homing versus multi-homing in markets with two-sided platforms is investigated, e.g., in Armstrong/Wright, Two-sided markets, competitive bottlenecks and exclusive contracts, (2007) 32 *Economic Theory*, 353; Belleflamme/Peitz, Platform competition: Who benefits from multihoming?, (2019) 64 *International Journal of Industrial Organization*, 1; and Bakos/ Halaburda, Platform competition with multihoming on both sides: Subsidize or not?, (2020) 66 *Management Science*, 5599.

[18] Karle/Peitz/Reisinger, Segmentation versus agglomeration: Competition between platforms with competitive sellers, (2020) 128 *Journal of Political Economy*, 2329.

time. For simplicity, focus on the extreme case that all contestable users will join the firm generating the highest gains from trade. In this case, competition becomes what has been called "competition for the market." Here, a firm that enters does so with the bet of offering the largest net benefit. If this bet turns out to be correct, indeed none of the contestable users will go to a rival.

Competition concerns arise if this firm becomes eventually difficult to displace and, as a result, the firm relaxes its effort in providing a high net benefit to users. This may be reflected by high prices, low service quality, and little innovation.

As a starting point, suppose that firms offer some utility $U(N)$ to each consumer who buys; for simplicity, all users are assumed to have the same intensity of use and the firm sets the same usage price. However, because of network effects, this utility may depend on the firm's total number of users N. A firm provides this utility through a combination of fixed and unit cost. Denoting the average per-unit cost by $AC(N)$, the per-unit gains from trade of each unit are $U(N) - AC(N)$. They are increasing in the number of users if (i) there are scale economies, that is, $AC(N)$ is decreasing in N or (ii) there are positive network effects, that is, $U(N)$ is increasing in N. For example, for computational reasons, a large fraction of the literature on network effects and two-sided markets assumes that network benefits are proportional to network size, that is, $U(N) = U_0 + N\, U_1$. When analyzing the impact of network effects on the sustainability of competition and associated theories of harm, the shape of the network benefit function $U(N)$ drives market outcomes and market structure.

A simple numerical illustration may be useful to highlight the importance of the shape of the benefit functions. Suppose that there are two firms operating at zero costs offering incompatible products. There are two groups of consumers of equal size. Both groups may buy from the same firm or one group may buy from one firm and the other group from the competitor. Firms offer a pure network good with $U(0) = 0$ and $U(2) = B$, where the number in brackets stands for how many groups buy the product in question. We distinguish between two polar cases: $U(1) = B$ and $U(1) = 0$. In the former case, the size of one group is sufficient for all network benefits to materialize, whereas in the latter case, both groups must consume the same product for network benefits to arise. Indeed, when $U(1) = 0$, there are social costs when the two consumer groups do not buy from the same firm: any market outcome that keeps both firms in the market with each firm catering to one group is inefficient. Prices will be equal to zero and consumers will obtain a net benefit of zero. Consumer welfare is the same or greater if both consumer groups join the same firm.[19] In such a market, a successful newcomer must quickly achieve the point at which consumers coordinate their decisions.[20] Here, for example, the lock-in of one consumer group can make market entry impossible. From a competition perspective, in such a situation it is essential to keep "competition for the market" open. Any successful attempt by a firm to lock-in a group of consumers is lethal. Maintaining competition in the market would however be highly inefficient. The situation in which only one network is active is likely to be beneficial to consumers. The task of a market investigation then is to understand whether the market admits more than one active firm. We recognize that in practice identifying the number of firms that the market would admit is inherently difficult, but the market investigation may have a "precautionary" or "preventive" role and point to tools that an incumbent may use and that would lead to having only one network being active; also, firms may be forthcoming with information that allows for a better assessment. We also note that some dominant incumbent firms claim that network effects fade out quickly and that the market admits more than one firm. In our simple setting, this means that they claim that the former rather than the latter case applies, and the firm should be taken at its word.

The case with $U(1) = B$ looks more benign to sustaining competition since both firms can attract sufficient consumers to generate benefit B. Put differently, network effects are such that a fraction of consumers is sufficient for network benefits to materialize. If any upfront investment is less than profits obtained in this situation, both firms can survive in the market and there is "competition in the market." However, if one of the two firms is the incumbent and has been able to attract both consumer groups, the potential entrant has to convince at least one

---

[19] If $U(1) = 0$, then consumers receive gross (and net) utility equal to zero if each firm sells to one group. If both groups consume the same good, then gross utility is positive since $U(2) = B$, and net consumer surplus will be positive if the firm cannot extract all the surplus that is generated. For instance, the firm may offer an ad-financed social network service for free and make revenues from advertisers who deliver ads to consumers.

[20] For simplicity, we are assuming that the two consumer groups are of equal size. It is important that market size does not grow over time or that its growth is modest. Otherwise, consumer lock-in is not much of an issue for an entrant.

group to switch sides to make entry viable. Thus, even though a firm's offer does not improve if it serves two instead of one group of consumers (since $U(2) = U(1) = B$), it has a strong incentive to attract more than one group so as to reduce the ability of the rival to become a serious competitor. This shows that despite the firm's claim that it is actually not subject to positive network effects when further increasing its consumer base, it may have strong incentives to strategically deter entry. The claim that serving all consumers proves superior quality of its product is not necessarily correct. By depriving the rival of a sufficient user base the firm can make the rival's offer unattractive. In effect, the market tips (if it is not straightforward that all consumers switch to the entrant almost simultaneously) and market tipping does not increase the gains from trade. While, in such a market, it is possible (and desirable) to have competition in the market, some features may lead to market tipping – some of these features may be given and others affected by the action of the firm that has become dominant. In such markets, interventions that enable consumers to switch easily from one product to another create an environment in which potential entrants try their luck. Such interventions that make future competition viable may be the preferred option compared to a wait-and-see approach and a market investigation may well be one such intervention. If an abuse can be shown, an Article 102 TFEU case can possibly be made; however, such a case would typically go against a certain business practice, while broader measures may be needed to make sure that the market is contestable in the sense that a more efficient potential entrant will successfully enter.

In the example in which $U(1) = 0$, a large critical base is required for network effects to materialize. This led to competition for the market. In the example in which $U(1) = B$, only a smaller critical base is required for network effects to materialize. Here, the market may sustain competition in the market. In both instances, an incumbent firm has a strong incentive to lock in consumers. In the first example it is sufficient to lock in a small number of them, while in the second example an incumbent firm has to lock in a large number to remove a competitive threat. In general, it is not obvious whether consumers actually benefit, for example, from lower prices or better products when a firm attempts to attract them in the first place. Through a market investigation, the authority can take a closer look at the strategies adopted by firms to attract consumers. A particular concern is coordination failures among consumers and delayed monetization. In this case, inferior products may continue to dominate the market, even though other products could be made available that are more attractive for at least one group of consumers.

It should also be recognized that characteristics of the market that are partly shaped by firms' actions may affect the strength of network effects. This is well recognized at least since Katz and Shapiro (1985).[21] The degree of interoperability determines to what extent network effects are firm-specific or apply to the whole industry. A market investigation may uncover a lack of interoperability that leads to a less efficient outcome. We acknowledge, however, that a lack of operability may have efficiency rationales and mandated interoperability has therefore to be considered carefully.

In a market in which competition in the market is viable, it may even be desirable to intervene and keep competition in the market alive because it may be difficult to revert to actual competition once one firm has become dominant, for example, because rivals could not benefit from learning-by-doing, could not upgrade the offerings to consumers, and thus would have fallen behind. Of course, negotiating the trade-off between possibly distortive effects of an early intervention and the benefits of keeping competition open is not easy and would require a more careful analysis. However, these considerations illustrate that dynamic considerations are important. They also suggest that standard competition tools may become available too late in the process.

Consider next an intermediate case to the ones considered so far (with *U(1)* a bit smaller than *U(2)*), where the same firm serving the second group of consumers leads to a benefit increment of *U(2) − U(1)* for each consumer. However, if the firm that attracts both groups is able to extract more surplus per consumer than firms competing in the market,[22] it may still be desirable from a consumer welfare perspective to sustain competition in the market.

The intermediate case also points to an inherent difficulty in such markets, namely, that efficiencies and anti-competitive effects often

---

[21] Katz/Shapiro (fn. 8).

[22] For instance, in an extreme case, the firm serving both groups being a monopolist, it may be able to extract all surplus from consumers; whereas two firms with one group each may compete so fiercely that consumers are able to obtain most of the generated surplus.

come together: once a firm has achieved dominance through a superior offer in the past and network effects, it will be able to sustain this position over time. In one example, this requires that the dominant firm makes switching difficult for at least one consumer group; in the other example, this occurs for both consumer groups. While it would be undesirable to impose remedies that lead to competition for the market when $U(1)$ is very small relative to $U(2)$, such remedies may be desirable when $U(1)$ is close enough to $U(2)$.

The contestability of a network industry depends on the ability of a firm with a superior stand-alone quality or larger marginal network effects to attract users. As mentioned above, in the presence of network effects, users often face a coordination problem. All may agree that a particular product or service is superior, but if they are currently using a different product or service, it may be difficult to convince some of them to go first. Coordinating user expectations is a key concern for new entrants to succeed against established entrants. The lack of entrants may hint at a "kill zone": potential entrants may have given up challenging certain incumbents protected by network effects and a lack of willingness (or ability) of users to coordinate on alternative products or services.

Of course, the market environment may be such that entrants can devise counterstrategies. If an entrant can address specific subgroups, and network effects mostly materialize for such special audiences, this disadvantage may be overcome by the entrant. Also, if the entrant has rich price instruments and can convince a key group of users to adopt (by lowering the price for this key group), it is in a better position to succeed.[23] Furthermore, if using the entrant's offer does not require users to drop the incumbent's offer, it becomes easier for an entrant to overcome the incumbency advantage. As illustrated above, the shape of the network benefit function determines the fraction of users that need to be convinced to adopt the new product or service. A market investigation may shed light on possible counterstrategies, as it may inform the EC about the need of remedying the status quo and the type of remedies needed (e.g., facilitating multi-homing by users).

---

[23] One manifestation are divide-and-conquer strategies, when a firm manages to reach two groups of users connected by network effects. See Caillaud/Jullien, Chicken & egg: Competition among intermediation service providers, (2003) 34 *Rand Journal of Economics*, 309.

2.2.2.3 Switching Costs

Entrants may also find it difficult to challenge incumbents because there may exist consumer *switching costs*.[24] When changing from one provider to another, a consumer may incur costs of a different nature: for instance, one may have always done things in a certain way and not be keen on changing, out of laziness, habit, or to avoid the costs of learning how to operate the new product or service. As with network effects, switching costs may exist independently of firms' conduct, but incumbents may in some cases create or reinforce them. Think of a bank that imposes "administrative fees" to close a current account or to extinguish a mortgage, a telephone provider that (absent regulatory intervention) will delay the technical process necessary for a user to switch to a new company, or airlines offering "frequent-flyer programs" that reward those who have accumulated sufficient miles (which might be lost if one starts flying with a competing airline), and so on.[25]

---

[24] For early work on the (now huge) literature on switching costs, see Klemperer, Markets with consumer switching costs, (1987) 102 *Quarterly Journal of Economics*, 375; and Klemperer, The competitiveness of markets with switching costs, (1987) 18 *Rand Journal of Economics*, 138. For surveys, see Klemperer, Competition when consumers have switching costs: An overview with applications to industrial organization, macroeconomics, and international trade, (1995) 62 *Review of Economics Studies*, 515; and Farrell/Klemperer, Coordination and lock-in: Competition with switching costs and network effects, in: Armstrong/Porter. *Handbook of Industrial Organization*, vol. 3., 2007, p. 1967–2072.

[25] According to the organization of this chapter, such practices belong to the following section on firm behavior that may not be adequately addressed by traditional competition law tools, but we cover endogenous switching costs already in this footnote. If firms reward consumers for repeat purchases, such reward programs (e.g., by providing coupons) constitute endogenous consumer switching costs. Their impact on competition is in general ambiguous.

Caminal/Matutes, Endogenous switching costs in a duopoly model, (1990) 8 *International Journal of Industrial Organization*, 353, show in a differentiated-product duopoly model with a covered market that overall consumers are worse off when firms implement reward programs in the form of lump-sum coupons. Caminal/ Claici, Are loyalty-rewarding pricing schemes anti-competitive?, (2007) 25 *International Journal of Industrial Organization*, 657, argue that two conditions have to be satisfied for reward programs to affect consumers negatively: (i) only few firms compete in the market and (ii) firms use a reward program with a weak commitment capacity. The general message is that in some highly concentrated markets, competition problems arise due to coupons and other reward programs but that often they are pro-competitive. However, we

In all these situations, one may think that a trade-off is at work. On the one hand, once customers are acquired, they will tend to be captive and be charged high prices. On the other hand, anticipating that this will be the case, and that each customer will be lucrative in the future, firms may compete fiercely to acquire the consumers in the first place. The overall effect may be positive or negative for consumers.[26] When new and old consumers coexist in an overlapping-generations setting and firms cannot distinguish them, then, if the composition of old and new consumers does not change, there is a single price charged to all consumers and this price does not change over time. If consumers keep their tastes such that there is no switching in equilibrium, this price is higher with switching costs than without.[27] This suggests that switching costs harm consumers when these costs are significant in the sense that hardly any consumer does switch.

Like network effects, the existence of switching costs makes it more difficult for entrants to contest the market position of firms that have already acquired a large customer base: other things being equal, the entrant will need to compensate the costs of switching by offering price cuts if it wants to attract consumers who have already bought from an incumbent.

In theory, the incumbent may behave less aggressively when it already has a large customer base and it faces a new rival, because it would be more profitable to exploit its existing customers (e.g., by setting high prices) than to fight entry, which is costly. If this was the

---

acknowledge that incumbent firms might resort to coupons or other fidelity rebates to make entry more difficult. See Giardino-Karlinger/Motta (fn. 11).

[26] Klemperer (fn. 24 no. 2) develops a simple two-period duopoly model with differentiated products in which a fraction of consumers of the first period stay on and the others are replaced by new consumers in the second period. If those consumers who stay on inherit their tastes from the first period, all consumers pay strictly higher prices in both periods compared to the setting without switching costs. By contrast, if those consumers newly draw their taste in the second period, all consumers pay weakly lower prices in both periods (and strictly lower in the second period) compared to the setting without switching costs.

[27] See Beggs/Klemperer, Multi-period competition with switching costs, (1992) 60 *Econometrica*, 651. With switching in equilibrium, it is possible to overturn this result. See, e.g., Rhodes, Re-examining the effects of switching costs, (2014) 57 *Economic Theory*, 161.

case, then switching costs may actually facilitate entry. However, (i) an incumbent behaving strategically may actually set even lower prices than what would be optimal in static terms if it expected entry, in order to build an even stronger customer base; and (ii) if the incumbent is able to price discriminate across different cohorts, then it could set lower prices to new prospective consumers and higher prices to old ones (thereby at the same time making entry difficult and exploiting their customer base). We should also recall that if industries characterized by network effects (such as digital markets) are at issue, then price considerations are often less relevant, because consumers may have access to the network products for free.

We acknowledge that in markets with scale economies, network effects, or switching costs there may be fierce competition during the period prior to market consolidation, with profit sacrifices being made on the expectation of future profit recovery after the market has consolidated. Ex post intervention should therefore include considerations of the legitimacy of such dynamic business strategies; that is, firms should not necessarily be denied the recovery of upfront investments and profit sacrifices.

2.2.2.4 Asymmetric Information and Limited Information
Limited Information and Consumer Search
Firms may not include all price elements when advertising products or putting them up for sale, or they may not include value-added taxes (VAT), or credit card charges. All this, combined with consumer search costs, consumers' impatience, etc., hinders transparency on the consumer side and thereby limits their "shopping around," in turn reducing firms' incentives to compete aggressively. Note that one may think of policy interventions that oblige firms to disclose add-on prices, increase transparency for consumers, promote comparability of offers, and reduce their search costs as "consumer protection" policies, but (apart from the fact that not all EU countries have strict enforcement of consumer protection laws) we should stress that if consumers cannot properly compare the different offers, a competition problem arises. At the extreme, obfuscation of prices and other contractual terms would make it impossible to compare offerings and could possibly make consumers captive of the firms. As a result, instead of having effective competition, one may end up with independent "local" (or segmented) monopolies.

This could be a manifestation of the Diamond paradox,[28] according to which even small informational frictions can lead to massive price distortions relative to a market with perfect information. Indeed, it can be shown that if consumers obtain price information for free from their local firm but incur a small search cost to obtain price information from rivals, then the market will be characterized by monopoly pricing.[29]

A less extreme situation arises if *some* consumers are fully informed. Suppose that this is the case and that all other consumers have significant search costs. In a market in which firms offer homogeneous products, the market will feature price dispersion and consumers almost always pay a price above marginal cost in an oligopoly.[30] Thus, the lack of price information suffered by some consumers leads to higher prices for all consumers.

The same general message holds in oligopoly markets with differentiated products. Suppose that firms cannot engage in price discrimination. If all consumers were fully informed, firms would enjoy some profit since products are horizontally differentiated. If, however, a fraction of consumers do not know about other offers than those of their "local" firm (and each firm has the same share of such uninformed consumers), each firm faces a trade-off: it wants to compete for informed consumers but also milk the uninformed consumers. In equilibrium, all

---

[28] See Diamond, A model of price adjustment, (1971) 3 *Journal of Economic Theory*, 156.

[29] Suppose consumers have a small search cost s. To see why the monopoly price is the equilibrium, reason by contradiction and imagine there exists an equilibrium outcome where firms set a price p lower than the monopoly price. In such an equilibrium, consumers expect that all firms set the price p. However, if one firm deviates to a higher price between p and $p+s$ then consumers who have this firm as their local provider would have no incentive to search (because they would incur the cost s, which would add to the price p) and, thus, they (correctly) expect that it is not worth it to engage in a search. Hence, each firm would have an incentive to set a price higher than p. Thus, no price lower than the monopoly price could be the market outcome. Obviously, firms do not have an incentive to set a lower price.

[30] The seminal paper that led to long stream of academic work on markets with search costs is Varian (1982) who considers a homogeneous product market with positive fixed costs and free entry. A paper that considers consumers who engage in sequential search is Stahl, Oligopolistic pricing with sequential search, (1989) 79 *American Economic Review*, 700. Because of some consumers who have to search to obtain price information, this model also delivers price dispersion.

firms set a price that is increasing in the share of uninformed consumers.[31]

Lack of price information makes it more difficult for consumers to find the lowest-priced goods. While price comparison websites have facilitated price comparison, there are at least two reasons why this does not completely remove informational frictions: (i) price comparison websites can only make money if firms are interested to pay for the service to be listed and this limits the incentive of a price comparison website to offer full transparency regarding all available products and the fees charged by the website leads to an upward pressure on the retail price;[32] (ii) firms may still employ obfuscation strategies that hide the true price at the price comparison stage and thus make a price comparison rather cumbersome for consumers.

When consumers are engaged in costly product search, remedies may improve the information available to consumers. It has been shown that under some conditions this makes consumers better off.[33] This insight applies to search advertising, personalized recommendation, filtering, and new display technology, which are important features of many digital markets.

Asymmetric Information in the Firm-Consumer Relationship[34]

If consumers are less informed than firms about, for example, product quality, consumer protection policies (partly through sector regulation) can aim at addressing the market failure that results from asymmetric

---

[31] This is an implication of the analysis in Grossman/Shapiro, Informative advertising with differentiated products, (1984) 51 *Review of Economic Studies*, 63.

[32] Ronayne, Price comparison websites, 2020 (unpublished manuscript).

[33] Zhou, Improved information in search markets, 2020 (unpublished manuscript).

[34] Asymmetric information may also arise in an oligopoly outside the firm-consumer relationship. Firms may have private information about cost or demand that competitors lack. Such environments may lead to higher prices and consumer harm compared to the full-information counterfactual. The economic literature has developed models of signal jamming that clarify the economic mechanism at play. See Riordan, Imperfect information and dynamic conjectural variations, (1985) 16 *Rand Journal of Economics*, 41; and Mirman/Samuelson/Urbano, Duopoly signal jamming, (1993) 3 *Economic Theory*, 129. However, information sharing may facilitate collusion and, therefore, such obligations may backfire. We do not further discuss the associated literature on information sharing.

information.[35] However, asymmetric information may not only be a consumer protection issue but also lead to a competition problem, which may in turn be outside the reach of standard competition tools, but which market investigations might be able to address.

Many product markets have the feature that product quality is only partially observable by consumers. This affects the incentives of high- and low-quality firms to enter. We sketch how a possible theory of harm in an oligopoly could be formulated.[36] Consider an environment in which firms have to make observable investment decisions to enter the market and then draw their quality from some joint quality distribution. Each firm's quality is its private information.[37] In addition to quality differences that are unobservable to consumers, products are exogenously horizontally differentiated (and this is observed by consumers). After observing their own quality and the number of firms, each firm decides whether to stay and pay the quality-dependent fixed cost. Higher quality comes with higher fixed costs, but marginal cost is independent of quality.[38] Since entry leads to more intense competition and thus lower prices for a given distribution of quality, this would lead to adverse selection: the implied change in the distribution of qualities puts further pressure on price. As a result, to have at least some high-quality firms in the market, entry is limited, and firms receive above normal profits. This suggests that asymmetric information about product quality may be reflected in above normal profits in an oligopoly. Remedies addressing asymmetric information then affect market structure. Alleviating the asymmetric information problem

---

[35] Consumer protection policy may be adopted and enforced by a specific consumer protection body or a sectoral regulation.

[36] This sketch of a model is inspired by the formal analysis of Creane/Jeitschko, Endogenous entry in markets with unobserved quality, (2016) 64 *Journal of Industrial Economics*, 494. Their setting is different in a number of ways; in particular, they look at competitive markets with an infinite number of active firms. In an earlier version, they also analyzed the asymmetric information setting under Cournot competition. See Creane/Jeitschko, Endogenous entry in markets with adverse selection, Royal Holloway Discussion Paper 2009-7.

[37] Thus, a firm does not observe the rivals' product quality. Otherwise, difficult signaling issues arise as a firm may want to try to signal information about its own and the rival's quality. See Fluet/Garella, Advertising and prices as signals of quality in a regime of price rivalry, (2002) 20 *International Journal of Industrial Organization*, 907.

[38] Otherwise, firms may try to signal their problem. We discuss this issue in the following paragraph.

would lead to a less concentrated market (which affects price and average quality in the market) and higher consumer welfare.[39] Existing competition tools cannot address such asymmetric information-induced competition problems. In some markets, the NCT may be able to adequately remedy them.

If high quality comes with higher unit cost, the issue of price signaling arises. Consider an oligopoly with a fixed number of firms that have private information about the quality of their own product. Quality may be high or low. Firms with higher quality may try to signal their quality through higher prices. In the market with quality uncertainty, low- and high-quality firms may set higher prices than under certainty. Thus, due to the interplay of imperfect competition and asymmetric information, consumers have to pay higher prices for all products.[40] Standard competition tools cannot address this problem, but there may exist adequate remedies under the NCT.

In some markets, the asymmetric information problem between firms and consumers goes in the opposite direction: firms may lack information about consumer characteristics that affect the firm's cost. This clearly applies to insurance and credit markets, but it is also relevant in online and offline retailing. The costs from product returns can be significant. Return rates are often consumer specific (consumers with low return rates are low-cost and those with high return rates are high-cost for the firms) and incumbent firms can make less attractive offers to high-cost consumers (in particular, in a digital environment with consumer tracking). Since entrants do not yet know prospective customers and high-cost consumers do not get attractive deals from incumbent firms, these high-cost consumers are more likely to switch to the entrant's offer. This implies that entrants will start with a – from

---

[39] Recall also that under full information the market may feature a finiteness property because of vertical product differentiation or endogenous quality. With endogenous quality, a quality race leads to more concentration. However, under asymmetric information (i.e., when consumers cannot observe or infer quality) firms do not have an incentive to provide quality; it is then not clear whether in such a market fewer or more firms are accommodated than under full information; in any case, under asymmetric information, there is no investment in quality and free entry leads to zero profit. Thus, these two market environments deliver markedly different results.

[40] This has formally been analyzed and shown in Daughety/Reinganum, Imperfect competition and quality signalling, (2008) 39 *Rand Journal of Economics*, 163.

their point of view – bad pool of consumers leading to barriers to entry due to asymmetric information.[41]

Mandatory return rights granted to consumers may make matters worse for entrant firms. One takeaway is that well-meant consumer protection policies (here the protection of consumers allowing them to return products without hassle that do not fit their taste) can backfire and lessen competition. A market investigation may uncover that regulation-induced market features lessen competition.

2.2.2.5 Consumers' Behavioral Biases That Are Favorable to Incumbent Firms

Consumer behavior may be subject to "biases" that include non-standard preferences and biases in decision making. Alternatively, one may distinguish between "biases" affecting choice through (i) willingness to pay, (ii) quality biases, and (iii) search biases.[42]

The willingness-to-pay channel may stem from reference point formation with loss aversion or misperceptions of demand. The search bias channel includes behavioral inertia and misjudgment of prices. The quality bias channel includes misjudgment of quality and a misperception of desired attributes. These biases affect oligopoly outcomes. Public interventions can be successful in some market environments to alleviate consumer harm that may stem from these market features. This may be part of a mandate of consumer protection. However, consumer harm is often the outcome of the interplay between behavioral bias and lack of competition. Then, it may also be seen as the task of the competition authority to alleviate consumer harm stemming from such market features that do not allow the market to work well.[43] Thus, in cases of consumer harm in oligopolistic industries due to market features associated with behavioral

---

[41] See, e.g., Dell'Ariccia/Friedman/Marquez, Adverse selection as a barrier to entry in the banking industry, (1999) 30 *Rand Journal of Economics*, 515.

[42] This alternative classification has been proposed by Huck/Zhou/London Economics, Consumer behavioral biases in competition: A survey, Final report prepared for the Office of Fair Trade (OFT), 2011. While we do not use their classification, this section draws on their analysis.

[43] As discussed by Huck et al., ibid., an increase of the number of firms reduces consumer harm in some cases but not in all. The relevant issue is whether the increase in the number of firms increases the incentive of firms to offer better deals to consumers. If this is the case, then a larger number of firms reduces consumer harm.

biases, a market investigation may be an appropriate approach to address the issue at hand; possible remedies include the standardization of information.

Consumers may form reference points about how to value products with loss weighted more strongly than gains from this reference point. Thus, loss aversion affects consumers' willingness to pay but nevertheless reflect preferences. Formation of such reference points may be based on past experiences or built on (rational) expectations. Karle and Peitz (2014) analyze a duopoly with differentiated products and price setting firms when consumers are expectation-based loss-averse.[44] They show that loss aversion in the price dimension intensifies competition, while loss aversion in the dimension of the product fit softens competition. Firms do not have an incentive to "educate" consumers if they can, whereas there may exist remedies that do. Relatedly, Zhou (2011) considers a duopoly model with sequential search with a given order in a duopoly with differentiated products and price-setting firms.[45] Consumers choose the first result in their search process as reference point; thus, they form history-based reference points. Also, in this setting, loss aversion intensifies competition when consumers are loss averse in the price dimension and soften competition when consumers are loss averse in the dimension of product fit.

Consumers may make wrong predictions about their own demand.[46] This may lead to exploitation of consumers in the sense that they pay more than what they are willing to pay if they had correct expectations. For example, if consumers purchase a product because they overestimate future usage, a monopoly firm may be able to extract the surplus from the predicted high demand. Under competition, such exploitation will not occur as firms compete for users.

[44] Karle/Peitz, Competition under consumer loss aversion, (2014) 45 *Rand Journal of Economics*, 1.

[45] Zhou, Reference dependence and market competition, (2011) *Journal of Economics & Management Strategy*, 1073.

[46] For instance, consumers wrongly predict their demand if they use the product or service over time and are naïve hyperbolic discounters. See DellaVigna/Malmedier, Contract design and self-control: Theory and evidence, (2004) 119 (2) *Quarterly Journal Economics*, 353; and DellaVigna/Malmendier, Paying not to go to the gym, (2006) 96 *American Economic Review*, 694. Consumers may also be exploited by firms offering nonlinear contracts if they underestimate the variance of their demand, as in Grubb, Selling to overconfident consumers, (2009) 99 *American Economic Review*, 1770.

A similar issue arises if consumers make misjudgments of quality. If consumers hold biased beliefs about desired attributes and believe that products are more differentiated than they actually are, this relaxes competition among oligopolists, leads to higher prices, and, thus, consumer harm. One such instance is that consumers do not form expectations on average performance of a product but instead base their expectation on a small sample of observations. Thus, two products of the same quality are often seen as of different quality by consumers. Overall, market demand becomes less sensitive to price differences and the oligopoly market features higher markup than if consumers correctly understood the quality of the market.[47]

Consumer search costs and switching costs may arise from behavioral inertia; people may be too "lazy" to shop around. The possible associated harm in cases of such inertia has been mentioned above. Search may be affected through prominence; and incumbency advantage (and strategies that increase this advantage) may lead to prominence and thus make entry more difficult if consumers are unlikely to consider non-prominent choices as they come late in the search process.[48]

2.2.3 Firm Behavior That May Not Be Adequately Addressed by Traditional Competition Law Tools

In this section, we consider situations in which some particular actions or business practices by incumbent firms lead to market inefficiencies. It is well understood that while the collection of individual decisions by market agents would often result in efficient outcomes for society, there are many situations where they might collide with society's objectives. Most relevant for our discussion, a firm may decide to impose anti-competitive vertical clauses, engage in collusive behavior, resort to abusive practices, or acquire a rival, thereby suppressing competition.

It is to prevent such actions, beneficial to the agents who take them but not to society, that competition laws find their main raison d'être, establishing provisions such as those contained in Articles 101 and 102

---

[47] For a formal analysis, see Spiegler, The market for quacks, (2006) 73 *Review of Economic Studies*, 1113.

[48] See Armstrong/Vickers/Zhou, Prominence and consumer search, (2009) 40 *Rand Journal of Economics*, 209.

of the TFEU and in the merger regulation. However, such provisions, and their enforcement, may take care of some but not necessarily all of those anti-competitive actions.

2.2.3.1 Common Ownership and Cross-Ownership

Some markets are characterized by a high degree of common owner-ship (when one person or institution owns shares of two or more firms) or cross-ownership (when two firms own each other's shares).[49] The concern is that an increase in common or cross-ownership of firms belonging to the same sector leads to a less competitive outcome.[50]

According to economic theory, a market with common or cross-ownership tends to deliver outcomes somewhere between a market without common and cross-ownership and a monopoly market.[51] While there is some similarity between common or cross-ownership and a merger, it is more difficult to defend increasing common owner-ship or cross-shareholdings on efficiency grounds. Thus, prima facie, competition policy should be stricter regarding common and cross-ownership than regarding mergers. We acknowledge, though, that individual risk-averse investors may have a legitimate interest in hold-ing stocks of multiple firms in the same industry (or in firms increasing cross-shareholdings) not because of competitive effects, but to reduce earning risks.

Consider an extreme situation of a fragmented market in which one firm or person controls all firms in the industry. By exerting its control right, it can implement business practices that limit competition between all the firms it controls and can, if under full control, achieve the monopoly outcome. Note that even if this common owner does not

---

[49] For a report on common ownership in Europe, see Frazzani/Noti/Schinkel/ Seldeslachts/Banal Estañol/Boot/Angelici, Barriers to competition through joint ownership by institutional investors, Report requested by the European Parliament's committee on Economic and Monetary Affairs, 2020. For an investigation of the United States, see Backus/Conlon/Sinkinson, Common ownership in America: 1980–2017, (2021) 13 *American Economic Journal: Microeconomics*, 273.

[50] For assessments accessible to non-economists, see Gilo, The anticompetitive effect of passive investment, (2000) 99 *Michigan Law Review*, 1; and O'Brien/ Salop, Competitive effects of partial ownership: Financial interest and corporate control, (2000) 67 *Antitrust Law Journal*, 559.

[51] See, however, Brito/Ribeiro/Vasconcelos, Can partial horizontal ownership lessen competition more than a monopoly?, (2019) 176 *Economics Letters*, 90.

hold a majority position it may de facto exert control and fear little opposition from the other owners because they enjoy supernormal profits and may not want to push for more aggressive behavior of the firm. This can be a wait-and-see game: the other owners do not push for a change of control, as long as owners of the rival firm do not push for a change of control at their firm.

Even absent control by common owners, the management of a firm may have an objective function that accounts for the interest of common owners. Common ownership requires us to take a closer look at managerial incentives. In case of cross-ownership, it has clear incentives to include profits of the rival in its own objective function provided that its compensation is based on profits that include profits from participation in other firms (as dividends or higher share values).

The basic economic theory on how common ownership and cross-ownership lead to less competitive outcomes in the form of higher prices is straightforward and has been around for a while.[52] For illustration, consider a symmetric duopoly in which firms offer substitutes and compete in prices or quantities. Suppose that under cross-ownership each firm holds a fraction λ of the shares of its rival. A particularly simple setting is the one in which each firm maximizes the profit of its owners and owners will receive a fraction $1 - \lambda$ of the profit π_1 the firm makes from its own operations plus the fraction λ of the profit π_2 the rival makes from its operations, $(1 - \lambda)\pi_1 + \lambda \pi_2 = (1 - 2\lambda)\pi_1 + \lambda\Pi$, where Π denotes industry profit. Thus, each firm maximizes a weighted average of its own profit and industry profit. Note that in a market without cross-ownership (namely, one where $\lambda = 0$), each firm just wants to maximize its own profits, it does not care about the rival's or industry profits. As a result, a market with cross-ownership leads to a less competitive outcome than a market without it. Intuitively, the higher the share λ a firm owns of its rival, the less aggressive it would like to be, because by capturing an extra sale from the rival it does not appropriate an extra euro of profits but just a proportion $(1 - \lambda)$ of them.

---

[52] See, e.g., Reynolds/Snapp, The competitive effects of partial equity interests and joint ventures, (1986) 4 *International Journal of Industrial Organization*, 141; Flath, When is it rational for firms to acquire silent interests in rivals?, (1991) 9 *International Journal of Industrial Organization*, 573; and Flath, Horizontal shareholding interlocks, (1992) 13 *Managerial and Decision Economics*, 75.

Suppose instead that there is common ownership of the form that a common owner holds a fraction λ of the shares in each firm. Suppose furthermore that the management of each firm maximizes the weighted sum of shareholder value where the weight corresponds to the share in ownership. The common owner is interested in industry profit whereas the other owners are interested in the profit of each firm. Thus, the management of firm 1 maximizes $(1 - \lambda)\pi_1 + \lambda\Pi$. Also, this objective function consists of a weighted average of the firm's profit and industry profit. Hence, a market with common ownership also leads to a less competitive outcome than a market without it.[53]

An important question is the channel by which managers make their decision depending on the common ownership structure. One obvious channel is that common ownership may affect the managerial compensation scheme.[54] However, even absent managerial compensation schemes to explicitly account for rivals' or industry profits, managers may set prices less aggressively in response to an increase of common ownership. For instance, if they were paid a fixed compensation, they may operate under the implicit understanding that their compensation will be reduced in the future if industry profits go down and vice versa.

Finally, common owners may have some control rights and use their power to directly influence managerial decisions. Shekita (2020) documents a number of cases in which such direct interventions have happened.[55]

The mechanisms by which common ownership may affect competition, and the extent to which they play a role in practice, are currently at the center of a heated debate. More generally, the jury is still out with respect to the empirical evidence on the link between competition and common ownership. A prominent empirical investigation regresses prices on MHHI as a measure of market concentration, which reflects the degree of common ownership. In the US airline industry, they find that airline ticket prices are around 3 percent to 7 percent higher in the

---

[53] We acknowledge that our presentation is rather simplistic. For a more flexible treatment of cross-ownership see, e.g., Flath, ibid.; for a more flexible treatment of common ownership that allows for varying control rights. See, e.g., O'Brien/Salop, Competitive effects of partial ownership: Financial interest and corporate control, (2000) 67 *Antitrust Law Journal*, 559.

[54] Antón/Ederer/Giné/Schmalz, Common ownership, competition, and top management incentives, CESifo Working Paper Series No. 6178, 2020.

[55] Shekita, Interventions by common owners, 2020 (unpublished manuscript).

average US airline route than would be the case under separate ownership.[56]

Firms and ownership portfolios are often asymmetric. Theory can account for these asymmetries and provide testable predictions. In their survey, Backus et al. (2021) summarize their reading of existing empirical evidence as follows: "Evidence of an effect of common ownership on prices is, at this point, suggestive at best. Early methods used to investigate the question are problematic, and so more work is required before broad conclusions should be drawn."[57] They suggest future research to focus "on attempts to measure the impact of within a single industry, with a focus on pairwise profit weights rather than market-level concentration measures as the variable of interest." Such research may also provide guidance to the EC if it were to launch a market investigation into an industry that looks suspicious at the outset.

While simple theory focuses on price effects of common and cross-ownership,[58] other effects may exist and strongly affect consumer welfare. For instance, common or cross-ownership may stifle or encourage investment and innovation. In the case of large R&D spillovers, there are benefits from common and cross-ownership as this tends to provide managerial incentives to partly internalize those spillovers; however, theory predicts that absent such spillovers, common and cross-ownership reduce investment incentives and innovation.

Cross- and common ownership may also affect incentives to exit the market. If exit boosts rivals' profits, cross- and common ownership make it more attractive to leave the market. Such exit would often lead not only to higher prices but also to lower product variety in the market. Symmetrically, theory predicts that common ownership (where firms are included as belonging to a market even if not active)

[56] Azar/Schmalz/Tecu, Anti-competitive effects of common ownership, (2018) 73 *Journal of Finance*, 1513. However, their empirical approach has been criticized by Backus/Conlon/Sinkinson, The Common ownership hypothesis: Theory and evidence, Brookings report, 2019; and Backus/Conlon/Sinkinson, Theory and measurement of common ownership, (2020) 110 *American Economic Review P&P*, 557. Elhauge, How horizontal shareholding harms our economy – and why antitrust law can fix it, (2020) 10 *Harvard Business Law Review*, 207, defends the approach against some other critiques and refers to other empirical studies in support of the view that common ownership leads to less competitive market outcomes.
[57] Backus et al., ibid. no. 1, at p. 25.
[58] See Lopez/Vives, Overlapping ownership, R&D spillovers, and antitrust policy, (2019) 127 *Journal of Political Economy*, 2394.

leads to less entry. Supportive evidence is provided by Newham et al. (2019) for the pharma industry: in their empirical analysis the more the branded pharma company and a potential generic entrant are connected by common ownership the less this generic is likely to enter the market.[59] They also show that this finding goes beyond a specific pair of firms and holds at the market level.

Merger control could in principle deal with common and cross-ownership. However, acquisitions are often under the radar of the competition authority, in particular, if owners do not hold controlling stakes, their cash-flow rights are small, or if they acquire stakes in small start-ups in a dynamic industry. Common ownership may be prevalent in an industry even though there may not be a single common owner with large shares but multiple common owners. In our illustrative example, there may be N owners each holding a fraction λ/N of the cash-flow rights. Clearly, it is then possible that this fraction λ/N is small whereas the overall fraction λ is large. In this case, a market investigation would allow the competition authority to become aware of immanent issues of common and cross-ownership in an industry and to provide guidance on how to deal with such cases.

2.2.3.2 Tacit Collusion

Another case where despite the coexistence of several firms in the industry (that is, we are not in a situation of single-firm dominance) the market outcome is inferior to a counterfactual with effective competition is that of tacit collusion. Here it is the conduct of the firms that is resulting in higher prices (and/or lower quality, lower capacity, less investment, narrower product range, etc.). However, the firms' conduct is not illegal and cannot hence be sanctioned by competition law. Indeed, it is well-known that firms may be able to achieve a collusive outcome without explicitly coordinating their actions with rivals but simply by adapting their actions so that each oligopolist behaves in a way that is consistent with collusion. Economic theory has recognized for a long time the possibility that tacit collusion may emerge and mimic the outcome of explicit cartels, and the jurisprudence of the EU has clarified that as long as firms do not talk to each other and do

---

[59] Newham/Seldeslachts/Banal-Estañol, Common ownership and market entry: Evidence from the pharmaceutical industry, DIW Discussion Paper 1738, 2019.

not engage in other practices that allow them to enforce collusion (think of agreements to exchange sensitive, timely, and disaggregate information) or to coordinate on certain outcomes (think of unilateral announcements about future price or output decisions, which allow firms to indirectly coordinate on certain actions), their conduct is not in violation of Article 101 of the TFEU.

Of course, there may be many reasons why firms may sooner or later want to talk to each other in order to sustain collusion: in particular, when the industry faces demand or supply shocks, firms will be tempted to talk to each other, because the current outcome that has been reached through tacit collusion is not optimal any longer and some adjustment would be optimal. However, some forms of collusion are more stable and need less "renegotiation" than others. For instance, customer allocation or division of the markets in areas of influence allow firms to respond to shocks without the need of coordinating their reactions to shocks and without the risk of triggering price wars. Further, explicit collusion is not easy to prove anyway. In order to prove it, antitrust authorities would need hard evidence that firms have talked to each other, and firms' employees are well aware that they should not leave traces of their meetings.

Whether the collusive outcome is enforced through tacit collusion or through explicit but well-hidden coordination, the conclusion is that a market may be subject to collusion, but competition authorities may have little chance to break it by using traditional anti-cartel laws. This does not mean that a market investigation may always be able to stop the collusive outcome; but in some situations, the EC could intervene so as to make the market environment less prone to collusion.

Vertical Integration and Collusion
Economic theory shows that vertical integration often improves the ability of upstream firms to tacitly collude;[60] it also improves the ability of downstream firms to tacitly collude.[61] Thus, vertical

---

[60] Nocke/White, Do vertical mergers facilitate upstream collusion?, (2007) 97 *American Economic Review*, 1321; Normann, Vertical integration, raising rivals' costs and upstream collusion, (2009) *European Economic Review*, 461.
[61] Biancini/Ettinger, Vertical integration and downstream collusion, (2017) 53 *International Journal of Industrial Organization*, 99.

integration appears in a negative light in industries prone to collusion. Divestiture obligations as a structural remedy under the NCT would lead to vertical separation. While this makes tacit collusion more difficult to sustain, there is a priori no guarantee that tacit collusion breaks down; therefore, possible efficiencies stemming from vertical integration should be taken into account when balancing expected costs and benefits of this remedy.

Vertical Collusion

Recent theory has looked beyond collusion among firms in just one layer of the production chain. In particular, tacit collusion between downstream firms may involve common suppliers. If vertical contracts are secret, downstream firms cannot use the contracts between supplier and rivals as a commitment device to sustain high prices in the downstream market.[62] Nevertheless, under some conditions, collusion is easier to sustain than "standard" tacit collusion in the downstream market.[63] Common suppliers are part of the game as they reject contract deviations. To make suppliers stick to such a strategy, they are compensated through higher prices for the input they supply; in return, they have to pay a slotting fee. Since downstream firms have to use a common supplier for some types of inputs for the collusive mechanism to work, exclusive dealing agreements can make sure that this is indeed the case. Thus, exclusive dealing agreements may facilitate tacit collusion even when exclusivity is for only a short period of time.

Cross-Ownership and Common Ownership: Pro-collusive Effects

Cross-ownership and common ownership may increase collusive concerns for two reasons: communication channels between firms may be established and, even absent any communication, deviation incentives are affected. In the latter case, the interaction between ownership structure and deviation structure is complex. However, even there,

---

[62] Observability may require information sharing and thus constitute a violation of Article 101 TFEU. For a setting with observable vertical contracts, see Piccolo/ Miklós-Thal, Colluding through suppliers, (2012) 43 *Rand Journal of Economics*, 492.

[63] See Gilo/Yehezkel, Vertical collusion, (2020) 51 *Rand Journal of Economics*, 133.

tacit collusion may be easier to sustain in the presence of cross-ownership and common ownership.[64]

Algorithmic Collusion

Another risk of tacit collusion is that firms in an industry may delegate their pricing decision (or decisions that directly affect them, such as stocking decisions) to self-learning algorithms. Some legal scholars have raised the concern of "algorithmic collusion."[65] While some cases of algorithmic collusion may well be considered as explicit collusion (e.g., if several firms in an industry use the same pricing algorithm so that this constitutes a hub-and-spoke cartel), the risk that independent self-learning strategies "learn" to collude appears to be outside the realm of Article 101 of the TFEU.

Different views exist in the literature about whether algorithmic collusion can arise when firms use different algorithms that aim at maximizing private profit. This discussion is not settled.[66] Our understanding is that the discussion is evolving from whether algorithmic collusion by independent algorithms is possible (the short answer is "yes") to how plausible or probable this is depending on the market environment. Collusion becomes more difficult if the environment changes frequently (and different firms are affected differently). Also, to be able to adjust, the algorithm must be frequently fed with new data. For an algorithm to learn, it must be also fed with data that measure the success of an action (e.g., quantity sold or number of purchases made).

An important class of learning mechanisms are those using reinforcement learning (RL). A simplistic explanation is that an RL-algorithm uses trial and error and puts over time more weight on actions in a given context that were successful in the past. Such

[64] See Gilo/Moshe/Spiegel, Partial cross ownership and tacit collusion, (2006) 37 *Rand Journal of Economics*, 82.

[65] See, in particular, Ezrachi/Stucke, *Virtual Competition*, 2016.

[66] Useful discussions include: Harrington, Developing competition law for collusion by autonomous artificial agents, (2018) 14 *Journal of Competition Law and Economics*, 331; Schwalbe, Algorithms, machine learning, and collusion, (2019) 14 *Journal of Competition Law and Economics*, 568; and Gautier/Ittoo/Van Cleynenbreugel, AI algorithms, price discrimination and collusion: A technological, economic and legal perspective, (2020) *European Journal of Law and Economics*, https://doi.org/10.1007/s10657-020-09662-6.

algorithms are model-free, that is, they do not rely on any maximization or adjustment based on forecasts involving a model.

Q-learning is a very natural version of reinforcement learning. Calvano et al. (2020) let different Q-learning algorithms play against each other in various imperfectly competitive market environments.[67] As their simulations show, these algorithms learn to tacitly collude over time, leading to prices above the level under noncooperative behavior but below prices charged by a monopolist. This can be seen as a proof of concept: algorithms from a particular class are able to learn to collude in the "wild," and this includes stochastic market environments.

There is little empirical evidence on algorithmic collusion at this point. The retail gasoline market is a good place to collect such evidence because the product is well defined and gas stations frequently change prices. In the German retail gasoline market, algorithmic-pricing software became widely available by mid-2017. Different chains were providing incentives to affiliated gas stations to implement such software to a different degree. Assad et al. (2020) employ high frequency price data. Using a convincing instrumental variable approach to infer whether a gas station uses algorithmic pricing software, they find that in duopoly markets, profit margins do not change when only one of the two gas stations adopts the software, but they increase by almost 30 percent in markets where both do.[68] The latter increase occurs around one year after the implementation of the pricing software. The takeaway from this article is that algorithmic collusion may indeed be a real concern, at least in some environments.

Where data and information are not publicly available, a market investigation might be a promising approach to generate evidence whether in a particular sector decentralized pricing leads to supranormal prices, that is, price levels that are higher than in a counterfactual in which firms did not use sophisticated price strategies that include punishments for competitors. However, we acknowledge that even if such evidence is obtained through the NCT, the difficult issue of finding effective remedies remains.

---

[67] Calvano/Calzolari/Denicolò/Pastorello, Artificial intelligence, algorithmic pricing and collusion, (2020) 110 *American Economic Review*, 3267.

[68] Assad/Clark/Ershov/Xu, Algorithmic pricing and competition: Empirical evidence from the German retail gasoline market, CESifo Discussion Paper No. 8425, 2020.

2.2.3.3 Contracting and Business Practices by Non-dominant Firms
In this section, we briefly consider examples of contractual or implicit clauses, as well as of other price-related practices, which may dampen competition.[69]

Endogenous Consumer Search
Market features such as search cost may lead to less competitive outcomes. Firms, however, may strategically affect consumer search. Armstrong and Zhou (2016) investigate buy-now options, exploding offers, and other tactics to convince consumers that the price will rise if they do not buy immediately but return from their search later on.[70] Firms may have unilateral incentives to choose such search deterrents. In a duopoly, firms adopt such search deterrents, to the detriment of consumers (and possibly firms). With differentiated products, consumers suffer from high prices and bad matches, but profits would also be higher if none of the firms were allowed to use search deterrents. Intervening through the NCT here leads to a Pareto improvement: firms and consumers are better off.

Bundling
Bundling is a common practice in an oligopoly. The economics literature distinguishes between pure and mixed bundling. Under pure bundling, firms offer only a bundle of several products, whereas under mixed bundling, they offer the products separately as well as the bundle at a discount. Bundling can lead to higher or lower consumer welfare depending on the specificities of the market.[71]

A simple intuition is that pure bundling leads to lower prices compared to the total price under separate selling and is overall beneficial to consumers because the price elasticity of demand is increased. Regarding pure bundling, the state of the art is Zhou (2017), who

---

[69] Some of these clauses may also facilitate collusion, but we abstract from this effect in what follows.

[70] Armstrong/Zhou, Search deterrence, (2016) 83 *Review of Economic Studies*, 26.

[71] For a survey of the early literature, see Koyabashi, Does economics provide a reliable guide to regulating commodity bundling by firms? A survey of the economic literature, (2005) 1 *Journal of Competition Law and Economics*, 707. We observe that bundling may be used as a device to partially or fully foreclose competitors, as shown, e.g., by Whinston, Tying, foreclosure, and exclusion, (1990) 80 *American Economic Review*, 837. Here, we focus on bundling in oligopoly for a given number of firms.

provides an oligopoly framework and shows that, under rather general conditions, pure bundling reduces consumer welfare.[72]

When consumers have heterogeneous evaluations for the products on offer, competitive effects of mixed bundling are in general ambiguous and depend on the distribution of consumer tastes. However, when there are more than two firms, consumers benefit from mixed bundling.[73] A different setting is one in which some consumers enjoy a benefit from consuming the products from the same firm (this is a one-stop shopping advantage), while others are only interested in buying one of the products, as analyzed by Thanassoulis (2007).[74] He shows that on average consumers are worse off under mixed bundling than under separate selling.

Low-Price Guarantees

The economic literature has provided a number of theoretical models that explain that supra-normal prices and profits can be achieved through the use of low-price guarantees, that is, a clause that states that if the consumer finds a cheaper product, then that price will be matched or even improved (such clauses are also called "best price" or "meet-or-release" clauses). The simplest setting considers a symmetric oligopoly with fully informed consumers in which firms set prices. Absent low prices guarantees, firms compete fiercely in prices and the competitive outcome results.[75] However, if firms provide low price guarantees, the monopoly outcome will be implemented.[76] Intuitively, a firm would not decrease its price to win additional customers, because it knows that a consumer served by a rival could

---

[72] Zhou, Competitive bundling, (2017) 85 *Econometrica*, 145.

[73] See Zhou, Mixed bundling in oligopoly markets, 2019 (unpublished manuscript).

[74] Thanassoulis, Competitive mixed bundling and consumer surplus, (2007) 16 *Journal of Economics & Management Strategy*, 437.

[75] The logic applies to homogeneous and to differentiated products. With differentiated products, firms can expect positive economic profits absent low price guarantees, also in such an environment such clauses remove the incentive for competitors to offer better deals and thus lead to less competitive outcomes. See Belton, A model of duopoly and meeting or beating competition, (1987) 5 *International Journal of Industrial Organization*, 399.

[76] See Salop, Practices that (credibly) facilitate oligopoly coordination, in: Stiglitz/ Mathewson (eds.), *New Developments in the Analysis of Market Structure*, 1986.

always obtain an as good or even lower price by buying from its original provider.[77]

While low price guarantees considered so far apply across firms, an alternative price guarantee is to promise the same price over time (and thus across consumers). Such a "most-favored customer" or "most-favored nation" clause may provide commitment for a firm not to lower its price. A firm implementing such a guarantee induces competing sellers to price less aggressively.[78]

Lear (2012) provides a detailed account of low-price guarantees and most-favored nation clauses.[79] To summarize, price guarantees may lead to high prices in markets in which neither firm has a high market share. While consumer welfare effects from such clauses are not necessarily negative, they do have the potential to harm consumers.

Price Parity Clauses
Some firms, particularly in digital markets, operate as two-sided platforms bringing together consumers and sellers. These platforms often take a cut from the revenues generated by sellers on the platform. In an oligopoly environment, platforms may impose price-parity clauses; that is, participating sellers cannot offer a lower price elsewhere. This removes the otherwise existing incentive of a consumer to bypass the platform and directly contract with the seller or to contract with the help of a competing platform that charges less to the seller. A seller takes the higher cost to transact with buyers into account and adjusts its prices. Absent the pricing restriction, the seller would have an incentive to steer the consumer to a sales channel on which it incurs lower costs. Price-parity clauses eliminate this possibility and thus have

[77] Price competition may be partly replaced by competition in service quality. However, this is often not feasible and, when it is, often does not provide the same benefits to consumers (this also holds in market environments characterized by price fixing).
[78] See Cooper, Most-favored-customer pricing and tacit collusion, (1986) 17 *Rand Journal of Economics*, 377. A possible implication of such clauses is that they may facilitate entry (in general, if potential entrants expect less aggressive competition in the industry, they will have an incentive to enter). Edlin, Do guaranteed lowest price guarantee high price? How price matching challenges antitrust, (1997) 111 *Harvard Law Review*, 528, argues that entry will be excessive.
[79] Lear, Can "fair" prices be unfair? A review of price relationship agreements, report prepared for the OFT, September 2012, available at https://www.learlab.com/publication/1145/, last accessed March 9, 2021.

the potential to sustain higher fees paid by sellers to the platform.[80] Eventually, consumers suffer from such contractual restrictions because of higher price levels in the product market;[81] this applies also to consumers who continue to buy directly, do not benefit from the services provided by the platform, and are in no contractual relationship with the platform.

There have been a number of abuse of dominance cases in EU countries on hotel booking platforms. For instance, in Germany the Bundeskartellamt first investigated the use of price parity clauses by HRS, at the time the leading hotel booking platform, and only later investigated Booking which was gaining market share. With a theory of harm that applies to all platforms in an oligopolistic industry, a simultaneous intervention (using the NCT) is preferable. Possible remedies include the prohibition of price-parity clauses and the prohibition of other practices that make it unattractive for sellers to serve consumers through different channels.

Strategies in Response to Behavioral Biases

Firms respond to consumers' behavioral biases by adjusting their business strategies, as already hinted at when considering the relationship between market features and consumers harm. Firms may use nonlinear prices and engage in practices that increase consumer inertia and increase prominence. Some of these practices may generate immediate consumer benefits (by providing convenience, consumers may not search elsewhere). However, such actions can create habits such that consumers stick to suboptimal choices.

Firms may become prominent through advertising. Consider a differentiated-product oligopoly with price-setting firms in which consumers are fully informed absent advertising. Firms may engage in advertising to make consumers ignore the competing offers. If firms can identify which consumers have been reached by competitors, they have an incentive to first advertise to those consumers who have not yet been addressed by competitors. Such a model shows that each firm

---

[80] The efficiency defense of such a practice is a seller's free-riding behavior on a platform's investment into recommending high-quality matches to consumers. This issue arises because of a missing-market problem for information provision, as the platform is only paid for a completed transaction.

[81] For a formal investigation, see inter alia Edelman/Wright, Price coherence and excessive intermediation, (2015) 130 *Quarterly Journal of Economics*, 1283.

exclusively advertises to a fraction of consumers (if advertising is sufficiently costly) and the market outcome is less competitive than absent the consumers' behavioral bias.[82]

Consumer harm may be more severe in digital markets (compared to non-digital ones) as firms instantly learn about consumer reactions. As Scott Morton et al. (2019) observe regarding digital platforms, "framing, nudges, and defaults can direct a consumer to the choice that is most profitable for the platform. A platform can analyze a user's data in real time to determine when she is in an emotional `hot state´ and then offer targeted sales."[83]

Behavioral biases or lack of information may make consumers (or at least some group of consumers) very valuable for firms. Thus, firms may compete in another dimension to attract those consumers who will later generate high profits. This implies that if firms have such strategies available, they will compete hard for consumers in some other dimension and, under competition, a large part of profits will be dissipated. However, while firms may gain little or even lose compared to the environment absent bias or lack of information, consumers may still be harmed. For example, if firms advertise to attract the attention of consumers and the advertising does not generate value (or only very little) for consumers (while affecting behavior), consumer harm may be severe but will not be reflected in high profits.

Apart from obtaining a worse deal, consumers may be harmed by the infringement of their privacy rights or by harm from a malfunctioning of the product and this harm may be particularly large if they engage with firms that have deep and broad consumer data. Theories of harm may thus have to look beyond rent extraction in the seller-consumer relationship and include non-monetary losses. While it remains true that initially firms may compete aggressively for consumers, the extra benefit from extracting rents from consumers may well be less than the harm inflicted on consumers and, therefore,

---

[82] The analysis would be very similar to Grossman/Shapiro, Informative advertising with differentiated products, (1984) 51 *Review of Economic Studies*, 63, with the opposite interpretation that advertising reduces the share of fully informed consumers (here all consumers know at least one firm).

[83] Scott/Morton/Bouvier/Ezrachi/Jullien/Katz/Kimmelman/Melamed/Morgenstern, Report from the Committee for the Study of Digital Platforms Market Structure and Antitrust Subcommittee, Stigler Center, University of Chicago, 2019, at p. 36.

consumers suffer overall even when accounting for consumers receiving more attractive offers. While this is clearly a consumer protection issue, it may also be a competition issue since large firms have a data advantage and, thus, may be able to keep competitors at bay with more aggressive offers and achieve supra-competitive profits. Developing appropriate remedies requires a sound understanding of the specific market failure and of how consumers can be protected, for example, from failing to take future losses into account.

Vertical Integration and Exclusive Dealing
In an industry characterized by vertical integration, a complementary relationship in the upstream market and competition in the downstream market may have the feature that the market is less competitive when upstream inputs are pooled. In particular, patent pools are anti-competitive when there is a lot of vertical integration between licensor and licensees and they propose information-free policies to screen anti-competitive pools.[84]

Competitive effects of vertical integration (or exclusive dealing) are also of relevance in the context of two-sided platforms. For example, some work has looked into one premium content and its provision through exclusive dealing.[85] Exclusive dealing and vertical integration can also be used as an instrument of product differentiation on the consumer side. For instance, providers of video streaming such as Amazon, Hulu, and Netflix engage in exclusive deals and vertical integration. To understand market forces in this world, it is important to understand to what extent consumers are willing to consider multi-homing. It will be difficult to evaluate without an NCT whether exclusive dealing and vertical integration in such markets are likely to be anti-competitive.

2.2.3.4 Dominant Firms' Practices That May Be Difficult to Address under 102 TFEU
It is also conceivable that a dominant firm might engage in practices that may be difficult to address under Article 102 TFEU and for which an alternative competition tool may therefore be desirable.

---

[84] Reisinger/Tarantino, Patent pools, vertical integration, and downstream competition, (2019) 50 *Rand Journal of Economics*, 168.
[85] See, e.g., Weeds, TV wars: Exclusive content and platform competition in pay TV, (2016) 126 *Economic Journal*, 1600.

NCT *in Response to the Protection of Intellectual Property*
Rights (IPR)

One such case is where competition policy may overlap and somehow
be in contrast with IPR laws or other laws/regulations. For instance,
imagine a situation where a dominant firm possesses a key input or
technology that enjoys IPR protection and that it refuses to give access
to rivals, thereby locking competition in the market. As we know, the
jurisprudence sets (rightly) a high standard of proof for intervention.
For a refusal to supply to be abusive, the following cumulative conditions must coexist: the input must be indispensable; refusal must lead
to complete foreclosure, that is, elimination of all competition; and it
must prevent the emergence of markets for new products for which
there is substantial demand.[86] The last condition ("new product test")
in particular is motivated by the protection of IPRs: if competition
policy allowed a competitor to offer exactly the same product as that
offered by the IPR holder, then effectively the IPR protection would
not be respected. However, IPR laws may award a patent or copyright
protection in cases where it would be difficult to see an innovation
worth protecting, and it is unclear that competition law may intervene
in such cases, in the light of the above conditions established by the
case law. It is conceivable that in such cases a market investigation may
also assess the extent to which IPR is worth protecting, to the detriment of competition.

In some cases, the problem may be at the other extreme, that is, there
may be insufficient IPR protection for start-ups coming up with new
business models or products, and they are systematically imitated by
dominant firms, which reduces the chances of growth of their smaller
rivals and may also affect their incentives to introduce new products or
services in the first place. This is the phenomenon that is often defined
as "sherlocking" (because Apple included in its Sherlock search tool all
the functionalities that an independent software developer had been
offering, under the name "Watson"), and which was adopted by
several large platforms, including Facebook (one of the most famous
cases is Instagram's "stories" copying Snapchat's model) and Amazon
(which allegedly often starts selling its own products after seeing that

---

[86] In *Microsoft* (see fn. 13), this condition was reformulated in broader terms, to
include also the cases where the refusal to deal limits further technical
development to the detriment of consumers.

some of the sellers in its platform are successful). In the latter case, though, an additional and possibly more important issue comes from the fact that Amazon can observe all transaction data of the sellers present on its platform and use this asymmetry to its own advantage. We understand that this feature is being investigated by the EC under 102 TFEU.

It is not clear to us to what extent these business models or products or ideas are worth protecting and/or can be protected and whether such "cloning" is really harmful to consumers (clearly, in the short run it is not, because they would have access to more variants and presumably competition would drive prices down; but in the long run this may prevent innovative solutions from existing in the first place, because start-ups would anticipate that cloning of their ideas would occur). However, this is clearly an area where an Article 102 TFEU case would not help.

Conduct by Dominant Firms That Bypass Regulations

In some cases, one or more firms may take advantage of existing imperfect laws and regulations by using loopholes or bypassing them. Consider, for instance, the pharmaceutical market. Competition law has in the past managed to use abuse of dominance provisions to address such issues, for example, in *AstraZeneca*.[87] But similar cases may be "borderline" and there may be less indirect ways to solve the problem than 102 TFEU. We think, for instance, of those cases where some drug prices have spiked almost overnight and by exceptionally high proportions. Competition law has used excessive prices provisions to try to deal with some of them, but with mixed success.[88] A market investigation may have been more adequate, since it may have identified those pitfalls in the existing regulations or institutional settings that may create issues more widespread than in the particular cases at hand.

---

[87] Case C-457/10 P, *AstraZeneca AB and AstraZeneca plc v European Commission*, EU:C:2012:770.

[88] While the *Aspen* case conducted by the Italian CA was upheld by the Consiglio di Stato (Consiglio di Stato Sezione IV, Aspen contro Autorità Garante della Concorrenza e del Mercato, Sentenza 13 marzo 2020, n. 1822), in a similar case in the United Kingdom (*Competition and Markets Authority v Flynn and Pfizer*, Case No: C3/2019/1293, [2020] EWCA Civ 617), the UK Court of Appeal broadly upheld the judgment of the Competition Appeal Tribunal that the case be remitted back to the CMA.

NCT as a "Better" Substitute to an Assessment under 102 TFEU
In other cases, resorting to Article 102 may be appropriate and feasible
in principle, but either it would not allow for prompt intervention or
the assessment under 102 may be extremely complex and uncertain.
Consider the former point: in some cases, it may take simply too long
to address the relevant issues within a reasonable horizon, especially in
dynamic fast-changing markets such as the digital ones. *Google shopping* may be a case in point: the EC investigated Google's practices
over a very long period, during which Google's business model – and
the market itself – changed considerably.[89] This was problematic for at
least two reasons: first, during the period of the investigation, the
industry had evolved considerably and by the time the EC issued its
decision, its structure was completely different from what it used to be
at the beginning of the investigation; and if harm had been made, it
could not be undone. Second, it also made the assessment of the case
more complex, as the conduct at issue and the market environment in
which it was taking place had changed considerably.[90]

As for the latter point, one should be aware that abuse of dominance
cases may be extremely difficult and uncertain, especially when their
assessment may require trading off possible short-term benefits with
long-term harm.[91] Consider, for instance, a situation where a firm
engages in bundling of a product that is dominant in a certain market
with another complementary product that is supplied also by other
competitors. Suppose also that in the short term this practice generates
small but certain benefits to consumers (for instance, because they may
save transaction costs by shopping from one firm only) but it may also
have exclusionary effects, with a small probability but with pronounced
impact in the long term (for instance, because a sufficient number of
consumers would desert competitors, which would be unlikely to be
viable for the competitors). Likewise, in a situation in which the

---

[89] Case AT.39740, Google Search (Shopping), European Commission, 27/06/
2017, C(2017) 4444 final.
[90] Recently, EU competition practice has rediscovered an old tool so as to allow for
injunctions to be issued to avoid the situation just depicted, namely, that a
dominant firm may continue to use (allegedly) anti-competitive practices that
may have permanent effects. Arguably, such injunctions may in some cases also
be a possible instrument to resort to.
[91] There may also exist uncertainty on the side of the EC as to whether a firm's
alleged dominance will hold water, while the alleged abuse can also lead to a
lessening of competition in a narrow oligopoly.

dominant firm starts to integrate databases from two different markets, such data integration may have a short-term benefit for consumers but may have long-term irreparable effects to competition.[92]

Under Article 102 TFEU, the EC would need to *prove* that the conduct at issue is abusive, which may require a sophisticated economic analysis and possibly the quantification of the probabilities and magnitudes of the different possible future events,[93] and a finding that the net effect of the conduct is adverse to welfare might be very difficult to substantiate with data. (Note that even if events were certain, it might be very difficult to carry out a quantitative balancing between an exclusionary effect and a pro-consumer effect.)

Conceivably, a market investigation might allow intervention even without proving that the conduct is abusive: quite simply, if it is thought that the adverse (dynamic) effect on competition is sufficiently high, then by applying a sort of *precautionary principle* the conduct could be discontinued.

Admittedly, in a sense this approach might be seen as amounting to lowering the standard of proof for competition intervention relative to the 102 practice. However, such an intervention might allow the preservation of competition in the industry. Further, there would be no fine and no finding that the firm has done anything unlawful: quite simply, suspicious conduct would be prevented in the name of preserving competition. The intervention may be temporary and, after market conditions have changed, the EC may no longer object to a certain business practice.

If there exist several 102 cases that are similar but involve different firms and different markets, it may be more efficient to deal with all of

---

[92] See de Cornière/Taylor, Data and competition: A general framework with applications to mergers, market structure and privacy policy, 2020 (unpublished manuscript); and Condorelli/Padilla, Data-driven envelopment with privacy-policy tying, 2020 (unpublished manuscript). The latter also discuss possible remedies. For a discussion of envelopment strategies, see Condorelli/Padilla, Harnessing platform envelopment in the digital world, (2020) 16 *Journal of Competition Law and Economics*, 143.

[93] It is not clear to us whether the judges would be ready to reason in terms of expected values, which would be the correct way to proceed, rather than simply assess whether the exclusionary outcome would be more likely than not. Imagine, for instance, that the conduct at stake gives a small welfare benefit b for sure but with a probability p it has an exclusionary harm h. Under a balance of probabilities standard, the court may find the conduct abusive only if $p>1/2$. Under an expected terms approach, abuse should be found if $p*h>b$, which may hold good also for $p<1/2$.

them at once. This is something that an NCT investigation may in principle make possible, whereas an Article 102 case would not. Again, one can think of *Google Shopping*: not only Google itself engaged in similar "self-preferencing" practices in services other than vertical search, but other platforms also allegedly resorted to similar practices.[94] In such circumstances, an NCT investigation into these practices in the digital industry may allow a uniform approach to be achieved that avoids the vagaries of the case law and might hence be superior to the attempt of setting a policy through the precedential values of Article 102 cases.

Related to the previous point, it is also possible that the very fact that a 102 case would necessarily concern one firm and one product may not address the competition issue. For instance, consider the situation arising after liberalization in the telecom sector in Europe, where each national market was characterized by a dominant firm (the previous public monopolist) and where entrants had a difficult time in gaining market share. Initially, difficulties were also created by the dominant incumbent claiming that a consumer moving to a rival provider would not have the right to keep her telephone number (since the number should be considered as its IPR – see the discussion above of unworthy protection of IP). To promote competition, mobile number portability was imposed. This was a much better solution than what a 102 case could have achieved. The latter could have obliged the dominant firm to offer portability, but this would likely be insufficient, since consumers needed to know that they could move back (without losing their number) if unsatisfied with an alternative provider. Otherwise, they may not have tried the rival in the first place.[95]

2.2.4 On Remedies in Market Investigations

As argued in Sections 2.2.2 and 2.2.3, there is a wide set of theories of harm that may justify a market investigation. As exemplified there, to address consumer harm in a meaningful way, the EC must have the

[94] For instance, the European Commission is investigating Apple after complaints by Spotify and by an e-book/audiobook distributor on the impact of the App Store rules on competition in music streaming and e-books/audiobooks. See European Commission, Antitrust: Commission opens investigations into Apple, Press Release of 19/06/2019, IP/20/1073.
[95] See Fletcher, Chapter 8.

power to implement appropriate remedies. In other words, if certain remedies are ruled out, market investigations based on particular theories of harm will be meaningless. In this section, we make a few considerations to help understand (i) which types of remedies may be appropriate in correspondence with the different theories of harm; and (ii) when an investigation should be closed with an imposition of remedies, and when it should not. On the latter point, we anticipate that the EC should carry out a cost-benefit analysis that allows for probabilistic assessments. While some remedies may have virtually no "side-effects" and hence could be imposed relatively safely, others may have adverse consequences, not only on the firms at issue (which would be protected by the principle of proportionality) but also on consumers – and hence trade-offs should be carefully considered before being imposed.

To state the obvious, a suitable remedy is intimately related to the theory of harm. The market investigation should identify the mechanisms that lock competition in the market at hand and thereby allow for understanding which interventions could possibly neutralize those mechanisms and unlock competition. Inevitably, though, markets are complex, different characteristics and conduct interact to determine market outcomes, and uncertainty may exist about the impact of a concrete intervention. We briefly discuss which remedies may correspond to the different theories of harm we have discussed in Sections 2.2.2 and 2.2.3. We recall that we have distinguished between those that relate to market features broadly independent of firms' conduct and those that relate to particular practices or behavior by the firms.

2.2.4.1 Market Features and Remedies

In Section 2.2.2, we elaborated on market features that may hinder markets from working properly or that may jeopardize competition. Such features include scale economies on the supply side, network effects, asymmetric information, consumer switching costs, and behavioral biases on the consumer side.

Note that some of these features may actually lead to pro-competitive effects; thus, one has to be reasonably sure that the proposed remedies will reduce the harm. For instance, while network effects often make it difficult for a new firm without an established customer base to enter the market, this is not always the case.

Also, consumers may benefit from positive externalities. Hence, one should look for an intervention that facilitates entry or expansion of younger firms while not depriving the set of consumers of the increased utility derived from such network effects. Remedies that foster *interoperability* would, in some situations, be a good example of such an intervention.

Relatedly, incumbent firms may have more data and better information about consumers: this may lead them to offer more targeted and better products, which is certainly benefiting consumers but gives them an advantage relative to younger and smaller rivals, who have no such detailed information. Again, a desirable remedy does not inhibit the pro-competitive effects while favoring a level playing field. In some instances, *data sharing* or *data portability* obligations may fit the bill. Note that this is a type of remedy that is not exclusive to digital industries: data and information matter in most industries. For instance, it was used in the *retail banking* and in the *home credit* market investigations in the UK: in the former case, the largest retail banks were obliged to develop and adopt an API (Application Program Interface) open banking standard so as to share information. In the latter case, the home credit companies were required to share data on their existing customers' payment records with other lenders.[96]

In such interventions, pro-competitive effects may be large and possible adverse effects, if any, are likely minimal. In some cases, incumbent firms may argue that the data and information in their possession is the result of their investments and efforts, and obliging them to share them with rivals amounts to depriving them of the fruits of their efforts. These claims should be carefully assessed and, to the extent they are justified, a solution may consist of a fair and reasonable compensation for disclosure.

Such considerations may also apply to inputs other than data or information. For instance, there may be regulatory restrictions that may hinder entry; for example, in a town there may be only one or two bus stations that could host bus services without leading to too much traffic congestion, and their management may have been assigned to incumbents. In those cases, a remedy might take the form of imposing

---

[96] See also Fletcher, Chapter 8.

access obligations (if not already part of the regulation) and would likely have much higher benefits than costs.[97]

Whenever there are regulatory barriers to entry, remedies may be aimed at lowering or removing them.[98] In many cases, procurement by public institutions may be designed in such a way as to – often involuntarily – reinforce scale-related competitive advantages of incumbents, or at least make it very difficult for smaller rivals to be effective competitors. Consider, for instance, a national government that intends to procure some good or service, say, to build a broadband infrastructure in peripheral areas of the country or to provide computers for all the public administration. It is unlikely that small (or regional) firms may be able to make offers at such a national scale, whereas they might be competitive if procurement was divided into different "lots." If a market investigation identified a problem of this type, a possible remedy may consist in advocating the relevant public authorities to design their public tenders in such a way to foster participation from smaller firms. To the extent that fragmentation of contracts may involve loss of positive externalities, or loss of economies of scale (and consequently a higher price), these considerations should be traded off with the advantages resulting from fostering competition (an analysis which may be admittedly complex), before imposing the remedy. More sophisticated procurement practices may accommodate such concerns.[99]

In Section 2.2.2, we also argued that a number of theories of harm find their roots in consumer-related features, be they switching costs, lack of information, or behavioral biases. In such cases, we believe that remedies aimed at improving transparency of prices and contractual terms, promote search and comparability of offers, or attenuate biases are also relatively safe, in the sense that they are less likely to generate "side-effects" that are adverse to competition. Examples of such remedies may include obliging suppliers to indicate from the outset all prices, rather than just a base price, with "add-on" components more or less hidden, including VAT; ensuring that consumers have all the relevant information about the product or service, including also

---

[97] See the *local bus services* market investigation in the UK.

[98] See again Fletcher, Chapter 8, for a list of cases where remedies to market investigations in the UK involved regulatory changes.

[99] These concerns extend to private procurement and thus barriers to entry due to market design choices by private entities.

measures of quality;[100] requiring producers to timely communicate all their prices so that they can be published or shown in the same place, thereby allowing consumers to compare prices;[101] and, in case of periodic payments for a service, requiring providers to send periodic statements written in a comprehensive and informative way and/or informing them that cheaper providers may be available elsewhere;[102] and obliging an integrated platform to show services competing with its own in a random order, rather than showing its own first, which would benefit it due to the prominence bias that consumers typically display.

In some industries, competition may not function properly because (i) there is a high sectoral concentration and (ii) high barriers to entry (say, due to large fixed costs) imply that incumbents are not disciplined by new firms. Even absent consumer distortions such as those mentioned above, and without particular business practices (see Section 2.2.4.2), the very fact that few firms coexist leads to weak competition and high prices relative to similar industries in less concentrated markets. There may be many reasons for this concentrated structure, including a liberalization process that has not been properly managed or an antitrust authority that has been too lenient when reviewing past mergers. Whatever the reason, though, there may not be obvious remedies to unlock competition apart from a structural intervention consisting of a divestment order. This type of remedy is obviously more complex than those examined above. Apart from possible issues of proportionality (there must be clear evidence of significant consumer harm to justify a divestment order), there may be incentive issues (part of the assets of the oligopolists may be the result of investment, innovation, effort), but – perhaps less evident – there may also be inefficiencies created by the breaking up of a company, as well as risks inherent from the artificial redesign of the industry. The experience of

---

[100] For instance, the *retail banking* market investigation in the UK included a remedy that required banks to display prominently a number of core indicators of service quality.

[101] This is a measure that has been adopted in several countries to favor comparability of gasoline prices (for instance, through websites or billboards located on major roads to allow drivers to know prices of nearby stations); in the *home credit* market investigation in the United Kingdom, one of the remedies required lenders to publish prices on a website where customers can compare the prices of loans on offer.

[102] See *store cards* and *home credit* market investigations in the United Kingdom.

remedies in merger control demonstrates that there may be many things that can go wrong when breaking up companies or divisions of companies.[103] First of all, the owner of the divested assets should have the *ability* to effectively compete. A company is an integrated set of assets of a different nature that may interact in non-obvious ways: by breaking it up, inefficiencies may arise. For instance, some management, say located in the headquarters, may serve different subsidiaries or products: divesting a subsidiary without assigning experienced human capital may make it less viable (and if assigning it to the divested company, the incumbent may suffer). Divestment of a subsidiary without giving it the contracts with existing customers would limit its competitiveness. In some cases, there may be common inputs and it may not be easy to ensure shared access.[104]

But for competition to be restored, the buyer of the divested assets should have not only the ability but also the *incentive* to compete effectively. In an industry with a history of weak competition, one has to ensure that the buyer of the divested assets will have the incentive to introduce competition, and this incentive may again depend on the design of the divestment (and hence the assets it buys).

In sum, structural remedies require an appropriate design and implementation, and it cannot be taken for granted that, say, a divestment will by itself lead to more competition. The awareness of the risk of such remedies may in turn inform the decision of whether it should be imposed in the first place.

2.2.4.2 Firms' Conduct and Remedies

In Section 2.2.3, we investigated theories of harm resulting from firm behavior that may not be addressed adequately by traditional competition law tools. These included cases such as common ownership and cross-ownership; tight oligopolies able to reach collusive outcomes; dominant firms that use business practices that would be difficult to address using Article 102 TFEU; or firms that are not dominant yet (and hence whose conduct cannot be investigated as abusive) but that may likely become absent an intervention by the EC.

---

[103] See Federico/Motta/Papandropoulos, Recent developments at DG Competition: 2014, (2015) 47 *Review of Industrial Organization*, 399.

[104] See again ibid., on why merger remedies involving the "carving up" of firms involving vertical relationships is especially problematic.

Forced divestitures as remedies in case of common ownership and cross-ownership have been discussed above. Such structural remedies are less problematic than in the case of fully integrated firms since in the case of common ownership and cross-ownership businesses they should be able to continue operate without disruptions after divestitures.

Tacit collusion-based theories of harm may be addressed by a number of remedies. Some remedies are unlikely to have negative side effects and are desirable if considered effective. For instance, if reducing the possibility of monitoring each other (e.g., reducing the possibility to exchange information) is feasible and likely to be effective, such a remedy appears unproblematic (unless it has negative repercussions on the consumer side).

Structural remedies might be more problematic. Consider a symmetric tight oligopoly that is considered to be prone to tacit collusion. Economic theory and conventional wisdom suggest that asymmetries and fragmentation would make tacit collusion less likely to occur. However, imposing divestiture obligations may be justified only in very particular circumstances, inter alia, because of the considerations we made above on the "risk" of divestments. Similarly, imagine that there is a duopoly and (tacit) collusion was achieved after one firm vertically integrated (the other was already vertically integrated). A remedy that requires undoing of the vertical merger would likely not be "proportional," unless there is strong evidence that the merger has led to consumer harm due to tacit collusion.

In case of dominance, we elaborated on the possible limitations of running a case under 102 TFEU. A market investigation may not only investigate a particular allegedly abusive practice but also address a competition issue more broadly, for example, by ruling out not only certain practices that are currently observed but also possible substitute practices that may follow after prohibition of a particular practice. As argued in Section 2.2.3, the practice may be problematic even absent dominance and its prohibition may be the appropriate remedy. Certain practices may have hidden efficiency rationales and therefore a prohibition has to be preceded by a cost-benefit analysis.

If a firm is not yet dominant, but there exists a risk that it will become dominant if certain practices continue or certain market features are not remedied, interventions may be appropriate so as to avoid competition problems in the future, which may be more difficult to remedy at that point. In particular, once a market has tipped and network effects have consolidated it may be more difficult to "reanimate" competition. If there are clear risks of a firm becoming entrenched, even interim measures appear to be appropriate. Moving fast before an investigation is completed always means moving under more uncertainty. However, in exceptional circumstances, this may be the better option. This may apply in particular to industries in which not yet dominant firms enjoy a strong position elsewhere.

2.2.4.3 Trigger for "Remedies Intervention"

Finally, there is the issue of when it is worth triggering the remedy after a market investigation. As mentioned above, the EC will have to perform a cost-benefit analysis before deciding whether to impose a particular remedy. Since some of the risks are probabilistic, a balance-of-harm approach is preferable according to which expected costs and expected benefits are to be accounted.[105] An optimal policy will have to account for type-1 and type-2 errors.

2.2.5 Takeaway Points

We have explained why market forces alone will not necessarily "fix it all" and automatically restore competition in a market characterized by market power. First, some exogenous market features – including scale and scope economies, network effects, switching costs, asymmetric information, and behavioral biases in consumers' decisions – make it difficult or impossible for entrants or smaller rivals to challenge the incumbents, lead to less competitive market outcomes, or are such that as-efficient competitors are doomed to fail. Since these features are not determined by firms' decisions (although their behavior may sometimes exacerbate the distortive effects of those features) traditional competition law tools would not be likely to correct the competitive distortions

---

[105] For instance, Furman/Doyle/Fletcher/McAuley/Marsden, Unlocking Digital Competition. Report of the Digital Competition Expert Panel, 2019, at p. 19, propose such an approach in the context of mergers that remove a potential competitor. The approach could be applied in NCT investigations when the EC faces uncertainty; it constitutes a cost-benefit analysis under uncertainty. An intervention may be desirable even if consumer harm is not very likely. This is the case if in the negative event consumer harm is severe, while it is only moderate in the positive event.

they create or are likely to create in the future. Secondly, the firms in an industry may engage in conduct that prevents self-correcting forces from operating. For a number of reasons, traditional competition law tools may not be able to prevent or correct such conduct. For instance, tacit collusion is (rightly) not sanctioned, common and cross-ownership are typically allowed, and firms may engage in a number of practices (e.g., price clauses) that cannot be characterized as unlawful under Articles 101 (if they are not agreements) or 102 (if the firms at hand are not dominant) but are harmful to consumers nonetheless. For all of these reasons, an NCT in the shape of a market investigation would usefully complement the existing competition policy "arsenal" at the EU level.

2.3 Intervention Triggers

In this section, we deal with possible "intervention triggers," namely, variables that can act as screens or indicators that may signal the need for the deployment of the NCT. To do so, we shall build upon the theories of harm (or circumstances under which a market may not work properly and traditional competition law tools may not help) developed in Sections 2.2.2 and 2.2.3: the triggers of a market investigation must be intimately connected with a conjectured theory of harm. We shall suggest focusing on simple indicators, because before starting a market investigation it is unlikely that the EC will have sufficient information and data to be able to apply sophisticated econometric methods.

2.3.1 From Theories of Harm to Intervention Triggers

We distinguish between market environments in which a dominant firm cannot be challenged or in which the risk that such a dominant position arises is high enough and oligopoly environments where there is some competition problem. In Section 2.2, we developed some theories of harm and in this section, we link them to intervention triggers. Before going into some detail, we sketch the links between the two classes of market environments and possible intervention triggers.

2.3.1.1 Uncontestable Dominant Position or Foreseeable Risk of One

A Dominant Position That Cannot Be Challenged
The market may be one where a firm is already dominant, and *barriers to entry* or *barriers to expansion* exist that make it difficult/impossible

for actual or potential rivals to challenge the market position of the dominant incumbent. Such barriers may arise because of scale and/or scope economies; (positive) direct or indirect network effects; factors that hinder the shopping around of consumers, such as lock-in effects and switching costs; and/or behavioral biases that make it difficult for challengers to contest the dominant incumbent's position.

In this case, the theory of harm is one whereby, for the aforementioned reasons, the dominant firm is not being challenged by actual or potential rivals. Accordingly, possible indicators of that situation include the following ones (which we shall describe more in detail in Section 2.3.3): persistently high market share of the dominant incumbent; little evidence of entry (and if so, only at small scale); evidence of high prices and/or high profitability; complaints by buyers/consumers that they get poor services (note that in multi-sided markets one side of users, say consumers, may appear to be happy but the other side of users, say advertisers, software developers, or sellers seeking access to the platform may not be); and little innovation or introduction of new products/services. Note that when we mention "high" prices, "insufficient" innovation, "poor" quality, and so on, we mean relative to a counterfactual situation in which competition is effective; but in practice, this should translate into trying to identify similar benchmark markets and compare prices and services offered in the market at issue with the benchmark/control market.

The Risk That the Market May Evolve into One Where Competition Is Locked

Some markets may have not yet generated a dominant firm but show clear signs of increasing market power in the hands of one firm. Certain business practices that could be seen as more innocent during the infancy of the industry (say, exclusive contracts, fidelity rebates, tying) may become more problematic as the industry matures and becomes more concentrated. These business practices may have some efficiency rationales but also contribute to barriers to entry, and the trade-off between costs and benefits may tilt toward the former as competitors are shaken out of the industry or relegated to unprofitable market niches. In combination with other factors (such as scale economies or network effects) they may lead to monopolization (but similar considerations may also arise for very narrow oligopolies, say a situation where two firms more or less equally share the market).

Some of the variables seen above may also offer some indications of a tendency for competition in the market to become locked. However, the situation will likely be more dynamic, and a more careful reading of the indicators may be needed. For instance, it may not be excluded that to increase its market power, a firm on the verge of becoming dominant may offer good deals to at least some customers. More generally, it will be more difficult to identify a sector that is prone to tipping or about to become dominated by one firm than a sector in which this process has already taken place. The role of a clear understanding of the likely theories of harm cannot be overstated in such circumstances: the EC will have to spell out clearly what it believes the evolution of the industry might look like and why it might give rise to locked competition. This will in turn point to possibly useful indicators/triggers, which should carefully be considered before starting a market investigation. (Recall also that it would be a good idea to preliminarily explore whether there are likely feasible remedies, before starting a market investigation.)

2.3.1.2 Lack of Effective Competition among Oligopolists

As we have explained in Section 2.3.1.1, there may also exist situations where the market does not deliver good outcomes for consumers (in terms of prices, product range and quality, innovation, and so on) even though there is no dominant position, nor is it likely that there will be one soon. One possible reason may be due to the existence of a collusive situation. We shall deal with possible collusive screens (that is, indicators of collusion) more in detail in Section 2.3.4, but the general idea will be to look for data and outcomes that are typically associated with collusive outcomes but not competitive industries. For instance, prices tend to be stable under collusion, but not under effective competition, even as there are cost shocks.

Another case may be one where there exist a few oligopolistic firms that behave similarly to "local" monopolists with respect to an important fraction of consumers, in the sense that each of them sells to consumers some of whom are somehow "captive." In such an environment, captive consumers do not shop around, for instance, because of lack of transparency of the market, switching costs (which may or not be at least in part endogenous, i.e., arise due to firm behavior), asymmetric information, or the existence of parallel restrictive clauses or vertical contracts (e.g., most or all sellers use exclusive dealing or single-homing – which may have not been introduced from the beginning). In all such cases, attention should probably be given to demand-side indicators and, in particular, to the understanding of whether and how many consumers may be ready to shop around or if, instead, they are unlikely to do so.

The case where several oligopolistic firms coexist but competition is locked and hence consumers are not obtaining good deals (relative to comparable but more competitive markets) may also serve to illustrate the importance of being guided by a theory of harm when looking for intervention triggers. If the sector was characterized by tacit collusion, we would have to look for features or practices that make it more likely for firms to monitor each other, to credibly punish each other in case of deviations, and to coordinate (see Section 2.3.4 for intervention triggers in case of collusion). If instead the issue seems to consist in the market being too segmented, so that each firm effectively has a local market (or even monopoly) power, then the problem lies elsewhere, most likely in market features or contractual conditions, or others, which make it difficult for consumers to shop around. For instance, looking at intervention triggers related to consumer behavior, one may find that consumers would be ready to switch. This speaks against carrying out a market investigation if the problem was of the latter type ("local" market power). However, such a trigger would not help in understanding whether a market investigation may be worthwhile if the problem was of the former type, namely, collusion (among other things, because if firms are indeed colluding, consumers would simply not have the opportunity to find better deals elsewhere).

2.3.2 Intervention Triggers: The Need for Simple Indicators

As just discussed, the conjectured theory of harm should offer insights on the type of observable data that indicate that something may not be working properly in the market. But how sophisticated, refined, and complete should such data gathering be?

We start from the presumption that the formal decision of opening a market investigation needs to be taken before any sophisticated data analysis could be carried out and only after some preliminary evidence could be gathered and studied by the EC, within a reasonably short time.

An alternative approach would be to conceive of a two-stage procedure for the market inquiry, where the first stage would consist of an exploratory market study in which the EC would already announce the opening of the investigation. Depending on the time window, firms could be approached for data; survey questionnaires or interviews could be requested from customers, final consumers, and other interested parties; and the EC could already conduct some (more or less) sophisticated market analysis. After the first-stage investigation, it would issue a first-phase motivated decision on whether there is reason to suspect adverse effects on competition and continue toward the second phase or not (any interested party could appeal this decision). Even under this alternative structure, though, there must be an initial decision by the EC whether to open the first phase. Hence, having some "intervention triggers" to look at in order to inform the decision of opening the market investigation or not would still be useful.[106]

We believe that intervention triggers should consist of simple indicators and (more or less) readily available data, since it is unlikely that the EC could have access to detailed and complete datasets before opening a market inquiry investigation in an official way. A fortiori, it is also unlikely that it could elaborate sophisticated econometric analyses, which would require a wealth of data.

One important source of information that does not require the opening of an investigation would be complaints from customers, consumer groups, or rivals.[107] Although it is well understood that not all such complaints are always justified from the viewpoint of competition protection (customers and consumers may complain about prices that they consider too high but may be the necessary reward for costs including those for innovation and investment; rivals may be unhappy about superior products of a market leader or lack of access to a resource developed by the market leader for its own use), they could nonetheless provide a signal that something in the industry

---

[106] We note that if the two-phase procedure was adopted, starting the investigation would be less costly (and hence relatively less attention may be put into the intervention triggers) than if the market inquiry consisted of just one period, since the EC could decide to stop the investigation after the first phase.

[107] Indications that the market does not perform properly may also include poor customer reviews in specialized magazines or websites.

may not work as it should.[108] Other sources of information could come from newspaper articles, specialized websites and press, trade reports, and so on. Information may also come from an ongoing case (at the EU or a national jurisdiction) that suggests competition problems going beyond the specific case at hand.

The kind of indicators or markers that the EC should look at in order to decide whether to open a market investigation would be to a large extent similar to those that it should look at when it decides whether to open a 101 or 102 investigation. We shall elaborate more on those in the following paragraphs, where we first deal with possible intervention triggers when unilateral behavior (by this, we mean a situation where there is no suspicion of collusive behavior, without necessarily having a dominant position in the market) is at issue; and we next deal with possible triggers when there is the risk that the market is characterized by (tacit or explicit) collusion.

2.3.3 Intervention Triggers for Unilateral Cases

2.3.3.1 High Prices (and Margins)
High prices (and inferred high margins) may be a signal of uncontested dominance, lack of effective competition among oligopolists, or collusion. Of course, the issue is how to assess when prices are "high" enough to be suspicious, and we shall argue that looking at "control markets," namely, markets that are similar but operate in a more competitive environment may offer a useful benchmark.

An additional complication may be that the firms' prices are interrelated. For example, supermarkets use loss leaders (that is, they offer very low prices on some products) to attract consumers in the hope they do all of their shopping there: thus, the overall price structure of a consumer basket matters. Another example are two-sided platforms in which one side may be subsidized whereas the other side may face high prices as part of the platform's function to manage network effects.[109]

---

[108] A discussion of how the EC should deal with such complaints – whether, for instance, it would be obliged to take a motivated decision on them or not – is beyond the scope of this chapter, although we cannot help but stress that the EC should be given the choice to prioritize its cases and assess which ones to pursue and which ones not.

[109] See, e.g., Armstrong (fn. 16).

This is just another instance where the EC will have to look at the overall price structure rather than one individual price.

Similar considerations also apply to *low quality, narrow product range, and lack of innovation* (in competition law one often uses the term "high prices" as a shortcut for a situation in which consumers do not have access to a "good deal," and we often implicitly use this term with the same meaning). Of course, as for high prices, the main issue is how to identify a situation where, say, quality is low. Even in this case, we believe that comparisons with control markets could offer helpful hints. Price increases within the same market can be indicative of *emerging* dominance, lack of effective competition among oligopolists, or tacit collusion. In the case of digital platforms, lower quality can be associated with increased advertising nuisance, more intensive data collection, and reduced customer support.[110] It is important to stress, though, that if reasonably good comparators were not available, then these variables would be unlikely to be helpful indicators.

In the case of two-sided platforms, similar considerations apply to the degree of sellers' competition. Many such platforms operate as intermediaries between sellers or advertisers, on one side, and consumers, on the other side. An important decision of a platform is how to steer competition on the platform. As Belleflamme and Peitz (2019) observe, "imperfect competition between sellers has the standard property that an additional seller on the platform leads to lower per-buyer profit for each seller already on the platform – a negative within-group external effect. It also often leads to lower prices and more variety, which buyers like. Thus, the additional seller may generate more participation on the buyer side, which, in turn, will benefit all sellers – the combination of two positive cross-group external effects."[111] A platform with market power but imperfect instruments to extract surplus from consumers (e.g., a platform that only charges a seller commission) is then interested in limiting the degree of competition on the platform. If this platform faced competition from other platforms, it would be concerned about losing consumers and may

---

[110] On indicators of platform market power, see, e.g., Franck/Peitz, Market definition and market power in the platform economy, CERRE report, May 2019.

[111] Belleflamme/Peitz, Managing competition on a two-sided platform, (2019) 28 *Journal of Economics & Management Strategy*, 5, at p. 6.

therefore enable or encourage more seller competition.[112] Thus, limited competition on the large platform can be seen as an indicator of uncontested dominance.

Similar considerations as for price levels may also hold true for *high profitability (or margins)*, although serious concerns may exist even absent high profitability because, in a situation where effective competition does not exist, firms are not under pressure to become more efficient and hence their productive efficiency may be lower, leading to higher costs and hence lower margins, or monetization may be delayed. Regarding the latter, high stock market valuations may also be informative.

2.3.3.2 Persistence of Market Shares and Lack of (Effective) Entry

Persistent and stable market shares and lack of *effective entry* may also signal competition problems: they could be consistent with a situation in which smaller or new firms are unable to contest the market power of incumbents – whether a single dominant firm or oligopolistic firms – and because of the lack of contestability, competition problems will arise. As we have stressed above, there are many reasons why small firms or new entrants may not be able to challenge the status quo, despite the fact that there are no legal barriers to entry. We should also note that episodes of small-scale entry are not necessarily a proof that entrants can challenge the incumbent: indeed, there are many markets in which fringe firms continue to operate by catering to a very small segment of the market and without ever representing a danger for the large incumbent(s). What is crucial in case of actual entry is to understand whether an entrant would ever be able to grow and challenge the market leader(s) or it is instead likely that it will always be relegated to a market niche.

Persistent market shares may also be indicative of a collusive environment: as argued in Section 2.3.4, collusive schemes often operate by holding market shares fixed. Lack of entry may appear at first inconsistent with a collusive industry, because high collusive prices should in principle attract new rivals, but (i) current incumbents may be protected by entry barriers of various type; or (ii) they might be able to tacitly coordinate so as to make new entry more difficult. For instance, if firms are vertically integrated and an entrant needs access to inputs

---

[112] See, however, Karle/Peitz/Reisinger (fn. 18).

produced by the incumbent, it may be relatively easy for the incumbent to tacitly collude not to give access to the prospective entrants.[113]

2.3.3.3 Suspicious Exclusionary Practices

A number of business practices may be associated with market environments where competition does not work properly and possibly contribute or reinforce that situation. Such practices may include *tying and bundling, exclusive dealing, refusal to supply or to give access* in different degrees (including constructive refusal to supply, delayed access, preferential treatment for its own affiliate, reduced interoperability, etc.). In some cases, these practices may have a pro-competitive explanation, but when used in an environment where competition is already locked, they may be an additional risk factor and may well be considered an additional indicator (together with persistence of market shares, lack of entry, or other signals that the market does not function well) that there is a problem.

Indeed, we know that such practices may play an exclusionary role and deter entry or expansion by rivals. We tend to think of them as potentially anti-competitive instruments when used by dominant firms,[114] but conceivably they may also be problematic in situations in which oligopolists enjoy high and stable market shares and significant entry is unlikely.[115]

The imposition of unusual (relative to similar enough products and services) onerous contractual conditions for customers (e.g., long-term contracts, asymmetric liability, tied-in services, request of renouncing

---

[113] The case of gasoline retail has often been discussed as an example: in several countries, supermarkets that intended to open pump stations and sell gasoline at low prices (also as a way to attract shoppers), found it difficult to obtain gasoline from the integrated oil producers. Calcagno/Giardino-Karlinger, Collective exclusion, (2019) 63 *International Journal of Industrial Organization*, 326, prove that vertically integrated incumbents could tacitly collude so as to all refuse to supply the input to a new entrant.

[114] See Fumagalli/Motta/Calcagno, *Exclusionary Practices: The Economics of Monopolisation and Abuse of Dominance*, 2018.

[115] The economic literature has mostly focused on models where such practices are used by a monopolistic incumbent, in part because they allow for a simpler treatment, in part because for a long time it was controverted that even a monopolist could engage in anti-competitive tying, exclusive dealing, or refusal to supply. But we conjecture that one could expand many of those theories to consider situations in which oligopolists – rather than a single dominant firm – are using them in an anti-competitive way.

to privacy of personal data) may also represent a possible signal that competition is not at work: unless consumers do not pay attention, it is to be presumed that if competition was working, then consumers would turn to some other providers rather than accepting such conditions.

2.3.4 *Intervention Triggers for Collusive Conduct*

Suppose the EC receives complaints about possible collusive behavior in an oligopolistic industry and it intends to look for indicators that signal that indeed there may exist (tacit or express) collusion in this industry before triggering a time-consuming market investigation. What indicators would it be worth looking at?

There exists a large literature in economics, both theoretical and empirical, on the factors facilitating collusion.[116] This literature identifies a number of variables that may foster, or hinder, collusion and may be of some help to guide the agency in having some understanding about whether the industry at issue may be prone to a collusive outcome. For instance, if there are few oligopolists accounting for most of the market sales; they are characterized by symmetric market shares, capacities, and organization structure (e.g., they are all vertically integrated); the market is mature, with stable and predictable demand; oligopolists are connected by a web of relationships (such as joint ventures, purchasing and/or distribution agreements, cross-ownership or cross-directorates); there are few and similar product categories, with price transparency that makes it easier to monitor each other's actions; then most of the industry features are favorable to collusion, and one would have reason to be suspicious.

But more often than not, things are not so clear-cut, and while some sectoral characteristics may appear to facilitate collusion, others may not. For instance, in the industry, there may be a very high concentration index, but some firms are vertically integrated whereas others are not; there may be few and relatively homogenous products, but also powerful buyers, and so on. Therefore, looking at structural factors – though relevant – may be of limited help. Furthermore, it is also possible that an industry where most structural factors appear to

---

[116] A full discussion of facilitating factors is beyond the scope of this chapter. See, e.g., Motta, *Competition Policy: Theory and Practice*, 2004, Chap. 4.

facilitate collusion will not necessarily be one where collusion occurs. At best, the analysis of the factors that facilitate collusion (let us call it a "structural approach") may answer the question: "How likely is it that *collusion may form* in this market?"

2.3.4.1 Behavioral Screens for Collusion

A different, and probably more fruitful, approach could be a "behavioral approach," where one tries to answer the question "how likely is it that *collusion has formed* in this market?" The analysis here would consist in looking at data of certain variables – the so-called screens, or markers (mainly prices and market shares) – to see whether their pattern is consistent with either tacit or explicit collusion and whether there are competing plausible explanations for those observed patterns.[117]

2.3.4.2 Price Levels

Since the ultimate aim of colluding firms is to raise prices, *unusually high prices* might provide some hint of collusion. As we have discussed, the problem is to understand what a high price in a particular market is. Ideally, one would look to compare the price of the market at issue with those emerging in a counterfactual market, that is, a market where reasonably competitive conditions exist. Theoretically, one could proceed by estimating a model that predicts prices in a competitive environment, but of course such an approach would require detailed data, a lot of time and skills, and would likely result in estimates that are highly uncertain and depend on modeling choices. Another route could be to compare prices with costs of production, to try to have a feeling for whether the firms at hand are commanding high margins on the goods or services sold. Unfortunately, costs of production can rarely be observed, and estimating them is a complex exercise, sometimes even for the firms themselves.

---

[117] See also Harrington, Behavioral screening and the detection of cartels, in: Ehlermann/Atanasiu (eds.). *European Competition Law Annual: 2006, Enforcement of Prohibition of Cartels*, 2007, p. 51–68; Abrantes-Metz/Bajari, Screens for conspiracies and their multiple applications, (2009) 4 *Antitrust*, 66; and Fabra/Motta, Assessing coordinated effects in merger cases, in: Corchón/ Marini (eds.), *Handbook of Game Theory and Industrial Organization*, 2017, p. 91–122.

A more useful approach could then be to compare the prices in the market at issue with some benchmark market, characterized by similar cost and demand factors. This is a well-established method for identifying excessive prices in abuse cases, but it may well be used also as an indicator that collusion is taking place. For instance, Abrantes-Metz and Bajari (2009) mention the case of the concrete market in New York, where organized crime created during the 1980s a "concrete club" that led to prices some 70 percent higher than in other large cities: even taking into account the higher New York prices, the comparison suggested suspiciously high prices.[118]

2.3.4.3 Prices Do Not Track Costs

Although cost levels are generally difficult to estimate, one may have information about changes in costs or shocks that affect some of the cost components. This information can be exploited, since the fact that prices do not reflect costs (for instance, prices do not move despite an observed shock that is significantly affecting costs) might signal collusive behavior.

Indeed, theory suggests that in competitive environments prices tend to move with costs of production. Bajari and Ye (2003), for instance, show that in a first-price sealed-bid auction with private values, equilibrium bids are a function of costs when firms behave competitively. Instead, in an efficient cartel, firms would share their cost estimates and then the lowest-cost firm would submit a serious bid while all other cartel members would either refrain from bidding or submit extremely high bids (to ensure they would not win the auction).[119]

---

[118] Abrantes-Metz/Bajari (fn. 117),

[119] Bajari/Ye, Deciding between competition and collusion, (2003) 85 *Review of Economics and Statistics*, 971. See also Athey/Bagwell/Sanchirico, Collusion and price rigidity, (2004) 71 *Review of Economic Studies*, 317, who analyze a model where firms' cost realizations are independently and identically distributed over time and are private information. In each period, colluding firms exchange messages over their costs before setting prices. The first best from their point of view would be for the firm with the lowest cost realization to sell. But if they choose a high (collusive) price, even a high-cost firm would want to declare that it has a low cost. Hence, for firms to have the incentive to report their true costs, the collusive price would have to be sufficiently low. But setting a low sales price would result in foregone profits. The authors show that, facing this trade-off, at the best collusive equilibrium, collusion entails stable prices and stable market shares over time.

More generally and intuitively, *price rigidity* can also be the colluding firms' reaction to the fact that agreeing to adapt to changing
market conditions is difficult and costly. Markets are constantly
affected by unexpected events, and even if explicitly colluding, firms
cannot foresee any possible future circumstances, and how to react to
them, when they set their collusive agreements.[120] As a result, when
such unexpected events occur, they would like to meet so as to renego-
tiate prices (or outputs). But communicating among each other might
leave traces and is dangerous (if discovered, the antitrust authorities
would use it to prove the infringement of cartel laws). As a result, firms
may prefer not to meet, and they may keep on setting the same prices
even if sub-optimal.

The same reasoning also applies in case of tacit collusion. Suppose,
for instance, that firms are currently setting high prices without talking
to each other, perhaps as a result of a lengthy process and several
adjustments. Imagine that now each oligopolist perceives a decline in
its demand, which would call for lowering prices. But (absent a mechanism to exchange information in a timely and disaggregate way) a
firm does not know whether the rivals are facing the same shock. In
these circumstances, decreasing its sales prices may be misinterpreted
by rivals not as a reaction to a negative demand shock, but as an
attempt to deviate and gain market share. As a consequence, each firm
may prefer to stick to the current prices, despite a shock that would call
for a downward price adjustment.

In line with this reasoning, it has been suggested by Abrantes-Metz
and Bajari that price volatility could be a useful collusive screen.[121] An
interesting example consists of their analysis of a cartel in procurement
auctions for food supply to military agencies in the United States,
which revealed that prices in frozen perch were much less volatile
(and less responsive to costs) during the life of the cartel than when
the cartel broke down.

Overall, therefore, whenever prices are readily available, a possible indicator that collusion may be at work in a given industry

---

[120] See Genesove/Mullin, Rules, communication, and collusion: Narrative evidence
from the Sugar Institute case, (2001) 91 *American Economic Review*, 379, who
offer an insightful description of how the participants to the (initially legal)
sugar cartel in the United States would have troubles in dealing with
unexpected shocks such as sudden changes in imports, in costs, and in capacity.
[121] See Abrantes-Metz/Bajari (fn. 117).

could be obtained by the analysis of price volatility and/or of whether prices track costs.[122]

Stability of Market Shares or Customers

Note that the same reasoning would also work for customer or market share (rather than price) stability. Firms may find it optimal to divide the market among each other, so that each of them sells to a certain and well-identified group of customers. In this way, there would be no need to "negotiate" prices with rivals after a shock: each firm just keeps on selling to its own customer at whatever price it desires, while abstaining to win customers who "belong" to rivals. Similarly, firms may have developed some modus vivendi whereby each of them has a market share that fluctuates within a narrow interval over time.

As an example, imagine that there are two sellers of some product that is relatively costly to transport and is used by another industry as an input. Suppose the two sellers are located in two different countries and that their customers are located neatly across national borders, irrespective of the distance from their plants and that this pattern is continuing over time and is not subject to changes in demand or supply shocks. This would be suggestive of a collusive outcome (whether tacit or explicit is another matter).

Note also that the stability of market shares may exist at a more aggregate (in time or product) level, despite observing variability of sales at a more disaggregate one. For instance, if the market under scrutiny is a procurement market, collusion may take the form of rivals winning certain auctions in turn. So, at first sight one may not identify collusion, while bid rotation would typically be constructed so as to guarantee stable market shares overall.

Sudden Price Changes

Although at first sight it may appear to contradict what was stated above, abrupt increases in prices that are not justified by cost or

---

[122] Of course, such a screen could also indicate that it is unlikely that firms are behaving in a collusive way. For instance, in Case ME/1647/04, DS Smith/ LINPAC Containers, 19 May 2004, buyers claimed that there was collusion in the industry. The UK Competition Commission looked at the time series of DS Smith's unit prices and costs, and since changes in prices followed quite closely changes in costs, it concluded that it did not offer evidence of collusion. (However, if firms were able to exchange information then even under collusion would prices follow costs.)

demand shocks may indicate that the industry is colluding. If, in an industry, one observes that out of the blue and without any apparent underlying reason, prices start to spike up, then one may think that somehow firms have managed to move to a more collusive outcome. Note, however, that cartels are aware that unusual price changes might attract unwanted attention from customers (and ultimately regulators) and accordingly often adopt progressive price increase policies.[123]

Abrupt price decreases might also reveal the existence of a cartel. As Green and Porter (1984) have shown,[124] in markets where sellers cannot easily monitor each other's prices, price wars are a necessary ingredient for collusion: if a firm observes a drop in its sales and cannot identify whether this is due to a fall in aggregate demand or the undercutting of rivals, it is optimal to price aggressively for a period of time as a way to avoid deviations from collusive prices before returning to high prices. However, we suspect that price wars associated with collusion are rare events: cartels that are more stable – and hence more harmful – will find a way to avoid price wars that are very costly for them.

It is important to note that evidence consistent with collusion does not necessarily imply that collusion is indeed taking place. It is highly recommended to check that there are no evident alternative plausible explanations for the observed behavior. Indeed, a sudden price increase (or decrease) may have nothing to do with collusive behavior, but instead be the result of demand or supply shocks. For instance, in the well-known *Woodpulp* case,[125] the Court of Justice found that significant price changes implemented by rival producers in parallel, within a short time period, and in similar proportions, might well have been caused by exogenous events such as shocks in the North American market (which determined changes in imports to Europe) and changes in Swedish policies, such as the introduction of a storage-

---

[123] See Harrington (fn. 117).

[124] Green/Porter, Non-cooperative collusion under imperfect price information, (1984) 52 *Econometrica*, 87. For an empirical analysis of price wars and collusion in the Joint Executive Committee (a railroad cartel) that operated in the United States at the end of the nineteenth century, see Porter, A study of cartel stability: The Joint Executive Committee, 1880–1886, (1983) 14 *Bell Journal of Economics*, 301.

[125] Joined cases 89, 104, 114, 116, 117, and 125 to 129/85, *Ahlström Osakeyhtiö and others v Commission of the European Communities*, EU:C:1988:447.

subsidy scheme, which led Swedish producers – which held an important share of the market – to reduce their supply.[126]

Possible Use of Leniency Applications
In some cases, firms submit leniency applications that may not be sufficient to start a cartel investigation – for instance, because it is unlikely that documentary evidence that proves coordination can be found – but it does point nonetheless to the existence of (tacit or explicit) collusive outcomes. Such leniency applications may conceivably trigger a market investigation.

To the extent that the market investigation would entail fines or other forms of punishment (which we understand there is agreement about), the leniency applicant should not receive fines, guaranteeing the incentives to disclose information in the first place.

If, after the market investigation, the EC decided that there is enough evidence to open a cartel investigation, then presumably the original leniency application should still guarantee immunity.[127]

Business Press Reporting and Activities of Business Associations
Reporting in the business press may provide information on price hikes and some underlying narrative that may suggest a collusive outcome. Also, advice by business associations to its members may give indications of attempted or achieved collusive outcomes. For example, suggestions regarding how to inflate variable cost may be seen as an attempt to reduce competitive pressure. Such suggestions may even be successful in fragmented industries if they lead to a "social norm" within the industry to refrain from price-cutting measures or measures that increase the opacity in the market for consumers.

2.3.5 Takeaway Points

In this section, we have argued that intervention triggers – that is, data that may signal that a market investigation may be worthwhile – are intimately connected to the theory of harm. We have also stressed that

---

[126] See Motta (fn. 116).
[127] If under the current legal framework this were not the case, then the EC should grant a sort of 'conditional leniency': if an infringement case is ever opened after a market investigation, then the applicant would be granted leniency. If not, the question of the leniency application would be immaterial.

it is important to look for simple indicators and data, since it is highly unlikely that before starting a market investigation the EC will be in possession of rich databases. Without trying to be exhaustive, we have also suggested a few variables that may be used as possible screens for market environments where the likely problem is of a unilateral (in the sense of not coordinated) nature or of a collusive one. The EC will have to use its resources carefully to investigate those cases in which potential consumer harm is particularly large, which may be due to long-run effects or due to immediate serious harm.

2.4 Conclusion

In this chapter, we have explained why, under some circumstances, markets do not perform as they should. We have argued that this may be due to features of the market that are not necessarily the making of firms (but that their conduct may exacerbate) and hence cannot be addressed by traditional competition law tools or by some practices that are undertaken by the existing firms but for some reasons competition law may not address them, or may do so only partially. In these situations, which may arise in very different industries and not only in digital ones, market investigations may be a possible NCT to remedy the market problem.

We have then dwelt upon some of these "theories of harm" (that is, reasons why a market is not as competitive as it should be), although it is important to stress that an exhaustive listing of such theories of harm would be meaningless: markets differ widely and evolve over time and so do business practices.

The role of a theory of harm is to suggest why market outcomes are less competitive and hence deliver less consumer benefit than a counterfactual where some market features may be corrected or where firms cannot engage in some particular behavior. Theories of harm thus provide an economic mechanism that explains the observed outcome and why it would differ from a more satisfactory counterfactual. Note also that the counterfactual should be a realistic one, which could likely be achieved by an NCT intervention, and where such an intervention is likely preferable to others, in particular sectoral regulation. On this last point, we argue that already at the stage where a theory of harm is formulated and a market investigation is considered, the EC should try to understand whether such an investigation may lead to an appropriate and feasible remedy.

In the cases where competition is at risk (rather than already seriously affected) so that consumer harm is likely to arise in the future, the additional difficulty is that not only the counterfactual that would arise following an intervention but also the outcome absent intervention has to be predicted.

To start a market investigation, we proposed simple intervention triggers that must be based on the conjectured theory of harm. For instance, if the EC is working under the hypothesis that the competitive problem in a certain market is due to tacit collusion, then looking at simple indicators such as whether prices are aligned with costs, or whether market shares are stable over time, may help. But those same indicators would be of little help if the hypothesized theory of harm was different, say that consumers do not shop around so that existing firms may behave as if they had monopoly power on some groups of consumers or some regions of the market.

The NCT will allow the EC to collect information, shed light on the economic channel leading to the observed market outcome (and, in particular, whether the data are consistent with the hypothesized theory of harm), and – importantly – assess whether the problem at issue can be appropriately remedied under the NCT; and if so, the investigation should devote sufficient attention to remedy design. This also highlights the need for an NCT reform to allow for a sufficiently broad and powerful set of remedies. For instance, if the excessive concentration of assets were seen as the cause of a lack of competition, the EC must have divestiture obligations as a remedy at its disposal. If a particular market were prone to market tipping due to network effects, interoperability requirements may be an adequate remedy, and the EC should be able to impose them.

We believe there should be a close interaction between theory of harm, intervention triggers, and possible remedies. A market investigation may know the following (logical but not necessarily sequential) steps. (1) At some point, there is growing perception of the existence of some competition problem. This perception might come from the informal or occasional observation of some variables (say, high prices, stability of market share, complaints about refusal to supply, and so on). (2) The EC will formulate a theory of harm, that is, it will make some hypotheses about what the problem may be and what may cause it. (3) The theory of harm will suggest a more thorough exploration of some concrete indicators (or intervention triggers), that is, of looking more closely at some particular data or empirical regularities. (4) If such indicators are consistent with the hypothesized theory of harm, before starting a market investigation, the EC will also have to consider whether the NCT might lead to an appropriate remedy and that the EC itself or perhaps another entity (say, NCAs, or sectoral regulators) have the capacity to monitor their implementation. (5) It will also have to consider whether this NCT is a better instrument to solve the problem than traditional competition law tools such as Articles 101 or 102 or sectoral regulation.

Needless to say, if a market investigation is conducted, then it might well reveal that there is no clear competition problem after all, for instance, because some rivals may be negatively affected but competition is unlikely to be locked; or it may show that consumers are not likely to benefit if certain market features are corrected or certain business practices are discontinued. In a similar vein, a market investigation may reveal new facts that suggest a different tool may be desirable. For example, some evidence may be uncovered according to which suspected tacit collusion might actually be explicit collusion, suggesting that a cartel infringement case under 101 TFEU may be started.

It is also conceivable that the EC builds a convincing case that certain market features (or firm behavior) are responsible for low consumer benefits but that there simply are no adequate tools that the NCT can rely upon in order to remedy the problem. Either because of the lack of remedies or high costs of implementing them, the market investigation may then stop without adopting any measures. However, such finding may still be useful as they may lead to further actions outside the NCT if the underlying competition problem is deemed to be severe. In particular, depending on the issue, legislation – at the EU or national level – may be considered to address the identified problem. Also, existing sector regulation may be applicable.

This chapter identifies a wide set of theories of harm that are not exclusive to digital markets. While we acknowledge that some types of harm might be of particular concern in digital markets, an artificial limitation of the scope of the NCT to digital industries would also appear to be an inferior option (not to mention the difficulties and possible arbitrariness in defining what is digital and what is not). Accordingly, we believe that if an NCT in the shape of market investigations is to be adopted, it should have a horizontal scope, rather than be applicable to only digital markets.[128]

---

[128] Crawford/Rey/Schnitzer, Chapter 7, reach the same conclusion.

3 A European Market Investigation
Institutional Setup and Procedural Design

HEIKE SCHWEITZER

3.1 Introduction

In 2020, the Commission considered legislation that would have introduced a "New Competition Tool" (NCT) into the European competition policy regime – in other words: a market investigation, EU style. Its general goal would have been to undergird the protection of undistorted competition in the internal market with a new pillar. It was meant to enable the Commission to tackle competition problems that are not covered or cannot be addressed effectively under the current EU competition rules. It would have differed from and complemented the existing competition rules in various respects: (1) it should not focus on the wrongdoing of individual undertakings but on identifying specific features of the market that impede or hamper competition; it should therefore not be of a "quasi-criminal" nature, and its application would not have involved fines; (2) in certain settings where special market characteristics and the conduct of the companies operating in the markets concerned create a threat for competition, it should allow for a precautionary intervention that is not feasible under existing competition rules; (3) it should allow for a particularly timely intervention; and (4) it should enable the Commission to address the root cause of the competition problem identified.

This chapter explores the institutional setup that such a European market investigation could take (Section 3.4), its procedural design (Section 3.5), the scope of remedial powers and the criteria for choosing remedies (Section 3.6), the need for a commitment procedure (Section 3.7), the need for interim measures (Section 3.8), sanctions in case of non-compliance with remedial obligations or commitments (Section 3.9), and judicial review (Section 3.10). The chapter will not discuss the correct legal basis for such an instrument. The analysis, however, has to start with a brief look at the legal nature of a potential European market investigation (Section 3.2).

The type of competition problems to be addressed by a European market investigation are analyzed in another chapter of this book.[1] However, substance and procedure necessarily interact. Among other things, it is very likely that there will be an overlap between a future European market investigation and the traditional competition rules. Consequently, certain competition problems could, in the future, be addressed under the existing competition rules (Article 101 and 102 TFEU) and proceedings (infringement proceedings, Article 7 Reg. 1/2003; commitment proceedings, Article 9 Reg. 1/2003; sector inquiries, Article 17 Reg. 1/2003) or with a European market investigation. The interaction with traditional competition law enforcement will be discussed in Section 3.3.

Regarding the scope of application of a European market investigation, the Commission has outlined four different policy options in its Inception Impact Assessment: A European market investigation could be designed as a dominance-based competition tool with a horizontal scope (option 1), as a dominance-based competition tool limited to specific sectors (option 2), as a market structure–based competition tool with a horizontal scope (option 3), or as a market structure–based competition tool limited to specific sectors (option 4). With the proposed Digital Markets Act, the Commission has de facto opted for the narrow option – namely, a sector-specific tool restricted to gatekeepers. This chapter will discuss procedural issues that would need to be addressed in all four settings – but with a focus on a market structure–based market investigation with a horizontal scope.

While a European market investigation would be a novel instrument within the EU competition policy framework, some jurisdictions have already implemented regimes that are similar by their goal and structure.[2] Among them, the CMA market investigation stands out as a full-fledged, sophisticated regime that has already been widely used. While the institutional setup of competition law enforcement and policy in the United Kingdom differs from that in the EU, the CMA market investigation can nonetheless help to identify critical issues and choices to be made and will therefore serve as a reference point throughout this study.

---

[1] See Motta/Peitz, Chapter 2.   [2] See Whish, Chapter 5.

3.2 The Legal Nature of a European Market Investigation and the Style of the Administrative Proceeding

A European market investigation regime would differ from established competition law proceedings in two important ways: by striving for a correction of market defects to protect and improve competition irrespective of objectionable conduct, it stands somewhere between competition law and economic regulation[3] (Section 3.2.1); furthermore – and similar to economic ex ante regulation – a European market investigation regime would not be of a quasi-criminal but of a purely administrative nature (Section 3.2.2). These two features will affect the design of the proceeding throughout. Third, a European market investigation would want to allow for a particularly quick intervention. It would therefore need to work under a strict timetable (Section 3.2.3).

3.2.1 Market Investigations between Competition Law and Ex Ante Regulation

Generally, a distinction is made between competition law and economic regulation. Where competition law is meant to protect a well-functioning competitive process by prohibiting the abuse of dominance and anti-competitive agreements or concertation, regulation typically pursues a broader set of goals and strives to correct a broader set of market failures. Apart from merger control, competition law enforcement takes place ex post, whereas economic regulation intervenes ex ante. And typically, regulatory law takes a more proactive stance in promoting competition, rather than merely protecting existing competition – the traditional domain of competition law.

A market investigation is placed somewhere between these poles. While belonging to the sphere of competition law by its goals, it does not focus on conduct but on features of the market that tend to adversely affect competition in ways that are not addressed by competition law. Apart from well-known gaps of competition law – such as tacit collusion or other forms of strategic interdependence between firms – demand-side conduct can be considered, and remedies may be imposed that would traditionally rather be looked at as a form of

---

[3] See Larouche/de Streel, Chapter 4; and Fletcher, Chapter 8.

consumer protection.[4] Also, market investigations combine aspects of an ex post and an ex ante enforcement. Where they address a *lack* of competition, the special features of the relevant market(s) and potentially resulting market failures will be investigated from an ex post perspective. Where *risks* for competition are to be addressed, the analysis will involve a prognostic element. When it comes to possible remedies, a forward-looking approach will need to be adopted in both settings – not only, but in particular, where dynamic, fast-changing markets are involved and the impact of novel technologies and business models on these markets must be taken into account.

Despite some regulatory elements, a European market investigation would need to consider its limitations. Remedies would need to be implemented and monitored without the backing of a sectoral regulator.[5] Ideally, they would address the underlying causes of a relevant competition problem to ensure that the market(s) can function competitively in the future without constant regulatory oversight.

One of the goals of a European market investigation – apart from addressing the above-mentioned gaps of competition law and allowing for a more holistic analysis of possible market failures – would be to enable the Commission to more effectively address certain market features that tend to produce anti-competitive outcomes in the longer run but will typically be beyond the reach of remedial action in infringement proceedings:[6] Article 7 remedies are focused on putting an end to an infringement, not on addressing the features of the market that hamper competition.[7] The recent debate on "restorative remedies" has not done away with this inherent limitation. A European market investigation, on the other hand, would strive to preserve or restore the possibility for competition in reaction to the special features of the market identified that may hamper competition. This shift in perspective can turn a European market investigation regime into an important complement to the current system of protecting undistorted competition in the internal market.

---

[4] Fletcher, Chapter 8.

[5] Where remedies are imposed in a regulated sector, the sectoral regulator may, however, be tasked with the monitoring of their implementation – for further analysis, see Larouche/de Streel, Chapter 3.

[6] See also Fletcher, Chapter 8.

[7] For an in-depth analysis, see Monti, Behavioural remedies for antitrust infringements – opportunities and limitations, in: Lowe/Marquis/Monti, *European Competition Law Annual 2013*, 2016, p. 185–206.

3.2.2 Administrative Nature of a European Market Investigation: A More Participative Process and Procedural Guarantees

The shift in perspective implies that a European market investigation would not involve the finding and sanctioning of wrongdoing nor the imposition of fines (apart from sanctions imposed for the non-compliance with procedural obligations imposed in the course of the investigation). Rather, it would be geared toward an analysis of whether specific features of a market tend to lead to a malfunctioning of the competitive process. Since European market investigations would not be used to investigate and sanction rule infringements, they would not qualify as quasi-criminal proceedings within the meaning of Article 48 of the Charter of Fundamental Rights and Article 6 ECHR.[8]

Given the potentially vast and intrusive powers that a European market investigation regime would confer upon the Commission, strong procedural rights and checks will need to be in place nonetheless. In particular, the procedural rights of fairness as set out in Article 41 of the Charter of Fundamental Rights would apply.[9] Wherever market actors are directly and individually affected by a market investigation, they would have a right to be heard (Article 41(2)(a) of the Charter of Fundamental Rights), a right of access to the file (Article 41 (2)(b) of the Charter of Fundamental Rights), a right to careful and impartial examination,[10] a right to a reasoned decision (Article 41(2) (c) of the Charter of Fundamental Rights and Article 296 TFEU),[11] and a right to judicial review (Article 47 of the Charter of Fundamental

---

[8] See European Court on Human Rights, Guide on Article 6 of the European Convention on Human Rights: Right to a fair trial (criminal limb), updated on April 30, 2020, p. 9–10: Market investigation proceedings would not have a punitive or deterrent purpose, would not rely on the finding of guilt, and no penalties would be imposed (apart from fines for the non-compliance with procedural obligations).

[9] According to Article 6(1) TEU, the Charter "shall have the same legal value as the Treaties."

[10] Case C-269/90, *Technische Universität München*, EU:C:1991:438, at para. 14. From the Articles 101 and 102 TFEU case law, see Case T-371/17, *Qualcomm and Qualcomm Europe v Commission*, EU:T:2019:232, at para. 101.

[11] Case C-269/90, *Technische Universität München*, EU:C:1991:438, at para. 14; Case T-394/15, *KPN v Commission*, EU:T:2017:756, at para 49. From the Articles 101 and 102 TFEU case law, see Case C-39/18 P, *Icap and Others v Commission*, EU:C:2019:584; Case T-433/16, *Pometon v Commission*, EU: T:2019:201, at paras. 348–394; Case T-371/17, *Qualcomm and Qualcomm Europe v Commission*, EU:T:2019:232, at paras. 35–55.

Rights and Article 6 ECHR). Furthermore, the right to protection of business secrets and other confidential information (Article 7 and 8 of the Charter of Fundamental Rights) and the protection against arbitrary or disproportionate intervention by public authorities in the sphere of private activities[12] would apply.

Any limitations of these guarantees, as well as of the freedom to conduct a business (Article 16 of the Charter of Fundamental Rights) and the right to property (Article 17 of the Charter of Fundamental Rights), must be justified under Article 52(1) of the Charter of Fundamental Rights: they must be provided for by law, respect the essence of those rights and freedoms, they must be necessary and genuinely meet objectives of general interest recognized by the EU, and they must comply with the principle of proportionality.

However, the presumption of innocence (Article 48(1) of the Charter of Fundamental Rights and Article 6(2) ECHR) would not be applicable. Nor would the principles of legality and proportionality of criminal offenses and penalties and of "*ne bis in idem*" (Articles 49 and 50 of the Charter of Fundamental Rights) play a role. Likewise, the rights of defense in a criminal law sense (Article 48(2) of the Charter of Fundamental Rights) would not be pertinent.

Ideally, the non-criminal nature of market investigation proceedings would allow for a less adversarial and more participative style of interaction between the Commission and the undertakings concerned.[13] The procedural design should strive to promote such a participative and cooperative setting.

3.2.3 Speed of Intervention as a Defining Feature of a European Market Investigation Regime

One of the goals of a European market investigation would be to ensure an effective and timely intervention where this is necessary to

---

[12] For this, see Article 7 of the Charter of Fundamental Rights. From the Case Law: Case C-92/09, *Schecke*, EU:C:2010:662, at para. 72; Case C-465/00, *Österreichischer Rundfunk*, EU:C:2003:294, at para 86. The Articles 101 and 102 TFEU case law see Case 46/87 and 227/88, *Hoechst v Commission*, EU:C:1989:337, at para. 19; Case C-583/13 P, *Deutsche Bahn v Commission*, EU:C:2015:404, at paras. 19–36; Case T-135/09, *Nexans France and Nexans v Commission*, EU:T:2012:596, at para. 40; Case T-325/16, *Ceske Dráhy v Commission*, EU:T:2018:368, at para. 34.

[13] For this the experience in the United Kingdom, see Fletcher, Chapter 8.

protect undistorted competition in the internal market. This would require a strict timetable and a highly efficient design of the procedure.

3.3 The Interaction between a Market Investigation and Infringement Proceedings (Article 7 Reg. 1/2003), Sector Inquiries (Article 17 Reg. 1/2003), and National Enforcement Proceedings

A market investigation as envisioned by the Commission would allow the Commission to intervene into markets based on a significantly broadened set of competition concerns that are the subject of another chapter of this book.[14] The procedural design should ideally be fine-tuned to the substantive concerns to be addressed. One of the important questions to be answered is how a European market investigation would interact with the traditional competition rules and their enforcement at the European and national level.

This question arises, firstly, when the Commission decides on whether to initiate a market investigation procedure: If the Commission suspects the existence of special features of the market that may justify the imposition of remedies under the market investigation regime, but cannot exclude infringements of Articles 101 and/or 102 TFEU, which legal rules and/or principles of competition policy shall determine its choice of procedure? Secondly, the question arises whether the Commission may later switch to an infringement proceeding when evidence suggests that Articles 101 and/or 102 TFEU have been infringed. This may be determinative for the willingness of undertakings affected by a market investigation proceeding to engage in a more cooperative spirit.

3.3.1 Interaction with Articles 101/102 TFEU at EU Level

The main goal of a European market investigation regime would be to address competition problems that are not – or not effectively – addressed by Articles 101 and/or 102 TFEU. Some of these gaps have been highlighted in the Commission's Inception Impact Assessment:

---

[14] See Motta/Peitz, Chapter 2.

the risk of anti-competitive monopolization; tacit collusion that cannot be addressed under Article 101 or 102 TFEU; demand-side market failures, for example, market failures due to consumer inertia; or a lack of competition due to an unequal distribution of data access. Most of them have long been known and discussed with regard to different settings and industries. Some of them, like the unequal access to data, have raised particular concern more recently due to technological and market developments.

Even though the focus of a market investigation would be on specific features of markets that tend to produce anti-competitive outcomes, and not on the types of market conduct that Articles 101 and 102 TFEU address, the scope of the two legal regimes can overlap: potential infringements of the existing competition rules can contribute to the (risk of a) market failure that a market investigation strives to cover. If a European market investigation were designed as a dominance-based tool (options 1 and 2), an overlap with Article 102 TFEU would be likely. If it were to apply irrespective of dominance (options 3 and 4), overlaps with both Articles 101 and 102 TFEU may occur. Some commentators have suggested that such overlaps must be avoided. A European market investigation regime should only address clear "gap cases." Whenever Articles 101 and/or 102 TFEU could potentially apply, infringement proceedings should enjoy priority. However, primary law does not require a market investigation's subsidiarity. If the use of a market investigation were to be made strictly subsidiary to the application of Articles 101 and/ or 102 TFEU, it would become useless for all practical purposes (Section 3.3.1.1).

The alternative is to allow the Commission some degree of discretion in the choice of the instrument – albeit with some limits and combined with a requirement to explain their choice (Section 3.3.1.2). Once the Commission has opted for a market investigation, shifting to an infringement proceeding would normally be barred (Section 3.3.1.3).

3.3.1.1 Subsidiarity of a European Market Investigation?

The subsidiarity of a market investigation vis-à-vis the existing competition rules is not required by primary law.

Articles 101 and 102 TFEU set out important intervention thresholds. While the protection of a system of undistorted competition[15] necessitates that certain anti-competitive conduct is outlawed, it is, at the same time, based on the principles of independent planning and decentralized coordination, rooted in the freedom to conduct a business (Article 16 of the Charter of Fundamental Rights) and the right to property (Article 17 of the Charter of Fundamental Rights). The incentives to invest and innovate that are crucial for the functioning of competition ultimately follow from these individual rights to compete. Interventions into these rights must be justified under Article 52(1) of the Charter of Fundamental Rights. A European market investigation regime – which would be meant to become an additional pillar of the protection of competition – would need to respect these principles and the economic logic on which a system of undistorted competition is based. It must not become a regime of boundless discretionary intervention into markets.

However, nothing suggests that the boundaries of intervention meant to protect a system of undistorted competition are conclusively defined by Articles 101 and 102 TFEU. Rather, the EU legislator has complemented these rules before. The European Merger Control Regulation tackles competition problems that partially also fall under Articles 101 and 102 TFEU;[16] but a regime of ex ante control for mergers proved to be necessary for an effective protection of competition. Obviously, this regime is not subsidiary to the application of Articles 101 and 102 TFEU. Rather, the Commission has declared that it will normally not intend to apply Articles 101 and 102 TFEU to concentrations falling under the EU Merger Control Regulation. Article 21(1) of the European Merger Control Regulation makes Reg. 1/2003 non-applicable where the European Merger Control Regulation applies.

Moreover, a number of sectoral regulations have been passed that complement Articles 101 and 102 TFEU and partially overlap with

---

[15] For this goal, see Article 3(3) TEU with Protocol No. 27 and Article 119 (1) TFEU.

[16] See Case C-6/72, *Europemballage and Continental Can v Commission*, EU: C:1973:22, at para. 25; Case C-142/84 and C-156/84, *BAT & Reyonolds v Commission*, EU:C:1987:490, at paras. 37–38. Mestmäcker/Schweitzer, *Europäisches Wettbewerbsrecht*, 3rd ed., 2014, § 24 paras. 6 et seq. (p. 618 et seq.).

them.[17] In these cases, Articles 101 and 102 TFEU continue to apply alongside the regulatory regime.[18] But the application of the regulatory regime is not subsidiary to the competition rules, although competition law will prevail in case of conflict.

The general picture that emerges from these examples and that is backed up by the Charter of Fundamental Rights is that the EU legislator enjoys a broad margin when specifying which rules and interventions into markets and individual economic rights are needed to ensure the well-functioning of competition. Furthermore, the EU legislator is free to grant broad discretion to the Commission to choose the best, most effective path to proceed in different settings. Regulation 1/2003, for example, essentially leaves it to the EU Commission to decide when to proceed by way of an Article 7 infringement decision and when to opt for an Article 9 commitment decision.

Discretion in choosing the appropriate instrument case by case will also be necessary should a market investigation regime be introduced at the European level. If the use of a market investigation were limited to cases where the applicability of Articles 101 and/or 102 TFEU can be excluded from the start, the use of the tool would become impracticable: before activating a market investigation, the Commission would need to engage in a full-blown infringement analysis. The advantage of a specifically timely intervention would be lost.[19]

Also, a subsidiarity principle would neglect the fact that in some cases, competition law infringements may exist but would not enable the Commission to impose remedies that effectively address the underlying cause of the competition problem that may be rooted in specific features of the market.

---

[17] See, in particular, Directive (EU) 2018/1972 of 11 December 2018 establishing the European Electronic Communications Code, OJ 2018 No. L 321/36; Directive (EU) 2012/27 of 25 October 2012 amended by Directive (EU) 2013/12 of May 2013, Directive (EU) 2018/844 of 30 May 2018, Directive (EU) 2018/2002 of 11 December 2018, Reg. (EU) 2018/1999 of 11 December 2018, Commission Delegated Reg. (EU) 2019/826 of 4 March 2019, and Directive (EU) 2019/944 of 5 June 2019.

[18] Case C-280/08 P, *Deutsche Telekom v Commission*, EU:C:2010:603, at para. 84.

[19] See, however, OFT, Market Investigation References, https://assets.publishing .service.gov.uk/government/uploads/system/uploads/attachment_data/file/ 284399/oft511.pdf, at 2.12–2.13.

To conclude: if a European market investigation is to be turned into an effective instrument complementing the existing competition rules, a subsidiarity principle in relation to the existing competition rules is inexpedient.

3.3.1.2 Integrating Market Investigations into the Competition Law System

Nonetheless, a market investigation regime would need to be integrated into a competition law system the central pillar of which are, and arguably should remain, Articles 101 and 102 TFEU. It would complement but not replace traditional competition law enforcement. As market investigations would not involve the imposition of fines, they would be weaker on the deterrence side. They would also be weaker on legal certainty.

The effect that a market investigation regime would have on the existing regime of EU competition law would, to a large extent, turn on the legal specification of the intervention criterion: Which competition concerns shall be addressed and shall justify the imposition of remedies? In Chapter 2, Massimo Motta and Martin Peitz provide an overview of structural competition problems that are currently outside the reach of EU competition rules or cannot be addressed effectively on their basis. Some of them are based on features of the market that have always been an important part of competition analysis, albeit with an additional conduct requirement in infringement proceedings. Some of them have rather been considered the domain of consumer protection policies so far, their effect on competition notwithstanding. This is true in particular for information asymmetries in consumer markets or behavioral biases of consumers. One of the decisions to be taken by the EU legislator will be how far to expand the scope of a European market investigation regime in this regard. In doing so, it will need to consider that – as demonstrated by the evolution of digital markets – competition concerns can arise from an intricate mixture of market features, including economic characteristics, technological factors, firm conduct, and consumer behavior that interact with one another in potentially complex ways.[20]

The drafting of the intervention criterion will therefore be a challenging task. Three options can be distinguished: The types of competition

---

[20] See also Fletcher, Chapter 8.

problems that a market investigation is meant to address could be specified conclusively in a Regulation (model 1). Alternatively, a very broad and open-ended criterion could be chosen – for example, an "adverse effect on competition" criterion (like in the CMA market investigation regime) or a "significant impediment of effective competition" criterion (similar to the European Merger Control Regulation) (model 2). In an intermediate model, a broad intervention criterion would be accompanied by a non-conclusive list of concrete and meaningful examples that illustrate the type of problems that the market investigation regime is meant to address (model 3). Out of these models, model 3 would appear to be the preferable choice.

Model 1 would maximize legal certainty. It would clearly delineate the scope of application of the market investigation regime and thereby narrow down the potential for overlaps with Articles 101/102 TFEU enforcement. It would, however, not only risk missing certain types of problems that are not yet prevalent or well understood[21] but would also invite litigation on the precise scope of the market investigation regime.

The open-ended and highly discretionary intervention mandate under model 2, on the other hand, would provide for a maximum of flexibility. But it would come at the cost of legal certainty and potentially broad overlaps between the market investigation regime and Articles 101/102 TFEU enforcement as well as with consumer policy (where demand side problems are addressed). The threshold for market intervention would be lowered and the risk of erring on the side of intervention ("false positives") would significantly increase. The Commission's discretion in engaging in market investigations would arguably need to be counterbalanced by a particularly stringent judicial review of the necessity and proportionality of eventual remedies imposed.

Model 3 is the model followed by Articles 101 and 102 TFEU, and it would seem that it would best ensure a coherent interaction between them and a future market investigation regime. It would retain a substantial degree of flexibility to react to new competition problems,

---

[21] See also Motta/Peitz, Chapter 2: "It would go against the spirit of introducing the NCT to aim at providing a complete list of detailed theories of harm since in emerging industries novel market-specific theories of harm may emerge as part of an investigation."

but the list of examples would simultaneously delineate the scope of application of the market investigation regime. Also, it would serve to determine a relevant intervention threshold and it would give an indication of what the Commission would need to prove to the requisite standard of proof in order to impose remedies.

Whichever model is chosen, there would be an area of potential overlap between a future market investigation regime and Articles 101 and 102 TFEU. Consequently, the Commission would sometimes have to make a choice. If market investigations were to address dominance-based competition concerns only (options 1 and 2), the market investigation regime would mainly overlap with Article 102 TFEU.

Arguably, the legislator would and should sketch, in the recitals to a Market Investigation Regulation, the principles that should guide the Commission in the exercise of its enforcement discretion.[22] Given the downsides of market investigations in terms of both deterrence and legal certainty, they should be reserved to settings where the evidence available at the time of the opening of the proceeding suggests that the competition problem, instead of resulting primarily from market conduct, is rooted in the features of the market, such that – even where an element of conduct is present – Article 7 Reg. 1/2003 remedies will not suffice to effectively restore or protect undistorted competition. If the market investigation regime were confined to specific sectors (options 2 and 4), guidance for when to use market investigations would follow from the reasons given for this legislative choice: A sectoral confinement would make sense only if the competition concerns to be addressed by market investigations were particularly acute in the sector(s) where new regime would apply.[23]

---

[22] Similarly: Commission Recommendation of 9 October 2014 on relevant product and service markets within the electronic communications sector susceptible to ex ante regulation (Market Recommendation) 2014/710, rec. 16 – with regard to the appropriateness of ex ante regulation in electronic communications markets.

[23] For a critique of an approach that would confine the scope of application of a market investigation regime to "digital markets" – which I share – see Motta/Peitz, Chapter 2: "The distinction between digital and non-digital markets is not very useful (and to a certain degree arbitrary); market features such as the degree of consume switching costs and the scalability of economic activities may well be related to a market being 'digital,' however they are neither necessary nor sufficient for a market to be classified as a digital market."

In any case, the Commission, when initiating a market investigation proceeding, should be required to explain its choice. The explanation should include an exposition of the type of competition problem(s) that the Commission suspects and of why it finds it more appropriate to tackle the suspected problem on the basis of a market investigation instead of an infringement proceeding. Possible explanations include an assessment that the competition problem to be tackled is one that is not addressed by Articles 101 and 102 TFEU; or an assessment that an action under traditional competition law is likely to be ineffective or significantly less effective in dealing with the competition problem identified, for example, because the competition problem results from industry-wide market features or multi-firm conduct (e.g., non-collusive parallel vertical agreements) that are more adequately addressed within the market investigation framework; or an assessment that the remedies available under Articles 101 and/or 102 TFEU would not suffice to address the root cause of a competition problem. This explanation would not only allow for a public sanity check whether a market investigation is used for the purposes for which it was created. It would also serve as a legal reference point for potential early interim measures, and it could delineate the field in which the Commission would be barred from switching back to Article 101 and/or 102 TFEU proceedings, thereby providing assurance to the undertakings concerned that their cooperation will be honored (see Section 3.3.1.3).

3.3.1.3 Initiating Infringement Proceedings Based on the Findings in a Market Investigation Proceeding?

Where the Commission would decide to initiate a market investigation proceeding instead of an infringement proceeding, this decision would determine the subsequent investigatory procedure. If, on the occasion of a market investigation proceeding, the Commission would find evidence of clear breaches of Articles 101 and/or Article 102 TFEU (e.g., evidence of a cartel), the Commission would need to be free to open an infringement proceeding alongside a market investigation proceeding. Information collected under the rules of a market investigation proceeding must not be directly used as evidence in an infringement proceeding. But nor would the Commission be "required to ignore the information disclosed to them and thereby undergo ...

'acute amnesia.'"[24] Rather, the information could, where appropriate, be taken into account to justify the opening of an infringement proceeding[25] and, subsequently, a new request for a document.[26]

It is a separate question whether the Commission, once it would decide to initiate market investigation proceedings, could reverse that choice and switch over to an infringement proceeding because it finds that, contrary to its initial suspicion, the relevant competition problem rather follows from anti-competitive conduct and not (primarily) from specific (structural) features of the market. Alternatively, a rule similar to Article 21(1) EU Merger Control Regulation could bar the applicability of Reg. 1/2003 with regard to the core competition problem as defined in a market investigation opening decision for a certain period of time.

Such a bar could reassure firms to cooperate with the Commission in market investigation proceedings[27] – despite the fact that private enforcement of Articles 101 and 102 TFEU, as well as a decentralized enforcement by national competition authorities, could not be precluded.

The best option may be that the Commission binds itself by way of a soft-law approach: the Commission could signal that it will, subject to exceptional circumstances, refrain from opening infringement proceedings that relate to the competition problem that justified the opening of the market investigation proceeding for the duration of the proceeding and, where remedies are imposed, a certain period afterwards. Should an infringement proceeding be opened, cooperation during a market investigation proceeding should be taken into account in the calculation of fines.

---

[24] See Case C-67/91, *Asociación Española de Banca Privada and Others*, EU:C:1992:330, at para. 39, referring to the judgment in Case C-85/87, *Dow Benelux v Commission*, EU:C:1989:379, at paras. 18 and 19.

[25] Case T-79/14, *Secop v Commission*, EU:T:2016:118, at para. 82; with reference to: judgments of Case C-85/87, *Dow Benelux v Commission*, EU:C:1989:379, at paras. 18–20, and Case C-67/91, *Asociación Española de Banca Privada and Others*, EU:C:1992:330, at paras. 39 and 55.

[26] Case C-238, 244, 245, 247, 250–252, 254/99 P, *Limburg Vinyl Maatschappij*, EU:C:2002:582 and EU:C:2001:574, at paras. 304–305.

[27] Note, however, that drawing a line between those infringement proceedings that are barred and those infringements that are discovered "on occasion of" market investigation proceedings may be difficult at times.

3.3.2 Interaction of Market Investigations with Sector Inquiries (Article 17 Reg. 1/2003)

Market investigations bear some resemblance with a sector inquiry (Article 17 Reg. 1/2003): both instruments comprise an analysis of the features of a market and the competition problems they may give rise to. However, the primary purpose of a sector inquiry is to detect potential Article 101/102 TFEU infringements.[28] A market investigation, by contrast, would allow the Commission to understand how specific features of a market may tend to produce anti-competitive outcomes irrespective of competition law infringements. Also, contrary to Article 17 Reg. 1/2003, a Market Investigation Regulation would endow the Commission with remedial powers.

If one were to write on a clean slate, one might consider a regime with an initial investigation phase with a broad trigger (e.g., "significant impediment of effective competition"), irrespective of the type of action to be taken later. At the end of this phase, the Commission would decide how to proceed further (ending the investigation, infringement proceedings, market investigation). In such a setting, the purpose of the Article 17–sector inquiry would need to be broadened and its procedural framework may need to be tightened to ensure a sufficiently timely proceeding. The inquiry would then provide a strong basis for the Commission to make an informed choice regarding its further enforcement strategy. This model would resemble the UK model where market investigation references frequently follow up on a "market study,"[29] and "market studies" are meant to map the market including its supply and demand side features to uncover potential competition issues that are not necessarily linked to competition law infringements.

So far, the Commission has not committed to such a broader-scale overhaul of the whole of the enforcement system, including a reform of Reg. 1/2003, but has considered the introduction of a new selfstanding instrument alongside the traditional competition law enforcement regime.

---

[28] See Article 17(1), 2nd sentence – the Commission's investigatory powers are limited to this purpose.
[29] On market studies, see Whish/Bailey, *Competition Law*, 2018, Chap. 11.4.

In principle, this would not preclude the Commission from opening a market investigation proceeding as a follow-up to an Article 17 sector inquiry. But where one of the main reasons for introducing a market investigation regime would be to allow for a particularly timely intervention, a sector inquiry should not become a mandatory or quasi-mandatory first phase. Consequently, the Commission would frequently have to choose between a sector inquiry and a market investigation. Again, this choice should turn on the type of competition problem that the Commission suspects and intends to address: where it suspects a competition law infringement that could adequately be addressed by way of Article 7 Reg. 1/2003 remedies, infringement proceedings, potentially preceded by a sector inquiry, should remain the instrument of choice. If the Commission suspects a type of competition problem that would best be addressed by a market investigation, that investigation would potentially comprise both a full-fledged investigatory phase and an exploration of potential remedies (see Section 3.5).

3.3.3 Effects of a European Market Investigation Regime on National Competition Law and Policy

3.3.3.1 Article 3 Reg. 1/2003 and National Market Investigation Regimes

Under Reg. 1/2003, national competition law must currently not be stricter – nor more lenient – than EU competition law when it comes to Article 101 TFEU. It may be stricter than EU competition law when it comes to unilateral conduct (see Article 3 Reg. 1/2003).

The introduction of a market investigation regime at the EU level would be based on a conviction that significant gaps exist in the current regime of effective protection of undistorted competition. Under options 3 and 4, the market investigation regime would extend to non-dominance-based competition problems. This could prompt Member States to introduce similar instruments at the national level. While in line with the general idea of parallel competition law and enforcement regimes at EU and national levels, the conflict rule set out in Article 3(1), 1st sentence Reg. 1/2003 could thereby be undermined. Furthermore, decentralized market investigation regimes at the national level could lead to an unwelcome fragmentation of the internal market, in particular as such regimes would endow competition authorities with a significantly broader discretion than the enforcement of the comparatively well-defined competition rules. The following principles could contain these risks:

(1) National market investigation regimes could be confined to competition problems that are overwhelmingly national in scope.

(2) At the very least, the use of market investigations at the EU and national levels should be integrated into the ECN reporting system such that the Commission and the NCAs are aware of the ongoing investigations. This will also allow for the requisite coordination: the ECN regime for case allocation should be expanded to cover market investigations. Where a market investigation is used in a context that is not purely national and more than one competition authority plans to start a market investigation, the ECN should seek to agree between the Network members on who is best placed to handle the investigation successfully. In most settings, a market investigation into the same relevant market(s) should be done by a single competition authority ("one-stop shop"). Where a single action is not possible, the Network members should coordinate their action and seek to designate one competition authority as the lead institution.[30] The Commission should be considered to be particularly well placed to handle a market investigation proceeding if more than three Member States are substantially affected by the suspected competition problem.

(3) NCAs will have to make sure that the principles set out in Article 3 Reg. 1/2003 are complied with. The Commission should have a possibility to intervene where a market investigation at the national level would risk undermining a uniform application of competition rules. Article 16(2) of Reg. 1/2003 may need to be expanded to cover this scenario.

The coordination mechanism should not be limited to the use of market investigations at the national level. Where the Commission would initiate a market investigation in a context that would relate to national markets with cross-border effects, NCAs should have the possibility to get involved in the investigation. One way of ensuring

---

[30] See Joint Statement of the Council and the Commission on the Functioning of the Network of Competition Authorities, at paras. 15–18.

involvement would be to give the relevant NCAs the possibility to second officials' participation in the EU investigation.

3.3.3.2 Effects of EU Market Investigations on National Infringement Proceedings

A Market Investigation Regulation would not affect the full applicability of Articles 101 and 102 TFEU. National competition authorities will continue to have full competence to apply Articles 101/102 TFEU. Given the different focus of market investigations and infringement proceedings, the initiation of a market investigation proceeding would not relieve the competition authorities of the Member States of their competence to apply Articles 101 and 102 TFEU in cases relating to the same factual setting. Also, national courts would still be able establish an infringement of Articles 101/102 TFEU and award damages, irrespective of an ongoing market investigation proceeding or of remedies imposed on the basis of a market investigation proceeding.

While the private enforcement of competition rules should not and arguably cannot be excluded, frictions in the realm of public enforce ment should be addressed. A rule analogous to Article 11(6) of Reg. 1/2003 may be legally contestable, given the primacy of the competition rules over a future market investigation regime. The Commission, when opening a market investigation proceeding, should, however, coordinate with the NCAs. Market investigations should be included in the mandate of the ECN. Based on the duty of loyalty (Article 4(3) TEU), NCAs may be required to suspend pending proceedings based on Article 101 and/or 102 TFEU while a European market investigation proceeding is ongoing. Also, remedies imposed by the NCAs must not conflict with remedies imposed or contemplated by the Commission under the market investigation regime (in analogy to Article 16 Reg. 1/2003).

3.4 The Institutional Setup of a European Market Investigation Regime

On the institutional side, the proposed introduction of a European market investigation regime raises the following issues:

– With whom should the decision lie to make use of this instrument? (Section 3.4.1)

– Should there be a reference mechanism? (Section 3.4.2)
– Should there be a complaints mechanism? (Section 3.4.3)

Another important institutional aspect will be the interaction of the market investigation regime with sector-specific regulation. This aspect is addressed in Chapter 4 of this book.

3.4.1 Decision to Open a Market Investigation

The market investigation regime would be meant to complement the system of protecting undistorted competition. Under the European Treaties, the responsibility to ensure that competition in the internal market is not distorted lies with the Commission. The decision to initiate a market investigation should therefore be a decision of the College of Commissioners. As the market investigation regime interacts in manifold ways with traditional competition law enforcement, market investigations should be conducted by DG Competition.

3.4.2 Market Investigation References to the Commission?

In the United Kingdom, certain institutions, including sectoral regulators, are vested with a right to refer a market investigation to the CMA. The interaction between sectoral regulation and market investigations is discussed in Chapter 4 of this book. A separate choice to be made in the EU is whether the Member States should be endowed with a right to make referrals.

Where a Member State suspects an infringement of Articles 101 and/ or 102 TFEU, it is entitled to lodge a formal complaint under Article 7 (2) Reg. 1/2003. This right derives from each Member State's legitimate interest in a coherent enforcement of competition rules as a basis of an internal market with undistorted competition.[31] According to Article 22(1) EUMCR, one or more Member State may request the Commission to examine any concentration as defined in Article 3 EUMCR that does not have a Community dimension but affects trade between Member States and threatens to significantly affect

---

[31] Member States are therefore deemed to have a legitimate interest for all complaints they choose to lodge. See Commission Notice on the handling of complaints by the Commission under Articles 81 and 82 of the EC Treaty, 27.4.2004, C 101/65, at para. 33.

competition within the territory of the Member State or States making the request. The Commission may then decide to examine the concentration (Article 22(3) EUMCR).

Obviously, information by the Member States on competition concerns resulting from structural features of a market and potentially affecting trade between the Member States will always be considered by the Commission. Nonetheless, a formalized referral procedure would raise some concerns. Within the overall competition policy framework, infringement proceedings under Articles 101/102 TFEU shall continue to be the standard way to proceed. The market investigation regime should merely address gaps or settings where competition law enforcement will likely be ineffective, and the Commission should exercise its best judgment when its use is exceptionally required. A formalized referral procedure would oblige the Commission to allocate resources to deal, at a formal level, with any given request to initiate market investigation proceedings. A more appropriate path to follow would be to deal with national propositions to open a market investigation in the course of an informal concertation. Where such suggestions would come from a national competition authority, the issue should be discussed in the ECN.

3.4.3 Complaints Mechanism for Private Parties?

Similarly, it is not obvious that the complaints mechanism under Article 7(2) Reg. 1/2003 and Articles 5-7 Reg. 773/2004, which entitles any natural or legal person who can show a legitimate interest to ask the Commission to find an infringement of Articles 101 and/or 102 TFEU, should be extended to market investigation proceedings.

An infringement of Articles 101 and 102 TFEU violates the rights of individuals. Within the enforcement regime established by Reg. 1/2003, the Commission – unlike civil courts – is not obliged to safeguard these individual rights whenever they may be infringed. For private persons harmed by anti-competitive conduct, there are different routes to get legal protection. Apart from turning to the Commission, there is the possibility to file private lawsuits or to turn to the Member States' competition authorities. An effective enforcement of competition law shall result from the interplay of these different enforcement regimes that complement each other. The Commission, as an administrative authority with limited resources, cannot investigate all possible infringements but must set priorities in its enforcement action. In exercising its discretion, it is guided by the Union interest.[32] It focuses its enforcement action on the investigation of the most serious infringements and on cases that help to define the Union's competition policy, as well as on those cases that help to ensure a coherent application of the competition rules.[33]

However – with a view to the alleged infringement of its individual rights and the purpose of the overall enforcement regime to provide effective protection – the Commission is obliged to consider carefully the factual and legal issues brought to its attention by the complainant, in order to assess whether those issues indicate an infringement of Articles 101/102 TFEU.[34] And where the Commission rejects a formal complaint, the complainant is entitled to a reasoned decision of the Commission that is appealable to the Court. The rights and duties are tied to a showing by the complainant that s/he is liable to be directly and adversely affected by an infringement of Articles 101 and/or 102 TEU and therefore harmed in his or her individual rights. There is no right to lodge a complaint *"pro bono publico."*[35]

A market investigation, on the other hand, does not presuppose a violation of individual rights. As described above, it would be a regime of "small-scale ex ante regulation." In such a setting, a right to lodge a formal complaint would introduce a right to complain *"pro bono publico"*[36] that is alien to the current system and would consume valuable resources that the Commission may better invest in active competition law enforcement. Obviously, this would not exclude informal complaints.[37] Also, whenever a market investigation would overlap with traditional competition law enforcement and an infringement of Article 101 and/or 102 TFEU *is* suspected, a complainant could still lodge a "normal" Article 101/102–complaint.

Similar considerations argue against creating a complaints mechanism for consumer protection bodies[38] – comparable to the

---

[32] Ibid., at paras. 27–28.   [33] Ibid., at para. 11.   [34] Ibid., at para. 53.
[35] Ibid., at para. 38.   [36] Ibid.
[37] For informal complaints regarding infringements of Articles 101 and 102 TFEU, see ibid., at para. 2.
[38] For example, a complaints mechanism for entities qualified to bring an action under Article 2 of Directive 2009/22/EC on injunctions for the protection of consumers' interests – see Directive 2009/22/EC of 23 April 2009, OJ L 110/30.

"super-complaints" mechanism in UK competition law.[39] Such a complaints mechanism would, again, risk placing a significant burden on the Commission.[40] The idea of a market investigation regime to allow for fast intervention might be compromised if a significant part of the staff were kept busy with preparing fast-track reports. In addition – and while recognizing the manifold interactions – a European market investigation regime would be meant to be an instrument of competition policy that fills very specific gaps, not of consumer protection policy.

3.5 The Procedural Design of a European Market Investigation Regime

The procedural setup must be driven by the goal to ensure

- a *rigorous, robust analysis* of the features of a relevant market, of the competition problems that may possibly result, and of conceivable remedies;
- a *fair and transparent procedure* that effectively protects the procedural guarantees of the parties to the proceeding and ideally allows for an open and participative exchange;
- an efficient procedure that ensures a timely and effective intervention where needed; and
- the necessary degree of *flexibility* to adapt the procedure to the type of market and competition problem at issue.

This chapter shall first specify the general setup of a European market investigation procedure (Section 3.5.1). Options for speeding up the procedure will be discussed separately (Section 3.5.2). This chapter shall furthermore look at possible legal instruments to increase the

---

[39] See Section 11 of the Enterprise Act 2002: In the United Kingdom, designated consumer bodies can make "super-complaints" to the CMA where they find that a market for goods or services has a feature, or combination of features, that is or appears to be significantly harming the interests of consumers and should therefore be investigated. The CMA must respond to a super-complaint by publishing a "fast-track" report on what action, if any, it intends to take within ninety days. For more on this, see Whish/Bailey (fn. 29), at Chap. 11.3. See also Super-complaints: Guidance for designated consumer bodies, OFT 514, July 2003, available at www.gov.uk/cma.

[40] For the UK experience, see Whish/Bailey (fn. 29), at Chap. 11.3.

incentives to cooperate of the parties to a market investigation proceeding (Section 3.5.3) and at the need to provide for a possibility to modify the scope of a market investigation proceeding (Section 3.5.4).

Generally speaking, a European market investigation procedure must find a sound compromise between flexibility, the need for administrative efficiency and speed, and the aim to create a participative procedure that allows for a more open and less adversarial exchange between the Commission and the undertakings concerned, on the one hand, and the recognition that a market investigation can severely affect the interests of undertakings, on the other, and that formal procedural guarantees will consequently need to be respected.

The goal of an open exchange with market actors based on a shared interest in well-functioning markets may be easier to achieve in some settings than in others – depending not least on the remedies envisioned. Market investigation proceedings will arguably remain more or less adversarial the more the remedies intrude into strategic business interests of selected undertakings. A cooperative attitude becomes more likely the less intrusive and selective the remedies are.

To get the full benefit of an open and participative proceeding, it may therefore make sense to provide for two alternative procedural paths in market investigation proceedings: Where market-wide, non-selective remedial measures would be envisioned, some procedural guarantees as foreseen in Article 41 of the Charter of Fundamental Rights may not be applicable and could be replaced by a transparency regime. Such a regime would allow for an earlier and more open exchange between the Commission and the market. Where the Commission would consider the imposition of remedies on selected undertakings, the Article 41–guarantees would, however, apply and would require a more formalized proceeding. The proposition for a two-pronged proceeding will be further explained below. It will be discussed in particular under Section 3.5.2.5.

3.5.1 The Structure of Market Investigation Proceedings

As discussed in Section 3.3.2, a future European market investigation regime is currently conceived of as a separate and self-standing procedure that would comprise both a full-fledged investigatory phase and an exploration of potential remedies. Different from the CMA market

investigation that follows up on a market study,[41] a European market
investigation would not be meant to function as a second phase to a
preceding "phase 1" investigatory proceeding.

This has a number of implications:

- The opening decision for a European market investigation would
  frequently be rather preliminary, based on an informal scoping
  phase, and would provide a relatively rough sketch of the potential
  competition problem to be explored. As further investigations into
  the market could substantially change the understanding of the
  competition problem, it would be important to provide for the
  possibility of a modification of the scope of the market investigation
  proceeding[42] (see Section 3.5.4).
- In such a setting, the CMA model to integrate the analysis and
  discussion of the competition problem and the discussion of potential remedies from the start would not work. There would be a need
  for a first evidence gathering phase (phase I) during which the focus
  is on understanding the special features of the relevant market and
  exploring the suspected competition problem. Only once the competition problem is – at least provisionally – specified and verified
  would it make sense to discuss potential remedies with the undertakings concerned in a second phase of the proceeding (phase II).
- In order to ensure a speedy proceeding, a Market Investigation
  Regulation would need to set out clear deadlines. At the same time,
  a significant degree of flexibility would be needed, given the broad
  range of competition problems that market investigations may
  potentially address and the varying degree of complexity of market
  investigation proceedings.

3.5.1.1 The Basic Structure of Market Investigation Proceedings: An Overview

European market investigation proceedings would typically comprise
the following stages:

- An initial informal scoping phase
- An opening decision

[41] See Fletcher, Chapter 8.
[42] This notwithstanding, the Commission's commitment not to open Article
101 and 102 TFEU infringement proceedings where the relevant allegation
coincides with the competition problem described in the original opening
decision should continue to be honored.

- Depending on the type of remedies envisioned:
  - Where the remedies potentially envisioned are addressed to a selected group of undertakings active in the market
    - An evidence gathering phase I of a maximum of twelve months (with a possibility of a one-off six months extension), which could end either with a closure of the proceedings or with a rough informal summary of the findings, of the theories of harm explored, and presentation of bright-line principles for suitable remedies that would not necessarily be published, but provide a basis for state-of-play-meetings and commitment negotiations;
    - A phase II of a maximum of twelve months (with a possibility of a one-off six months extension) during which further evidence gathering would be accompanied by market consultation, discussions with the potential addressees of remedies and an informal market testing of the remedies envisioned
    - The sending out of a provisional draft of the decision to the potential addressees of remedies
    - Access to the file for the potential addressees of remedies and hearings
    - Publication of a decision adopting the final remedies
  - Where market-wide remedies are considered:
    - An initial evidence gathering phase (phase I)
    - The publication of a provisional findings report that would present the evidence gathered during phase I, as well as the theories of harm explored and potential remedial options if a relevant competition problem would appear to be corroborated by the evidence
    - Informal consultations on the findings and remedial options and – if needed – a continuation of evidence gathering (phase II)
    - Decision adopting the final remedies
- Implementation of remedies

3.5.1.2 The Scoping Phase

Market investigation proceedings – like other competition policy proceedings – would normally be preceded by a preliminary, non-public investigation that would collate all the market information available and discuss the existence of a competition of the type to be addressed by the market investigation. At the end of this phase, the Commission may decide to dismiss the suspected competition concerns, to open an infringement proceeding, or to open a market investigation proceeding.

3.5.1.3 The Opening Decision

In its opening decision, the Commission would have to sketch the suspected competition problem, define the scope of the proceeding and explain why it has opted for a market investigation (see Section 3.3.2.2). The opening decision could be a relevant reference point for any interim measures (see Section 3.8) and it would delineate the field within which the undertakings in the market would be subject to an obligation to cooperate (see Section 3.5.2.4) – but simultaneously protected from the opening of an infringement proceeding (see Section 3.3.1.2).

A market investigation could be used to address a competition problem specific to a given market, or it could address a specific type of market practice used across multiple markets that, combined with specific features of the relevant markets, could lead to relevant competition problems in multiple markets.[43] The procedure would be the same in both cases.

Contrary to the UK practice,[44] no consultation should be required before initiating a European market investigation proceeding. Given that, in the EU, market investigations would typically not be preceded by a sector inquiry or other form of formalized market analysis, there would not be enough substantial information on which to consult meaningfully.

Where a market investigation proceeding would primarily relate to national markets with cross-border impact, the opening decision could be preceded by an internal consultation within the framework of the ECN. Such a consultation should be mandatory if infringement proceedings or market investigations relating to the same factual setting are pending at the national level.

The opening decision would be published.

3.5.1.4 Two Procedural Options for European Market Investigation Proceedings

Arguably, the Commission should be able to proceed along two alternative paths after the publication of the opening decision: where the

---

[43] This mirrors the distinction between "ordinary references" and "cross-market references" in the CMA market investigation regime – see Enterprise Act 2002, s 131(6).

[44] Enterprise Act 2002, s 169.

Commission would consider the imposition of remedies upon a limited number of selected market participants – for example, on a dominant undertaking or on a small number of oligopolists – access to the file and hearing requirements would need to be observed, as they follow from Article 41 of the Charter of Fundamental Rights (see Section 3.5.2.5). To a relevant degree, these requirements would structure the proceedings: the potential addressees of a remedial decision would need to be able to express their view on the full findings of the Commission, as well as on the theory of harm on which the Commission has ultimately settled, and they would need to be granted access to the full file (except for confidential information). Where the Commission would consider the imposition of market-wide remedies – for example, a general obligation on all undertakings active in the market to provide information to consumers, a general portability or interoperability requirement or a generalized prohibition to make use of MFNs – Article 41 of the Charter of Fundamental Rights would arguably not be applicable. A more open and participative approach to market investigation proceedings may then be feasible (see Section 3.5.2.5).

Market Investigation Proceedings That May Result in the Imposition of Remedies upon a Limited, Selected Group of Undertakings

Where the Commission would consider the imposition of remedies on selected market participants only, the procedural guarantees of Article 41 of the Charter of Fundamental Rights would apply. After the publication of the opening statement – which should already consider the remedial options in this regard – the potential addressees of a remedial decision would need to be informed that they will henceforth be treated as parties to the investigation. Before a final remedial decision is taken, the Commission would then be required to present the undertakings concerned with a document that is functionally similar to a "statement of objections" in infringement proceedings, and might, in the market investigation context, take the form of a provisional draft of the remedial decision. This draft decision would then be the basis of the hearings and for access to the file.

The provisional draft decision would be based on a two-step evidence gathering proceeding: an initial phase I of a maximum of twelve months (with a possibility of a one-off extension of six months based on justified reasons) would be fully dedicated to evidence gathering.

Despite the fact that the market investigation should ideally enable a
less adversarial interaction between the Commission and the market
actors, as it does not involve the finding of an infringement, the
Commission would not be able to rely solely on the voluntary cooperation of the market actors. Contrary to merger control proceedings, the
undertakings potentially affected by remedies in a market investigation
proceeding would not necessarily have an incentive to provide the
information requested in a timely fashion. The Commission would
therefore need to dispose of the full set of investigative powers. It
would need to be able to issue requests for information, and it would
need to have the power to take statements and the power to conduct
inspections – essentially all the powers it would have in an infringement proceeding or a sector inquiry (see Articles 18–22 Reg. 1/2003).
Furthermore, it must be able to enforce compliance by way of imposing
sanctions. After an initial evidence gathering period of a maximum of –
arguably – twelve months, the Commission should assess whether the
evidence gathered and the remedial options available[45] justify a continuation of the proceeding or whether the proceeding should be
closed.

If the Commission would decide to continue, it should, in a phase II,
consult more broadly with the market and with the potential addressees of remedies. The latter should be able to discuss the preliminary
findings and possible remedial options with the market investigation
team in the course of state-of-play meetings.[46] They should have the
possibility to present their own remedial proposals. Commitment
negotiations may take place at this point (see Section 3.7). The
Commission could also informally discuss remedial options with other
market actors.

[45] For the need to consider remedial options early on, see Motta/Peitz, Chapter 2:
"We shall stress that the EC should start thinking of remedies already at the very
early stages of a NCT process. In particular, it should start thinking of remedies
as soon as a theory of harm is formulated ... and even before starting a NCT
investigation officially." Similarly: Fletcher, Chapter 8: "Potential remedies are
now considered from the start of the process, and sometimes even (informally)
before the formal Market Investigation launch."

[46] On State of play-meetings in the context of infringement and merger
proceedings, see Wils, The oral hearing in competition proceedings before the
European Commission (April 21, 2012), 35 *World Competition: Law and
Economics Review* (2012), 397, from the updated version, last revised: May 7,
2020, available at SSRN: https://ssrn.com/abstract=2050453, at IX., p. 37/38.

Phase II should be limited to a maximum of twelve months (with a possibility of a one-off extension of six months based on justified reasons).

Based on the insights gained in phase I and II, the Commission would prepare a provisional draft decision and send it out to the potential addressees of the remedies envisioned. These undertakings must then be granted access to the file,[47] subject to the legitimate interest of undertakings in the protection of their business secrets (see Article 18(3) EUMCR) and have an opportunity to present their views. A remedial decision could only be based on facts and theories of harm on which these parties have been able to submit their observations. In addition to the opportunity to submit their comments in writing, the parties should have a right to request an oral hearing.[48]

Other natural or legal persons may be heard insofar as the Commission deems it necessary. Applications to be heard on the part of such persons should be granted where they show a sufficient interest.[49] They would, however, not benefit from a right to access to the file.[50]

[47] Access to the file shall be limited to those parties. For access to the file in merger/infringement proceedings, this is in line with Article 15(1) Reg. 773/2004 and Article 17(1) Reg. 802/2004: In these cases, access to the file is granted to the addressee of the statement of objections.

[48] Analogous to Article 12(1) of Reg. 773/2004 and to Article 14(1) of Reg. 802/2004. An oral hearing should arguably be offered irrespective of the fact that the fundamental right to be heard does not entail a right to be heard orally, as long as there is a possibility to effectively make known one's views in writing – for this, see Wils (fn. 46) at p. 397 et seq., from the updated version, last revised: May 7, 2020, available at SSRN: https://ssrn.com/abstract=2050453, at II, p. 5/6.

[49] See Article 27(3) Reg. 1/2003 and Articles 10, 11, and 13 of Reg. 773/2004; Article 18(4) EUMCR; and Article 11 Reg. 802/2004.

[50] A right to access to the file would not follow from the Transparency Reg. 1049/2001, either: the same general presumption that has been accepted in other competition law proceedings should apply: the disclosure of such documents would undermine the protection of the purpose of inspections and investigations as well as the protection of the commercial interests of the undertakings party to the proceeding as it has been accepted in other competition law proceedings (See Case T-677/13, *Axa Versicherung v Commission*, EU:T:2015:473, at para. 39; C-365/12 P, *Commission v EnBW et. al.*, EU:2014:112, at para. 93). No specific examination of each document would hence be required. If access were granted under the Transparency Reg. 1049/2001, the careful balance of the protection of procedural rights of the parties, the legitimate interests of undertakings in the protection of their business secrets and other confidential information, and the public interest in ensuring a manageable procedure that would underlie a

The final decision should normally be published two years after the opening decision – where use is made of the possibility for an extension, the final decision would be published within no more than three years after the opening of the proceeding.

In some cases, a market investigation proceeding may follow up on a sector inquiry or on an infringement proceeding that has convinced the Commission of the existence of a broader competition problem that cannot be adequately addressed based on the traditional competition rules, or it may otherwise be based on a substantial amount of information and evidence available already when the market investigation is opened. In such a case, the Commission may be able to move much more quickly. In particular, phase I may then be much quicker. For such settings, in which the Commission would already dispose of a good informational and analytical basis at the outset, a future Market Investigation Regulation might fix a legally binding deadline of eighteen months from the opening decision to the final remedial decision.

Market Investigation Proceedings That May Result in Remedies Imposed on a Limited Number of Selected Market Participants
Market investigation proceedings may be structured differently where market-wide remedies are considered. This may be appropriate in particular where demand-side problems – such as asymmetric information or consumers' behavioral biases – play a relevant role. In these cases, Article 41 of the Charter of Fundamental Rights may not be pertinent. Instead of formal "access to the file" proceedings, the Commission could and should ensure a high degree of transparency and opportunities for market participants to comment in other ways. Market investigation proceedings could greatly benefit from such an open and participative approach.

Again, the Commission would start with an initial phase I evidence gathering phase of no more than twelve (+ six) months. At the end of this phase, it would decide whether to close proceedings or to proceed. In case of continuation, the Commission would publish a preliminary findings report that would summarize the evidence (with full respect to confidentiality), explain the potential theories of harm, and set out bright-line principles for suitable remedies.

European Market Investigation Regulation's access to the file regime would be upset.

The report would then be the basis for a broad consultation with market participants and stakeholders in a phase II of no more than twelve (+ six) months. The final decision would follow.

The advantage of this proceeding would be its openness: the preliminary report would inform the market actors and stakeholders about the direction of the investigation early on. Phase II would benefit from an active and open discussion.

3.5.2 Options to Promote a Timely Intervention in Light of the Fundamental Guarantees of Procedural Fairness

One of the core goals of introducing a European market investigation regime would be to allow for a particularly timely intervention before competition problems become so entrenched that they are difficult to remedy. While there is some tension between the goal to identify and address the potentially highly complex competition problems that cannot be effectively addressed with the traditional competition rules, and to do so particularly fast, the CMA market investigation provides an example that the tension can be managed.

Compared to infringement proceedings, market investigation proceedings may sometimes enable the Commission to move faster because no infringement need be proven.[51] This in itself will not suffice, however. If the market investigation regime is to allow for a significantly faster correction of relevant failures of competition, options for accelerating the proceedings need to be explored.

Time savings could possibly result (a) from acknowledging that proving a relevant competition problem will not necessarily presuppose a formal market definition,[52] (b) from the introduction of strict and legally binding deadlines, and (c) from the adoption of some procedural innovations that would allow for a speedier course of action.

Overall, a lean, streamlined, yet sufficiently flexible procedural framework will be needed. This includes a need for effective investigatory powers (Sections 3.5.2.2 and 3.5.2.3). Possibilities for strengthening the incentives of market actors to cooperate shall be explored in turn (Section 3.5.3). Finally, where the market analysis

---

[51] See Motta/Peitz, Chapter 2.
[52] If the EU legislator were to opt for a dominance-based market investigation regime, a formal market definition will obviously be required.

suggests a shifting of the focus of market investigation proceedings as it was set out in the opening decisions, such a modification should be possible without the need to open a new market investigation proceeding (Section 3.5.4).

3.5.2.1 Structure of the Analysis: Need for a Formal Market Definition?

Defining the relevant market(s) at the outset of a proceeding would frequently provide a helpful framework for the subsequent economic analysis. Generally, it will serve to identify the relevant competitive constraints faced by firms in any given field of market activity. Also, it can help to identify barriers to entry and thus provides a basis for assessing the market power of incumbent firms.

However, in some settings, market definition can become a highly complex and uncertain exercise. The Special Advisors Report has expounded some of the conceptual difficulties that a traditional market definition faces in an environment characterized by strong network externalities, zero-price offers, business strategies based on the construction and expansion of ecosystems, and in highly dynamic and fast-changing settings.[53] In such settings, established methods of market definition often fail to produce unambiguous results.[54] The problem can be particularly acute where the potential competition law intervention takes place not with a view to sanctioning past infringements but to preserve competition in the future. In fast changing, innovative markets, consumer perceptions of viable substitutes can quickly change.[55]

A European market investigation regime would combine an ex post analysis with a forward-looking perspective: it would frequently be based on the finding of an existing structural competition problem but sometimes on a risk to competition. Where remedies are imposed, this would always be done with a forward-looking attitude.

[53] Crémer/Montjoye/Schweitzer, Competition Policy for the Digital Era, https://ec.europa.eu/competition/publications/reports/kd0419345enn.pdf, p. 42–48. See also Fletcher, Chapter 8.
[54] See Franck/Peitz, Market Definition and Market Power in the Platform Economy, May 2019, https://www.cerre.eu/sites/cerre/files/2019_cerre_market_definition_market_power_platform_economy.pdf, p. 19–67, for a discussion of the conceptual difficulties of a market definition in the platform economy.
[55] Crémer/Montjoye/Schweitzer, Competition Policy for the Digital Era, https://ec.europa.eu/competition/publications/reports/kd0419345enn.pdf, at p. 47.

In such a setting, a formal market definition with a clear drawing of the boundaries may not always be necessary.[56] Depending on the theory of harm to competition, it can be useful to allow the Commission to explicitly consider existing uncertainties and to acknowledge different degrees of substitutability that can then be considered in the subsequent competitive analysis. This may, inter alia, allow the Commission to better take account of the role that certain input factors (like data) can play across market boundaries, the role of ecosystems, and forms of "conglomerate power."

3.5.2.2 Duty of Expedition and/or Binding Deadlines

The goal to ensure a particularly timely intervention may argue for the fixing of binding deadlines for the various procedural steps that a market investigation involves. The European merger control regime provides a good example for the accelerating effect that tight legal deadlines[57] can have – albeit in a setting where the parties to the concentration have strong incentives to cooperate and to submit all relevant information in a timely fashion. Likewise, the CMA market investigation regime provides for a tight time frame: the CMA must complete its investigations within eighteen months of the date of the reference,[58] with a possibility for a six months extension for "special reasons."[59]

A future European Market Investigation Regulation could adopt this model. However, consideration should be given to the fact that, unlike CMA market investigations, market investigation proceedings would not be preceded by a market study and that a European market investigation can potentially require an analysis of many more national

---

[56] See also Fletcher, Chapter 8. For proposals for a more flexible approach to market definition within the realm of "traditional" competition law, see Economic Advisory Group on Competition Policy, an Economic Approach to Article 82, https://ec.europa.eu/dgs/competition/economist/note_eagcp_july_05 .pdf, p. 2–4; Salop, The first principles approach to antitrust, *Kodak*, and antitrust at the millennium, (2000) 68 *Antitrust Law Journal*, 187; Kaplow, Market definition: Impossible and counterproductive, (2013) 79 *Antitrust Law Journal*, 361; Schweitzer/Haucap/Kerber/Welker, *Modernisierung der Missbrauchsaufsicht für marktmächtige Unternehmen*, 2018, p. 42 et seq.

[57] See Article 10 European Merger Control Regulation.

[58] S 137(1) as amended by the ERRA 2013.

[59] S 137(2A) as amended by the ERRA 2012. According to the CMA, the inquiry period may be extended in complex cases, where, for example, there are multiple parties, issues, or markets. See CMA's Supplemental guidance, para. 3.7.

markets than the UK market investigation regime. A European market investigation may apply to very different settings, ranging from a European market the competition problems of which are already well understood, to relatively novel – potentially interrelated – markets the functioning of which is not yet well understood and that are national in scope. Consequently, some flexibility would be needed. Also, the need for speed notwithstanding, the time frame must allow for a thorough and robust investigation of all relevant facts[60] and for full respect for the procedural guarantees.

Against this background, it seems advisable that a future European Market Investigation Regulation would require the Commission to normally complete a market investigation procedure within 24 months from the date of the opening decision, and within no more than 36 months under exceptional circumstances (see Section 3.5.1). A "stop the clock" mechanism should be foreseen in case the parties to the proceeding would delay the evidence gathering.

In addition, a statutory duty of expedition may be foreseen in a future European Market Investigation Regulation. Market investigation proceedings can imply a significant degree of legal uncertainty for firms active in the relevant market. The duty of expedition would protect the interest of the parties to regain a sound basis for longer-term planning as soon as possible. Furthermore, a duty of expedition would lie within the logic of a market investigation, namely, the goal to protect undistorted competition in an effective and timely manner.

Procedurally, the time-sensitivity of market investigation proceedings provides a justification for codifying binding deadlines for requests for information in order to disincentivize strategic delays from the start. However, the Commission must be able to modify the deadline where a request for information is particularly complex,[61] and undertakings must be able to request extensions if needed. The deadline "must enable the addressee of the decision not only to provide its

---

[60] A potential judicial review of a Commission's final remedial decision will include a review whether "the evidence presented contains all the information which must be taken into account in order to assess a complex situation and whether it is capable of substantiating the conclusions drawn from it." See Case C-12/03 P, *Tetra Laval*, EU:C:2005:87, at para. 39.

[61] According the Union Courts' jurisprudence, RFI deadlines must not impose a disproportionate burden. See, in the context of Article 18 Reg. 1/2003: Case T-306/11, *Schwenk v Commission*, EU:T:2013:123, at paras. 72 et seq.

reply in practical terms, but also to satisfy itself that the information supplied is complete, correct and not misleading."[62] When considering requests for an extension of the statutory deadline, the Commission would need to consider the economic situation of the addressee.[63] At the same time, the proportionality of the deadline would be affected by the need for speed:[64] the fact that the Commission would itself be subject to legally binding deadlines would influence the proportionality review.[65]

3.5.2.3 Importing Information from Other EU Proceedings and Information Exchange with National Competition Authorities (NCAs)

Importing Information from Other EU Proceedings (Infringement Proceedings, Sector Inquiries, Merger Proceedings)

In some settings, a market investigation may follow up on an infringement proceeding (or a series of infringement proceedings with remedies that were not able to solve the underlying structural problem), or on information gained during a sector inquiry or a merger proceeding, or on investigations from regulatory authorities. In these settings, an abbreviated procedure (see Section 3.5.1.4) may be an option. However, this may depend on a possibility to draw on the information gathered in prior proceedings for the purposes of a market investigation proceeding, instead of collecting the relevant information anew.

Both Reg. 1/2003 and the EU Merger Control Regulation constrain such transfers of information: information acquired as a result of the application of the rules of either of the two regulations shall be used only for the purpose for which it was acquired.[66] According to the Union Courts' established jurisprudence, these limits are intended to protect the rights of defense of the undertakings that submit

---

[62] Case T-306/11, *Schwenk v Commission*, EU:T:2013:123, at para. 73.
[63] Case T-302/11, *HeidelbergCement v Commission*, EU:T:2014:128, at para. 107.
[64] Case T-306/11, *Schwenk v Commission*, EU:T:2013:123, at para. 81.
[65] See Case T-310/01, *Schneider Electric*, EU:T:2002:254, at paras. 94 et seq.; para. 100: pointing to the "requirement for speed which characterises the overall scheme of Reg. No. 4064/89" for finding that the time-limit fixed was reasonable.
[66] See Article 28(1) Reg. 1/2003 and Article 17(1) European Merger Control Regulation.

information.[67] They also derive from the protection of professional secrecy.[68]

However, even if the information gathered under the Merger Regulation or under Reg. 1/2003 "may not be directly used as evidence in a procedure not governed by that regulation, they nevertheless amount to factors that may, where appropriate, be taken into account to justify the opening of a procedure under another legal basis"[69] and, subsequently, a new request for a document.[70] Neither the Commission nor the Member States are "required to ignore the information disclosed to them and thereby undergo ... 'acute amnesia.'"[71]

If the Commission has obtained information during a previous proceeding that indicates a competition problem, it could, under this case law, initiate a market investigation proceeding, using that information as circumstantial evidence and verifying or supplementing it on the basis of the investigatory powers provided for in a future European Market Investigation Regulation.[72]

---

[67] Case C-85/87, *Dow Benelux v Commission*, EU:C:1989:379, at para. 18: This requirement "is intended to protect the rights of the defence of undertakings, guaranteed by Article 14(3) [of Reg. 17/62]. Those rights would be seriously endangered if the Commission could rely on evidence against undertakings which was obtained during an investigation but was not related to the subject-matter or purpose thereof."

[68] Case C-67/91, *Asociación Española de Banca Privada and Others*, EU:C:1992:330, at para. 37: "Professional secrecy entails not only establishing rules prohibiting disclosure of confidential information but also making it impossible for the authorities legally in possession of such information to use it, in the absence of an express provision allowing them to do so, for a reason other than that for which it was obtained." Furthermore, Art 7, 8 of the Charter of Fundamental Rights require such a restrictive handling of data.

[69] Case T-79/14, *Secop v Commission*, EU:T:2016:118, at para. 82; with reference to: judgments in Case C-85/87, *Dow Benelux v Commission*, EU:C:1989:379, at paras. 18–20, and in Case C-67/91, *Asociación Española de Banca Privada and Others*, EU:C:1992:330, at paras. 39 and 55.

[70] Case C-238, 244, 245, 247, 250–252, 254/99 P, *Limburg Vinyl Maatschappij*, EU:C:2002:582 and EU:C:2001:574, at paras. 304–305.

[71] See Case C-67/91, *Asociación Española de Banca Privada and Others*, EU:C:1992:330, at para. 39, referring to the judgment in Case C-85/87, *Dow Benelux v Commission*, EU:C:1989:379, at paras. 18 and 19.

[72] See Case C-85/87, *Dow Benelux v Commission*, EU:C:1989:379, at para. 19 (in the infringement proceeding context): Barring the Commission from doing so would "go beyond what is necessary to protect professional secrecy and the rights of the defence and would thus constitute an unjustified hindrance to the performance by the Commission of its task of ensuring compliance with the

In order to further facilitate the transfer of information, the rules on investigatory powers under Reg. 1/2003 could be amended such that information gained on that legal basis could also be used in a market investigation that would be based on the same factual setting – for example, when an infringement proceeding is closed and a market investigation proceeding would be opened instead or when a sector inquiry would suggest the opening of a market investigation proceeding. Such an amendment could turn investigations under the rules of Reg. 1/2003 into a first phase investigation where the Commission is initially in doubt on whether an infringement proceeding or a market investigation proceeding would be more appropriate (see Section 3.3.2).

By contrast, a direct transfer of information obtained during a market investigation proceeding to an infringement proceeding will not be possible: to transfer information collected in a purely administrative proceeding to a quasi-criminal proceeding would violate the parties' rights of defense.

Exchange of Information with National Competition Authorities
With a view to infringement proceedings, Article 12 Reg. 1/2003 sets out the rules to be followed when information is exchanged between the Commission and NCAs. In principle, the Commission and the NCAs shall have "the power to provide one another with and use in evidence any matter of fact or of law, including confidential information" (Article 12(1) Reg. 1/2003). However, information exchanged shall only be used in evidence for the purpose of applying Articles 101/102 TFEU and in respect of the subject matter for which it was collected by the transmitting authority (Article 12(2) Reg. 1/2003). At the same time, NCAs may use the information exchanged also for the application of national law where national competition law is applied in the same case and in parallel to EU competition law and does not lead to a different outcome.

A question arises whether an NCA could provide the Commission with information gathered in the course of an infringement proceeding where that proceeding and a market investigation proceeding conducted at the EU level would refer to the same factual setting.

competition rules in the common market and to bring to light infringements of Articles 85 and 86 of the Treaty."

According to fundamental principles of procedural fairness as guaranteed by Article 41 of the Charter of Fundamental Rights, two conditions must be fulfilled for an exchange of information to be admissible: (1) the transfer of information must be provided for by law; and (2) the information transferred must not have been obtained under an investigatory regime that provides for a lower degree of procedural protection than the one that is applicable in the context in which the information shall be used after the transfer. Consequently, information collected in the course of a proceeding in which the further reaching guarantees of a quasi-criminal proceeding apply could be used in a market investigation proceeding, provided that a future European Market Investigation Regulation would provide for a clear legal basis.

3.5.2.4 Information Gathering in a Data-Driven Economy: Duty to Cooperate

Given the specific features of an economy driven by data processing and algorithmic decision-making, the question arises whether the "normal" investigatory powers that the Commission disposes of in infringement proceedings and should likewise possess in market investigation proceedings (see Section 3.5.1.4) would need to be complemented by a duty of cooperation. Ever more frequently, the Commission will not only need access to information. Rather, it will need to understand data collection and processing strategies and the precise ways in which the algorithms employed by relevant market actors function. As observed by Lord Tyrie in a letter to the Secretary of State for Business, Energy and Industrial Strategy,[73] broad varieties of complex data, including usage data, is now frequently stored in the cloud, and pricing decisions, as well as other decisions, are delegated to algorithms. It may be technically impossible to transfer algorithms, the historical data that serves as input, and the decision outputs to the Commission in any way that would be useful for competition investigation. Also, it may be difficult to impossible for the Commission to understand the purposes for which data is used or the way an

---

[73] Letter by Lord Tyrie, Chairman of the CMA, to the Secretary of State for Business, Energy and Industrial Strategy, February 21, 2019, https://assets .publishing.service.gov.uk/government/uploads/system/uploads/attachment_ data/file/781151/Letter_from_Andrew_Tyrie_to_the_Secretary_of_State_BEIS .pdf, Annex, at p. 32, fn. 51.

algorithm works even if it is transferred to the Commission.[74] What the Commission will need, therefore, is support from the firms in understanding the ways in which data is collected, processed, and stored, including the ways in which algorithms function. Such support may be a necessary precondition for drafting precise requests for information that help to clarify the relevant facts and that the addressees of such requests can sensibly answer.

A starting point may be the adoption of an expanded power to take statements as it is provided for in the ECN+ – Directive 2019/1. According to Article 9(1) of that Directive, "Member States shall ensure that national administrative competition authorities at a minimum are empowered to summon any representative of an undertaking or association of undertakings, any representative of other legal persons and any natural persons, where such representative or person may possess information relevant for the application of Articles 101 and 102 TFEU, to appear for an interview." On this basis, the Commission could obtain oral or written explanations from any market actor subject to the investigation or their representatives and staff[75] on which data is stored where and how to access it, which algorithms are employed, and how they function.

A further-reaching provision that could be adapted to the competition realm and be particularly useful in complex digital settings is Sec. 166 of the Financial Services and Markets Act 2000.[76] According to this provision, the financial regulator may require financial firms subject to its regulation to provide the regulator with a report on a matter of concern or to appoint a skilled person to be approved by the regulator to provide the regulator with a report and to provide that person with all such assistance as the person may reasonably require.

Such provisions could be backed up by a broader duty of undertakings to cooperate with the Commission in a market investigation proceeding. A duty to cooperate actively in the investigation is recognized already in infringement proceedings:[77] undertakings may be

---

[74] See Monopolkommission, Biennial Report XXIII, Chap. 1, Control of abusive practices in the digital platform economy, at para 98.

[75] For such a right, see also Article 11 (1)(c) of the SSM Reg. 1024/2013.

[76] See letter by Lord Tyrie (fn. 73), Annex, at p. 33, who refers to this provision.

[77] See Case C-374/87, *Orkem v Commission*, EU:C:1989:387, at paras. 22 and 27; Case T-46/92, *Scottish Football Association v Commission*, EU:T:1994:267, at para 31: individuals concerned by a request for information "must make

required to provide all necessary information concerning such facts as
may be known to it and to disclose all documents in its possession that
are related to the subject matter of an investigation. However, in
infringement proceedings, the Commission "may not compel an undertaking to provide it with answers which might involve an admission on
its part of the existence of an infringement."[78] For example, the
Commission may require the disclosure of factual information but
must not seek clarification of the objectives pursued by the undertakings if this would compel the undertakings to acknowledge a violation
of competition rules.[79]

In a future European market investigation proceeding, no infringement would be at issue. It would be a purely administrative procedure,
with no risk of self-incrimination.[80] A duty to cooperate may, therefore, include a duty to clarify the purpose of certain market action, a
duty to explain the functioning of an algorithm, or to perform certain
data-related tests on the Commission's behalf. Such a duty to cooperate would obviously be confined by a proportionality criterion.

A violation of the duty to cooperate could be sanctioned by fines. At
the same time, it may, where appropriate, allow the Commission to
conclude that a certain fact is to be regarded as proven[81] and preclude
the party concerned from challenging that fact finding in an appeals

available to the Commission all information relating to the subject-matter of the
investigation . . .. Consequently, the applicant's argument that the contested
decision could only have been justified if it had manifestly obstructed the
Commission in carrying out its task must be rejected. Given that the individuals
concerned have such an obligation to cooperate actively in the initial
investigation procedure, a passive reaction may in itself justify the adoption of a
formal decision."

[78] Case C-374/87, *Orkem v Commission*, EU:C:1989:387, at para. 35.
[79] Ibid., at paras. 38–39.
[80] For the right not to be compelled to admit a participation in an infringement as it
is interpreted and applied in EU Competition law, see Case C-374/87, *Orkem v
Commission*, EU:C:1989:387, at paras. 35–40; Case C-301/04 P, *Commission v
SGL Carbon*, EU:C:2006:432 and EU:C:2006:53, (at paras. 40–44); Case T-
371/17, *Qualcomm and Qualcomm Europe v Commission*, EU:T:2019:232, at
paras. 177–194.
[81] For the legitimacy of such a conclusion, see the German Bundesgerichtshof
decision of 14 July 2015, KVR 77/13 – Wasserpreise Calw II, at para. 30:
A dominant company has an obligation "to transmit data from its sphere of
influence to the competition authority which the authority cannot obtain in
another reasonable way . . .. If the company refuses to collaborate in this way,
the competition authority may draw conclusions from this within the scope of its
free assessment of evidence . . .. In an individual case, it may conclude that a

proceeding (see Section 3.5.3). Also, a violation of the duty of cooperation may be considered when it comes to the question whether to engage in commitment negotiation

3.5.2.5 Access to the File in European Market Investigation Proceedings

An essential part of the right of every person "to have his or her affairs handled impartially, fairly and within reasonable time" by the institutions of the EU is "the right of every person to have access to his or her file" (Article 41(2)(b) of the Charter of Fundamental Rights). The right to access to the file is not limited to quasi-criminal proceedings but applies likewise in purely administrative proceedings. It is intended, in particular, to enable the parties to a proceeding "to acquaint themselves with the evidence in the Commission's file so that on the basis of that evidence they can express their views effectively" on the conclusions reached by the Commission.[82] While this case law has developed in the context of infringement proceedings, its rationale would extend to proceedings like future European market investigation proceeding that – while purely administrative in nature – could negatively affect undertakings rights and interests in potentially far-reaching ways. From the Commission's perspective, access to the file – as well as the right to be heard – could help to enhance the accuracy and robustness of the Commission's findings. Furthermore, the guarantees of procedural fairness should contribute to the general acceptance of the outcomes of administrative proceedings and increase the willingness to comply.

At the same time, the granting of access to the file could become *the* most cumbersome and time-consuming part of the proceeding. This is so, in particular, because the Commission, when granting access to the file, is obliged to respect "the legitimate interests of confidentiality and of professional and business secrecy" (Article 41(2)(b) Charter of

---

certain fact is to be regarded as proven on account of the company's refusal to cooperate."
[82] See Case C-238, 244, 245, 247, 250–252, 254/99 P, *Limburg Vinyl Maatschappij*, EU:C:2002:582 and EU:C:2001:574, at paras. 315–316, with a view to Statement of Objections in infringement proceedings. See also Case C-51/92 P, *Hercules Chemicals v Commission*, EU:C:1999:357, at paras. 75–76.

Fundamental Rights and Article 339 TFEU).[83] The same is true for the right to anonymity of information providers at risk of reprisals.[84]

Market investigation proceedings could potentially be very complex proceedings, involving an extensive gathering of evidence. The process of first identifying confidential information in all those documents and subsequently weighing up the interests for and against disclosure and drawing up a non-confidential versions of the documents or, where appropriate, sufficiently comprehensible and precise summaries of their content, as the Commission does in infringement and merger control proceedings,[85] could become an impossible exercise in market investigation proceedings. It may have the potential to impair the ability of the Commission to manage market investigation proceedings in an effective and timely manner.

What is more, depending on the type of remedy that the Commission would envision, the number of undertakings potentially affected and possibly requesting access to the file could be large.

A future European Market Investigation Regulation would therefore need to deal carefully with "access to the file" issues. The question may, however, present itself in a different light depending on the remedial regime envisioned. It is not evident that Article 41(2)(b) of the Charter of Fundamental Rights will apply in all settings.

Where the Commission considers the imposition of remedies on individualized market actors – for example, on one, possibly dominant, undertaking or a limited number of large oligopolists in a market – Article 41(2)(b) of the Charter would obviously apply. In such cases,

---

[83] According to Article 339 TFEU, EU officials must not disclose "information of the kind covered by the obligation of professional secrecy, in particular information about undertakings, their business relations or their cost components."

[84] Case T-5/02, *Tetra Laval*, EU:T:2002:264, at paras. 98–101, 105, and 107; Case T-221/95, *Endemol Entertainment v Commission*, EU:T:1999:85, at para. 70; Case C-145/83, *Adams v Commission*, EU:C:1985:448, paras. 34, 35, and 37. For further discussion and references, see Wils/Abbott, Access to the file in competition proceedings before the European Commission (June 6, 2019), (2019) 42 *World Competition*, 255, from the updated version, last revised: May 15, 2020, available at SSRN: https://ssrn.com/abstract=3399935 or http://dx.doi .org/10.2139/ssrn.3399935, at III.B., p. 11/12.

[85] See Wils/Abbott (fn. 84) at p. 25, 29 with further references. For a specification of the right to access to the file in light of these principles in infringement proceedings and in merger proceedings, see Article 27(2) Reg. 1/2003 and Article 15 of Reg. 773/2004 (infringement proceedings); and Article 18(3) EUMCR and Article 17 of Reg. 802/2004 (merger control).

procedures would be needed that allow the Commission to handle the "access to the file" process efficiently.

Where the Commission would consider the imposition of market-wide remedies, on the other hand, Article 41(2)(b) of the Charter would arguably not be applicable. In these settings, a transparency regime could be envisaged instead (2).

Imposition of Remedies on Individualized Market Actors
Where the Commission contemplates the imposition of remedies on a limited number of selected undertakings in a market, these undertakings would benefit from the guarantee of Article 41(2)(b) of the Charter of Fundamental Rights. A proportionate balance would need to be struck between the right to access to the file and the protection of confidential information.[86] Administrative efficiency would be another relevant aspect to be considered in this balancing exercise, as has been recognized by the General Court.[87] This is true in particular where excessive demands upon the administration have the potential to compromise the Commission's ability to effectively protect a system of undistorted competition in the internal market – one of the EU's core aims.[88] In merger control proceedings, the General Court (GC) has furthermore recognized that the application of the principles governing the granting of access to the file "may reasonably be adapted to the need for speed."[89]

Given the goal of a future European market investigation regime to ensure an effective and timely intervention in case of competition problems falling under the scope of the instrument, measures should be considered to keep the "access to the file" process manageable. In the context of infringement and merger proceedings, certain procedures have been developed in order to lessen the tension between the

---

[86] See Wils/Abott (fn. 84), at p. 25.
[87] Case T-210/01, *General Electric*, EU:T:2005:456, at para. 694: "The need for the parties to have access to the Commission's case-file in order to be able to defend themselves, ultimately, against the objections raised by the Commission in the SO should not be interpreted as requiring the Commission to grant them access to its file in portions throughout the proceedings, a requirement which would represent a disproportionate burden on it."
[88] See Article 3(3) TEU with Protocol No. 27.
[89] Case T-221/95, *Endemol Entertainment v Commission*, EU:T:1999:85, at para. 68; Case T-210/01, *General Electric v Commission*, EU:T:2005:456, at paras. 631 and 684. See also: Wils/Abott (fn. 84), at p. 30.

right to access to the file and the legitimate interest in preserving confidentiality. The data room procedure is one relevant example.[90] It may also play a role in market investigation proceedings.

Confidentiality rings are another useful instrument to appropriately balance the right to access to the file and confidentiality interests. Voluntary confidentiality rings[91] have already been used in several competition "access to the file" proceedings. These rings are based on negotiated agreements between information providers and SO addressees by which both agree that a restricted circle of persons (the members of the confidentiality ring; for example, external counsel) will get access also to confidential information and select from all documents those for which a non-confidential version must be prepared. In antitrust proceedings, the Commission can propose a confidentiality ring to the information provider and the SO addressee. The conclusion of a disclosure agreement remains voluntary, however. A mandatory confidentiality ring is excluded by Article 27(2) Reg. 1/2003, according to which "the right of access to the file shall not extend to confidential information."

In the context of market investigation proceedings, the EU legislator should consider whether to empower the Commission to mandate the formation of a confidentiality ring.[92] Obliging information providers to accept that external counsel gets access will interfere with the right to professional and business secrecy as it follows from Articles 7, 8, 16, and 17 of the Charter of Fundamental Rights, as well as from Article 339 TFEU. Under Article 52(1) of the Charter of Fundamental Rights, the interference could be justified when provided for by law, and provided that it respects the essence of the rights and is proportionate to the legitimate aim of ensuring administrative efficiency and an effective and timely protection of undistorted competition. The essence of the right to confidentiality would be respected if access to the

---

[90] See DG Competition, Guidance on Data Room Procedures, https://ec.europa.eu/competition/mergers/legislation/disclosure_information_data_rooms_en.pdf; and Wils/Abott (fn. 84), at p. 44–45 with further references.

[91] For the procedural design in such cases, see https://ec.europa.eu/competition/antitrust/conf_rings.pdf; Wils/Abott (fn. 84), at p. 46.

[92] For this proposal – with a view to infringement proceedings – see Albers, Aktuelle Entwicklungen in der Praxis des Anhörungsbeauftragten, in: *Schwerpunkte des Kartellrechts 2011*, 2012, at p. 35, 49.

information were limited to a narrow circle of external counsel who would be subject to a duty of professional secrecy and subject to sanctions in case of its violation.

Generally, the right to access to the file is limited to documents that are of relevance to the decision taken by the Commission. There must be an "objective link" between the document and the objections raised by the Commission.[93] Failure to communicate evidence that is *adverse* to the interests of a party can be successfully challenged only if the Commission relied on that evidence to support its theory of harm and/ or remedial decision.[94] Moreover, if there is other documentary evidence that conclusively proves the Commission's findings and can be accessed by the party, a publication of further supporting evidence is not be required.[95] On the other hand, a party must have access to all *evidence that is potentially favourable to it*, for example, because it is not consistent with the inferences drawn by the Commission.[96] If there is at least "a small chance of altering the outcome of the administrative procedure," access must be granted.[97] The same is true if access would facilitate the defense of the party's interests in the administrative proceedings.[98] These principles have been developed by the Union courts in infringement proceedings. However, they likewise apply in merger proceedings. They are not limited to quasi-criminal nature of a proceeding but are based on Article 41(2)(b) of the Charter of Fundamental Rights and follow from the fact that an individualized administrative measure intervenes into fundamental rights. It is, therefore, very likely, that they would be applicable to future European market investigation proceedings, too.

---

[93] Case C-204, 205, 211, 213, 217, and 219/00 P, *Aalborg Portland and Others v Commission*, EU:C:2004:6, at paras. 126 and 128.

[94] Case T-53/03, *BPB v Commission*, EU:T:2008:254, at para. 42.

[95] See Case C-204, 205, 211, 213, 217, and 219/00 P, *Aalborg Portland and Others v Commission*, EU:C:2004:6, at para. 73; Case C-407/08 P, *Knauf Gips v Commission*, EU:C:2010:389, at para. 13; Case T-151/07, *Kone v Commission*, EU:T:2011:365, at para. 146; Case T-419/14, *Goldman Sachs v Commission*, EU:T:2018:445, at para. 215.

[96] Case C-407/08 P, *Knauf Gips v Commission*, EU:C:2010:389, at para. 23; Case T-441/14, *Brugg Kabel and Kabelwerke Brugg v Commission*, EU:T:2018:453, at para. 70.

[97] Case C-204, 205, 211, 213, 217, and 219/00 P, *Aalborg Portland and Others v Commission*, EU:C:2004:6, at para. 131.

[98] See references in Wils/Abott (fn. 84), at p. 56, fn. 243 and 244.

Transparency Rules in Case of Market-Wide Remedies
The legal setting differs in proceedings where market-wide remedies
would be considered. According to Article 41(2)b) of the Charter,
every person has a right to access to "his or her file," as part of the
right to have "his or her affairs handled impartially" and fairly.
Consequently, Article 41(2)(b) is applicable only where a person is
individually affected by the decisions to be taken in an administrative
proceeding. Where remedies of a market-wide nature are imposed that
affect all undertakings active in the market equally, a strong argument
can be made that none of these undertakings will be affected individually. According to settled case law in the field of state aid law, an
undertaking will not have standing under Article 263(4) TFEU to
contest a Commission decision that is not addressed to it directly if it
is concerned by that decision solely by virtue of belonging to the
relevant market in question.[99] Market-wide remedies imposed in
market investigation proceedings would resemble sectoral regulation.
Even if – contrary to the position taken here – the Union courts would
find Article 41(2)(b) of the Charter to be applicable in these types of
cases, the lack of individualization within the group of competitors
active in the same market and the typically lower depth of intervention
of market-wide remedies would justify more intense constraints on the
right to access to the file under Article 52(1) of the Charter.

In such a setting, it would therefore appear to be justified to substitute the normal "access to the file" proceeding with a general transparency regime to be developed for such market investigation proceeding,
which could build on the experience of the transparency regime prac-
ticed in CMA market investigations.[100] For example, a preliminary
findings report could be published following the phase I evidence
gathering, and hence relatively early on in the proceedings (see
Section 3.5.1.4). This would enable a more intense interaction with
undertakings in the market on the findings, their interpretation, and
potential remedies early on and in a more participative setting. A high
degree of transparency in the administrative proceeding would, in turn,
attenuate the intensity of the intervention into fundamental rights.

[99] See, from the area of state aid law, Case C 367/04 P, *Deutsche Post und DHL v Kommission*, EU:C:2006:126, at paras. 40, 41; Case C-525/04 P, *Spain v Lenzing*, EU:C:2007:698, at paras. 32, 33.
[100] See CMA, Transparency and disclosure: Statement of the CMA's policy and approach, January 2014.

At the same time, a well-designed transparency regime would keep market investigation proceedings more manageable for the Commission.

3.5.3 Additional Incentives to Cooperate

In principle, the burden of proving a relevant competition problem and the necessity and proportionality of any given remedy to the requisite legal standard will be on the Commission.

However, the parties to a future market investigation proceeding may be in possession of information and evidence that is essential for the correct understanding of the (mal-)functioning of the market. This is true in particular where information from inside a firm becomes relevant to the analysis. Sometimes, what prima facie appears to be a competition problem may ultimately benefit customers.[101]

In an infringement proceeding, the burden of proving efficiencies is on the infringer. A market investigation proceeding would not be an adversarial proceeding. Nonetheless, it should be considered part of the general duty to cooperate (see Section 3.5.2.4) of the parties to the proceeding (and normally in their own best interest) to come forward with relevant evidence in time. As a matter of clarification, a future European Market Investigation Regulation may specify that they bear the evidentiary burden for relevant information that clearly originates in their sphere.

In order to effectively dissuade firms from strategically delaying a market investigation proceeding by withholding relevant information, a rule may be considered that would preclude parties from bringing facts and arguments at the appeals stage when they could have been raised by the applicant during the administrative procedure but were not then raised.[102] While leaving the Commission's best effort

---

[101] In parallel to Article 101(3) TFEU. The UK market investigation regime speaks of "relevant customer benefits" – see s 134(7) and (8) of the Enterprise Act and UK Competition Commission, Guidelines for market investigations, 2013. https://assets.publishing.service.gov.uk/government/uploads/system/uploads/attachment_data/file/284390/cc3_revised.pdf, p. 76 et seq.

[102] Such a rule would limit the parties' right to be heard and/or right to judicial review. See Case C-407/08 P, *Knauf Gips v Commission*, EU:C:2010:389, at paras. 90–92. In Knauf, the ECJ found that "[i]n the absence of a specific legal basis," the onus on a party "to react during the administrative procedure, or be faced with the prospect of no longer being able to do so before the Courts of the Union" would be a limitation on the exercise of the rights and freedoms

obligation unchanged to base its decision on all relevant information, it would sanction undertakings that violate their duty of cooperation.

3.5.4 Modifications of the Scope of a Market Investigation Proceeding

In the course of the more profound factual and economic analysis of a market, the initial understanding of the competition problem may change. Depending on the framing of the competition problem in the opening decision, the focus may then shift significantly. A future European Market Investigation Regulation should explicitly foresee that in such a case a reframing of the competition problem is possible without a need to open a new proceeding.[103]

3.6 Remedies

3.6.1 The Role and Goal of Remedies in Market Investigation Proceedings

A market investigation proceeding may have different outcomes:

- It could end with the finding that no competition problems exist that justify taking specific measures under a future European Market Investigation Regulation, or that a relevant competition problem exists but no adequate tools are available that could remedy the problem
- Possibly, it could end with a commitment decision (see Section 3.7)
- It could end with the imposition of remedies of a structural, behavioral, or hybrid kind
- Or with non-binding recommendations for new legislation or to companies[104] or to sectoral regulators

Where remedies were imposed, their goal would be to protect or reestablish competition – ideally by addressing the root cause of the competition problem that was found.

---

recognised by the Charter of Fundamental Rights and would need to be provided for by the law. It could, however, be justified under Article 52(1) of the Charter of Fundamental Rights.

[103] See, for example, Enterprise Act 2002, s 135 and UK Competition Commission, Guidelines for market investigations (fn. 101), at para. 27.

[104] E.g., for a code of conduct.

The different focus of a market investigation as compared to an infringement proceeding, namely, the structural competition concerns, would be reflected in a different focus of the remedies. The objective of Article 7–remedies is "to bring [the] infringement to an end." Remedies must be "proportionate to the infringement committed and necessary to bring the infringement effectively to an end." Remedies imposed under a market investigation procedure, on the other hand, would need to be suitable to address the competition problem identified and proportionate to that concern. They would not try to undo the consequences of an allegedly unlawful conduct but would be forward looking and strive to make the market function competitively in the future. A focus would be on reducing barriers to entry and expansion for competitors, on ensuring the continued contestability of positions of market power, on reducing incentives to coordinate or to impede or distort competition, and on maintaining or increasing the ability and incentives to compete.

3.6.2 General Legal Requirements: Effectiveness, Proportionality, Legal Certainty, and Duty to State Reason

Remedies imposed under a market investigation regime would affect the freedom to conduct a business (Article 16 Charter of Fundamental Rights) and the right to property (Article 17 Charter of Fundamental Rights). They must, therefore, be provided for by law, respect the essence of those freedoms and rights, and be proportionate. Also, they must genuinely meet objectives of general interest recognized by the Union and be necessary to achieve that goal (Article 52(1) of the Charter of Fundamental Rights).[105]

Undistorted competition is a fundamental and high-raking goal of the European Union (see Article 3 TEU with Protocol No. 27). Its effective protection justifies remedial intervention, provided that it is proportionate to the harm.

---

[105] For the case law to Art 52(1) of the Charter of Fundamental Rights, see Case C-283/11, *Sky Österreich*, EU:C:2013:28, at paras. 42 et seq.; Case C-277/16, *Polkomtel*, EU:C:2017:989, at para. 50, 51; Case C-540/16, *Spika and Others*, EU:C:2018:565, at paras. 34, 36; Case C-534/16, *BB construct*, EU: C:2017:820, at paras. 34–37; Case C-184/02 and C-223/02, *Spain and Finnland v Parlament and Council*, EU:C:2004:497, at paras. 51, 52; Case C-544/10, *Deutsches Weintor*, EU:C:2012:526, at para. 54.

A future European Market Investigation Regulation should provide for a remedial regime that is suitable to effectively address the types of market failures that the market investigation regime is meant to address and to reestablish and safeguard the competitive process. Obviously, the imposition of remedies would only be lawful to the extent that it would fit the theory of harm. The choice of a remedy (or of a package of remedies) should be guided by the aim of effectively addressing the competition problem comprehensively. Where possible, the Commission should address the root cause of the problem. Remedies that merely mitigate the problem(s) may be considered where other measures would not be available or practicable. Or they may be imposed as interim remedies where the final, more comprehensive remedy would need time to take effect. At the same time, the remedies would need to be practicable and proportionate. Also, competition should be reestablished within a reasonably short period of time.

Remedies must meet the requirements of legal certainty: undertakings must unambiguously know their rights and obligations. Any remedy imposed must therefore be precise and clear – both for the addressees and for other persons potentially affected by the remedy.[106]

The Commission would need to provide for a mechanism that would ensure an effective implementation and, if necessary, monitoring of the remedies.

Finally, Article 41(2)(c) of the Charter of Fundamental Rights and Article 296 TFEU would require the Commission to state the reasons that guided the imposition of the remedy in order to enable the Union Courts to review the legality of the measure and provide the addressees with an adequate indication as to whether the decision is well-founded or whether it may be vitiated by some defect enabling its validity to be challenged.[107] A failure to sufficiently state a reason may lead to the quashing of a remedy.[108]

---

[106] See Joined Cases 92 and 93/87, *Commission v French Republic et al.*, EU: C:1989:77, at para. 22.

[107] E.g., Case C-181/90, *Consorgan v Commission*, EU:C:1992:244, at para. 14; Case C-39/18 P, *Commission v Icap and Others*, EU:C:2019:584, at para. 23.

[108] Case T-395/94, *Atlantic Container Line AB and Others v Commission*, EU: T:2002:49, at paras. 412–416 (in the context of Article 7 Reg. 1/2003 remedies).

3.6.3 Types of Remedies and Choice between Remedies

A future European market investigation regime would be meant to address a wide spectrum of potentially multi-faceted competition problems. The suitable remedy or remedial package would need to be found case by case. A broad degree of flexibility would be required to design remedies that fit as precisely as possible the relevant theory of harm and market setting. A future European Market Investigation Regulation should not constrain the choice of remedies.[109]

Generally, a distinction is made between structural remedies, that is, one-off measures that directly alter the competitive structure of a market; behavioral remedies, that is, ongoing measures that regulate or mandate or constrain a certain conduct of market actors; and access remedies that may have characteristics of structural or behavioral remedies or both.[110] Whereas Article 7 Reg. 1/2003 states, with a view to remedying infringements of Articles 101 and 102 TFEU, that "[s]tructural remedies can only be imposed either where there is no equally effective behavioral remedy or where any equally effective behavioral remedy would be more burdensome for the undertaking concerned than the structural remedy," and thereby expresses a preference for behavioral remedies, the contrary is true for merger control, which is meant to preserve a competitive market structure, and where, consequently, "divestitures are the benchmark for other remedies in terms of effectiveness and efficiency. The Commission therefore may accept other types of commitments, but only in circumstances where the other remedy proposed is at least equivalent in its effects to a divestiture."[111]

Depending on the competition concern identified, remedies imposed as a result of a market investigation may need to focus on structure

---

[109] For a similar experience in the CMA market investigation regime, see Fletcher, Chapter 8.

[110] See, for example, Commission, Notice on remedies acceptable under Council Reg. 139/2004 and under Commission Reg. 802/2004, OJ 2008 No. C 267/1, at para. 17; Loertscher/Maier-Rigaud, On the consistency of the European Commission's remedies practice, in: Gerard/Komninos (eds.), *Remedies in EU Competition Law – Substance, Process and Policy*, 2020, p. 53–72, available at SSRN: https://ssrn.com/abstract=3450614 or http://dx.doi.org/10.2139/ssrn .3450614, at p. 7–12; UK Competition Commission, Guidelines for market investigations (fn. 101), at p. 78. The distinction is not always clear-cut, and in any given case, a remedy package may combine structural, behavioral and access elements.

[111] Commission, Notice on remedies (fn. 110), at para. 61.

and/or conduct. Where the competition concerns to be addressed by a
market investigation would be of a structural nature, the remedies
imposed should have a structural effect. But depending on the market
setting, structural effects may sometimes result from behavioral or
access remedies. Where the features of the market that tend to produce
anti-competitive effects would be linked to specific business strategies,
behavioral remedies might be required. Consequently, a future
European Market Investigation Regulation should not express a preference for either structural or behavioral remedies. Rather, the essential requirement would be that the remedy fits the relevant competition
problem.

3.6.3.1 Structural Remedies/Divestitures

Where a market investigation would be meant to address serious
competition problems of a structural nature, it may require structural
remedies, which may range from the removal of structural links with
competitors – for example, a divestiture of a minority shareholding in a
joint venture or a competitor where they contribute to the competition
concern[112] – to a full divestiture of a business to a new market
participant or a preexisting but independent market participant, where
this would be necessary to maintain competition.

As the imposition of structural remedies intrudes into fundamental
rights,[113] it would need to comply with the requirement of necessity
and proportionality as set out in Article 52(1) of the Charter of
Fundamental Rights. While they would be unlikely to become a standard remedy within a European market investigation regime, they may,
depending on the competition problem identified, come with the
advantage of changing the market dynamics and incentive structure
for the firms durably, and with no further monitoring and enforcement
cost once the measure has been implemented. They might, for example,
be considered where earlier infringement decisions and Article 7 remedies were not effective in restoring competition because they were
unable to address the underlying competition concern. In any given
case, the Commission would need to show convincingly that no other

---

[112] Ibid., at para. 58.
[113] This is true for all remedies. However, structural remedies will typically imply a
particularly strong form of intervention, in particular into the right to property
(Article 17 Charter of Fundamental Rights) and into the freedom to conduct a
business (Article 16 Charter of Fundamental Rights).

remedy is available that would be less intrusive but likely to be equally effective.

The divestiture commitments negotiated under Article 9 Reg. 1/2003 indicate that structural remedies can at times be appropriate also from a business point of view. As one-off measures, they would not necessarily be more burdensome on firms than behavioral remedies: contrary to a behavioral remedy that may constrain the strategic choices of businesses over a long period of time and will typically involve constant monitoring, a structural remedy comes with the benefit that its addressee will enjoy full flexibility after the implementation of the remedy.[114] Where the only alternative would be a durable sector regulation, structural remedies should be seriously considered.

3.6.3.2 Behavioral Remedies
Behavioral remedies would require a certain conduct or omission from the addressees of the remedial order. A relatively simple and clear-cut behavioral remedy would be an obligation imposed on companies to terminate or change certain types of agreements[115] or to refrain from using certain types of contract clauses.[116] Other behavioral commitments can be significantly more complex and would require further specification and ongoing monitoring. This could be true, for example, for a remedial order to facilitate switching or multi-homing, or for an order addressed to a vertically integrated or conglomerate firm to avoid self-preferencing in certain situations.

In merger settings, the Commission accepts behavioral remedies "only exceptionally in very specific circumstances."[117] A main concern is that it can be difficult to design and implement an effective compliance and monitoring mechanism for such remedies. Compliance costs and monitoring needs and costs will need to be considered in a market investigation context, too. Also, behavioral remedies that directly

---

[114] See Maier-Rigaud, Behavioural versus structural remedies in EU competition law, in: Lowe/Marquis/Monti (eds.), *EU Competition Law Annual 2013: Effective and Legitimate Enforcement of Competition Law*, 2016, available at SSRN: https://ssrn.com/abstract=2457594, at p. 210–211.
[115] For example, to terminate distribution agreements between competitors or agreements resulting in the coordination of certain commercial behavior between competitors or to terminate or change existing exclusive agreements. See Commission, Notice on remedies (fn. 110), at paras. 60 and 67–68.
[116] For example, MFN clauses.
[117] Commission, Notice on remedies (fn. 110), at para. 17.

intervene into business decisions over longer periods of time may reduce economic efficiency, dynamic incentives to invest and innovate, and may come with the side-effect of constraining competitive rivalry.[118]

Whether behavioral remedies are nonetheless suitable to address the relevant structural competition problem effectively and comprehensively and at reasonable cost to both the addressee of the remedy and the Commission[119] would need to be determined case by case.

3.6.3.3 Access Remedies

Access remedies seek to address the competition concern by mandating specified firms to grant access to key infrastructure, networks, key technology, patents, know-how,[120] or other essential input such as, possibly, data, at appropriate terms and conditions. Interoperability remedies that are much debated in the context of the digital economy are another sub-category of access remedies.

Access remedies may be considered where access to a certain input is essential for the competitive opportunities of existing and/or the entry of new competitors. In certain settings, the granting of access could remove or lower barriers to entry or expansion and effectively contribute to opening up competitive opportunities and markets.

In order to effectively implement access remedies, complex monitoring and enforcement regimes may be necessary, however. Like in merger control, the effectiveness of access remedies imposed within a market investigation framework would frequently depend on whether market participants themselves can effectively monitor and enforce these remedies – for example, via access to a fast dispute resolution mechanism. Like in merger control, the Commission should therefore only impose access remedies where the complexity does not lead to a risk of their ineffectiveness and where monitoring devices ensure that remedies would be implemented and enforced in a stringent and timely manner.[121]

---

[118] For this concern, see UK Competition Commission, Guidelines for market investigations (fn. 101), at paras. 336 and 352.

[119] For the limited power of the Commission to delegate monitoring powers to a trustee, see Case T-201/04, *Microsoft v Commission*, EU:T:2007:289, at paras. 1251–1279.

[120] Commission, Notice on remedies (fn. 110), at para. 62.

[121] Ibid., at para. 66.

3.6.3.4 Other Types of Remedies in Market Investigation Proceedings/Overlaps between Rule-Setting in a Market Investigation Context and Legislative Competences

Contrary to Article 7 Reg. 1/2003 remedies and merger remedies, remedies imposed as a result of a market investigation proceeding can address specific features of the market as such, with no link to a potential infringement or concentration. The Commission can therefore impose different and further-reaching remedies. The UK Guidelines for Market Investigations mention "enabling measures" in particular, and distinguish between (a) "market-opening measures" that, inter alia, "limit parties' abilities to require their customer to enter into long-term or exclusive contracts or to otherwise create switching costs for customers"; (b) "informational remedies, which are aimed at giving customers information to help them make choices and thereby increase competitive pressure on firms in the market"; and (c) "remedies that restrict the adverse effects of vertical relationships," such as "restriction of access to confidential information ('firewall provisions')," or FRAND obligations.[122]

Where market-wide remedies are imposed, they can at times resemble legislation. Within certain limits,[123] the EU legislator can delegate legislative powers to the Commission and has done so also in competition law.[124] In order to avoid a potentially excessive expansion of legislative powers of the Commission and an inappropriate overlap of competences of the Commission and the EU legislator, a future European Market Investigation Regulation could require that rule-like market-wide remedies come with a sunset clause. The Commission would then be able to provide for a fast fix for the relevant competition problem. But any such remedy would cease to have effect after a maximum of, say, five years, unless further legislative action is taken.

---

[122] UK Competition Commission, Guidelines for market investigations (fn. 101), at para. 376.
[123] Craig/De Búrca, *EU Law: Text, Cases and Material*, 2015, at p. 114–116.
[124] See, e.g., Council Reg. 19/65 of 2 March 1965 amended by Council Reg. 1215/ 1999 of 10 June 1999 and Council Reg. 1/2003 of 16 December 2002; Council Reg. 2821/71 of 20 December 1971 amended by Council Reg. 2743/72 of 19 December 1972 and Council Reg. 1/2003 of 16 December 2002.

3.6.4 *Procedure for the Imposition of Remedies*

3.6.4.1 Timing of Consultation on Remedial Options

In a proceeding that comes with strict time limits, the question of when the exploration and discussion of remedial options should start becomes crucial: while the competition problem must be sufficiently clear and well understood before the exploration of potential remedial options can start, it should not begin too late.[125] In the course of market investigation proceedings, the Commission should have a sound understanding of the competition problem and remedial options by the end of phase I. The parties to the proceeding should then have the possibility to comment and to propose and discuss other remedial options. Such propositions on alternative options should be possible even outside the framework of commitment negotiations (on commitments, see Section 3.7): they bring important information to the proceeding regarding the range of possibilities and will allow for a better assessment of which option is most appropriate and proportionate.

At the same time, the GC's finding that, where several Article 7 Reg. 1/2003 remedies exist for bringing an infringement to an end, "it is not for the Commission to impose upon the parties its own choice from among all the various potential courses of action which are in conformity with the Treaty,"[126] while already questionable in the Article 7 context, should not apply in a market investigation setting: it is not for the firms, but for the Commission to exercise judgment on what is the best way to address a specific competition problem. Given that market investigations will normally relate to economically complex facts and involve a prognostic element, the Commission would enjoy a significant margin of appreciation in designing the remedial regime. Simultaneously, it would be required to clearly state the reasons for its choice.

---

[125] The CC lost two cases before the Competition Appeal Tribunal (CAT) on remedies in 2009 – once in the Groceries Market Investigation (CAT, *Tesco v Competition Commission*, Case 1104/6/8/08 [2009] CAT 6, summary available at https://www.catribunal.org.uk/judgments/11046808-tesco-plc-judgment), a second time in the Payment Protection Insurance Market Investigation (CAT, *Barclays Bank PLC v Competition Commission*, Case 1109/6/8/09 [2009] CAT 27, summary available at https://www.catribunal.org .uk/judgments/11096809-barclays-bank-plc-2009-cat-27-judgment-16-oct-2009).

[126] Case T-24/90, *Automec v Commission*, EU:T:1992:97, at paras. 51–52.

The discussions about remedies must not unreasonably delay the closing of a market investigation procedure. Therefore, clear deadlines for remedial proposals by market participants must be fixed.[127] Only in exceptional circumstances may the Commission accept that proposals are submitted for the first time after the expiry of this period. The Commission should be available to discuss any proposals already in advance of the end of this period.

3.6.4.2 Mandatory Market Test for Remedies and Consultation of Outside Experts

There is a question whether remedies that the Commission proposes to impose on only a limited number of selected undertakings should be subjected to a mandatory market test, analogous to the market test foreseen in Article 27(4) Reg. 1/2003.[128] Under Reg. 1/2003, the market test is only foreseen for commitment decision (Article 9 Reg. 1/2003). Within the framework of market investigation proceedings, an argument may be made that the informal market consultation prior to the provisional draft decision would suffice.

A feature that could significantly contribute to the suitability of the remedial regime to address the competition concerns identified, as well as to its robustness and credibility, would be the involvement of outside expertise, be it economic or technical, in the remedy design. Ideally, a future European Market Investigation Regulation should provide for such a mechanism at a relatively early point of time – that is, during phase II. Due to institutional differences, a European market investigation regime would not involve independent expertise to the same extent as the CMA market investigation does.[129] Incorporating a mechanism that provides for a "fresh pair of eyes" at this crucial stage may, however, significantly contribute to the quality of the outcome and turn out to be an important neutrality check at the same time.

Whenever remedies are imposed in a regulated sector, the sectoral regulators should be involved in the discussion of remedies.

---

[127] Some guidance may be taken from the Commission's Notice on remedies (fn. 110), at para. 88, although the deadlines in market investigation proceedings could arguably be shorter.

[128] This has also been considered for Article 7 Reg. 1/2003 remedies. See Hellström/Maier-Rigaud/Bulst, Remedies in European antitrust law, (2009) 76 *Antitrust Law Journal*, 43, at p. 62; and Monti (fn. 7), at p. 199.

[129] See, for example, Fletcher, Chapter 8.

3.6.4.3 Possibility to Adjust Remedies in the Case of a Material Change in the Facts on Which the Remedies Were Based

The Commission could order a remedy with a limited duration – for example, by specifying an end date in a "sunset-clause" – where it would conclude that the competition problem will be of a limited duration or where a specific remedy in a broader remedy package shall only provide for a temporary arrangement.

With a view to cases where the competition problem to be addressed is considered to be a durable one, a future European Market Investigation Regulation should provide for a possibility to waive or alleviate a remedy either upon the request of an addressee of a remedy or ex officio where there has been a material change in any of the facts on which the remedial decision was based, such that the remedy becomes obsolete or disproportionate.

In the context of infringement proceedings, such a possibility is foreseen with a view to commitment decisions (Article 9(2)(a) Reg. 1/2003). Likewise, non-divestiture merger remedies usually include a review clause that allows the Commission, upon request by the parties showing good cause, to waive, modify, or substitute the commitments in exceptional circumstances. According to the Commission's Remedy Notice[130] (para. 74), it is "more relevant for non-divestiture commitments, such as access commitments, which may be on-going for a number of years and for which not all contingencies can be predicted at the time of the adoption of the Commission decision."

Where a waiver or adjustment of a remedy would be requested by the addressee of a remedy, the burden of showing exceptional circumstances should be on him/her. Exceptional circumstances should be accepted where market circumstances have changed significantly and on a permanent basis or where the addressees can show that the experience gained in the application of the remedy demonstrates that the objective pursued with the remedy would be better achieved if modalities of the commitment were changed. Like with merger remedies, a sufficient long time-span – normally at least several years – between the Commission decision and a request by the parties would normally be required. Where the waiver request entails complex

---

[130] Commission, Notice on remedies (fn. 110).

economic assessments, the Commission would have a certain discretion in its assessment.[131]

Vice versa, where the remedies imposed would prove to be inadequate with a view to the goals pursued – that is, where they would turn out to be ineffective or pose other significant problems at the implementation phase – a possibility should be foreseen to revisit the remedies ex officio within a fixed period of time while continuing to rely on the substantive findings regarding the competition concern. Such a mechanism is currently discussed for the CMA market investigation.[132] As Amelia Fletcher has pointed out, such a flexibility may be especially important in dynamic markets that are subject to fast and significant changes. "In such markets, the identified concerns may be fairly persistent ... but the appropriate remedies may well require flexing as the markets and technologies change."[133] Such a flexibility may ultimately benefit firms as well as consumers: "no one gains from costly, ineffective regulation."[134]

3.6.4.4 Mandatory Ex Post Evaluations

The legislator should think about providing for a mandatory ex post evaluation of remedies/commitments after a period of – say – five years, in order to allow the Commission to learn from past experience over time and to improve the framework. The evaluation may be done by independent outside experts in order to safeguard the Commission's resources and to ensure a "fresh pair of eyes."

3.7 Voluntary Commitments by Market Actors within the Framework of a European Market Investigation

Following the example of Article 9 Reg. 1/2003 (for infringement proceedings) and of the EU Merger Control Regulation, a future European Market Investigation Regulation should legally provide for the possibility of accepting undertakings offered by market actors and making them binding.

---

[131] Case T-712/16, *Deutsche Lufthansa v Commission*, ECLI:EU:T:2018:268, at para. 38.

[132] On this, see Fletcher, Chapter 8, referring to the letter of then Secretary of State Greg Clark MP from CMA Chair Lord Andrew Tyrie, 21 February 2019, at fn. 27.

[133] Fletcher, Chapter 8.   [134] Ibid.

3.7.1 *Justification for a Commitment Procedure within a European Market Investigation Proceeding*

Commitment proceedings are based on considerations of procedural economy: they shall allow for a more rapid solution to competition problems than would be feasible if the Commission were required to proceed by way of a formal remedial decision, and they shall thereby allow the Commission to make the most efficient use of its limited enforcement resources.

In the context of market investigation proceedings, commitment decisions could somewhat abbreviate the market investigation phase (albeit to a limited extent – see Section 3.7.2). More importantly, they could help to abbreviate the proportionality analysis linked to the comparison of different remedial options. While parties potentially affected by remedies would be able to come forward with their own remedial proposals anyhow, the making binding of a consensual solution may come with increased incentives of the parties to implement their proposed solution effectively. In addition, lengthy appeal proceedings would normally be avoided as the voluntary commitments would benefit from a presumption of proportionality.[135] Last but not least, a well-organized commitment procedure would widen the opportunities for a participative, non-adversarial style of proceeding and invite a productive cooperation between the Commission and the companies affected. The concerns sometimes raised against Article 9 Reg. 1/2003 commitment proceedings[136] would not apply to

---

[135] Opinion of Advocate General Kokott in Case C-441/07 P, *Commission v Alrosa*, EU:C:2009:555, at para. 55.

[136] The concerns sometimes raised against Article 9 Reg. 1/2003 commitment proceedings (see e.g., von Kalben, *Verpflichtungszusagen im EU-Wettbewerbsrecht*, 2016, at p. 21–27, Dunne, Commitment decisions in EU competition law, (2014) 10(2) *Journals of Competition Law and Economics*, 399, at p. 435–442) would be of significantly less weight in the market investigation context; firstly, because of the restriction of the commitment negotiations to a second phase where the competition concerns are already well understood, secondly, because the negotiations would take place in a balanced setting: for the companies engaged in the talks, there is no finding of an infringement and no sanctions to be avoided. Where they fundamentally disagree with the Commission's initial findings, substantial incentives to litigate will persist. Where the Commission and the companies largely agree on the findings, on the other hand, the Commission and the companies may have a joint interest to avoid a lengthy follow-up investigation and legal uncertainty. At the same time, the provisional findings report (as well as a mandatory

commitment negotiations in the course of future market investigation proceedings: since a finding of an infringement and fines are excluded from the start, companies would be under no (perceived) pressure to cooperate. Where the Commission and the companies would have come to a shared understanding of the competition concerns, on the other hand, they may have a joint interest to avoid lengthy follow-up investigation and legal uncertainty.

Which role there will be for commitment proceedings in practice would remain to be seen. The UK experience cautions against too high expectations.[137] Where parallel commitments would need to be negotiated with a large number of companies, commitment proceedings may become burdensome. Potential efficiency gains of a commitment decision over a formal remedial decision are then reduced and commitment negotiations may rather delay than accelerate the finding of a solution. Commitment decisions may be more relevant where a competition problem arises from the conduct of one or a very few firms.

3.7.2 Timing

In the United Kingdom, undertakings can be accepted at two different points of time: They can be accepted "in lieu of a market investigation reference," such that a market investigation will not take place (Section 154(2) of the Enterprise Act 2002),[138] or they can be accepted at the end of a market investigation.

In the European setting, commitment negotiations should not start before phase II, in order to ensure a sufficient informational basis for assessing the relevant competition concern and the menu of remedial options.

market test – see Section 3.6.4.2) will serve as a safeguard against an overly lenient approach by the Commission. A "collusion" between the Commission and the companies offering commitment seems unlikely.

[137] See OFT, Guidance on Market investigation references, https://assets .publishing.service.gov.uk/government/uploads/system/uploads/attachment_ data/file/284399/oft511.pdf, at para. 2.21: "Trying to negotiate undertakings with several parties in circumstances in which possible adverse effects on competition have not been comprehensively analysed, is likely to pose serious practical difficulties." See also Whish/Bailey (fn. 29), at p. 483, 484.

[138] Where the CMA accepts undertakings in lieu of a reference, it will not be able to make a reference within the 12 months that follow – Enterprise Act 2002, s 156(A1) – cross-market references; and s 156(1) – ordinary references; except where an undertaking has been breached – Enterprise Act 2002, s 156(2)(a).

3.7.3 *Procedural Rules for Commitment Negotiations*

The procedural rules to be followed when negotiating commitments should be specified in guidelines. Given the strict time limits that European market investigations would be subject to, time limits should also be fixed for commitment negotiations. Merger control proceedings provide a useful template in this regard.

In analogy to Article 9 Reg. 1/2003 commitment proceedings, commitments should only be accepted if they are unambiguous and self-executing.[139]

As procedural economy is one of the major justifications for a commitment procedure, accepting commitments should be conditional on the parties accepting that access to the file will only be granted to the main documents on which the Commission relies for the identification of the relevant competition problem.[140]

Before the Commission would decide to make commitments binding, the commitments should be subjected to a market test procedure.[141]

In its commitment decision, the Commission should be required to summarize the findings of the market investigation and competition analysis and explain the appropriateness of the commitments in addressing the relevant competition concerns. This would be an important benchmark in case an adjustment of the commitments would later be needed.

Following a commitment decision, the Commission should not be allowed to make use of the market investigation procedure again within the following twelve months with a view to the same competition problem, unless there would be a breach of the commitments or unless the commitments were accepted on the basis of false or misleading information.[142] It should, however, be allowed to open market investigations afterwards in case the competition problem would persist despite the implementation of the commitments.

---

[139] See Commission, Notice on Best Practices for the conduct of proceedings concerning Articles 101 and 102 TFEU, [2011] OJ C 308/6, at para. 128.

[140] In analogy to Article 9 Reg. 1/2003 proceedings, see ibid., at para. 123; and Wils/Abbott (fn. 84), at III.C., p. 13.

[141] For the Article 9 market test procedure, see Commission, Notice on Best Practices (fn. 140), at para.129.

[142] For such a rule, see Enterprise Act 2002, s 156(1) and (2).

The parties who have offered the commitments should be allowed to request the reopening of the proceedings where there has been a material change in any of the facts on which the decision was based (see Section 3.6.4.3).

3.8 Interim Measures within the Market Investigation Framework

3.8.1 The Need for Interim Measures in Market Investigation Proceedings

Market investigations shall address severe gaps in the protection of the competitive process. Among other things, they should allow the Commission to prevent specific *risks* for competition from materializing, in particular, the risk of market "tipping." Also, protecting competition in fast-moving markets characterized by strong economies of scale and network effects may be an important area of application for market investigations. In such settings, serious and irreparable harm to competition can occur quickly in the absence of a timely and effective intervention. While market investigation proceedings are meant to be relatively fast, they could nonetheless take up to (possibly) three years before a final decision is taken. The Commission would need to dispose of an instrument that ensures that no irreparable damage occurs in the meantime while the necessary investigations are carried out. Otherwise, the added value of market investigation proceedings could turn out to be limited.

The introduction of interim measures into the "markets regime" is also discussed in the United Kingdom.[143] In this context, Lord Tyrie has argued that the power to impose interim measures pending full investigation would "provide a stronger incentive for these firms to listen, engage and take steps to address the CMA's concerns in advance of formal work, than currently."[144] This is in line with the French experience in infringement proceedings: the more active use of, and greater ease in adopting, interim measures that is characteristic for the French model has tended to increase the companies' willingness to cooperate and their interest in a consensual settling of the proceedings

---

[143] See letter by Lord Tyrie (fn. 73), Annex, at p. 10 and 12.   [144] Ibid., at p. 17.

by way of voluntary commitments.[145] In the EU, the *Broadcom* proceeding[146] appears to confirm this experience: following the imposition of an interim measure, Broadcom has proposed commitments. Finally, this is in line with the experience in the field of enforcement of intellectual property rights, where provisional measures for the immediate termination of infringements[147] will frequently lead to a settlement of the case.

Given this experience, it is all the more important to ensure the proportionality of any interim measure and to provide for fast and full judicial review. Where these guarantees are available, interim measures may, however, come to play an important role.

3.8.2 A Legal Framework for Effective Interim Measures

In infringement proceedings, the European Commission has rarely made use of interim measures so far. Up until now, there are only ten interim measures decisions in total, nine of which were passed between 1980[148] and 2001.[149] Only one interim measure has been imposed under Reg. 1/2003, namely, in the *Broadcom* case.[150] Three features of the interim measures regime as it is now laid down in Article 8 Reg. 1/2003 are considered to have contributed to a rather hesitant use of this instrument: (a) the fact that the substantive standard for imposing interim measures is considered to be rather high, (b) the high procedural requirements that have to be met before ordering an interim measure, and (c) the substantial risk that the EU General Court will suspend the interim measure for the duration of an action for annulment. As these features might also affect the effectiveness of interim measures in market investigation proceedings, they shall be considered in turn.

---

[145] Lowe/Maier-Rigaud, Quo vadis antritrust remedies, in: *Annual Proceedings of the Fordham Competition Law Institute*, 2008, at p. 610.

[146] AT.40608 *Broadcom*.

[147] See Art. 9 and rec. 22 of the Directive 2004/48/EC of 29 April 2004 on the enforcement of intellectual property rights, OJ 2004 L 157/45.

[148] CFI, Case C-792/79 R, *Camera Care Ltd v Commission of the European Communities*, EU:C:1980:18.

[149] Commission Decision of 3.7.2001 in Case COMP D3/38.044 – *NDC Health/IMS Health*.

[150] Case AT. 40608 *Broadcom*.

3.8.2.1 Substantive Preconditions for Imposing Interim Measures

Article 8 Reg. 1/2003 requires a prima facie finding of a competition law infringement and a showing of urgency due to the risk of serious and irreparable damage to competition. As regards the evidentiary burden for establishing a prima facie finding of an infringement, the GC has found that a *"prima facie* infringement cannot be placed on the same footing as the requirement of certainty that a final decision must satisfy."[151] At the same time, when considering the adoption of an interim measure, the Commission must have "regard to the legitimate interests of the undertakings concerned by them"[152] and to the public interest in effective competition that may be negatively affected where interim measures are adopted without good cause.

It seems that under French competition law,[153] where interim measures are ordered much more frequently,[154] the requirements are similar on paper, but the test of "immediate harm" is interpreted more leniently.[155] In principle, the EU case law on interim measures in competition law provides for a substantial degree of flexibility, however: according to the European Court of Justice, the ordering of an interim measures is based on an overall assessment and weighing up of the interests concerned – the interest in the protection of competition and the interest of the companies affected by the interim measure.[156]

---

[151] Case T-44/90, *La Cinq SA v Commission*, EU:T:1992:5, at para. 61.

[152] Case C-792/79 R, *Camera Care Ltd v Commission*, EU:C:1980:18, at para. 19.

[153] See L. 464-1 du code de commerce: The main preconditions are the likelihood of a competition law infringement and serious and immediate harm to the general economy, the economy of the sector, the interest of consumers, or the interests of the claimant.

[154] Giraud/Blanc, Les mesures conservatoires à la francaise: Un modèle réellement enviable?, (2018) 3 *Concurrences*, available at https://fr.lw.com/ thoughtLeadership/mesures-contradictoires-une-solution-souhaitable.

[155] Both with regard to the test of "immediate harm" and with a view to the evidentiary burden regarding the infringement ("likely to infringe" competition law compared to "prima facie breach" of competition law), see Thill-Tayara, Presentation, available at https://www.concurrences.com/IMG/pdf/concurrences_ presentations_180608.pdf?42722/9476cb9c0f55ec6994e463bc4a719ac9a3d3 b173, at p. 3. Cf. Burnside/Kidane, Interim Measures: An overview of EU and National Case law, at p. 7, available at https://www.concurrences.com/IMG/pdf/ alec_j._burnside_adam_kidane_-_interim_measures_-_an_overview_of_eu_and_ national_case_law.pdf?42067/88ef3e2932cc547cc56d9630b273aca4582c3a7a.

[156] CFI, Case C-481/01 P (R), *IMS Health v Commission*, EU:C:2002:223, at para. 63.

In market investigation proceedings, interim measures would need to be based on a substantiated prima facie finding of a competition problem of the type that the market investigation regime is meant to address and limited to cases of urgency due to a risk of serious and irreparable harm to competition. The Commission should be required to assess the size of the harm to competition and the degree of certainty by which the harm will materialize. While the requirement of a prima facie competition problem would certainly call for a relevant minimum degree of substantiation that a relevant risk exists, the precise demands on the Commission could differ depending on the size of the potential harm.

Consequently, the Commission could – depending on the facts of the case – order interim measures already early on into a market investigation proceeding, provided it can substantiate the competition concern. The less comprehensive the evidence, the more cautious should the interim measures be. Where the competition problem is already well established and backed up by substantial proof, further-reaching measures would be acceptable if necessary to avoid serious and irreparable damage to competition. Such measures may include behavioral or even access obligations being imposed on an undertaking (see Section 3.8.2.4).

3.8.2.2 Procedural Safeguards

In Article 8 Reg. 1/2003 proceedings, the procedural requirements are high, as they are part of the Commission's toolbox in quasi-criminal infringement proceedings: before adopting an interim measure, the European Commission must issue a statement of objections, grant access to the files, give the opportunity to comment, hold a hearing, and consult the advisory committee. Interim measures under Article 8 Reg. 1/2003 therefore risk tying up substantial additional resources, affecting the rapidity of main proceedings.[157]

Market investigation proceedings would not be of a quasi-criminal nature, and they would not implicate the presumption of innocence. A somewhat lighter degree of procedural guarantees may therefore be justified. For the United Kingdom, the Furman Report, for example,

---

[157] Lowe/Maier-Rigaud (fn. 146), at 609.

recommended to restrict access to the file to documents clearly relevant to the interim measure.[158]

3.8.2.3 Suspension Decision by the GC
The imposition of interim measures can be challenged before the European GC. Actions for annulment do not have an automatic suspensory effect. However, the Court has a wide leeway in deciding whether the contested measure should be suspended for the duration of the action for annulment (Article 278 TFEU).[159]

The suspension of the interim measure in the *IMS Health* case has been taken as an indication of a high risk of suspension, particularly in novel cases or cases based on a change in the interpretation of the competition rules. Recently, there have been calls to limit judicial review of interim measures to a plausibility check.[160] Constraining judicial review of interim measures would, however, not only require a change of primary law. It would also interfere with the fundamental right to an effective remedy and a fair trial under Article 47 of the Charter of Fundamental Rights and be hard to justify under Article 52(1) of the Charter of Fundamental Rights.[161] Given that interim measures may interfere severely into a company's freedom to conduct a business (Article 16 of the Charter of Fundamental Rights), as well as into the right to property (Article 17 of the Charter of Fundamental Rights) – including by measures that will have effects on the market that cannot later be undone – tight judicial review will rather be needed.

At the same time, *IMS Health* should not be read to stand in the way of an effective use of interim measures, in particular, to generally disallow interim measures in cases of previously untested theories of harm. Rather, in the eyes of the Union Courts, the case combined an

[158] Furman/Coyle/Fletcher/McAuley/Marsden, Unlocking digital competition, March 2019, available at https://www.gov.uk/government/publications/unlocking-digital-competition-report-of-the-digital-competition-expert-panel, at para. 3.127.
[159] With respect to the standard of judicial review, Case C-481/01 P(R), *IMS Health v Commission*, EU:C:2002:223, at paras. 57 et seq.
[160] Art, (2015) 2(1) *Italian Antitrust Review*, 55, at p. 69; with respect to the United Kingdom: Furman/Coyle/Fletcher/McAuley/Marsden (fn. 159), at paras. 3.128 et seq.
[161] Likewise, Article 6 ECHR may be involved. See *Micallef v Malta* ([GC], §§ 80–86): Article 6 applies to interim measure where (1) a civil right within the meaning of the Convention is at stake and (2) the interim measure can be considered to effectively determine the civil right or obligation at stake.

interpretation of Article 102 TFEU that the Courts found to be prima facie unconvincing with a far-reaching remedy and therefore failed the error-cost test.

3.8.2.4 Proportionality of the Interim Measures

As interim measures will interfere, in some way or another, into fundamental rights, care must be taken that the intervention is necessary to genuinely meet recognized objectives of general interest and that it is proportionate (Article 52(1) of the Charter of Fundamental Rights). In the context of a market investigation proceeding, interim measures must be limited to what is strictly necessary to ensure that the identified risk to competition does not materialize in an irreversible way (e.g., in the case of a risk that a market will tip) or that the competitive process is irreversibly harmed (e.g., because the continuation of a specific business strategy will lead to durable barriers to entry).

According to the GC's existing case law on interim measures in infringement cases, these measures must be of a temporary and conservatory nature and restricted to what is required in the given situation.[162]

This requirement cannot and should not be strictly upheld when it comes to interim measures in market investigation proceedings: obviously, where competition can be protected by a measure that is merely conservatory in nature and can later be undone if no competition problem is found, interim measures must go no further. Also, very far-reaching remedies like a divestiture must not be ordered by way of an interim measure. The interests of the addressee(s) of an interim measure must always be taken into account and given weight.

However, interim measures should not be strictly limited to preserving the status quo.[163] The types of competition problem that a market investigation regime would be meant to address would sometimes require the imposition of positive obligations that go beyond the status quo ante – otherwise a market may, for example, tip and competition may durably fail. Consequently, interim measures such as the imposition of duties to temporarily ensure a vertical unbundling, to grant access to certain resources, or to ensure interoperability should be

---

[162] Case 792/79 R, *Camera Care Ltd v Commission*, EU:C:1980:18, at para. 19.
[163] See, however, the highly restrictive approach in Case T-184/01 R, *IMS Health v Commission*, EU:T:2001:200, at para. 25.

possible where necessary to maintain competition. In each single case, the proportionality of the measure would need to be verified.

3.8.2.5 Duty of Expedition
In market investigation proceedings, the Commission would be under a general duty of expedition (see Section 3.5.2.2). This duty would apply in a reinforced manner where interim measures were imposed, so as to confine the burden on the addressees of the interim measures as much as possible.

3.9 Sanctions in Case of Non-compliance with Remedies and/or Commitments and/or Interim Measures

The Commission would need to keep the implementation of any remedies or commitments made binding or interim measures under review to ensure that they are complied with. Where remedies are imposed in a regulated sector, the monitoring function may be delegated to the national regulatory authorities.[164]

In case of non-compliance, the Commission – or if applicable a regulatory authority – must possess sanctioning powers with a sufficient deterrent effect.[165] The fining powers set out in Articles 23 and 24 of Reg. 1/2003 and/or in Articles 14 and 15 of the EU Merger Control Regulation can serve as a role model.

In the United Kingdom, the duty to comply with orders and undertakings is owed to anyone who may be affected by a breach, such that breaches of the duty are actionable where they cause a loss or damage to another person.[166] This may also be a model for the EU.

3.10 Judicial Review

3.10.1 Decisions Subject to Judicial Review

According to Article 47 of the Charter of Fundamental Rights, everyone whose rights and freedoms guaranteed by EU law are violated has the right to judicial review. Likewise, a right of access to a court is

---

[164] For this proposition, see Larouche/de Streel, Chapter 4.
[165] For the insufficiency of the CMA's enforcement powers in this regard see Fletcher, Chapter 8.
[166] Enterprise Act 2002, s 167(2)–(3).

guaranteed under Article 6(1) ECHR. Under Article 263(4) TFEU, any
natural or legal person can institute proceedings against any procedural act addressed to him or her before the Union Courts.
Consequently, any addressee of a remedy resulting from a European
market investigation would be able to bring an action. The same is true
for the addressee of an investigatory measure or where procedural
rights in the administrative procedure were violated.

Other decisions taken in the course of market investigation proceedings would not be subject to judicial review. In particular, the opening
of a market investigation proceeding could not be appealed as it would
be a mere intermediate measure.[167] Nor should a decision by the
Commission not to open a market investigation be subject to judicial
review: contrary to infringement proceedings, no individual rights are
involved when it would come to market investigation proceedings. The
use of a market investigation would therefore be entirely at the
Commission's discretion.

There is a question whether proceedings against a final market
investigation decision could be instituted also by other market actors
who would consider that the Commission, in its closing decision, did
not comprehensively address the competition problem identified, or
failed to identify the competition problem accurately, and who would
claim to be negatively affected thereby. Under Article 263(4) TFEU, a
right of action is limited to those who are directly and individually
concerned. While a final market investigation decision would be of
direct concern to third party market actors,[168] an *individual* concern
would be questionable. According to the well-known *Plauman*
formula, "persons other than those to whom a decision is addressed
may only claim to be individually concerned if that decision affects
them by reason of certain attributes which are peculiar to them or by
reason of circumstances in which they are differentiated from all other
persons and by virtue of these factors distinguishes them individually
just as in the case of the person addressed."[169] According to settled
case law, an undertaking cannot contest a Commission decision if it is
concerned by that decision solely by virtue of belonging to the relevant

---

[167] Case T-902/16, *Heidelberg Cement*, EU:T:2017:846, at paras. 14–17.
[168] See GC, Case T-3/93, *Air France v Commission*, EU:T:1994:36, at paras.
80–81.
[169] ECJ, Case C-25/62, *Plaumann v Commission*, EU:C:1963:17, at p. 107.

market in question.[170] Nor would the fact that a person has participated in the administrative procedure based on which the Commission has adopted its decision afford that person standing to bring proceedings contesting the legality of that decision in terms of its substantive content. Rather, "[t]he precise scope of an individual's right of action against a Community measures depends on his legal position as defined by EU law with a view to protecting the legitimate interest thus afforded him."[171] As discussed in Section 3.4.3, a market investigation – contrary to Articles 101 and 102 TFEU – would not be based on or backed up by individual rights. The underlying model would rather be one of "small-scale ex ante regulation" to protect the system of undistorted competition more effectively and completely.

3.10.2 Standard of Judicial Review

The Commission's remedial decision will be subject to the regime of legality control under Article 263 TFEU. Where a Commission decision is appealed, the Union courts will – depending on the grounds of the appeal – review whether the relevant competition problem has been proven to the requisite standard of proof and whether the remedies imposed appropriately address the relevant competition problem, are necessary to achieve this goal, and proportionate with a view to the corresponding intervention into fundamental rights. The proportionality review would likely become a focus of judicial review of market investigations.[172]

The Court would also review charges that the Commission has violated procedural rights. A defect in this respect could lead to the decision in question being quashed.

Both in infringement and in merger control proceedings, the Union courts recognize that the Commission possesses a margin of appreciation in complex economic matters and confine the review to verifying whether the rules on procedure and on the statement of reasons have been complied with, whether the facts have been accurately stated, and

---

[170] See, from the area of state aid law, Case C 367/04 P, *Deutsche Post und DHL v Kommission*, EU:C:2006:126, at paras. 40, 41; Case C-525/04 P, *Spain v Lenzing*, EU:C:2007:698, at paras. 32, 33.

[171] GC, Case T-381/11, *Eurofer v Commission*, EU:T:2012:273, at para. 35; ECJ, Case C-355/08 P, *WWF-UK v Council*, EU:C:2009:286, at para. 44.

[172] For the UK experience see Whish, Chapter 5.

whether there has been any manifest error of assessment or misuse of powers.[173] The same would hold with regard to market investigations. Legality control is nonetheless demanding: "Not only must the Community Courts, *inter alia*, establish whether the evidence relied on is factually accurate, reliable and consistent but also whether that evidence contains all the information which must be taken into account in order to assess a complex situation and whether it is capable of substantiating the conclusions drawn from it."[174]

Contrary to infringement proceedings, European market investigations would not be of a quasi-criminal nature. The presumption of innocence would be of no relevance in these proceedings. Also, the choice of remedial action would have an important prognostic element. The Union courts legality review of market investigation decisions might therefore resemble the type of legality review currently exercised in merger proceedings. Considering that the remedies imposed as a result of a market investigation could intensely interfere with fundamental rights, judicial review of questions of fact would and should be intense.

When it comes to the review of the Commission's assessment of the competition problem and the necessity and proportionality of the remedy, the standard of judicial review would need to be appropriate to the subject matter of the dispute. For example, where the Commission would react to a potential problem of tipping, the prognostic uncertainties would need to be recognized. The same would be true with regard to the necessity and effectiveness of a remedy. Nonetheless, the harsher a remedy would intervene into individual rights, the more intense would the judicial review be.

3.10.3 Expedited Proceedings in Divestiture Cases?

Actions brought before the EU courts do not have suspensory effect (Article 278 TFEU). This will also be true for appeals against market investigation decisions. The decisions would continue to be in force pending the judgment of the GC on the substance. An applicant could,

[173] Case C-501, 513, 515, 519/06 P, *GlaxoSmithKline v Commission*, EU:C:2009:610, at para. 163. See generally, Van der Woude, Judicial control in complex economic matters, (2019)10 *Journal of European Competition Law & Practice*, 415.
[174] Case C-12/03 P, *Tetra Laval*, EU:C:2005:87, at para. 39.

however, apply for the decision to be suspended or for any other interim measure to be ordered. The standard for interim relief would be a high one: the applicant would need to establish a prima facie case (*fumus boni iuris*) and show that the suspension or other interim measure is urgent to avoid serious and irreparable damage for the applicant. The test would be applied strictly – pure financial loss would normally not suffice. In case of a divestiture, it would, however, normally be met. Arguably, a future European Market Investigation Regulation should, for these cases, include a rule that the expedited procedure is to be followed.[175]

---

[175] For the expedited procedure, see Amendments to the Rules of Procedure of the Court of First Instance of the European Communities, OJ 2000 No. L 322/4.

4 The Integration of Wide and Narrow Market Investigations in EU Economic Law*

PIERRE LAROUCHE AND ALEXANDRE
DE STREEL

4.1 Scope and Aim of the Chapter

In 2020, the European Commission embarked on a major reflection and consultation exercise aimed at adapting EU economic law to the challenges of our times, in particular to the competition issues raised by the deployment of digital technologies.[1] In June 2020, the Commission envisaged adding a new instrument – named then 'New Competition Tool' – to the EU economic regulation toolbox, in order to deal with structural competition problems which could not be addressed adequately by existing instruments.[2] Two main options were put forward for that instrument: a wide version applicable to all sectors of the economy and a narrow version applicable to the digital sector (or platforms) only. The wide version is similar to the market investigations that exist in several jurisdictions across the world. Conceptually, it is located between standard competition law and sector-specific regulation. The narrow version is a tailored instrument for regulation and thus falls more clearly within sector-specific regulation. In December 2020, the Commission opted for the narrow version in its

* This chapter is based in part on an expert study on the interplay between the New Competition Tool and Sector-Specific Regulation in the EU which was prepared in September 2020 for the Directorate-General Competition of the European Commission. The authors wish to thank Peter Alexiadis, Axel Desmedt, Richard Feasey, Giorgio Monti and Marieke Scholz for their very helpful comments and suggestions.
1 Already in 2019, the Commission had commissioned an influential report on the impact of the digital economy on EU competition law: Crémer/de Montjoye/Schweitzer, Competition policy for the digital era, Report to the European Commission, March 2019.
2 https://ec.europa.eu/info/law/better-regulation/have-your-say/initiatives/12416-New-competition-tool.

proposal for a Digital Markets Act (DMA), a sector-specific instrument applicable to 'gatekeepers' of 'core platform services', which includes three types of what is termed 'market investigation'.[3]

As market investigations would be part of the broader EU regulation toolbox under either the wide or the narrow option described above, this chapter analyses how to integrate both these options within EU economic law. To do so, the chapter is structured as follows. Following this introduction, Section 4.2 deals with the characteristics of competition law, sectoral regulation and market investigations. Then Section 4.3 sets out the existing relationships between competition law and sectoral regulation at the systemic, substantive and institutional levels. On that basis, Sections 4.4 and 4.5 make recommendations for a smooth integration of market investigations in EU economic law. As market investigation in the wide option is close to competition law, Section 4.4 deals with its interplay with sectoral regulation. Since, under the narrow option, market investigation is a form of sectoral regulation, Section 4.5 deals with its interplay with competition law. Finally, Section 4.6 concludes by summarising our main recommendations.

4.2 Characteristics of the Main Legal Tools of EU Economic Regulation

Next to competition law, EU economic regulation includes a number of more specific regulatory regimes, which are briefly reviewed below, in order to be able to situate a new EU market investigation tool.

4.2.1 Competition Law

4.2.1.1 Systemic and Substantive Issues

The regime of competition law in the European Union is well known;[4] we will briefly survey its main relevant features for the purposes of this

---

[3] Proposal of the Commission of 15 December 2020 for a Regulation of the European Parliament and of the Council on contestable and fair markets in the digital sector (Digital Markets Act), COM(2020) 842, articles 14–17. For a brief presentation on the rationale of the proposal, see Chirico, Digital Markets Act: A regulatory perspective, (2021) 12 *Journal European Competition Law & Practice*, 493.

[4] See Jones/Sufrin/Dunne, *EU Competition Law*, 7th ed., 2019; Whish/Bailey, *Competition Law*, 9th ed., 2018.

chapter. While discussion remains open on this issue, it is safe to say that the objectives of competition law include consumer welfare and the protection of the competitive process. EU competition law, as it applies to firms, comprises three main components: (i) a prohibition against restrictive agreements and concerted practices, at Article 101 (1) TFEU, coupled with an exemption clause at 101(3) TFEU; (ii) a prohibition against abuses of dominant position, at Article 102 TFEU; (iii) prior review of concentrations (mergers and acquisitions) having an EU dimension, pursuant to Regulation 139/2004 (commonly known as the EU Merger Regulation).[5]

These three components are all couched in fairly general legislative provisions, which are applied in individual cases following a largely common methodology. First, relevant markets are defined, followed by market assessment (in the light of the specifics of each component) and the imposition of appropriate remedies, if necessary. The remedial arsenal of competition law includes fines, damages, nullity of agreements in breach of Article 101 TFEU, prohibition of mergers that run afoul of the Merger Regulation, as well as a wide range of behavioural or even structural obligations to remove or prevent infringements of the law or to restore competition.

4.2.1.2 Institutional Issues

The enforcement of Articles 101 and 102 TFEU is now detailed in Regulation 1/2003.[6] Enforcement powers are shared between the European Commission and the respective National Competition Authority (NCA) of each Member State. Given the increasing importance of the NCAs since the decentralisation of competition law in 2004, EU law includes strengthened institutional requirements for those NCAs – in particular in terms of independence, accountability, expertise, procedural safeguards and remedial powers.[7] In addition, the respective competent court(s) in each Member State are competent

---

[5] Council Regulation (EU) 139/2004 of 20 January 2004 on the control of concentrations between undertakings, OJ 2004 No. L 25/1.

[6] Council Regulation (EU) 1/2003 of 16 December 2002 on the implementation of the rules on competition laid down in Articles 81 and 82 of the Treaty, OJ 2003 No. L 1/1, as amended.

[7] Directive (EU) 2019/1 of the European Parliament and of the Council of 11 December 2018 to empower the competition authorities of the Member States to be more effective enforcers and to ensure the proper functioning of the internal market, OJ 2019 No. L 11/3.

to apply those provisions as original jurisdictions; they are also in charge of judicial review of NCA decisions (with the possibility of reference to the Court of Justice), whereas European courts entertain appeals from Commission decisions. The Merger Regulation is enforced by the European Commission alone, with appeal to European courts.

Member States also have national competition laws along widely convergent lines to EU competition law, which are enforced by the NCA and national courts. Regulation 1/2003 contains a number of rules on the interplay between EU and national competition laws (rules on applicable law and conflict rules). It also provides coordination mechanisms between the categories of authorities involved in EU competition law enforcement, including consultation, coordination, case allocation and the creation of a European Competition Network (ECN) of authorities.[8] There is less need for coordination under the Merger Regulation, given the mutually exclusive scope of EU and national laws. Mechanisms are in place for the transfer of cases from the EU to the national level, and vice versa. Under Regulation 1/2003 as well as under the Merger Regulation, Member States are involved in Commission decision-making through advisory committees (Advisory Committee on Restrictive Practices and Dominant Positions, Advisory Committee on Concentrations).

4.2.2 Sectoral Regulation

4.2.2.1 Systemic and Substantive Issues

Next to competition law, EU economic regulation features a number of more specific regimes, usually dealing with a single economic sector. Dunne defines economic regulation as 'any State-imposed, positive, coercive alteration of – or derogation from – the operation of the free market in a sector, typically undertaken in order to correct market defects of an economic nature'.[9] While more specific in their scope of

---

[8] For constitutional reasons, coordination mechanisms between the Commission and NCAs are better developed and stronger than between the Commission and national courts.

[9] Dunne, *Competition Law and Economic Regulation: Making and Managing Markets*, 2015, at p. 40.

application, these regimes often cover a broader range of concerns than the three components of competition law listed above.

Sector-specific regulation is usually adopted and tailored to correct perceived market failures in part of the economy.[10] Market failures can have different causes, and economic literature on this point is constantly evolving. The main ones are market power, externalities, asymmetry of information and coordination issues.[11] Whereas competition law is mostly concerned with market failures on the supply side (in particular, market power), specific regulation often extends to both supply-side and demand-side failures. In addition, one could argue for an even broader conception of EU economic regulation, which would also include general regimes dealing with demand-side failures, that is, consumer protection rules. As will be seen in Section 4.3.1, there is no theoretical incompatibility in so doing. In terms of methodology, remedies and institutions, these general demand-side regimes tend to resemble sector-specific regulation rather than competition law.

Specific regulation tends to be formulated in more detailed provisions than competition law, and accordingly implementation and enforcement are often more focused on narrow issues. In so doing, authorities typically rely on economic knowledge and analysis in applying provisions that result from the economic assessment made by the legislative authority. Amongst sector-specific regulation, the EU electronic communications regulatory framework[12] stands out through its regime of asymmetric regulation for providers with Significant Market Power (SMP). The SMP regime features a more developed methodology, which leans more clearly on competition law. This regime aims to regulate providers that hold SMP (interpreted as equivalent to dominance) on relevant markets, defined according to competition law methods. However, the alignment with competition law is not complete, as the markets susceptible to ex ante regulation are selected on the basis of

---

[10] This chapter will not venture into the fundamental issue of the normative benchmark for market failure, which can be either a 'purely economic' concept such as efficiency or welfare or a more political benchmark established by reference to public policy objectives.

[11] Baldwin/Cave/Lodge, *Understanding Regulation: Theory, Strategy and Practice*, 2nd ed., 2012; Viscusi/Harrington/Sappington, *Economics of Regulation and Antitrust*, 5th ed., 2018.

[12] Directive (EU) 2018/1972 of the European Parliament and of the Council of 11 December 2018 establishing the European Electronic Communications Code [hereinafter EECC], OJ 2018 No. L 321/36.

three criteria which single out those markets where a dominant position could not be effectively policed by competition law and, therefore, the stronger force of regulation is required.[13] Note, however, that other than electronic communications regulation, most EU economic regulation regimes are not based on competition law methodology, since they respond to market failures – and may pursue economic policy objectives – that are different from those of competition law. They remain nonetheless mostly grounded in economic analysis.

The remedial arsenal of specific regulatory regimes, in comparison to competition law, tends not to rely on fines, but rather on the imposition of (mostly) behavioural obligations, on wholesale or retail markets. Wholesale obligations range from non-discrimination to price regulation and include all forms of separation/unbundling as well as wholesale access and service provision. Retail obligations include prudential obligations, consumer protection requirements or universal service obligations.

4.2.2.2 Institutional Issues

While, next to NCAs, the Commission can directly enforce EU competition law (which is exceptional in the broader context of EU law), EU economic regulation is usually enforced by Member States. Most regimes require Member States to set up a dedicated National Regulatory Authority (NRA) for implementation and enforcement. Given the importance of applying economic regulation effectively and in a non-discriminatory manner across the internal market, EU law generally sets institutional requirements for those NRAs – in particular in terms of independence, accountability, expertise, procedural safeguards and remedial powers[14] – compliance with which is strictly

---

[13] EECC, art. 67(1). Those three cumulative criteria are (i) high and non-transitory structural, legal or regulatory barriers to entry are present; (ii) there is a market structure which does not tend towards effective competition within the relevant time horizon, having regard to the state of infrastructure-based competition and other sources of competition behind the barriers to entry; and (iii) competition law alone is insufficient to adequately address the identified market failure(s). For a very good analysis of the three criteria test, see Never/Preissl, The three-criteria test and SMP: How to get it right, (2008) 1 *International Journal of Management and Network Economics*, 100.

[14] For instance, EECC, Art. 6-9; Directive (EU) 2019/944 on common rules for the internal market for electricity, OJ 2019 No L 158/125, art. 57.

enforced by the Court of Justice.[15] In order to guarantee the consistent application of EU law and some measure of coordination between NRAs, EU sectoral regulation regimes often establish an EU-level forum for NRAs, for instance, in the form of a network or an agency. In general, the Commission plays a very active role in those networks. Moreover, in some cases, NRA decisions are subject to review or even veto at the European level by the Commission or the EU-level forum.[16]

Exceptionally, EU economic regulation can be enforced directly by EU-level agencies or bodies. This is the case, in particular, for the financial supervision of systemic banks, which is undertaken by the Single Supervisory Mechanism at the ECB.[17] In other sectors, the EU agency comprising the network of NRAs may also have direct, but limited, enforcement powers on matters having cross-border dimensions,[18] cross-border externalities or a strong internal market dimension.[19]

4.2.3 *Wide and Narrow Versions of Market Investigation*

4.2.3.1 Systemic and Substantive Issues

According to its original inception impact assessment,[20] the Commission was envisaging to propose a new market investigation tool – the New

---

[15] E.g., for the telecommunications regulators: Case C–424/15 *Ormaetxea Garai et al. v Administración del Estado*, EU:C:2016:780. For energy regulators, see C-378/19 *Prezident Slovenskej republiky*, EU:C:2020:462; C-767/19 *Commission v Belgium*, EU:C:2020:984 and C-718/18, *Commission v Germany*, EU:C:2021:662. For the data protection authorities, see Case C-518/07 *Commission v Germany*, EU:C:2010:125.

[16] This is the case in telecommunications regulation: EECC, arts. 32–34.

[17] Council Regulation (EU) 1024/2013 of 15 October 2013 conferring specific tasks on the European Central Bank concerning policies relating to the prudential supervision of credit institutions, OJ 2013 No. L 287/63.

[18] See the powers conferred upon ACER throughout Regulation 2019/943 on the internal market for electricity.

[19] See, in particular, the power of ESMA to supervise and fine credit rating agencies. Article 28 of Regulation 236/2012 which regulates short selling and certain aspects of credit default swaps gives the ESMA the power to intervene through legally binding acts in the financial markets of Member States if there is a 'threat to the orderly functioning and integrity of financial markets or to the stability of the whole or part of the financial system in the Union'. This power has been validated by the Court of Justice in Case C-270/12 *United Kingdom v European Parliament and Council*, EU:C:2014:18.

[20] See fn. 2.

Competition Tool – to address certain structural competition problems (i) due to problematic market features; (ii) which have adverse consequences on competition and may ultimately result in inefficient market outcomes in terms of higher prices, lower quality, less choice and innovation and (iii) that standard competition law tools cannot tackle or cannot address in the most effective manner.

The inception impact assessment grouped those structural competition problems into two categories depending on whether harm is about to affect or has already affected the market. First, *structural risks for competition* occur where certain market features – such as network and scale effects, lack of multi-homing and lock-in effects – and the conduct of the firms operating in the markets concerned create a threat for competition. This applies to (i) tipping markets, where risks for competition can arise through the creation of powerful market players with an entrenched market and/or gatekeeper position, which could have been prevented by early intervention or (ii) unilateral strategies by non-dominant firms to monopolise a market through anti-competitive means. Second, a *structural lack of competition* happens when a market is not working well and not delivering competitive outcomes due to its structure. These include (i) markets displaying systemic failures – going beyond the conduct of a particular firm with market power – due to certain structural features, such as high concentration and entry barriers, consumer lock-in, lack of access to data or data accumulation or (ii) oligopolistic market structures with an increased risk for tacit collusion, including markets featuring increased transparency due to algorithm-based technological solutions.

Remedies may consist in imposing on firms certain obligations which may be structural, non-structural or hybrid. Since the market features or failures giving rise to structural competition problems are not imputable to any particular firm, there is no finding of infringement, nor are fines imposed on firms. Beyond those remedies, the market investigation tool could also lead to recommendations to legislative bodies (which could bring market investigations close to existing sector enquiries under competition law, as these sector enquiries are often followed by legislative proposals from the Commission);[21]

---

[21] Report from the Commission of 10 May 2017, E-Commerce Sector Inquiry, COM(2017) 229 which, among others, led to Regulation (EU) 2018/302 of the European Parliament and of the Council of 28 February 2018 on addressing unjustified geo-blocking and other forms of discrimination based on consumers'

recommendations to sectoral regulators; non-binding recommendations to firms, for instance, in form of code of conducts; or voluntary
commitments made by firms.

To tackle those structural competition problems and the related
market features, the inception impact assessment of the Commission
envisaged four different options depending on (i) the *scope* of the
market investigation: a wide scope applicable horizontally to all sectors
of the economy (as it is the case for standard competition rules) or a
narrow scope limited to certain sectors, in particular the digital or
digitally enabled markets or (ii) the *threshold* for intervention: a low
threshold applicable to all cases of structural competition problems
(and potentially to all firms in those markets) or a high threshold
limited to dominant firms as it is the case under Article 102 TFEU
(but without having to prove abuse).

On the basis of the results of the public consultation[22] and its own
internal thinking, the Commission decided in the end to propose an
instrument – the Digital Markets Acts (DMA) – with a narrow scope,
limited to digital gatekeepers. The DMA rests on three main concepts,
namely, a list of 'core platform services' (its material scope of application), 'gatekeepers' (the firms that are subject to the DMA) and a list of
obligations imposed on gatekeepers of core platform services. The
DMA features three types of market investigation that relate to these
concepts:[23] (i) The first type of market investigation allows the
Commission to *designate as gatekeeper* a provider of core platform
services, on the basis of a series of quantitative and qualitative indicators set out in the DMA.[24] (ii) The second type of market investigation

nationality, place of residence or place of establishment within the internal
market, OJ 2018 No. L 60I/1.

[22] See https://ec.europa.eu/competition/consultations/2020_new_comp_tool/
summary_stakeholder_consultation.pdf

[23] DMA Proposal (fn. 3). For a description of the propsosal, see de Streel/
Larouche, The European Digital Markets Act proposal: How to improve a
regulatory revolution, (2021) 2 *Review Concurrences*, 46.

[24] Ibid., arts. 3(6) and 15. The DMA Proposal (art. 2.2) lists eight core platform
services to which the obligations of the DMA may apply: (i) online B2C
intermediation services which include marketplaces such as Amazon
Marketplace and app stores such as Apple App Store or Google Play store; (ii)
online search engines such as Google search or Microsoft Bing; (iii) online social
networks such as Facebook; (iv) video-sharing platform services such as
YouTube; (v) a number independent interpersonal communication services such
as WhatsApp, Skype or Gmail; (vi) cloud computing services such as Amazon
webservice or Microsoft Azure; (vii) operating systems such as Google Android,
Apple iOS, Microsoft Windows and (viii) advertising services including ad

allows the Commission to impose behavioural and, if necessary, structural *remedies* when a designated gatekeeper systematically refuses to comply with the obligations and prohibitions imposed by the DMA.[25] (iii) The third type of market investigation allows the Commission to *extend the scope of application* (i.e., add new core platform services to the list) *and add to the list of obligations* contained in the DMA. Regarding the scope, the Commission could propose to the EU legislative bodies a revision of the DMA to include new digital services and business models in the regulation.[26] As for the obligations, the Commission could, with a delegated act (and thus without going back to the EU legislature), enlarge the list of obligations incumbent upon the designated gatekeepers.[27]

Thus, in practice, the narrow version of the market investigations proposed by the Commission in the DMA are merely flexibility clauses, aiming to adapt the DMA to the evolution of digital technologies and markets as well as update it in the light of the enforcement experience of the Commission. Using the 'market investigation' label for such a flexibility clause in sectoral regulation can be a bit of a misnomer,[28] because such a narrow tool has little in common with the market investigations existing in other jurisdictions.

4.2.3.2 Institutional Issues
At the institutional level, the DMA Proposal entails a centralised EU-level enforcement model. Indeed, the Commission will be in charge of the enforcement of the new sector-specific regulation applicable to digital gatekeepers, including the three types of narrow market investigation mentioned above. For the first time in the history of EU integration, fully-fledged sectoral regulatory powers would be entrusted to the European Commission.

---

networks, ad exchanges and any ad intermediation services such as Google AdSense.

[25] Ibid., art. 16.

[26] Ibid., art.17(a). As the extension of the DMA scope should be done with a legislative review (and not with a delegated act), this type of market investigation mechanism does not add much to the right of legislative initiative already granted to the Commission by the article 17 TEU.

[27] Ibid., arts. 10 and 17(b).

[28] As suggested by Camus, 'mal nommer les choses, c'est ajouter au malheur du monde'.

Conversely, the role of the Member States and their national authorities is more limited than in the other fields of EU economic law. For
the first type of market investigation (gatekeeper designation) and the
second type of market investigation (imposition of sanctions in case of
systematic non-compliance), the DMA Proposal provides for the establishment of the Digital Markets Advisory Committee (DMAC), a
comitology-type committee which could issue non-binding opinions
on Commission draft decisions.[29] For the third type of market investigation related to addition of new obligations, the standard dual control
mechanism for delegated acts will apply: before the adoption of the act,
representatives of the Member States will be consulted by the
Commission, and after the Commission adopts the delegated act, the
Council may oppose that act.[30]

4.3 Existing Interplay between Competition Law and Sector-Specific Regulation

A market investigation tool will therefore be introduced into a well-
populated landscape of legal regimes of economic governance in the
EU. Accordingly, its relationship with the existing legal regimes must
be carefully considered. For instance, in its response to the public
consultation, the network of national telecommunication regulators
BEREC pointed to the risks that 'a conflict between Electronic
Communications Services regulation and the New Competition Tool
could result in inconsistent application of ex-ante regulation, forum
shopping by market actors and potential regulatory uncertainty on
whom, how and under which circumstances a market actor is subject
to regulation. This legal uncertainty could have serious implications for
investment in a dynamic and competitive sector'.[31]

In order to structure the analysis of the relationship between a new
market investigation tool and existing EU economic regulation, we will
distinguish between three aspects thereof: (i) the *systemic* relationship
between market investigation as an instrument and other existing

---

[29] DMA Proposal (fn. 3), art. 32 and art. 15(1) for the first type of market
investigation and art. 16(2) for the second type of market investigation.
[30] Ibid., art. 37(4) and (6).
[31] BEREC Response of 7 September 2020 to the Public Consultations on the
Digital Services Act Package and the New Competition Tool, BoR(20) 138, at
p. 37.

regimes of economic governance – including consumer protection law – that is, boundary and hierarchy issues between these regimes; (ii) the *substantive* relationship, as concerns the respective substance and methodology of these regimes and (iii) the *institutional* relationship, as between the institutions who are in charge of implementing, interpreting and enforcing these regimes. In this section, we provide a survey of the state of the law and of existing options regarding the three aspects of the relationship between various regimes of economic regulation, by way of background to our analysis of how market investigation would fit into that landscape, which will be developed in the next sections.

4.3.1 Systemic Relationship: Complementarity between Economic Regulation Regimes

In the wake of the substantial expansion of sector-specific regulation at the EU level from the mid-1980s onward, as a result of harmonisation and liberalisation efforts to achieve the single market, the systemic relationship between these regulatory clusters came to the fore, and in particular the relationship between competition law and sectoral regulation. Practitioners and academics alike sometimes conceive of competition law and sector-specific regulation as substitutes or alternatives: each of them would have its domain, exclusive of the other.[32] Under this view, the main challenge would then be to properly classify concrete issues and disputes as pertaining to one or the other. Quite conceivably, this view is influenced by US law, where regulation has been seen as a substitute to antitrust law, and where leading case law tends to consider antitrust and regulation as exclusive of one another.[33]

---

[32] This was a prominent feature in the discussions around the future of sectoral regulation, and it is linked with the sometimes excessive use of the ex ante vs. ex post distinction, especially by economists. See, for instance, Bourreau/Dogan, Regulation and innovation in the telecommunications industry, (2001) 25 *Telecommunications Policy*, 167; or Newbery, Regulation and competition policy: Longer-term boundaries, (2004) 12 *Utilities Policy*, 93. On the legal side, see Breyer, *Regulation and Its Reform*, 1982, p. 156–161.

[33] Shelanski, The case for rebalancing antitrust and regulation, (2011) 109 *Michigan Law Review*, 638, chronicles and criticises the two leading US cases on point, *Verizon Communications v Trinko* 540 US 398 (2004) and *Credit Suisse v Billing* 551 US 264 (2007). See also OECD, Regulated conduct defence in

Yet both a theoretical analysis of EU law and the weight of practice and case law point to the opposite direction: in the EU, competition law and sectoral regulation should be seen as complements which pursue similar objectives but with different means, each of the two focusing on its particular strength.[34] To the extent it is at all useful to try to delineate their respective domains, these domains overlap. Hence, cases will arise where both are applicable, and coordination mechanisms will be necessary. The theoretical analysis is based on the architecture of EU law. Ultimately, all instruments of EU law are meant to pursue the overall objectives listed at Article 3 TEU (and Protocol 27), including, for the legal instruments concerned by the present chapter, the establishment of an internal market where competition is not distorted. These objectives inform the main provisions of primary EU law, such as Articles 101 or 102 TFEU (which establish the competition rules) or Articles 34, 45, 49, 56, 63 TFEU (which establish the four freedoms of movement within the EU internal market) as well as the corresponding legal bases used to enact secondary law (regulations, directives), including Articles 103, 114 or 352 TFEU which have been used for competition law and internal market law. Secondary law based on these legal bases is meant to contribute to the realisation of those overarching objectives. In other words, the architecture of EU law connects all these regimes and subsumes them under common objectives. It is accordingly not only possible but even preferable to conceive of them as components of a coherent whole, that is, an EU body of economic regulation.

Hence, over the years, it has become customary to refer to competition law as a general, across-the-board component of that body of economic regulation, next to which a number of specific regulatory

---

antitrust cases (2011) DAF/COMP(2011)3. Note that a nuanced reading of Trinko reveals that, in order to conclude that the application of antitrust law is excluded, the US Supreme Court is careful to point out that the prior regulatory process 'fulfilled the antitrust function'.

[34] See also Dunne (fn. 9); and Hellwig, Competition policy and sector-specific regulation in network industries, in: Vives (ed.), *Competition Policy: Fifty Years on from the Treaty of Rome*, 2009, p. 203–235. This is also the view of some US authors like Carlton/Picker, Antitrust and Regulation, (2007) NBER Working Paper 12902 noting that: 'Antitrust and regulation can also be viewed as complements in which regulation and antitrust assign control of competition to courts and regulatory agencies based on their relative strengths. Antitrust also can act as a constraint on what regulators can do.'

regimes are concerned with specific sectors or issues.[35] General competition law and specific regulation then go hand in hand as complements (and not substitutes or alternatives). Specific regulation contributes to achieving the overall objectives of EU economic regulation by dealing with questions that either lie outside the purview of general competition law because competition law was not conceived to deal with them or are recurrent systemic issues for which competition law is not the most effective instrument. Overlaps between competition law and specific regulation are therefore unavoidable.

The practice of the last decades bears witness to these overlaps and to the complementarity between economic regulation regimes. Electronic communications regulation offers many instances. The 1998 Access Notice already detailed the interplay between competition law and sector-specific regulation in the emerging competition practice of the 1990s.[36] In the 2000s, a string of high-profile refusal to deal and margin squeeze cases further highlighted the relationship between competition law and sector-specific regulation.[37] Examples come from other sectors as well. In the postal sector, the liberalisation of cross-border mail services came through the application of the Postal Services Directive and competition law.[38] In the energy sector, enforcement of Article 102 TFEU against the major network operators gave a decisive impetus to the unbundling of networks (transmission and distribution) from production, as provided in the sectoral directives.[39]

---

[35] Larouche, *Competition Law and Regulation in European Telecommunications*, 2000.

[36] Commission Notice on the application of the competition rules to access agreements in the telecommunications sector, OJ 1998 No. C 265/2.

[37] Case C-280/08P *Deutsche Telekom v Commission*, EU:C:2010:603; Case C-52/9 *Konkurrensverket v TeliaSonera*, EU:C:2011:83; Case C-295/12P *Telefonica v Commission*, EU:C:2014:2062. The relationship between competition law and regulation set by those cases is analysed in de Streel, The antitrust activism of the Commission in the telecommunications sector, in: Lowe/Marquis (eds.), *European Competition Law Annual 2012: Competition, Regulation and Public Policies*, 2014, at p. 189. More recently, Case C-165/19P, *Slovak Telekom v. Commission*, EU:C:2021:239.

[38] Directive (EC) 97/67 of the European Parliament and of the Council of 15 December 1997 on common rules for the development of the internal market of Community postal services and the improvement of quality of service, OJ 1997 No. L 15/14, as amended; Geradin, Enhancing Competition in the Postal Sector: Can We Do Away with Sector-Specific Regulation? (2006) TILEC Working Paper.

[39] Now: Directive 2019/944 of the European Parliament and of the Council of 5 June 2019 on common rules for the internal market for electricity OJ [2019]

In the financial sector, as well, the realisation of the internal market in insurance, for example, was a result of the interaction between competition law and sectoral directives.[40] Conversely, EU law has a long tradition of relying on complementary regulation when competition law has been ineffective in solving structural competition problems. This has happened in the telecommunications sector with the regulation of international roaming charges[41] or in the financial sector with the regulation of credit card interchange fees.[42] In all of these examples, the existence of an overlap between competition law and sectoral regulation was acknowledged and accepted. That overlap is the very foundation for the complementary interplay between these regimes that led to successful outcomes from the point of view of the overarching EU objectives.

For the purposes of this chapter, this EU body of economic regulation can be deemed to include demand-side regulation as well, dealing with consumer protection or data protection (in particular, the GDPR).[43] Indeed, consumer protection is primarily dealt with through secondary legislation based on Article 114 and 169 TFEU, thereby linking with the general objectives of Article 3 TEU as they relate to the functioning of the economy. Furthermore, a number of the sector-specific regulatory regimes, such as those in network industries, the financial sector, the audio-visual sector and e-commerce, span both supply- and demand-side regulation.

Figure 4.1 gives a rapid overview of some of the many regimes of economic regulation in the EU, as they were discussed above, using

---

L 158/125. See Hancher/Larouche, The coming of age of EU regulation of network industries and services of general economic interest, in: Craig/de Búrca (eds.), *The Evolution of EU Law*, 2nd ed., 2011, p. 743–782.

[40] As best exemplified in the role played by the sectoral block exemption, lately Regulation 267/2010, OJ [2010] L 83/1 (now expired), in charting a balance between the liberalisation of the sector and the need for insurance firms to cooperate on certain aspects of their operations.

[41] Regulation (EU) 531/2012 of the European Parliament and of the Council of 13 June 2012 on roaming on public mobile communications networks, OJ 2012 No. L 172/10, as amended by Regulation 2015/2120 and Regulation 2017/920.

[42] Regulation (EU) 2015/751 of the European Parliament and of the Council of 29 April 2015 on interchange fees for card-based payment transactions, OJ 2015 No. L 123/1.

[43] On the interplay between competition law and consumer protection, see Cseres, Competition and Consumer Policies: Starting Points for Better Convergence (2009), ACLE Working Paper 2009-06.

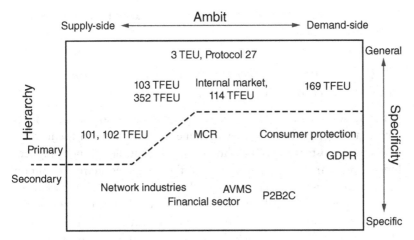

Figure 4.1 The EU body of economic regulation

mainstream abbreviations for some specific regimes, such as AVMS (Audiovisual Media Services),[44] GDPR (General Data Protection Regulation)[45] or P2B (for Regulation 2019/1150).[46] On the horizontal axis, these regimes are ordered according to whether they are predominantly concerned with supply-side regulation (towards the left) or with demand-side regulation (towards the right). On the vertical axis, these regimes are ordered according to how specific they are, from the whole economy on top to the narrowest sectors at the bottom. The regimes based on primary EU law (TEU and TFEU) are included above the dotted line, with the legal bases and the statements of policy aims coming at the very top, given their high level of generality. In this chart, the broader version of the new instrument, as envisaged earlier, would come close to the MCR, whereas the narrower version, as

---

[44] Directive (EU) 2010/13 of the European Parliament and of the Council of 10 March 2010 on the coordination of certain provisions laid down by law, regulation or administrative action in Member States concerning the provision of audiovisual media services (Audiovisual Media Services Directive), OJ 2010 No. L 95/1, as amended by Directive 2018/1808.

[45] Regulation (EU) 2016/679 of the European Parliament and of the Council of 27 April 2016 on the protection of natural persons with regard to the processing of personal data and on the free movement of such data, and repealing Directive 95/46 (General Data Protection Regulation), OJ 2016 No. L 199/1.

[46] Regulation (EU) 2019/1150 of the European Parliament and of the Council of 20 June 2019 on promoting fairness and transparency for business users of online intermediation services, OJ 2019 No. L 186/55.

proposed in the DMA, would be closer to network industries and AVMS regulation.

4.3.2 Substantive Relationship: Reliance on Common Economic Methodologies

If the various regimes of EU economic regulation are complements within a larger body of law, with some overlap between them, their respective substantive rules should be compatible, if not aligned. Indeed, the starting point is that all of these regimes share a common theoretical basis and methodology. With respect to theory, EU economic regulation typically follows a public interest approach: public authorities stand at some distance from markets and society, they observe the operation of markets and act in the public interest in order to remedy or correct market failures. Compared to the United States, public choice theory plays a less important role in Europe. Government failure is of more limited concern: it is assumed that the EU multi-level institutional setting is less vulnerable to capture and other government failures.[47] EU economic regulation is content with traditional safeguards such as judicial review, reporting obligations or periodical assessments and reviews.

This theoretical basis is reflected in the methodology used to develop and review regulation, which is derived from the principles of proportionality and subsidiarity.[48] That methodology is set out in the Better Regulation Guidelines, especially in the chapter on Impact Assessment.[49] In the case of EU economic regulation, the methodology incorporates the use of economic analysis in the development of regulation and, to the extent necessary, in its implementation and enforcement as well. In other words, economic regulation relies on recognised economic knowledge from fields such as industrial organisation, institutional economics, political economy, game theory or behavioural economics, to name but the main ones.

---

[47] On the different positive and normative explanations of regulation, including public interest and public choice theories, see Baldwin/Cave/Lodge (fn. 11) Chapter 4; Viscusi/Harrington/Sappington (fn. 11) Chapter 2.

[48] TUE, Art. 5 and Protocol No. 2.

[49] European Commission Staff Working Document of 7 July 2017, Better Regulation Guidelines SWD(2017)350, Chapter III.

In principle, the substance of a new EU market investigation tool, as a general regime of economic regulation, should fit within the theoretical basis and methodology set out above. No significant difficulties should arise. Nonetheless, it is worth mentioning a few substantive lessons arising from the experience with other economic regulation regimes, which could be useful in the elaboration of a market investigation tool.

Firstly, there is limited value in methodological convergence going beyond the general commitment to rely on recognised economic knowledge, as set out just above. As mentioned in Section 4.2.2, in the course of developing the current regulatory framework for electronic communications in the early 2000s, EU institutions decided to rely on competition law methodology for a core element of the framework, the SMP regime. It was hoped that this would ensure coherence between electronic communications and competition law and boost the ease-of-use and legitimacy of sector-specific regulation. Market definition and market analysis (in order to ascertain if a player held SMP) were built into the regulatory process, ostensibly to reproduce competition law analysis.[50] A good argument can be made that both market definition and SMP analysis never were done quite along the same lines as under competition law.[51]

In any event, starting at the latest with the second Recommendation on relevant markets in 2007,[52] the exercise became mostly one of market selection, with the famous 'three-criteria test' becoming the main focus of discussion. The market selection made in the Commission Recommendation was so influential that the 'competition law' analysis carried out by NRAs to define markets and then identify SMP operators on those markets receded in the background. The experience of electronic communications regulation with the introduction of competition law methodology is therefore at best

[50] de Streel, The integration of competition law principles in the new European regulatory framework for electronic communications, (2003) 26 *World Competition*, 489.

[51] Larouche, A closer look at some assumptions underlying EC regulation of electronic communications, (2002) 3 *Journal of Network Industries*, 129; de Streel, A program for review of the European economic regulation for electronic communications, (2008) 32 *Telecommunications Policy*, 722.

[52] Recommendation 2007/879 of 17 December 2007 on relevant product and service markets within the electronic communications sector susceptible to ex ante regulation, OJ 2007 No. L 344/65.

inconclusive.[53] On a more general note, Hellwig explains how the use
of market definition (within the meaning of competition law) in sectoral regulation would unduly prevent regulation from taking a more
systemic view of the market failures and theories of harm.[54]

Secondly, the commitment to rely on recognised economic knowledge does however have some concrete implications for regulatory
design. Here as well, electronic communications regulation provides a
good illustration. The current regulatory framework rests on the
principle of technological neutrality, which implies that the law must
be framed so as to be sustainable in the face of technological change
and evolution and that it must avoid picking technological winners
inadvertently.[55] As a consequence, most of the central concepts of
electronic communications law have been formulated in economic or
functional terms, eschewing technological categories.[56] This choice has
stood the test of time. In comparison, regulatory frameworks that
enshrine technological categories or models – such as the successive
electricity directives – have proven more difficult to manage over time,
with each round of legislative review leading to more regulation and
increased complexity.

Thirdly, since the early 2000s, with the reform of competition law
and the electronic communications regulatory framework, the
Commission relied mostly on soft-law instruments as the preferred
vehicle to achieve coordination, whether substantive or procedural.
These soft-law instruments include recommendations (within the
meaning of Article 288 TFEU) as well as less official types such as
communications, notices and guidelines. The Commission chose soft-
law instruments because of their informality and flexibility, given that
they were meant for fellow regulatory or competition law authorities.

---

[53] If the reliance on competition law methodologies proved inconclusive at the
substantive level, such reliance serves an institutional purpose, namely, to justify
the Commission veto over NRAs draft decisions regarding market definition and
SMP designation.
[54] Hellwig (fn. 34).
[55] EECC, art. 4(c). On the principle of technological neutrality, see Hancher/
Larouche (fn. 39); van der Haar, The principle of technological neutrality:
Connecting EC network and content regulation (2008), unpublished PhD
dissertation.
[56] Although the European Electronic Communications Code reintroduces some
technology-based concepts with the notion of 'very high capacity network' at
EECC, art. 2(2).

In practice, these soft-law instruments were largely followed, but their formal legal force was questioned and tested by litigants in a number of court cases. Unfortunately, European courts weakened the approach of the Commission by emphasising the lack of binding effect of soft-law instruments upon courts and other authorities than the Commission itself.[57]

Historically, amongst these soft-law instruments, only recommendations have been given any effect at all, even if limited, in that courts are bound 'to take them into account in order to decide disputes submitted to them, in particular where they cast light on the interpretation on national measures adopted in order to implement them or where they are designed to supplement binding Community provisions'.[58] It took years for the Court to finally accept, in 2016, that soft law – in this case a recommendation – could bind further and impose some actual constraints on NRAs and reviewing courts, in situations where legislation expressly requires the NRA to 'take utmost account' of such soft law. For the NRA, 'taking utmost account' implies following the recommendation, unless it finds that this is not appropriate, in which case the NRA must give reasons for its position.[59] Upon review, a national

---

[57] This can be observed in particular with respect to competition law, where the CJEU insisted upon the non-binding nature of the De minimis notice (now at OJ 2014 No. C 291/1) (Case C-226/11 *Expedia* EU:C:2012:795, at para. 4); the Notices on cooperation within the ECN, OJ 2004 No. C101/43 and on leniency, OJ 2006 No. C 298/17 (Case C-360/09 *Pfleiderer*, EU:C:2011:389, at para. 21); the Guidance paper on Article 102 TFEU, OJ 2009, No. C45/7 (CJEU, 6 October 2015, Case C-23/14 *Post Danmark I*, EU:C:2015:651, at para. 52); the instruments produced by the ECN, especially the Model Leniency Programme (Case C-428/14, *DHL Express (Italy)*, EU:C:2016:27, at paras. 41–44). The General Court also denied any binding nature to Commission comments issued under Art. 7(3) of Directive 2002/21 [now Art. 33(3) EECC]: Case T-109/96 *Vodafone España*, EU:T:2007:384, at para. 93 and Case T-295/06 *Base and Mobistar v Commission*, EU:T:2008:48.

[58] Case C-322/88 *Salvatore Grimaldi*, EU:C:1989:646, at para. 18, reconfirmed in the context of economic regulation in Case C–55/06, *Arcor v Bundesrepublik Deutschland*, EU:C:2008:244, at para. 94; and Case C-28/15 *KPN v ACM*, EU:C:2016:692, at para. 41.

[59] Case C-28/15 *KPN v ACM*, at para. 38. This ruling is confirmed in Case C-277/16 *Polkomtel v UKE*, EU:C:2017:989, at para. 37 and further clarified C-689/19P *VodafoneZiggo v Commission*, EU:C:2021:142. The CJEU gives more effect to 'utmost account' than the Gen Ct had previously done in Case T-109/96 *Vodafone España*, (fn. 57), at para. 93.

court may depart from a recommendation only for reasons having to do with factual circumstances.[60]

4.3.3 Institutional Relationship: The Importance of Cooperation

4.3.3.1 Overall Picture

When it comes to institutions, the relationship between regulatory regimes is multi-dimensional.[61] Typically, within each regime there is a *horizontal* relationship between the regulatory authorities of each Member State – in charge of implementing EU secondary law, as a default rule – as well as a *vertical* relationship between the Member State authorities and the European-level authority, usually the Commission. In addition, as between regimes, the respective authorities find themselves in a *transversal* relationship.

The overall picture is quite complex. At the apex of the pyramid, the European Commission plays a role in every EU economic regulation regime. In EU competition law, it holds direct implementation powers, shared with NCAs. Where national authorities are (also) in charge of implementation, the Commission is empowered – depending on the regime – to enact implementing or delegated legislation, to issue non-binding coordination documents (recommendations, guidelines, etc.) or to review, veto or take over the work of national authorities. In addition, the Commission is always a member or observer in the EU-level institutions regrouping national authorities.

At the bottom of the pyramid, each Member State created a national competition authority (NCA) as well as a number of national regulatory authorities (NRAs), in order to handle the implementation and enforcement tasks arising from EU economic regulation. Within each Member State, one or more courts are responsible for the judicial

---

[60] Case C-28/15 *KPN v ACM*, at paras. 42–43, expanding upon existing case law, as mentioned at para. 41.

[61] See Larouche, Coordination of European and member state regulatory policy: Horizontal, vertical and transversal aspects, (2004) 5 *Journal of Network Industries*, 277; Petit, The proliferation of national regulatory authorities alongside competition authorities: A source of jurisdictional confusion, in: Geradin/Munoz/Petit (eds.), *Regulatory Authorities in the EC: A New Paradigm for European Governance*, 2005, at p. 180; Monti, Attention Intermediaries: Regulatory Options and their Institutional Implications (2020) TILEC Discussion Paper 2020-18.

review of NRA and NCA decisions (or a similar mechanism of judicial control), and courts also hold original jurisdiction for the application of competition law.

In the middle of the pyramid, between the European Commission and the national authorities and courts, one finds for each regime that the NCAs or NRAs, as the case may be, are regrouped in an EU-level forum wherein they can – depending on the regime – exchange information, coordinate or allocate enforcement activity, develop best practice or issue recommendations or other soft-law instruments or in some cases even issue decisions. These European fora take various legal forms, and their size and powers vary.[62] They include the European Competition Network (ECN),[63] the Body of European Regulators for Electronic Communications (BEREC),[64] the Agency for the Cooperation of Energy Regulators (ACER)[65] or the European Supervisory Authorities (ESAs) in the financial sector.[66]

4.3.3.2 Horizontal and Vertical Coordination

In each EU economic regulation regime, EU law typically provides for means of horizontal and vertical coordination between the relevant authorities concerned with that regime.[67] It is beyond the scope of this chapter to describe them in detail. One prominent example is

---

[62] See de Visser, *Network-Based Governance in EC Law*, 2009.

[63] Directive 2019/1 (fn. 7).

[64] Regulation (EU) 2018/1971 of the European Parliament and of the Council of 11 December 2018 establishing the Body of the European Regulators for Electronic Communications, OJ 2018 No. L 321/1.

[65] Regulation (EU) 2019/942 of the European Parliament and of the Council of 5 June 2019 establishing an European Agency for the Cooperation of Energy Regulators, OJ 2019 No. L 158/22.

[66] Regulation (EU) 1093/2010 of the European Parliament and of the Council of 24 November 2010 establishing a European Supervisory Authority (European Banking Authority), OJ 2010 No. L 331/12, as amended; Regulation (EU) 1094/2010 of the European Parliament and of the Council of 24 November 2010 establishing a European Supervisory Authority (European Insurance and Occupational Pensions Authority), OJ 2010 No. L 331/48, as amended; Regulation (EU) 1095/2010 of the European Parliament and of the Council of 24 November 2010 establishing a European Supervisory Authority (European Securities and Markets Authority), OJ 2010 No. L 331/84, as amended.

[67] On the need and types of institutional cooperation in shared regulatory spaces, see Freeman/Rossi, Agency coordination in shared regulatory space, (2012) 125 *Harvard Law Review*, 1131.

found at Regulation 1/2003, as regards Articles 101 and 102 TFEU. This Regulation sets out a mechanism for cooperation between the Commission and the NCAs: they notify each other when proceedings are initiated and before they are closed, with a view to coordinating their action. Such coordination takes place within the European Competition Network (ECN).[68] Ultimately, the Commission retains the power of taking cases away from an NCA under certain circumstances, but that power has not been used formally so far.[69] Another model is found in electronic communications, under the SMP regime:[70] there, NRAs communicate their draft SMP measures to one another and to the Commission, for consultation. Coordination takes place within BEREC, which can also comment on NRA draft measures. Ultimately, the Commission retains the power to object to a draft measure and even veto it if it concerns market definition or SMP assessment. A small but not insignificant number of veto decisions have been issued over the years, while several comment decisions by the Commission have led to changes in NRA final decisions.[71]

The mechanisms described above are too detailed and probably too prescriptive to be applied to transversal relationships between two different economic regulatory regimes, if only because such regimes are contained in separate legal instruments. Indeed, no comparable mechanisms exist between two different regimes in EU economic law at the moment. Nonetheless, two features of these mechanisms could be useful in the design of what would be a more limited transversal coordination regime involving a new EU market investigation tool.

Firstly, the duty to consult is designed to be as effective as possible. For competition law, consultation takes place early in the process on the basis of a notice of intent to open an investigation, in order to avoid

---

[68] Regulation 1/2003, art. 11, save for consultations on draft Commission decisions, which take place through the Advisory Committee on Restrictive Practices and Dominant Positions: Regulation 1/2003, art. 14(1).

[69] Regulation 1/2003, art. 11(6) and Case C-857/19 *Slovak Telekom v Protimonopolný úrad Slovenskej republiky*, EU:C:2021:139. Note that some cases have been moved informally to the Commission.

[70] EECC, arts. 32–33.

[71] See https://ec.europa.eu/digital-single-market/en/consultation-procedures-telecom.

wasteful duplication of enforcement efforts.[72] Subsequently, a more extensive round of consultation takes place towards the end of the proceedings, when the authority has reached the point in its work where it can table a draft decision or measure. The Commission and other authorities have all the information in hand to be able to give meaningful comments to the authority that tabled the draft, and that authority has time to take these comments into account.

Secondly, one of the most interesting features of the SMP regime under the electronic communications framework is the obligation to 'take utmost account', which figures throughout Articles 32 and 33 EECC.[73] NRAs must take utmost account of the objectives of the EECC.[74] They must equally take utmost account of (i) comments received from other NRAs, BEREC or the Commission regarding a draft measure[75] and (ii) a Commission notification that it entertains serious doubts regarding a draft measure.[76] In return, the Commission is also bound to take utmost account of BEREC's opinion before issuing a veto or a recommendation to an NRA.[77] Similarly, NRAs must also take utmost account of Commission recommendations aiming to harmonise EECC implementation[78]. As mentioned above, the Court of Justice of the EU elaborated on the meaning of 'taking utmost account'.[79] It held that, in order to take utmost account of a Commission recommendation, an NRA is expected as a rule to follow the recommendation. The NRA can depart from the recommendation only if it finds the recommendation inappropriate in the circumstances of a given situation, and then the NRA must give reasons for its conclusion. In other words, 'taking utmost account' would correspond to a strong 'comply or explain' obligation. Even though the Court of

---

[72] Such a round of early consultation would be pointless under the EECC, since the NRAs are well aware of their respective enforcement agenda (being coordinated via the Commission Recommendation on relevant markets) and the risk of overlap is minimal.

[73] The notion of 'taking utmost account' figures in many other places in the EECC, and indeed throughout EU law. However, it is in the context of articles 32 and 33 EECC that it has received the most attention in practice and in academic work.

[74] EECC, art. 32(1)   [75] EECC, arts 32(8) and 33(1).   [76] EECC, art. 33(4a).

[77] EECC, arts. 32(6) and 33(5).   [78] EECC, art. 38(2).

[79] Here in the context of EECC, art. 38(2): Case C-28/15 *KPN v ACM* (fn. 58), at paras. 37–38.

Justice formulated its reasoning in general terms, it remains to be seen whether 'taking utmost account' will be interpreted similarly in other contexts.

4.3.3.3 Transversal Coordination

As mentioned above, as regards transversal relationships between authorities across regimes, EU law is much less developed. At a minimum, all authorities at the EU and national level, in their capacity as actors in the implementation and enforcement of EU law, are under a duty of loyalty (sincere cooperation) towards one another.[80] Such duty translates in an obligation to consult other authorities – usually between an NRA and the NCA – as explicitly stated in some EU regimes.[81] But effective coordination often requires more than consultations.

At the European level, some transversal coordination effort takes place internally, given that the Commission plays a role in every EU economic regulation regime. Such coordination is a matter for the internal rules and procedures of the Commission. In principle, internal coordination within a single institution – the European Commission – should happen without too much friction. The joint work of Directorates-General for Competition and for Communications Networks, Content and Technology in 2003–2006, the early years of the SMP regime, provides a successful example of intra-Commission coordination. Coordination between the EU-level regulatory fora is uneven: whereas in network industries the respective fora are perhaps too diverse to be able to coordinate effectively, the three financial-sector European Supervisory Authorities appear to be in closer contact, given their greater symmetry and their common design.

If anything, the most interesting developments regarding transversal coordination occurred at Member State level. A number of innovative formulae have been deployed. By way of example, Italy and the United Kingdom have created NRAs spanning multiple regimes in the converging ICT sector (electronic communications and audio-visual media services), in order to regulate more effectively. Given commonalities and also out of efficiency concerns, Germany has bundled all network-industry NRAs into one (Bundesnetzagentur or BNetzA), as well as all financial-sector NRAs into one (Bundesanstalt

---

[80] TEU, art. 4.   [81] For instance, EECC, art. 11.

für Finanzdienstleistungsaufsicht or BaFin).[82] In order to avoid frictions and forum shopping between competition law and sectoral regulation, the United Kingdom has given concurrent competition law powers to a number of NRAs in the network industries. Finally, Spain and the Netherlands have gone the furthest, merging the NCA with the NRAs in the network industries and the consumer protection authority into a wide authority (Comisión Nacional de los Mercados y la Competencia or CNMC, Autoriteit voor Consumenten en Markten or ACM). While these different formulas are attractive and worth studying,[83] none of them appears feasible in the context of the relationship between the authorities in charge of implementing an EU market investigation tool and other authorities tasked with the application of economic regulation.

4.3.4 Conflict Rule: Arbitrating Conflicting Obligations

In the end, despite the emphasis on cooperation and coordination, or perhaps because of it, a conflict rule is also needed. Such a rule was at the heart of *Deutsche Telekom*,[84] a case where the Commission found that DT had breached Article 102 TFEU by engaging into a margin squeeze between its wholesale access prices and its retail tariffs, leaving competing retailers with limited and sometimes even negative margins. One of DT's main points in defence was that both its wholesale and retail prices had been approved by the German sectoral regulatory authority.[85] Following the Commission and the General Court, the Court of Justice held that Article 102 TFEU remained applicable even if the German regulatory authority had already dealt with the case, unless DT would have been positively compelled by the authority to act as it did (which it was not).[86] The underlying message was clear: a

---

[82] In the same vein, the United Kingdom has created a UK Regulators Network (UKRN) bringing together regulators in the network industries and the financial sector, yet without the competition authority: https://www.ukrn.org.uk/.

[83] See Alexiadis/Pereira Neto, Competing Architectures for Regulatory and Competition Law Governance, (2019) EUI-FSR Energy Research Report.

[84] Case C-280/08P *Deutsche Telekom v Commission* (fn. 37).

[85] RegTP, as it then was. The corresponding regulatory powers are now vested in the BNetzA.

[86] Case COMP/37.451 Deutsche Telekom AG, OJ 2003 No. L263/9, at para. 54; Case T-271/03 *Deutsche Telekom v Commission*, EU:T:2008:101, at paras. 85–88; Case C-280/08P, at paras. 80–90.

firm remains subject to competition law for its course of conduct, even if such conduct would not fall foul of sectoral regulation. Competition law therefore prevails.[87] In the subsequent *Spain v Commission* case, a similar margin squeeze issue arose, with Spain arguing for the primacy of the decision taken by its sectoral authority. The General Court framed the issue more explicitly in terms of a conflict rule when it wrote the following:[88]

In any event, even if the sectoral regulation referred to by the Kingdom of Spain derives from European Union secondary legislation, it must be stated that, in view of the principles governing the hierarchical relationship of legal rules, such secondary legislation could not, in the absence of any enabling provision in the Treaty, derogate from a provision of the Treaty, in this case Article [102 TFEU].

The rule arising from *Deutsche Telekom* and *Spain v Commission* therefore flows from the primacy of competition law (specifically Article 102 TFEU) – as primary EU law – over sectoral regulation, which is secondary EU law. This rule is useful whenever Articles 101 or 102 TFEU is involved. What about other situations where no hierarchical element is present, such as between two regimes of secondary law? Of course, the regimes in question could contain their own conflict rules, as is the case for instance with the EECC for electronic communications and audio-visual media services regulation.[89] In the absence of such explicit rules, case law on this point is not well established. Available principles of legislative interpretation could apply, but they do not carry the same strength as a hierarchical rule.

---

[87] The reverse situation, where a firm would comply with competition law but not with sectoral regulation, has not yet been explored in the case law. In the 1998 Access Notice, the Commission states that in such a case, compliance with competition law does not prevent liability under sectoral regulation. In practice, such cases are unlikely to arise: since the 2004 reform (Regulation 1/2003), the Commission has ceased to issue non-infringement decisions under Articles 101 or 102 TFEU, and national competition authorities do not have the power to issue such decisions. Unless a firm would somehow have obtained a court judgment on the issue, it will accordingly not be in a position where it can invoke an actual decision to support a claim that it complies with competition law in the course of regulatory proceedings.

[88] Case T-398/07, *Commission v Spain*, EU:T:2012:173, at para. 55. In the same paragraph, the General Court explicitly dismissed Spain's argument that Trinko was a relevant authority on this point.

[89] EECC, art. 1(3).

In some situations, a general/specific articulation could be used. In such cases, the Court of Justice tries to apply both regimes in a complementary manner as far as possible. For instance, in the electronic communications sector, the Court of Justice clarified that the sector-specific consumer protection rules of the EECC are complementary – and not substitute – to the general consumer protection rules. Therefore, those general consumer protection rules apply fully to the electronic communications sector and should be enforced by the consumer protection authority.[90] Otherwise, the more specific regime should apply first, but at the same time it should not apply so as to contradict the more general regime, unless the more specific regime explicitly deviates from the more general one.

Another possibility would be a principal/accessory relation: for composite services, instead of applying two different regimes, only the regulation pertaining to the principal component would apply, leaving aside the regulation applicable to the accessory component. For instance, in *UPC Nederland*, a case concerning the delivery of audio-visual media content over electronic communications networks, the Court of Justice applied the legal regime of the principal component (electronic communications network) to the entire service and left aside the regime that only applied to an ancillary element of the service (audio-visual media service).[91] A similar approach was followed by the Court of Justice in the collaborative economy cases to decide whether the sharing platform should be qualified as a provider of an information society service or as a provider of the intermediated service (such as transport for Uber or hosting for Airbnb).[92] The Court sought

---

[90] Joined Cases C–54/17 and C–55/17, *Autorità Garante della Concorrenza e del Mercato (AGCM) v Wind Tre and Vodafone Italia*, EU:C:2018:710, at para. 60, noting that: 'The term "conflict" refers to the relationship between the provisions in question which goes beyond a mere disparity or simple difference, showing a divergence which cannot be overcome by a unifying formula enabling both situations to exist alongside each other without the need to bring them to an end.'

[91] Case C–518/11, *UPC Nederland v Hilversum*, EU:C:2013:709.

[92] Case C–434/15 *Asociación Profesional Élite Taxi v Uber Systems Spain*, EU: C:2017:981, at para. 40; Case C–320/16, *Uber France*, EU:C:2018:221, at para. 22, deciding that: 'The intermediation service (provided by Uber) had to be regarded as forming an integral part of an overall service the main component of which was a transport service and, accordingly, had to be classified, not as an "information society service" … but as a "service in the field of transport."' Case C–390/18, Airbnb Ireland, EU:C:2019:1112, at para. 69; Case C–62/19

to identify the main component of the service provided by the collaborative economy platform and then applied the legal regime relating to that main component to the whole service provided by the platform.

4.4 Recommended Interplay between a Wide Market Investigation and Sector-Specific Regulation

As explained above, the Commission had envisaged two versions, wide and narrow, of a market investigation at the EU level. The wide version applies to all sectors of the economy, including the regulated ones. This is the version generally applicable in jurisdictions having a market investigation tool. For instance, in the United Kingdom, the CMA may launch a market investigation in any sector of the economy, including regulated sectors, as no sector is legally excluded from Part 4 of the UK Enterprise Act. The sectoral regulators may themselves make market investigation references for which the investigation is to be conducted by the CMA. They will do so when it would be more appropriate to deal with a competition problem through a market investigation than under sectoral regulation.[93] In this regard, Whish indicates that 4 of the 20 market investigation references so far came from sectoral regulators.[94] Next to the market investigations done in regulated sectors at the request of the regulators, other investigations have been done in regulated sectors at the CMA's own initiative.[95] Similarly, in South Africa, all the provisions of the Competition Act,

---

Star Taxi App v Unitatea Administrativ Teritorialăa Municipiul Bucureşti prin Primar General, and Consiliul General al Municipiului Bucureşti, EU: C:2020:980.

[93] Market investigation references: Guidance about the making of references under Part 4 of the Enterprise Act, OFT 511, March 2006, at para. 2.3 in fine (fn. 37).

[94] See Whish, Chapter 5. Those were (i) the Office of Rail and Road made a reference of Rolling Stock Leasing in April 2007 and the Competition Commission reported in April 2009; (ii) OFCOM made a reference of Movies on Pay TV in August 2010 and the Competition Commission reported in August 2012; (iii) OFGEM referred Energy in June 2014 and the CMA reported in June 2016; (iv) the Financial Conduct Authority referred Investment Consultants in September 2017 and the CMA reported in December 2018. Moreover, in one other case in 2005, OFCOM accepted undertakings from BT in lieu of a market investigation reference

[95] This was the case of the market investigations in retail banking or in investment consultants.

including the market inquiries, apply to regulated sectors.[96] In practice, some market inquiries have been completed in regulated sectors such as the Banking Inquiry in 2008 and the Mobile Data Services in 2019.[97] This is also the case in Mexico where market examinations have been launched in regulated sectors such as transport or credit card payment systems.[98]

An advantage of a wide version of market investigation over a narrow one is that it alleviates uncertainty and costly litigation on the precise scope of the market investigation. The risks and costs of a narrow sectoral version could be illustrated by the constant frustration, in the long-standing process of ICT convergence, with the attempts to neatly delineate the respective ambits of sector-specific regulatory regimes through definitions. Intense negotiations have produced a complex definitional scheme involving 'electronic communications' networks and services, to be distinguished from 'Information Society services' and from 'audio-visual media services' (themselves divided in both linear and non-linear subcategories).[99] The resulting pigeonholing exercise is profoundly at odds with the technological and economic reality of the ICT sector.[100] A wide version avoids these pitfalls, but it requires a smooth interplay with sector regulation when market investigations are conducted in a regulated sector.

4.4.1 Systemic Relationship: Closing Regulatory Gaps

As explained above, the EU approach to economic regulation sees the various regimes – general and sector-specific – as complements rather than substitutes. Hence, a new wide market investigation could easily be integrated in European economic law and applicable to sectors

---

[96] South African Competition Act No. 89 of 1998 as amended, art. 3(1A). On the South African regime, see Bonakele/das Nair/Roberts, Chapter 6.

[97] http://www.compcom.co.za/banking-enquiry/, http://www.compcom.co.za/newsletter/data-market-inquiry/.

[98] https://www.cofece.mx/wp-content/uploads/2018/11/COFECE-047-2018-English-.pdf.

[99] Those respective definitions are now included in EECC, art. 2; Directive (EU) 2015/1535 laying down a procedure for the provision of information in the field of technical regulations and of rules on Information Society services, OJ 2015 No. L 241/1, art.1; AVMSD, art. 1(1).

[100] See, for instance, Case C-518/11, *UPC Nederland v Hilversum*.

which might be subject to specific regulation.[101] The presence of overlaps is a logical consequence thereof; to borrow from computer science, it is not a bug, it is a feature.

4.4.1.1 Market Investigation to Close Substantive Regulatory Gaps

The application of a new market investigation tool in a regulated sector – electronic communications, energy, transport, financial services, etc. – may be justified and useful to remedy a structural competition problem that either does not trigger regulatory intervention or for which available regulatory remedies would offer no effective solution. In this case, the market investigation could close a 'regulatory gap'. By way of illustration of such a 'gap', one could think of the tight oligopoly structure that appears to be prevailing in electronic communications markets, as evidenced in a number of merger control assessments.[102] At the beginning of the last review of the regulatory framework for electronic communications, BEREC pointed to the insufficiency of the (then) Directives to intervene in case of tight oligopolies and suggested legislative changes to broaden the possibilities of intervention.[103] However, the EU institutions did not adopt all the

---

[101] This is also recommended by Crawford/Rey/Schnitzer, Chapter 7.

[102] Such tight oligopoly is a result of concentration on mobile communications markets (given the limited number of spectrum licenses), coupled with the relative transparency of the market and extensive infrastructure sharing. See, for instance, Case T-399/16, *CK Telecoms UK Investments v Commission*, EU:T:2020:217, where the oligopolistic state of the UK mobile communications market is discussed at length, against the backdrop of Merger Regulation case law making comparable findings in other national markets. As for fixed communications markets, in most Member States they are at best duopolies.

[103] BEREC Opinion of 15 December 2015 on the Review of the EU Electronic Communications Regulatory Framework, BoR(15) 206, at p. 14, noting that: 'NRAs should be able to address duopoly scenarios – e.g. where NRAs are unable to find a single SMP operator in the relevant market but where two players are nonetheless not effectively competing. This is especially relevant, for example in the market for internet access, where the duopoly situations (with only two infrastructure-based competitors) is more likely to develop. As described in BEREC's report on oligopolies, duopolistic/oligopolistic communications markets face a high risk of evolving in a non-competitive manner and are less likely to support efficient and sustainable competition ('two are not enough').' BEREC's report on oligopoly analysis and regulation has identified several possible options for adapting the Framework regarding the regulatory treatment of oligopolies, including potential market indicators of non-competitive oligopolies. BEREC Report of 15 December 2015 on oligopoly analysis and regulation, BoR(15) 195.

changes proposed by BEREC and, doing so, may have left a regulatory gap which could be usefully closed by a marker investigation tool.[104]

A gap could also arise because a structural competition problem occurs so infrequently that establishing a regulatory regime for such a problem is deemed too costly for the benefits it would bring. These include the cost of carrying out the intervention (inquiry, proceedings, decision), the cost of maintaining, enforcing and reviewing regulation and of course the compliance costs and disincentives visited on market actors. A wide market investigation tool which can be used only when needed could be less costly to use than a fully-fledged sector-specific regulatory regime. Finally, a gap could also arise as a matter of regulatory dynamics: the structural competition problem in question could be a new occurrence that has not yet been acknowledged and identified by sector-specific regulation. Conceivably, experience could have been gained under the market investigation in dealing with such a problem in other sectors, in which case the market investigation could offer a comparative advantage over sector-specific regulation.

4.4.1.2 Market Investigation to Close Institutional Regulatory Gaps

It has also been suggested that the market investigation could be useful to intervene in situations where a structural competition problem could be addressed by sector-specific regulation but has not been remedied because of failure on the part of the NRA in charge of such regulation. For instance, the NRA may apply sector regulation in an incorrect manner and make mistakes,[105] the NRA may be captured[106] or the

---

[104] All the more since the General Court in Case T-399/16 *CK Telecoms* (fn. 102), severely restricted the applicability of the Merger Regulation to mergers involving such markets.

[105] This has been used to justify the Commission decision in Deutsche Telekom (fn. 37). See Geradin, Limiting the scope of article 82 of the EC treaty: What can the EU learn from the US Supreme Court's judgement in Trinko in the wake of Microsoft, IMS, and Deutsche Telekom?, (2004) 41 *Common Market Law Review*, 1519; contra Larouche, Contrasting legal solutions and comparability of the EU and US experiences, in: Levêque/Shelanski (eds.), *Antitrust and Regulation in the EU and US: Legal and Economic Perspectives*, 2009, p. 76–100. As discussed above, this is not how the Court of Justice explained the case: Case C-208/08P, *Deutsche Telekom* (fn. 37). On the use of competition law actions to correct intervention of NRAs, see also de Streel (fn. 37).

[106] There are few actual cases where regulatory capture was at stake, even though by all accounts capture is not unheard of in the EU. A more striking case of legislative capture occurred in the case of the removal of regulation of Next

NRA may fail to successfully defend its decision on appeal for reasons that are independent of its control.[107] In the jurisdictions that already have a market investigation tool, it has sometimes been used to correct the inaction of the regulators.

However, the EU context is different from these national jurisdictions. We would resist any suggestion that the market investigation tool is the appropriate means to correct the (in)action of an incompetent or captured NRA. There are other legal means to do that, in particular the specific coordination mechanisms set up by the sectoral regulation in question[108] or, in last resort, an infringement procedure against the Member State of the NRA in question under Article 258 TFEU. It would be detrimental to the integrity of both the market investigation tool and other economic regulation regimes if market investigation was seen as an additional means of recourse in regulatory proceedings. The existence of a regulatory gap should not depend on the quality of NRA enforcement activities but rather on the inability of the regulatory regime to deal with a structural competition problem in the abstract. In other words, the gap should be substantive and not institutional. Therefore, as will be suggested in Section 4.4.3, if the market investigation concludes that the obligations necessary to remedy the structural competition problem could in fact be imposed under existing regulation (hence, there is no substantive regulatory gap), then it would be better to solve such problem with existing sector regulation. To do so, the Commission, having done the market investigation, could make recommendations to the authorities, often national, in charge of sectoral regulation.

4.4.2 *Substantive Relationship: Using Economic Methodologies*

To fit into the broader landscape of EU economic law, market investigation should rest on solid economic analysis, as do the other

---

Generation Network in Germany: Case C-424/07 *Commission v Germany*, EU:
C:2009:749.

[107] See the example of termination rates in the Netherlands, leading up to Case
C-28/15 *KPN v ACM* (fn. 58) where the Dutch NRA duly applied EU law only
to see its decision vacated on appeal. The reasons given by the Dutch court of
appeal were severely criticised by the CJEU in its judgment at para. 42, with
reference to the opinion of the Advocate-General for more detail.

[108] For instance, EECC, arts. 32–34.

regulatory regimes. In the light of the experience with electronic communications regulation, however, we would like to emphasise that, even as regards the relationship with traditional competition law, there is no significant advantage to be gained by placing the economic inquiry to be carried out under the market investigation within the strait-jacket of competition law analysis (i.e., relevant market definition, followed by an assessment of whether the relevant market as defined – or the firms that populate it – meets certain criteria).

In particular, relevant market definition can introduce an element of rigidity that might impair the effectiveness of market investigation: it results in a snapshot view of markets, and the EU practice tends to define narrow markets. Competitive phenomena that might occur outside of or beyond the relevant market(s) have proven difficult to introduce into the analysis at the market assessment stage.[109] This is all the more critical when market investigation deals with structural competition problems in dynamic markets, where part of the competitive game involves reshaping markets through disruptive innovation, for instance.[110] Even if breaking with the standard formula of competition law analysis might perhaps wrongly create the impression that market investigation does not belong within competition law, the very rationale for market investigation is to bridge gaps in the coverage of competition law, some of which arise as a consequence of rigidities induced by relevant market definition.[111]

What is truly important for the market investigation tool to fit within the broader landscape of EU economic law is a clear

---

[109] By way of example, see how the relevant market definition exercise prevents the Commission from perceiving what is truly at stake in Facebook/WhatsApp, namely, the acquisition of one of the most likely springboards for disruptive innovation by the very powerful platform: Decision of the Commission of 3 October 2014, Case M.7217 Facebook/WhatsApp. See LEAR, Ex-post Assessment of Merger Control Decisions in Digital Markets (2019) Study for the Competition and Markets Authority; Fletcher, Chapter 8, cautioning against the reliance on rigid market definition in the digital sectors.

[110] In the specific context of the DMA Proposal, Larouche/de Streel, The European Digital Markets Act: A revolution grounded on traditions, (2021) 12 *Journal of European Competition Law & Practice*, at p. 548–552.

[111] In that respect, one could argue that the market investigation tool would merely follow the trend already underway in merger control, where the horizontal guidelines in both the United States and the EU put forward analytical methods that reduce the need for market definition to carry out a conclusive assessment in cases of monopolistic competition (markets with significant product differentiation amongst competitors).

commitment to the theoretical and methodological foundations of such law. In other words, market investigation should be solidly anchored in economics. Instead of insisting on the analytical structure of competition law, it is preferrable to invest time and resources to ensure that the rationale for a market investigation is well developed and that the provisions of the market investigation legislation properly render or translate the underlying economics. In all likelihood, this means that the market investigation tool should be formulated in more precise terms than current competition law (which relies on general notions such as 'agreement', 'restriction of competition', 'abuse' and 'dominant position'). A more precise formulation would also reduce the need to use concepts such as market definition in order to put boundaries on the discretion of the authority. We would also suggest that the market investigation tool contains devices designed to foster sound economic analysis, such as a requirement that a cogent theory of harm be formulated, tying all the economic features into a coherent analysis.[112] This implies that the tool should be based on structural problems and not on the finding of a dominant position. Furthermore, the experience with sectoral regulation shows the significance of technological neutrality and, with it, the use of economic or functional concepts.[113] Technological neutrality is especially important if the market investigation applies across the board to all economic sectors as suggested above.

Finally, the experience with sectoral regulation also indicates that the substantive development of market investigation and its coordination with other regulatory regimes should not rely too much on soft-law instruments. If the EU market investigation is enforced by the Commission alone, these soft-law instruments will bind the Commission, as recognised by case law. Nevertheless, some soft-law instruments could be used to set out the relationship between market investigation and other economic regulation regimes, and hence between the respective authorities. In certain cases, case law indicates that a 'comply or explain' effect can be achieved, but only with the use of recommendations or with the addition of an obligation to 'take utmost account' of the instrument. In our view, informed by the experience of the last 20 years, it is preferable to try to lay down the

---

[112] This is also the direction suggested by Motta/Peitz, Chapter 2.
[113] This is also recommended by Crawford/Rey/Schnitzer, Chapter 7.

fundamentals of the market investigation substance and of its relationship with other regimes in the legislation itself, even if it requires a greater expense of time and resources during the legislative process. Soft-law instruments can be used later to build and elaborate on these existing fundamentals, without running any risk for the validity and legal force of these fundamentals.

4.4.3 Institutional Relationship: Involving the National Regulatory Authorities

4.4.3.1 Vertical Cooperation between the Commission and the National Competition Authorities

Considering the number of regimes making up EU economic regulation at the institutional level, a new EU market investigation tool should not be set up as yet another stand-alone regime, an institutional island whose authorities need to coordinate and cooperate with those in charge of every other regime. Since market investigation is closely linked with EU competition law, its institutional structure would be best embedded within that of competition law. After all, market investigation is likely to be applied by the Commission or the NCAs or both. It would stand to reason that the mechanisms of Regulation 1/2003 would then be used to achieve coordination and cooperation with the authorities applying competition law.[114]

In concrete terms, this would mean that a round of consultation within the ECN would be undertaken every time the Commission (or an NCA) proposes to launch a market investigation.[115] This would allow for a discussion, within the ECN, of whether the use of the market investigation tool – as opposed to standard competition tools (Articles 101 or 102 TFEU) – is appropriate and of which authority is best placed to investigate. Similarly, at the end of the investigation, the proposed measure could be circulated for consultation within the ECN[116] or the Advisory Committee,[117] depending on whether an NCA or the Commission led the investigation. Relying on the tried-and-true mechanisms of Regulation 1/2003 for institutional coordination between the new market investigation tool and the rest of competition law would be an effective and efficient choice.

---

[114] This is in line with the analysis put forward by Schweitzer, Chapter 3.
[115] In line with Regulation 1/2003, art. 11(2) and (3).   [116] Ibid., art. 11(4).
[117] Ibid., art. 14(1).

4.4.3.2 Transversal Cooperation between the Commission and the National Regulatory Authorities

As the authorities in charge of sector-specific regulation are often national, transversal cooperation between the Commission and the NRAs is needed at every stage of the application of a market investigation in a regulated sector.[118] Indeed, in the jurisdictions having a market investigation tool, cooperation between the NCA and the NRA is often foreseen for all the tasks of the authorities, including the enforcement of the market investigation.[119] This is the case, for instance, in Greece[120] or in South Africa.[121]

At the initiation stage, a market investigation could be *launched* ex officio or upon a reference. There are pros and cons as to whether NRAs should be able to lodge a reference for market investigation with the competent authority. On the pro side, NRAs are ideally placed to identify regulatory gaps in the sectors that they scrutinize. On the con side, as we set out above, the integrity of both the market investigation tool and sector-specific regulation would be prejudiced if a market investigation is used as an additional battlefield for sector-specific regulation. Accordingly, the market investigation legislation should clearly define the circumstances under which an NRA can make a reference: there must be a substantive regulatory gap, that is, a situation where the NRA either has no competence to intervene or no adequate remedy at its disposal, in the abstract, even if it discharged its functions in the best possible fashion.

During the enquiry and the *information gathering* process about a possible structural competition problem in a regulated sector, the Commission should consult the relevant NRA(s). The Commission

---

[118] The possible market investigation stages are described in Schweitzer, Chapter 3.
[119] Generally, on the relationships between NCA and NRA, see OECD, Relationship between Regulators and Competition Authorities (1999) DAFFE/ CLP(99)8; OECD, Relationships between Competition Authorities and Sectoral Regulators (2005) DAF/COMP/GF(2005)2 and International Competition Network, Working Group on Antitrust Enforcement in Regulated Sectors (2004) Report to the Third Annual Conference in Seoul; International Competition Network; Working Group on Antitrust Enforcement in Regulated Sectors (2005) Report to the Fourth Annual Conference in Bonn.
[120] Greek Law 3959 of 2011 on the Protection of Free Competition, art. 24.
[121] South African Competition Act No. 89 of 1998 as amended, art. 82. On that basis, the Competition Commission of South Africa (CCSA) has concluded several Memoranda of Understanding with sector regulators: http://www .compcom.co.za/mou/.

should also be able to receive confidential information from those NRAs, provided it ensures the same level of confidentiality as the NRA which gathered the information.[122] Such exchange of information should be foreseen in the law and possibly organised through cooperation agreements between the Commission and the NRAs.[123] The same principles may apply to the sharing of information in the other direction, that is, information gathered in the course of a market investigation being shared with an NRA.

The *identification of the structural competition problem* should be done in close cooperation with the relevant NRAs and/or the EU-level forum regrouping those NRAs. In that regard, the Commission should be required to consult the relevant NRA(s) and the EU-level forum before issuing a decision on the structural competition problem.[124] Conversely, the relevant EU-level forum, if any, should be able to issue a non-binding opinion on the Commission draft decision, thereby extending its advisory power to market investigations.[125] In the light of the discussion above, the Commission should be under a requirement to 'take utmost account' of the NRA or EU-level forum opinion in order to add credibility to the consultation process. With such a requirement, the Commission is bound either to follow the opinion or to provide explanations as to why it is not appropriate to follow that opinion.

However, there is no need to go any further than cooperation and consultation. In particular, we do not see why, as some have suggested, the market investigation should be implemented by the NRAs

---

[122] A similar provision to exchange information between NCA and NRA is included in the EECC, art. 11. Such sharing of information should comply with the fundamental principles of procedural fairness guaranteed by Article 41 of the Charter of Fundamental Rights of the EU. To do so, Schweitzer, Chapter 3, explains that two conditions must be met: '(i) the transfer of information must be provided for by law; and (ii) the information transferred must not have been obtained under an investigatory regime [here the sectoral regulatory regime] that provides for a lower degree of procedural protection than the one that is applicable in the context in which the information shall be used after the transfer [here the NCT regime]'.

[123] Cooperation agreements between NCA and NRA often contain provisions on information sharing between agencies.

[124] Such cooperation is also foreseen between the NCA and the regulatory authority in Mexico: Mexican Federal Economic Competition Law of 2014, art. 94(III).

[125] For instance, the current advisory powers of BEREC are listed in Regulation 2018/1971, art. 4(1), esp. 4(1)(b).

themselves when applied in a regulated sector.[126] As market investigation forms part of the EU competition law regime, NRAs might not be suited to carry out a market investigation.[127] Moreover, in the context of a new tool, enforcement should be in the hands of the same authority irrespective of the sector where it is applied. It took almost 40 years of experience under EU competition law before the law was thought to be sufficiently well developed for Regulation 1/2003 to introduce fully decentralised application by national competition authorities without fear of fragmentation. If any national authority should get the power to apply market investigation, it should be the NCA, and then only in the medium to long term, provided it has sufficient resources for these tasks.

At the remedial stage, if a structural competition problem has been identified in a regulated sector, then the Commission should *design the remedies* in close cooperation with the relevant NRAs. This is all the more justified since, in designing the remedies, the Commission would be well advised to take into account the different objectives the NRAs might be pursuing. Inspiration may be taken from the UK system where the CMA should take into account the various objectives of sectoral regulation when designing the remedies in a market investigation.[128] As explained by Whish and Bailey 'those remedies may go beyond preventing adverse effects on competition: for example there is a legal obligation to ensure the maintenance of a universal postal service'.[129]

The *implementation of the remedies* depends on the competence of the NRAs. On the one hand, if the NRAs have the competence – under their national law transposing EU law or directly under EU law – to remedy the structural competition problem, then there is no regulatory gap. In such a case, the Commission could issue a recommendation to the NRAs to implement the designated remedies under their respective sectoral framework, with a requirement to take utmost account of the Commission recommendation. This case is perhaps unlikely but not

---

[126] This has been suggested by BEREC in its Response to the Public Consultation on the DSA and the NCT, at p. 37.

[127] Except maybe in Member States where the relevant NRA is merged with the NCA in a super-authority (e.g., the Netherlands or Spain for network industries); but there the super-authority in its quality as NCA would be in a position to undertake the investigation.

[128] UK Enterprise Act 2002, section 168.   [129] Whish/Bailey (fn. 4).

impossible: it is conceivable that, at the end of a long market investigation, the additional information and knowledge gained through the investigation leads to a different conclusion than what was expected earlier. What seemed like a regulatory gap, on the basis of the information available at the outset of the investigation, could turn out to be actually solvable with the existing array of regulatory remedies. This approach would be similar to the Mexican system where the NCA could notify the NRA regarding the finding of barriers to competition and free market access for it to determine, within the scope of its jurisdiction and according to the procedures in prevailing legislation, what actions should be taken to achieve competition conditions.[130] On the other hand, if the NRAs do not have the competence to remedy the structural competition problem (hence, there is truly a regulatory gap), then the Commission should be able to impose appropriate remedies, thereby ensuring that the market investigation usefully complements sector regulation.

Finally, the *monitoring and the control of compliance* with the remedies imposed after the market investigation could be delegated by the Commission to the NRA. In this case, the NRA should regularly report to the Commission, which would remain in charge of sanctioning any failure to comply with the imposed remedies.[131]

4.4.4 *Conflict Rule: Protecting the Internal Market*

Given the extensive cooperation and coordination mechanisms suggested above, there should be few cases where conflict between the application of the market investigation tool and the specific regulation occurs.[132] We have explained in Section 4.3.4 that standard competition law (Articles 101 and 102 TFEU) prevails over sectoral regulation mainly because of the hierarchy of law: competition law is primary EU law and therefore enjoys primacy over sectoral regulation, which is secondary law. A new EU market investigation tool would itself not be primary law. Since it would potentially have a broader scope than standard competition law, it may even not be considered as an

---

[130] Mexican Federal Economic Competition Law of 2014, art. 95.
[131] This setting was relied in the Decision of the Commission of 2 April 2003, Case M.2876 NewsCorp/Telepiu, at para. 259.
[132] Coordination between the market investigation tool and current competition law is discussed in Schweitzer, Chapter 3.

implementation of primary EU competition law like Regulation 1/2003 or, to some extent, the Merger Control Regulation.[133] Thus, an argument based on the hierarchy of law is more difficult to make.

As a starting point, we would be against an absolute hierarchical rule based on 'fields' or 'competences', without any regard for the concrete implementation and enforcement by the respective authorities. To wit, such a rule would state that there is a market investigation 'field' where sector-specific regulation cannot thread, irrespective of what has been done under the market investigation, or vice-versa. Indeed, absolute market investigation tool primacy over sectoral regulation would lead to difficulties when the two legal regimes have different objectives, for example, to remedy different market failures, which is often the case.

Conversely, sector-specific regulation should not prevail over the market investigation tool as an absolute rule. Some favour such a solution because sectoral regulation could be considered as a *lex specialis* in relation to the more general market investigation tool, applicable across the board to the whole economy.[134] Even if this argument could apply in a horizontal relationship (between two national regimes or two EU regimes), it is less convincing in a transversal situation pitting EU law enforced at the EU level (the market investigation tool) against another EU legal regime, often a Directive, applied at the national level (sectoral regulation). In such a situation, a primacy rule in favour of sectoral regulation risks undermining the internal market by fragmenting the effect of the market investigation tool.

We would accordingly propose a much narrower rule, based not on abstract notions of 'fields' but on the concrete actions of the respective authorities. As a starting point, both the market investigation tool and sector-specific regulation should apply concurrently, unless their concurrent application puts a firm in a situation where it cannot comply

---

[133] The legal basis of the market investigation may also play a role in this assessment. If the market investigation is based not only on Art. 103 TFEU, but also on another legal basis such as Art. 114 TFEU (as suggested in the Inception Impact Assessment) or Art. 352 TFEU (as it is the case for the Merger Regulation), then the direct link with EU primary law (Art. 101 and 102 TFEU) will be loosened.

[134] See BEREC Response to the Public Consultation on the DSA and NCT, at p. 36.

with both regimes at the same time. Such cases should be exceptional. There would thus be no conflict if, under one regime, a firm is put under a regulatory obligation, whereas under the other regime, regulatory analysis led the firm to be exempted from any obligation.[135] In such a situation, the firm can comply with both regimes. To the extent that the two regimes are complementary, there should not be any significant proportionality issue, since the respective interventions of each authority are presumably necessary and proportionate to the aims of the respective regimes. In any event, if – as is assumed – the application of the market investigation in a regulated sector is premised on the existence of a regulatory gap, there can be no divergence since sector-specific regulation cannot be applied. Under such a narrow conflict rule, the emphasis would be on institutional mechanisms for the Commission and the NRA to cooperate and coordinate their actions, along the lines described above, so as to avoid a situation where the firm is put in an impossible bind.

In spite of the above, should a firm find itself in a position where it cannot comply with one regime without breaching the other, then we would suggest the following conflict rule. Our starting point is that, in principle, the market investigation tool will be used to impose obligations across the EU. Sector-specific regulation, on the other hand, is usually applied at Member State level, with a specific set of obligations for each Member State.[136] In a case where the scope of the two conflicting regulatory obligations is different, then the regulatory obligation applicable across the EU (usually coming from the market investigation tool) should prevail, out of concern for the internal market.

4.5 Recommended Interplay between a Narrow Market Investigation and Competition Law

As explained in Section 4.2, the Commission decided to propose a narrow version of market investigations which, in practice, are merely

---

[135] With the possible exception of a situation where the exemption from any obligation is essential for the overall effectiveness of the regulatory instrument in question.

[136] Our reasoning would not necessarily hold if the starting assumptions (market investigation tool applied uniformly across the EU, sectoral regulation applied to the specific set of circumstances of a Member State) are not met.

flexibility clauses for the Digital Markets Act. As the narrow version places market investigations within sector regulation, we deal now with the interplay between DMA market investigations and (EU or national) competition law.

4.5.1 Systemic Relationship: Closing Competition Law Gaps

At a general level, the proposed DMA is a new EU sector-specific regulation applicable to the providers of a pre-defined list of eight 'core platform services'. The DMA aims to cover competition law 'gaps' and intervenes when competition law cannot act or can only act in an ineffective manner in achieving market contestability and B2B fairness in the digital economy.[137] Hence, as for any other EU sector-specific regulation, the DMA will complement – and not substitute for – competition law. In fact, the list of obligations and prohibitions in the DMA Proposal is very much inspired by past or ongoing EU or national competition cases which, it is claimed, did not prove effective in solving the competition problems beyond the scope of the instant cases.[138] Once the DMA is adopted, the Commission will intervene on the basis of the DMA against the courses of conduct targeted by such sectoral regulation and would no longer have recourse to competition law for that purpose. That should facilitate and speed up Commission intervention.

4.5.2 Substantive Relationship: Using Economic Methodologies

The DMA Proposal foresees three different types of market investigation: the first to designate digital gatekeepers on the basis on quantitative and qualitative economic indicators, the second to sanction gatekeepers that systematically violate the obligations and prohibitions to which they are subject by virtue of the DMA and the third to expand the scope or the obligations of the DMA. As recommended above for the wide market investigation, we think that the design and the implementation of the narrow version of market investigation should also be

---

[137] DMA Proposal (fn. 3), rec. 9 and 10.

[138] Impact Assessment Report of the Commission Services of 15 December 2020 on the Proposal for a Regulation of the European Parliament and of the Council on contestable and fair markets in the digital sector (Digital Markets Act), SWD(2020) 363, at para. 155.

based on sound economic analysis without being put in the strait-jacket of competition law methodologies.

In particular, regarding the gatekeeper designation, the DMA Proposal foresees three generic criteria which apply cumulatively, namely: (i) a large size and impact on the EU internal market, (ii) the control of an important gateway for business users to reach end-users and (iii) whether the control in question is entrenched and durable.[139] Those generic criteria are 'operationalised' with an open list of quantitative and qualitative indicators such as the financial size, the number of customers and their lock-in, the entry barriers or the scale and scope effects.[140] We welcome those criteria and indicators because, on the one hand, they reflect the economic theories on gatekeepers and bottlenecks[141] and, on the other hand, they do not rely on competition law market definition tools, whose methodologies are difficult to apply in the digital economy.[142]

Regarding the addition of new obligations or prohibitions, the DMA Proposal sets out two normative standards to guide the market investigation:[143] (i) ensuring contestability of digital markets, which means that markets should remain open to new entrants and innovators offering digital services that may substitute or complement the services already offered by the gatekeepers;[144] or (ii) ensuring fairness in the B2B relationship between the gatekeepers and their business users, which is defined as a balance between the rights and obligations of each party and the absence of a disproportionate advantage in favour of the gatekeepers.[145] Those standards are much more open than the criteria of the first type of market investigation on gatekeeper designation, hence they increase the discretion of the Commission. To ensure consistency with the other tools of EU economic law, it is crucial that those standards are applied and interpreted on the basis of sound

---

[139] DMA Proposal (fn. 3), art. 3(1).   [140] Ibid., art. 3(6).

[141] Caffara and Scott Morton define gatekeeper as 'an intermediary who essentially controls access to critical constituencies on either side of a platform that cannot be reached otherwise, and as a result can engage in conduct and impose rules that counterparties cannot avoid'. Caffara/Scott Morton, The European Commission Digital Markets Act: A translation (2021) Vox.eu. On the related concept of bottleneck, see Armstrong, Competition in two-sided markets, (2006) 37 *Rand Journal of Economics*, 668.

[142] See fn.106 and 107.   [143] DMA Proposal (fn. 3), art. 10.

[144] This is sometimes referred as fairness in some Executive Vice-President Vestager speeches.

[145] DMA Proposal (fn. 3), art. 10(2) and also art. 7(6) and rec. 57.

economic analysis. This will probably be easier for the contestability standard, which relates to economic efficiency (i.e., the size of the pie) and is intrinsically linked to entry barriers (and hence also part of competition law analysis), than for the vague fairness standard, which includes distributional considerations (i.e., the distribution of the pie) that are always more controversial.

4.5.3 Institutional Relationship: Involving the National Competition Authorities

4.5.3.1 Use by the Commission of Concurrent Powers

Once the DMA is adopted, the Commission will have concurrent regulatory and competition powers. To intervene against conduct of the digital gatekeepers which will (already) be regulated by the DMA, the Commission should rely on its DMA power and no longer on its competition law powers. The interesting question, however, is which route the Commission will follow when intervening against courses of conduct that are not (yet) covered by the DMA. Given the concurrency of powers, the Commission should choose between competition law or a market investigation of the third type under the DMA. Under the former, the Commission would open an abuse of dominance case and should build a theory of harm to the requisite legal standard imposed by the EU Courts. Under the latter, the Commission would launch a market investigation and then adopt a delegated act to add the course of conduct under consideration to the list of the DMA obligations. In order to do so, the Commission should prove that such conduct weakens market contestability or creates an imbalance between the rights and the obligations of the gatekeeper and its business users. This standard seems to be lower than the legal standard under competition law, all the more since judicial review of delegated acts adopted in the wake of DMA market investigations is likely to be less intensive than in individual competition law decisions. This difference in legal standards is not surprising, as the DMA aims to facilitate and speed up intervention compared to competition law, for a subset of firms designated as gatekeepers of core platform services.

However, given such difference in the applicable legal standard, it is reasonable to expect that the Commission will choose between its competition and DMA powers not only according to the type of gatekeeper conduct at play but also as a function of the ease of intervention. As the DMA standard is lower than the competition standard, we may reasonably expect the Commission to favour market investigation under the DMA over competition law enforcement when intervening against designated gatekeepers. Again, this is not a problem as such, since the regulated platforms have significant market power in their role as gatekeepers and cannot hence claim that they could not have been subjected to any intervention absent the DMA. Nonetheless, according to us, two important safeguards are necessary to ensure that the Commission does not abuse its extensive concurrent powers and to maintain legal predictability.

To prevent the risk of abuse of power and regulatory creep, the standard of intervention to propose a delegated act expanding the DMA list of obligations should be based on sound economic interpretation of market contestability and B2B fairness, as explained above. To ensure legal predictability, the Commission should explain in advance the criteria it will use to choose between its regulatory and competition powers.[146] To do that, the Commission may, for instance, rely on the criteria it uses to select markets for ex ante regulation in telecommunications. Such selection is based on three criteria, and the third one, in particular, indicates that[147]

This third criterion aims to assess the adequacy of competition law to tackle identified persistent market failure(s), in particular given that *ex ante* regulatory obligations may effectively prevent competition law infringements. Competition law based interventions are likely to be insufficient where frequent and/or timely intervention is indispensable to redress persistent market failure(s). In such circumstances, *ex ante* regulation should be considered an appropriate complement to competition law.

The Commission could also rely on the criteria proposed by Motta and Peitz to determine when a (broad) market investigation may be a better

---

[146] In the United Kingdom, where most of the regulators have concurrent power, they have concluded MoU with the competition authority which clarify how concurrent powers will be exercised. See, for instance, Memorandum of understanding of 8 February 2016 between the CMA and Ofcom on concurrent competition powers. Also Crocioni, Ofcom's Record as a Competition Authority: An Assessment of Decisions in Telecoms, EUI Working Paper RSCAS 2019/93.

[147] EECC, art. 67(1) clarified by Commission Recommendation 2020/2245 of 18 December 2020 on relevant product and service markets within the electronic communications sector susceptible to ex ante regulation, OJ 2020 No. L 439/23, recital 17. See fn. 13.

route than an Article 102 TFEU enforcement action. This may be the
case when a competition law assessment may be long, complex and
uncertain or when it would not solve a generalised problem but just
deal with one specific conduct or firm.[148] On those bases, possible
criteria to favour a DMA market investigation over competition law
enforcement could comprise the recurrence or the prevalence of conduct by different types of gatekeepers or the need to intervene quickly
or with remedies that require extensive monitoring.[149] Adopting such
criteria would be useful to ensure legal predictability but cannot
undercut the responsibility of the Commission to apply EU competition law. Indeed, competition law – which is primary law – cannot
legally be sacrificed on the altar of the DMA – which is secondary law.
More fundamentally, given that the initial list of obligations and
prohibitions found in the DMA appears largely based on experience
in competition law enforcement, it would seem appropriate to continue
to use competition law as a first line of intervention, in order to build
up experience and 'test-drive' theories of harm in actual cases before
courses of conduct are enshrined in the DMA list of prohibitions and
obligations.

4.5.3.2 Transversal Cooperation between the Commission and the National Competition Authorities

As the DMA will apply next to competition law, it is important that the
authorities in charge of both legal instruments coordinate amongst
themselves. The DMA will be enforced by the Commission while
competition law is enforced by the Commission and the NCAs. On
the one hand, coordination within the Commission (as DMA enforcer
and the leading EU competition authority) is inherent to the
Commission decision-making process, as decisions are prepared by
the relevant Directorates-General in a collaborative manner, with
inter-DG steering groups, and adopted by all Commissioners under
the principle of collegiality.[150] On the other hand, the coordination

---

[148] Motta/Peitz, Chapter 2.

[149] Those criteria may also be inspired by the reasons mentioned by the
Commission services for the insufficiency of competition law in dealing with
some structural competition problems in the digital economy: Impact
Assessment Report on the DMA Proposal (fn. 138), at paras. 119–124.

[150] Commission Decision 2010/138 of 24 February 2010 amending its Rules of
Procedure, arts. 1 and 23.

between the Commission as DMA enforcer and the NCAs may be more complex as there is no obvious existing forum where such coordination should take place. Indeed, the ECN and the coordination mechanisms of Regulation 1/2003 may not be appropriate because the DMA is not conceived of as a competition law tool.

However, such coordination is essential, as parallel intervention by the Commission under the DMA and by an NCA under national competition law is not improbable. Indeed, while the DMA Proposal prohibits Member States from imposing further obligations on designated gatekeepers for the purpose of ensuring contestable and fair markets, it does not prevent Member States from imposing obligations on the basis of EU or national competition rules.[151] In other words, national competition law can be used to impose obligations on designated gatekeepers, provided that this is compatible with Regulation 1/2003.[152] For instance, obligations could be imposed in parallel under the DMA and under the newly adopted §19a of the German Competition Act[153] which targets similar platforms. Such parallel imposition, at best, undermines the internal market and, at worst, leads to incompatibility.

In order to avoid such pitfalls, the DMA Proposal provides for two coordination mechanisms between the Commission and national authorities. Firstly, the DMA establishes a Digital Markets Advisory Committee (DMAC), a comitology committee which could issue non-binding opinions on Commission draft decisions under the first and the second types of market investigation[154] Secondly, the DMA requires prior consultation with Member State experts for the third type of market investigation.[155] However, such coordination mechanisms are

---

[151] DMA Proposal (fn. 3), art. 1.6.

[152] Council Regulation 1/2003 of 16 December 2002 on the implementation of the rules on competition laid down in Articles 81 and 82 of the Treaty, OJ 2003 No. L 1/1, as amended, art. 3(2) provides that: 'Member States shall not under this Regulation be precluded from adopting and applying on their territory stricter national laws which prohibit or sanction unilateral conduct engaged in by undertakings.'

[153] See Section 19a of German Competition Law on Abusive Conduct of Undertakings of Paramount Significance for Competition across Markets.

[154] DMA Proposal (fn. 3), art. 32 and art. 15(1) for the first type of market investigation and art. 16(2) for the second type of market investigation.

[155] Ibid., art. 37(4).

not enough. First, the national experts composing a comitology committee or consulted before the adoption of a delegated acts are not
necessarily coming from independent authorities, let alone the NCAs.
Second, the Commission is relatively free as to what to make of the
national experts' opinions and is not subject to a 'comply or explain'
principle. It would probably be better to establish a new permanent
forum where the Commission and the NCAs (possibly with other
independent national authorities) could meet to discuss the enforcement of the DMA. Such a forum would allow the national authorities
to bring their expertise and legitimacy in support of DMA market
investigations. It would also reduce the risk of divergent or incompatible decisions by the Commission under the DMA and by an NCA
under competition law.

4.5.4 Conflict Rule: Protecting the Internal Market

If the establishment of a discussion forum between the Commission
and the NCAs may reduce the risk of divergent or incompatible decisions, it may not alleviate it completely. Therefore, as for the wide
market investigation, a conflict rule needs to be in place. As before, we
adopt a narrow conception of conflict, which should be based on the
concrete existence of two incompatible decisions and not on an
abstract notion of incompatible 'fields'. As before also, we think that
the starting point for the conflict rule should be the preservation of the
single market (which is the objective of the DMA) while respecting the
hierarchy of law: this means that EU competition law would prevail
over the DMA, but not national competition law when it goes further
than EU law. Therefore, in case of an incompatibility between an
obligation imposed by the Commission under the DMA, which applies
across the EU, and a remedy imposed by an NCA under national
competition law, which applies to one Member State only, the DMA
obligation should prevail.

4.6 Conclusion

This chapter shows that, at the *systemic level*, the different components
of EU economic law (competition law and sectoral regulatory regimes)
often overlap. They stand in a complementary relationship to each
other. They all are meant to pursue the overall objectives of the

Treaties but with different means, each of them focusing on its particular strengths. At the *substantive level*, competition law and sectoral regulation share a common theoretical basis and typically follow a public interest approach. They also share a common methodology, based on economic analysis and the application of the principles of subsidiarity and proportionality. At the *institutional level*, both competition law and sectoral regulatory regimes are implemented and enforced by a complex set of EU and national institutions: the European Commission, National Competition Authorities (NCAs), National Regulatory Authorities (NRAs) and EU-level networks, with national and European courts playing a role as well. Coordination mechanisms are in place to cover horizontal (between national authorities), vertical (between the European and national levels) and transversal (across legal regimes) relationships. The success of the overall system depends mostly on a smooth coordination between the different institutions.

Therefore, a new market investigation tool could easily be integrated in the existing body of EU economic law. Two versions of market investigation have been mooted: a wide version applicable horizontally to all the sectors of the economy, including the regulated ones, and a narrow version applicable to specific sectors of the economy. While the wide version corresponds to the market investigation existing in other jurisdictions, the narrow one is akin to a flexibility clause for sector-specific regulation.

A wide market investigation could be integrated within EU economic law. At the *systemic level*, such a tool would apply horizontally to the whole economy, including regulated sectors, as it could usefully close eventual regulatory gaps. Such gaps could arise because a structural competition problem occurs so infrequently that the establishment of a fully-fledged regulatory regime has been deemed too costly for the benefits it would bring or because, as a matter of regulatory dynamics, the problem in question is a new occurrence that has not yet been acknowledged and identified by sector-specific regulation.

At the *substantive level*, such a wide market investigation tool should rest on the same theoretical basis and methodology as existing EU economic law. However, the tool should not be strait-jacketed within specific competition law methodology (including relevant market definition and assessment of the relevant market in the light of the provision at stake), as long as solid economics underpin its implementation, including a theory of harm in individual cases. This does not necessarily imply an increase in the discretion of the authority in charge of the market investigation but rather reliance on an economic methodology which is better adapted to the structural competition problems that the market investigation is aimed to address. Also, the tool should be formulated in technology-neutral terms, that is, using economic or functional concepts. Finally, the fundamental elements of the market investigation tool should be set out in legislation, and the role of soft-law – if any – should be limited to developing or elaborating on these fundamentals.

At the *institutional level*, wide market investigation enforcement should be embedded within the institutional framework for coordination under Regulation 1/2003 to ensure proper coordination with competition authorities. Furthermore, if and when a market investigation is applied in regulated sectors, the Commission (or any institution in charge of the market investigation) and the relevant NRAs should cooperate closely at every stage of the investigation: (i) at the *initiation* stage, NRAs should be able to make a reference when they cannot deal with a structural competition problem in their sector because of the existence of a regulatory gap; (ii) at the *information gathering* stage, the Commission and NRAs should be able to exchange confidential information provided confidentiality is respected at both ends of the exchange; (iii) at the *structural competition problem identification and remedy design* stages, the NRAs (and relevant EU-level networks) should be able to issue an opinion on draft Commission decisions, and the Commission should be bound to take the utmost account of such opinion; (iv) at the *remedy implementation* phase, the Commission should be able to impose remedies when the NRAs cannot act; however, if the NRAs are able to act (hence the market investigation shows that there is no regulatory gap in the end), then the Commission should make recommendations for action, of which the NRAs should take utmost account; (v) finally, at the *remedy monitoring* stage, the Commission may delegate to the NRAs the compliance monitoring as well as the evaluation of the remedy.

Given these coordination mechanisms, the potential for conflict between the market investigation tool and sectoral regulation is minimised. In any event, market investigation and sectoral regulation should apply concurrently, except in the rare case where a firm would be put in a position where it could not comply with one without breaching the other. In such case, the remedy under the market investigation – which has EU scope – should prevail over the sectoral remedy – which has a national scope – in order to protect the integrity of the internal market.

However, the Commission has decided to propose, in the Digital Markets Act, a narrow version of the market investigation. The integration of such a narrow version in EU economic law is somewhat easier than the integration of the wide version, as it comes closer to the more traditional relationship between sectoral regulation and competition law. At the *systemic level*, the DMA complements competition law where practice has shown that competition law is ineffective in solving competitive problems. At the *substantive level*, the standards, the criteria and the indicators used to implement the three types of DMA market investigation are not strait-jacketed within competition methodologies, but they should be applied and interpreted with sound economic analysis. At the *institutional level*, the Commission will acquire concurrent regulatory and competition powers and it should explain in guidelines the criteria it will use to choose between those different powers when addressing the conduct of the digital gatekeepers. Moreover, given the possible parallel application of the DMA by the Commission and national competition law by the NCAs, it is key that the cooperation between the Commission and the NCAs is ensured. Finally, a *conflict rule* needs to be established when the parallel application of the DMA and competition law leads to incompatible obligations.

5 | Market Investigations in the UK and Beyond

RICHARD WHISH

5.1 Introduction

On 2 June 2020, the European Commission announced that it was considering the possibility of proposing a 'New Competition Tool' that could be used to address structural competition problems arising in markets that are not covered, or not covered effectively, by Articles 101 and 102 TFEU. This initiative was part of a broader piece of work: the Commission's press release[1] stated that the Commission had been reflecting on the role of competition policy and how it fits in a world that is changing fast and is increasingly digital and globalised. The Commission's conclusion was that it should:

- continue to enforce rigorously the existing competition rules, including making use of interim measures and restorative remedies where appropriate;
- consider the establishment of a system of ex ante regulation of digital platforms, including additional requirements for those that play a gatekeeper role; and
- consider the establishment of a New Competition Tool.

In essence, the idea of the New Competition Tool was that, after having conducted a rigorous market investigation, the new Tool would allow the Commission to impose behavioural and/or structural remedies to overcome any structural harms to competition in the market investigated. This could be done without the establishment of a finding of an infringement of Article 101 and/or 102 by the undertakings under investigation, and no fines would be imposed on the market participants; nor would there be provision for the award of compensation to anyone harmed by the competition harms identified.

---

[1] IP/20/977 of 2 June 2020.

The Commission's Inception Impact Assessment of 2 June 2020 explained in greater detail the context of its examination of the possible creation of a New Competition Tool, the Commission's objectives and policy options, its preliminary assessment of expected impacts and the evidence base and data collection that would be involved in the process together with the Commission's proposals to consult with citizens and stakeholders. Specifically, the Commission announced that it intended to procure targeted research papers on policy options and key features of a New Competition Tool.

This chapter is based on a report that was one of the research papers commissioned as part of the Commission's initiative. The author was asked to produce a comparative study of existing competition tools aimed at addressing structural competition problems, with a particular focus on the United Kingdom's market investigation tool.

Following a period of consultation, the Commission announced how it intended to proceed in December 2020.[2] It published a draft Digital Markets Act which proposed that a series of obligations (both positive and negative) would be imposed on 'gatekeepers' that provide specified 'core platform services' such as search engines, social networking services and online intermediation services. Gatekeepers would be designated by reference to objective, transparent criteria based on size, control and durability. As far as the New Competition Tool was concerned, the proposals outlined in December were less ambitious than what had been suggested when the Commission launched its initiative the preceding June. Far from this power being available for addressing structural competition problems across the entire economy, and irrespective of the existence of a dominant position in a relevant market, the Commission is now proposing that there should be a power to conduct market investigations in three specific situations:

- to identify gatekeepers that are not captured by the designation criteria in the Digital Markets Act;
- to identify whether other services should be added to the list of core platform services; and
- to design additional remedies for when a gatekeeper has systematically infringed the rules of the Digital Markets Act.

---

[2] Commission Press Release IP/20/2347 of 15 December 2020.

This chapter will examine the use of market investigations in the competition laws of the United Kingdom, Greece, Iceland, Mexico and South Africa.

In Section 5.2, this chapter provides an overview of UK competition legislation generally. It then describes the system of market investigations in the United Kingdom: first, the substantive provisions (Section 5.3); then the institutional framework and the system of appeals (Section 5.4); and thereafter the procedure when a market investigation is carried out (Section 5.5). Section 5.6 examines how the market investigation provisions have been applied in practice. Section 5.7 describes analogous provisions in Greece, Iceland, Mexico and South Africa. The report ends with some concluding thoughts in Section 5.8.

5.2 Overview of UK Competition Legislation

The two principal competition law statutes in the United Kingdom are the Competition Act 1998 and the Enterprise Act 2002, as amended by the Enterprise and Regulatory Reform Act 2013 (ERRA 2013).

5.2.1 Antitrust

The Competition Act contains two prohibitions. The 'Chapter I prohibition', modelled upon Article 101(1) TFEU, prohibits agreements that may affect trade within the United Kingdom and that have as their object or effect the prevention, restriction or distortion of competition. The 'Chapter II prohibition', modelled upon Article 102 TFEU, prohibits the abuse of a dominant position if it may affect trade within the United Kingdom. These 'antitrust' provisions are enforced by the Competition and Markets Authority (CMA) and, within their jurisdictional perimeters, by the sectoral regulators such as the Office of Communications (OFCOM) and the Office of Gas and Electricity Markets (OFGEM). This is known as the 'concurrency regime', whereby each of the sectoral regulators has concurrent jurisdiction with the CMA to apply competition law within the sectors for which they responsible. There are nine sectoral regulators in the United Kingdom with concurrent powers to apply the competition rules. Rules on the concurrency regime are contained in the

Competition Act (Concurrency) Regulations 2014.[3] There is also
Guidance on concurrent application of competition law to regulated
industries.[4] The CMA and the sectoral regulators meet within the UK
Competition Network and work closely across a range of matters,
jurisdictional, procedural and substantive. An Annual Concurrency
Report is published.[5] Paragraph 3.16 of the *Market investigation
guidelines*[6] provides that where either the CMA or a sectoral regulator is considering making a market investigation reference, they must
consult one another.

The powers of the CMA and the sectoral regulators with concurrent
powers to enforce the antitrust provisions are similar to those of the
European Commission: for example, they can conduct on-the-spot investigations, request information, impose interim measures, adopt final decisions, impose penalties for infringements and issue directions to bring
infringements to an end. These powers are explained in the CMA's
*Guidance on the CMA's investigation procedures in Competition Act
1998 cases.*[7]

5.2.2 Merger Control

Part 3 of the Enterprise Act makes provision for the control of mergers.
Mergers that do not meet the jurisdictional thresholds set out in the EU
Merger Regulation and that satisfy the thresholds of the Enterprise Act
fall exclusively within the jurisdiction of the CMA.

5.2.3 Market Investigations

Part 4 of the Enterprise Act establishes a system whereby the CMA and
the sectoral regulators may make a *market investigation reference* in
order to discover whether any features of a market prevent, restrict or
distort competition.[8] Power also exists for the Secretary of State to
make a market investigation reference in limited circumstances,
although this power has never been exercised in practice. The market

---

[3] SI 2014/536.   [4] CMA10, March 2014, available at www.gov.uk/cma.
[5] Available at www.gov.uk/cma.
[6] CC3, January 2014, revised July 2017; these guidelines will be found at
www.gov.uk/cma.
[7] CMA8, updated 4 November 2020.
[8] Part 4 of the Enterprise Act will be at www.legislation.gov.uk.

investigation is carried out by a 'group' of the CMA.[9] If the CMA group conducting the market investigation finds that features of a market have an adverse effect on competition, it must consider how those adverse effects and any detriment to customers could be remedied and it must implement appropriate remedies, that is to say, remedies that are effective and proportionate. The CMA has wide-ranging powers available to remedy any features of the market causing adverse effects on competition or any detriment arising from those features, including the power to order the divestiture of assets.

Whereas a finding that the Chapter I and II prohibitions in the Competition Act have been infringed may lead to the imposition of penalties in the form of administrative fines on the undertakings responsible and to the award of damages to anyone harmed by the infringement, a finding in a market investigation that features of a market have an adverse effect on competition does not mean that the investigated undertakings are guilty of wrongdoing. A market investigation may lead to the CMA requiring changes in an undertaking's or undertakings' *future* behaviour, but there are no sanctions for *past* conduct nor is provision made for the payment of compensation to anyone harmed by the behaviour under investigation. As the CMA says in paragraph 21 of the *Market investigation guidelines*, the market investigation system is investigative and inquisitorial: it is not accusatorial.

5.2.4 Market Investigations: Substance

The substantive provisions on market investigations in Part 4 of the Enterprise Act, including their relationship with the Chapter I and II prohibitions in the Competition Act and with the powers of the UK's sectoral regulators, are described in Section 5.3.

5.2.5 Market Investigations: Institutions and Judicial Review

The power to make a market investigation reference is vested in the CMA and, within their jurisdictional spheres of competence,

---

[9] See Sections 5.2.5 and 5.4.3 on CMA groups.

in the sectoral regulators such as OFCOM and OFGEM. The Secretary of State also has power in limited circumstances to make a reference. It sometimes happens that a market investigation reference originates in a *super-complaint* by certain consumer bodies designated by the Secretary of State. Market investigation references typically follow on from a *market study* conducted by the CMA or (less regularly) a sector regulator. These institutional arrangements are described in Section 5.4 of this chapter.

Section 5.4 also explains that, when a market investigation reference is made, the actual investigation is conducted by a group of members of the CMA Panel, usually consisting of three, four or five people. This group will have had no involvement in the decision to make a reference in the first place; furthermore, the CMA group, when conducting the investigation and reaching a decision, is operationally independent of the Board of the CMA.

The CMA group's decision is final, except that there is an appeal by way of judicial review against the decision of the CMA group to the Competition Appeal Tribunal (CAT). Appeals will be discussed towards the end of Section 5.4.

5.2.6 Market Investigations: Procedure

The Enterprise Act, as supplemented by the ERRA 2013, explains the procedure to be followed in the conduct of market investigations. These provisions are described in Section 5.5.

5.2.7 Market Investigations: Guidelines

The CMA (and its predecessor, the Office of Fair Trading (OFT) and the Competition Commission) have issued a number of guidelines and other publications that explain the operation of the markets regime, which consists of both market studies and market investigations. These guidelines do not have binding statutory force: the CMA is able to adapt its procedures to the needs of individual cases, subject to certain procedural obligations established in the primary legislation, such as the duty to consult on certain matters and to meet statutory deadlines for the completion of particular tasks. Of particular importance are the following:

- *Guidance on making references*[10]
- *Market investigation guidelines:*[11] paragraphs 50–87 of these guidelines have been revised and incorporated into the CMA's Supplemental guidance
- *Supplemental guidance on the CMA's approach,*[12] which explains changes to the markets regime introduced by the ERRA 2013.

These three documents will be cited regularly in this chapter.

5.3 Market Investigations in the UK: Substance

This section will explain the substantive provisions in the Enterprise Act on market investigations. It will begin by considering the legal basis on which a market investigation reference may be made. The CMA, and the sectoral regulators within their jurisdictional perimeters, have a discretion whether or not to make a reference. Section 5.3.2 explains how this discretion is exercised. In particular, these paragraphs explain the relationship between the Chapter I and II prohibitions and the market investigation system and the way in which the sectoral regulators choose whether to use their sector-specific regulatory powers or the market investigation provisions to address competition concerns. The possibility of the CMA accepting 'undertakings in lieu of a reference' is then described. The questions to be determined by the CMA during the investigation are then explained, followed by a review of the remedies that can be imposed to remedy, mitigate or prevent any adverse effect on competition identified by the investigation.

5.3.1 *The Power to Make a Reference*

Section 131(1) of the Enterprise Act provides that the CMA and the sectoral regulators[13] may make an 'ordinary reference' when there are

---

[10] Market investigation references: Guidance about the making of references under Part 4 of the Enterprise Act, OFT 511, March 2006: this Guidance was adopted by the CMA when it took over the functions of the OFT on 1 April 2014; it is available at www.gov.uk/cma.

[11] Guidelines for market investigations: Their role, procedure, assessment and remedies, CC3, January 2014, revised July 2017.

[12] CMA3, January 2014, revised July 2017.

[13] The powers of the sectoral regulators in relation to market investigation references are set out in the Enterprise Act 2002, Sch 9, Part 2.

'reasonable grounds for suspecting'[14] that one or more 'features' of a market prevent, restrict or distort competition in the supply or acquisition of goods or services in the United Kingdom or in a part thereof. Power also exists to make a 'cross-market reference' where the features of concern exist in more than one market; in practice the provisions on cross-market references have not yet been used. Features of a market include:

- the structure of the market concerned or any aspect thereof;
- the conduct[15] of persons supplying or acquiring goods or services who operate on that market, whether that conduct occurs in the same market or not; and
- conduct relating to the market concerned of customers of any person who supplies or acquires goods or services.[16]

It is important to stress that the features of a market that may be investigated in a market reference include both structural and behavioural ones; and furthermore that demand-side considerations ('conduct ... of customers who ... acquires goods or services') can be investigated as well as the conduct of suppliers of goods and services on the supply-side of the market.

In paragraph 1.9 of its *Guidance on making references*, the CMA says that it may not always be clear whether a feature of a market that affects competition is best described as structural or an aspect of conduct: it regards this as a semantic issue. The CMA points out that section 131 of the Enterprise Act does not require it to state, when making a reference, whether the feature to be investigated is structural or an aspect of conduct. The market investigation system in the United Kingdom focuses on *features* of the market, including both the structure of the market and conduct on it.

---

[14] The 'reasonable grounds for suspecting' standard for the making of a reference is not a very high one: see Case 1054/6/1/05 *Association of Convenience Stores* [2005] CAT 36, paragraph 7, available at www.catribunal.org.uk. It is not higher than the standard to be satisfied when initiating an antitrust investigation under s 25 Competition Act 1998.

[15] 'Conduct' for these purposes includes a failure to act and need not be intentional: Enterprise Act 2002, s 131(3).

[16] Ibid., s 131(2).

Part II of the *Guidance on making references* discusses the CMA's interpretation of the reference test set out in section 131 of the Enterprise Act.

Chapter 4 of the *Guidance* discusses the meaning of 'prevention, restriction or distortion of competition'. Paragraph 4.4 repeats the point made earlier that there may not be a clear divide between structural features of a market and those relating to conduct: it gives as an example exclusionary conduct by firms in the market that affects structure to the extent that it raises barriers to entry. The CMA says that in most cases it is likely that an assessment that a reference is appropriate will be based on a combination of features and will include evidence about both structure and conduct. Chapter 4 of the *Guidance* also says that market definition can be a useful step in assessing harm to competition and that the CMA will approach market definition in market investigation cases as it would in other competition cases.

Chapter 5 of the *Guidance on making references* discusses what is meant by 'structural features of a market'. It considers in turn:

- concentration;
- vertical integration;
- conditions of entry, exit and expansion;
- regulations and government policies;
- informational asymmetries;
- switching costs; and
- countervailing power.

Chapter 6 of the *Guidance on making references* discusses firms' conduct. It considers in turn:

- the conduct of oligopolies;
- facilitating practices;
- custom and practice; and
- networks of vertical agreements.

As noted above, Chapter 7 of the *Guidance* considers the conduct of customers, which section 131(2)(c) of the Act considers to be a feature of a market, and specifically addresses the issue of search costs, that is to say, the cost that customers may have to incur in order to make an informed choice.

Section 135 of the Enterprise Act provides that the CMA may vary a reference.

5.3.2 The CMA's and the Sectoral Regulators' Discretion Whether to Make a Market Investigation Reference

The CMA and the sectoral regulators with concurrent powers have a discretion whether to make a market investigation reference when the reference test is met. Paragraph 2.1 of the *Guidance on making references* says that the CMA will make a market investigation reference only when the following criteria, *in addition to the statutory ones*, are met:

- it would not be more appropriate to deal with any competition issues under the Competition Act 1998 or by other means, for example, by using the powers of the sectoral regulators;
- it would not be more appropriate to accept undertakings in lieu of a reference;
- the scale of the suspected problem, in terms of the adverse effect on competition, is such that a reference would be appropriate;
- there is a reasonable chance that appropriate remedies will be available.

5.3.2.1 The Relationship between the Market Investigation Provisions and the Competition Act

The greatest utility of the market investigation provisions is that they can be used to investigate features of a market that have an adverse effect on competition, irrespective of whether there is a violation of the antitrust provisions in the Competition Act 1998. The powers in Part 4 of the Enterprise Act are much more comprehensive in scope than the Chapter I and II prohibitions in the Competition Act. As will be seen in Section 5.6, which considers the market investigation provisions in practice, investigations in which an adverse effect on competition has been identified involved markets where the detriment to competition was attributable to factors such as, for example, the oligopolistic structure of the market, switching inertia by consumers or governmental policy and economic regulation: these are not issues that could be addressed under the antitrust provisions in the Competition Act. The Competition Act seeks to suppress behaviour that violates the Chapter I and II prohibitions; Part 4 of the Enterprise Act takes a holistic view of markets and is intended to identify forward-looking remedies that will deliver better outcomes for consumers. However, it could be the case that features of a market having an adverse effect on competition might violate the Chapter I and/or II prohibitions. There is no formal provision in the Enterprise Act that says that conduct that infringes or might infringe the Chapter I or II prohibitions in the Competition Act cannot be the subject of a market investigation reference. It is therefore a matter for the CMA *in its discretion* to decide whether to deal with a particular situation under the Competition Act or the Enterprise Act. The CMA discusses the relationship between the market investigation provisions and the Competition Act 1998 in paragraphs 2.2–2.8 of the *Guidance on making references*.

Paragraph 2.3 of the *Guidance on making references* states that the CMA's policy is to consider first whether a suspected problem may be addressed under the Competition Act 1998. The CMA says that generally it would consider a market investigation reference where it has reasonable grounds to believe that market features restrict competition, but do not establish a breach of the Chapter I and/or Chapter II prohibitions, or when action under the Competition Act has been or is likely to be ineffective for dealing with any adverse effect on competition identified.

Paragraphs 2.4 and 2.5 of the *Guidance on making references* state that a market investigation reference might be appropriate for dealing with parallel behaviour in oligopolistic markets which falls outside the Chapter I and II prohibitions, not least given the uncertainty that surrounds the concept of collective abuse of a collective dominant position.

Paragraph 2.6 of the *Guidance* says that the market investigation provisions may be suitable for dealing with the problems that can arise from parallel networks of similar vertical agreements that may have the effect of preventing the entry of new competitors into a market without there being any evidence of collusion between the firms that caused this situation to arise.

Paragraph 2.7 of the *Guidance* makes the point that competition problems arising in oligopolistic markets and where there are parallel networks of vertical agreements involve industry-wide market features or multi-firm conduct. The *Guidance* says that the 'great majority' of references are likely to be of this type. It says that 'generally speaking' single-firm conduct will 'where necessary and possible' be dealt with under the Competition Act 1998 or sectoral legislation or rules. As the CMA states:

It is not the present intention of the [CMA] to make market references based on the conduct of a single firm, whether dominant or not, where there are no other features of a market that adversely affect competition.

However, paragraph 2.8 of the *Guidance* says that the general principle of not reviewing single-firm conduct under the market investigation provisions is subject to certain comments and qualifications, as follows:

In many cases anti-competitive conduct by a single firm may be associated with structural features of the market, for example barriers to entry or regulation and government policies or conduct by customers which have adverse effects on competition. These other market features are discussed in sections 5 and 7 of this guidance. Where they are present a market investigation reference may be more appropriate than action under [the Competition Act 1998] even though only a single firm appears to be conducting itself anti-competitively.

The principle will be reviewed should the development of case law relating to [the Competition Act 1998] Chapter II prohibition give good grounds for believing that the prohibition is inadequate to deal with conduct by a single firm which has an adverse effect on competition.

The [CMA] might decide to make a market investigation reference when there has been an abuse of a dominant position and it is clear that nothing short of a structural remedy going beyond what is appropriate under [the Competition Act 1998] would be effective in dealing with the consequential adverse effect on competition.

To date, 20 market investigation references have been completed by the CMA (or its predecessor, the Competition Commission). There has never been a case in which a firm or firms under investigation have argued that the market investigation provisions should not have been used because the powers in the Competition Act 1998 should have been used instead.

5.3.2.2 The Relationship between the Market Investigation Reference Provisions and the Powers of the Sectoral Regulators

The CMA may launch a market investigation reference into any sector of the economy: there are no sectors that are legally excluded from Part 4 of the Enterprise Act. The fact that a particular sector might be subject to sector-specific regulation does not preclude the CMA from making a reference.

As noted above, the sectoral regulators have powers, concurrently with the CMA, to apply competition law in the sectors for which they are responsible. The sectoral regulators can also make market investigation references to the CMA.[17] In the *Guidance on making references*, the CMA says, at the end of paragraph 2.3, that, when exercising their discretion whether to make a reference, the sectoral regulators may wish to consider whether it would be more appropriate for them to deal with any adverse effects on competition under any relevant sector-specific legislation or rules.

Four of the 20 market investigation references to have been made were referred by sectoral regulators:

– The Office of Rail and Road made a reference of Rolling Stock Leasing on 26 April 2007; the Competition Commission reported on 7 April 2009;
– OFCOM made a reference of Movies on Pay TV on 4 August 2010; the Competition Commission reported on 3 August 2012;
– OFGEM referred Energy on 26 June 2014; the CMA reported on 24 June 2016;
– the Financial Conduct Authority referred Investment Consultants on 14 September 2017; the CMA reported on 12 December 2018.

In one other case, OFCOM accepted undertakings from BT, the main UK fixed-line telecommunications provider, in lieu of a market investigation reference: see Section 5.3.3.

5.3.2.3 Scale of the Problem
Paragraph 2.27 of the *Guidance on making references* says that the CMA will make a reference only where it has reasonable grounds to suspect that the adverse effects on competition of features of a market are likely to have a significant detrimental effect on customers through higher prices, lower quality, less choice or less innovation; where the effects are insignificant, the CMA considers that the burden on business and the cost of a reference would be disproportionate.

Paragraph 2.28 of the *Guidance on making references* says that, generally speaking, the CMA would not refer a very small market, a market where only a small proportion is affected by the features having

---

[17] On these institutional arrangements, see Section 5.4.

an adverse effect on competition or a market where the adverse effects are expected to be short lived.

5.3.2.4 Availability of Remedies

Paragraphs 2.30–2.32 of the *Guidance on making a reference* say that the CMA would not refer a market if it appeared that there were unlikely to be any available remedies to deal with an adverse effect on competition, for example, where a market is global and a remedy under UK law would be unlikely to have any discernible effect.

5.3.3 Undertakings in lieu of a Reference

Section 154(2) of the Enterprise Act gives power to the CMA to accept an undertaking or undertakings in lieu of a making a market investigation reference. It can do this only where it considers that it has the power to make a reference and otherwise intends to make such a reference. In proceeding under section 154(2), the CMA must have regard to the need to achieve as comprehensive a solution as is reasonable and practicable to the adverse effect on competition concerned and any detrimental effects on customers, taking into account any relevant customer benefits. The CMA says in paragraphs 2.21 and 2.25 of its *Guidance on making references* that it considers that undertakings in lieu are unlikely to be common; following a preliminary investigation, the CMA may not be in possession of sufficient information to know whether undertakings in lieu would be adequate to remedy any perceived detriments to competition.

Section 155 of the Act provides that, before accepting undertakings in lieu of a reference, the CMA is obliged to publish details of the proposed undertakings, to allow a period of consultation (of not less than 15 days) and to consider any representations received; a further period of consultation is required should the CMA intend to modify the undertakings. As noted below, undertakings in lieu have been accepted in three cases over a period of 17 years. Section 155 lays down some basic rules for such cases: subject to this, the actual procedure will vary depending on the facts of the particular investigation.

Section 156 of the Act provides that, if an undertaking in lieu has been accepted, it is not possible to make a market investigation reference within the following 12 months, unless there is a breach of the undertaking or unless it was accepted on the basis of false or misleading information.

Undertakings in lieu of a reference have been accepted in three cases, *Postal franking machines*,[18] *BT*,[19] a case involving OFCOM and *Extended warranties on domestic electrical goods*.[20]

The undertakings in lieu of a reference in the *BT* case were of major significance. OFCOM accepted more than 230 separate undertakings from BT in order to achieve operational separation between 'Openreach', which owned and operated the monopoly part of BT's business, and those parts of its business where it is subject to competition. OFCOM remained concerned, however, that BT still had the ability and incentive to favour its own retail business when making strategic decisions about Openreach.[21] BT sought to address this concern by establishing Openreach as a distinct company with its own staff, management and strategy. In July 2017, OFCOM accepted BT's proposal and agreed to release BT from its undertakings in lieu.[22] The intention is that Openreach will serve all of its customers equally and BT will no longer be able to favour its own vertically integrated business units.

In February 2019, the Chairman of the CMA, Lord Tyrie, submitted proposals to the Secretary of State for Business, Enterprise and Industrial Strategy for possible reforms of the market investigation provisions.[23] One proposal was that the CMA should be given power to accept *partial* undertakings in lieu and, more generally, to accept undertakings at other points in its investigation where feasible and appropriate. Under current legislation, such undertakings must satisfy all the concerns of the CMA at the end of the market study: it would however be attractive to have the power to identify and remedy certain competition problems by agreeing undertakings during an investigation; others would then be dealt with at the end of the market investigation, as currently happens. The UK Government has not yet responded to this (or any other) of the CMA's proposals.

---

[18] OFT decision of 17 June 2005.   [19] OFCOM decision of 22 September 2005.
[20] OFT decision of 27 June 2012.
[21] Details of OFCOM's review can be found at www.ofcom.org.uk.
[22] OFCOM Statement of 13 July 2017.
[23] Available at www.gov.uk/government/publications/letter-from-andrew-tyrie-to-the-secretary-of-state-for-business-energy-and-industrial-strategy.

5.3.4 Questions to Be Decided on Market Investigation References

Once a reference has been made, section 134(1) of the Enterprise Act requires that the CMA must decide whether any feature, or combination of features, of each market referred prevents, restricts or distorts competition in the referred market(s). If the CMA considers that there is an 'adverse effect on competition',[24] section 134(4) of the Act provides that the CMA must decide three additional questions:

- first, whether it should take action to remedy, mitigate or prevent the adverse effect on competition or any detrimental effect on customers it has identified: detrimental effects are defined in section 134(5) of the Act as higher prices, lower quality, less choice of goods or services and less innovation;
- secondly, whether it should recommend that anyone else should take remedial action; and
- thirdly, if remedial action should be taken, what that action should be.

Section 134(2) of the Enterprise Act says that an adverse effect on competition (AEC) exists where features of a market are found to prevent, restrict or distort competition. Part 3 of the *Market investigation guidelines* provides detailed guidance on the AEC test based on experience in conducting numerous investigations since the Enterprise Act entered into force in 2003. Part 3 of the *Guidance* is divided into four sections dealing respectively with market characteristics and outcomes, market definition, the competitive assessment and concluding the AEC test. There are extensive references to decided cases under the market investigation regime.

Section 134(6) of the Enterprise Act requires that, when considering remedial action, the CMA must have regard to the need to achieve 'as comprehensive a solution as is reasonable and practical to the adverse effect on competition and any detrimental effects on customers'. Section 134(7) of the Act says that the CMA may, in particular, have regard to the effect of any action on any relevant customer benefits as

---

[24] One of the Tyrie proposals for reform of the market investigation provisions was that the 'adverse effect on competition test' might be replaced by an 'adverse effect on consumers' test; no response has yet come from the Government to these proposals.

defined in section 134(8). If the CMA finds that there is no anti-competitive outcome, the question of remedial action does not arise.

Section 136(1) of the Act requires the CMA to prepare and publish a report within the period permitted by section 137. Time limits are discussed in Section 5.5.

The CMA's report must contain its decisions on the questions to be decided under section 134, its reasons for those decisions and such information as the CMA considers appropriate for facilitating a proper understanding of those questions and the reasons for its decisions. As noted in Section 5.3.5, the questions to be decided include, if remedial action should be taken, what that action should be.

5.3.5 Remedies in Market Investigation Cases

When the CMA has prepared and published a report under section 136 and concluded that there is an AEC, section 138(2) requires it to take such action as it considers to be reasonable and practicable to remedy, mitigate or prevent the AEC and any detrimental effects on customers that have resulted from, or may result from, the AEC. When deciding what action to take, the CMA must be consistent with the decisions in its report on the questions it is required to answer, unless there has been a material change of circumstances since the preparation of the report or the CMA has a special reason for deciding differently.

In making its decision under section 138(2), the CMA must have regard to the need to achieve as comprehensive a solution as is reasonable and practicable to any AEC, having regard to any relevant customer benefits of the market features concerned. The market investigation provisions differ from antitrust cases. In the latter, any directions imposed by the CMA in an infringement decision under the Competition Act will be designed to suppress the offending conduct that took place in the past. Under the Enterprise Act, the CMA will seek to achieve a 'comprehensive solution' designed to bring about a well-functioning market in the future. Extensive consultation takes place in market investigation cases involving third parties as well as the firms under investigation. The evolution of remedies in a particular case can be actively followed on the relevant website of the CMA.

The CMA may implement remedies either by accepting undertakings from the firms under investigation (section 159 Enterprise Act) or by imposing orders upon them (section 161 Enterprise Act); the CMA has a choice of whether to seek undertakings or to make an order. Another possibility is for the CMA to make recommendations that someone else should take remedial action, perhaps a sectoral regulator or the Government. In some cases, the CMA may have recourse to a package of measures consisting of undertakings, orders and/or recommendations. In paragraph 92 of the *Market investigation guidelines*, the CMA says that it will proceed on the basis of practicality, such as the number of parties concerned and their willingness to negotiate and agree undertakings in the light of the CMA's report. Where a large number of firms are under investigation it may be more practical to adopt an order than to try to accept numerous undertakings from different entities.

An order may contain anything that is permitted by Schedule 8 to the Act. The powers contained in Schedule 8 include orders

- to restrict a particular kind of conduct on the part of firms: for example, to prohibit certain agreements, refusals to supply, tying transactions or discrimination. Provision is specifically made for the regulation of prices to be charged for goods or services;
- to supply goods or services;
- not to acquire a business;
- to divest a business.

Section 164(1) provides that the provisions that may be contained in an undertaking are not limited to those permitted by Schedule 8 in the case of orders. In paragraph 92 of the *Market investigation guidelines*, the CMA says that, in deciding whether to accept undertakings or to impose an order, it will consider whether a particular remedy falls within the order-making powers available to it under Schedule 8 of the Act.

Section 168 of the Enterprise Act provides that, where the CMA or the Secretary of State considers remedies in relation to regulated markets such as telecommunications, gas and electricity, they should take into account the various sector-specific regulatory objectives that the sectoral regulators have. These may go beyond preventing adverse effects on competition: for example, there is a legal obligation to ensure the maintenance of a universal postal service.

In paragraph 93 of the *Market investigation guidelines*, the CMA points out that it has power, in regulated sectors, to make an order to modify the licence conditions of regulated firms.

Part 4 of the *Market investigation guidelines* provides detailed guidance on remedies in cases where a market investigation leads to a finding of an AEC. Part 4 begins, in paragraphs 325–354, by explaining the framework for the consideration of remedies. It then discusses, in paragraphs 355–369, the concept of 'relevant customer benefits' as defined in section 134(8) of the Act. Paragraphs 371–384 provide an overview of the various types of remedy that can be imposed: these paragraphs should be read in conjunction with Annex B of the *Guidelines* which summarises some of the key considerations relevant to the evaluation, design and implementation of different classes of remedies. Annex B first discusses divestiture and intellectual property remedies, then behavioural remedies and finally recommendations. The final section of Part 4 of the *Market investigation guidelines* considers the selection of remedies in particular cases by considering different problems that may have been identified in the market investigation and possible remedial approaches that may be taken to deal with those problems.

Further guidance on remedies is to be found in paragraphs 4.14–4.25 of the CMA's *Supplemental guidance*, in particular on the duration of remedies and whether a 'sunset clause' should be included, specifying the maximum duration of a remedy.

One of the proposals submitted to the Secretary of State by Lord Tyrie in February 2019 was that power should be made available to the CMA to impose interim measures during the course of a market investigation, for example, to stop potential harm more quickly and/or in some cases to safeguard remedial options: no such power exists under the current legislation.

5.4 Market Investigations in the UK: Institutional Arrangements

This section will discuss the institutional arrangements for the conduct of market investigation references in the United Kingdom. It will begin by considering which institutions have the power to make a reference and the work that they will have done before making a reference. It will then explain that the actual market investigation is conducted by a 'group' of members selected from the CMA Panel and will conclude by describing the system of appeals from decisions of the CMA to the CAT.

5.4.1 Which Institutions May Make a Market Investigation Reference?

As noted earlier in this chapter, the power to make a market investigation reference is vested in the CMA and also, within their jurisdictional perimeters, the sectoral regulators. In limited circumstances, it is also possible for the Secretary of State to make a reference. Section 5.3.2 pointed out that 4 of the 20 market investigations to have been completed by the CMA were made by sectoral regulators.

Paragraph 23 of the *Market investigation guidelines* explains that, prior to making a reference, the referring body will already have looked into the market in question: a reference can be made only where the referring body has reasonable grounds for suspecting that features of a market prevent, restrict or distort competition. It may be that the CMA or sectoral regulator will have conducted a market study on its own initiative (Section 5.4.1.1); or it may have been prompted to do so by a complaint or complaints: in certain circumstances this may have been a 'super-complaint' (Section 5.4.1.2).

5.4.1.1 Market Studies

The CMA and the sectoral regulators may conduct market studies when they consider that markets are not working well. There is no statutory definition of a market study, but these institutions' function of keeping markets under review enables them to conduct market studies. The CMA has published *Market studies: guidance on the [CMA's] approach* (*Market studies guidance*).[25] *Market studies* are distinct from *market investigations*, although it is possible that a market study might lead to a market investigation reference. The most obvious distinction between a market study and a market investigation is that there are no legally binding order-making powers at the end of a market study.

---

[25] OFT 510, 2010, subsequently adopted by the CMA and available at www.gov.uk/cma.

Section 130A of the Enterprise Act requires the CMA to publish a market study notice on commencement of a market study under section 5 of that Act; this provision would also apply where a sectoral regulator initiates a market study to which the Enterprise Act applies. A market study notice must specify the timetable within which the CMA must complete the study, the scope of the market study and the period during which representations may be made to the CMA in relation to the market.

Chapter 4 of the *Market studies guidance* explains how the CMA goes about market studies. The major stages of a study include selection of a market, pre-launch work, the decision to launch a market study, gathering and analysis of evidence and consultation on the CMA's findings.

Where the CMA has published a market study notice, section 131B of the Enterprise Act requires the CMA to publish a 'market study report' setting out its findings and actions (if any) that will be taken as a result of the study; this must be done within 12 months of publication of the market study notice. If the CMA proposes to make a market investigation reference in relation to the subject matter of a market study, it must publish a notice of its proposed decision and begin the process of consulting relevant persons within six months of the market study notice. Strict time limits are imposed on the conduct of market studies in order to disturb the operation of the market as little as possible. They are discussed in paragraphs 2.9 and 2.10 of the CMA's *Supplemental guidance on the CMA's approach*.

Various outcomes may follow a market study by the CMA:

- a clean bill of health for the market in question;
- consumer-focused action, for example, to raise consumers' awareness in such a way that they make better purchasing decisions;
- making recommendations to business to change its behaviour, for example, on matters such as information about after-sales services, standard terms and conditions and improving consumer redress;
- making recommendations to Government to amend legislation or take some other action to remove 'public' restrictions of competition;
- investigation or enforcement action against firms that might be in breach of competition or consumer law;
- a market investigation reference or undertakings in lieu of such a reference.

If the CMA proposes to make a market investigation reference, section 131B of the Enterprise Act provides that the market study report must contain the decision of the CMA whether to make a reference (or accept undertakings in lieu of a reference), its reasons for that decision and such information as the CMA considers appropriate for facilitating a proper understanding of its reasons for that decision. If the CMA decides to make a reference, it will be made at the same time as the market study final report is published.

5.4.1.2 Super-Complaints

Market investigation references sometimes originate in complaints, including so-called super-complaints. Section 11 of the Enterprise Act provides for super-complaints to be made to the CMA and to the sectoral regulators. The purpose of a super-complaint is that a designated consumer body can make a complaint to the CMA or regulator about features of a market for goods or services in the United Kingdom that appear to be significantly harming the interests of consumers. This is a way of making the consumer's voice more powerful: individual consumers often lack the knowledge, motivation or experience to complain effectively, but a designated consumer body should have the resources and ability to do so. Consumer bodies are designated by the Secretary of State; seven have been designated:

The Campaign for Real Ale Ltd;
The Consumer Council for Water;
The Consumers' Association ('Which?');
The General Consumer Council for Northern Ireland;
The National Association of Citizens Advice Bureaux ('Citizens Advice');
The National Consumer Council;
The Scottish Association of Citizens Advice Bureaux.

The CMA must respond to a super-complaint by publishing a 'fast-track' report within 90 days. A super-complaint can lead to a number of responses including, though not limited to, competition or consumer law enforcement, referral to a sectoral regulator, the launch of a market study, a market investigation reference or recommendations that certain action be taken (for example, Government action).

5.4.2 *Consultation Prior to a Market Investigation Reference*

Section 169 of the Enterprise Act requires the CMA or sectoral regulator to consult before making a market investigation reference and section 172 requires it to give reasons for its decision to propose a reference. The Act leaves open the form and extent of the consultation process: the consultation may be a public one, though not necessarily so. The duty to consult is discussed in paragraphs 3.4–3.9 of the *Guidance on making references*. An example of the consultation provisions operating in practice is afforded by the most recent market investigation reference of *Funerals*. The CMA began a market study on 1 June 2018 and consulted on a possible reference on 29 November 2018. A reference was launched on 28 March 2019 and was completed in December 2020.

5.4.3 Decision-Making in Market Investigation Cases

As has been seen, market studies can be conducted by both the CMA and the sectoral regulators. However, market investigations are carried out solely by the CMA. Given that the CMA can conduct both market studies and market investigations, its governance and decision-making structure has been designed to ensure that key decisions in relation to each of these are made by separate parts of the CMA. These arrangements are described in paragraphs 1.22–1.28 of the *Supplemental guidance on the CMA's approach*.

When the CMA makes a market investigation reference, this decision is taken by the Board of the CMA. The Board consists of a Chair, a Chief Executive and a number of executive and non-executive directors. There is also a 'CMA Panel', appointed by the Secretary of State. The Panel has a Chair and three Inquiry Chairs. There are a number of Panel members (currently 30).

Once a market investigation reference has been made (whether by the CMA or by a sectoral regulator), the Chair of the CMA Panel will appoint a 'group' to conduct the actual investigation. The inquiry group will consist of at least three members of the CMA Panel. The Chair of the CMA Panel must ensure that no member of the inquiry group participated in the Board's decision to refer the market in the first place.[26] The inquiry group is required to decide whether there is an AEC in the market(s) referred and, if so, what remedial action

---

[26] At its Board meeting of 4 June 2020, the Board of the CMA confirmed its practice that Panel members who are Board members may not take part in decisions to make a market investigation reference for any investigation on which it is anticipated that they might sit on the inquiry group.

should be taken. The group is responsible for the implementation of remedies up to the point at which the reference is determined.

These arrangements are intended to imitate the division of functions between the OFT and the Competition Commission that existed prior to the ERRA, which abolished the OFT and Competition Commission and created a new, unitary authority, the CMA. Under the prior system, the OFT referred markets to the Competition Commission, and the Commission then conducted the market investigation 'with a fresh pair of eyes', a significant safeguard against the possibility of 'confirmation bias'. When the CMA was created, there was anxiety that this safeguard would be lost; for this reason, the decision-makers in the market investigation are separate from those who make the reference.[27]

The Board of the CMA has no say in the final outcome of a market investigation. However, paragraph 3.39 of the CMA's *Supplemental guidance on the CMA's approach* provides that the CMA Board may append an 'advisory steer' to a market investigation reference setting out its expectations regarding the scope of the market investigation and the issues that could be the focus of the investigation. The inquiry group is expected to take the advisory steer into account but is required by law to make its statutory decisions independently of the CMA Board. An advisory steer was given to the inquiry group by the CMA Board in the reference made in 2019 of *Funerals*.[28]

5.4.4 Review of Market Investigation Decisions under Part 4 of the Enterprise Act

Section 179 of the Enterprise Act makes provision for review of decisions under Part 4 of the Act. Section 179(1) of the Act provides that any person 'aggrieved by a decision' of the CMA may apply to the CAT for a review of that decision: the aggrieved person could be a third party with sufficient interest. The application must be made within two months of the date on which the applicant was notified of

---

[27] For reasons of operational efficiency, some of the CMA staff that carried out work that led to the reference will also work on the actual reference. See the CMA's Supplemental guidance on the CMA's approach, paragraph 1.22.

[28] The advisory steer is available at www.gov.uk/cma.

the disputed decision or of its date of publication, whichever is earlier. When dealing with applications under section 179(1), the CAT must apply the same principles as would be applied by a court on an application for judicial review:[29] that is to say, a decision can be challenged on the grounds of illegality, irrationality or procedural impropriety. As in the case of appeals from decisions of the European Commission to the General Court under EU law, there is no appeal *on the merits* of a decision in a market investigation case to the CAT. In principle, a challenge of 'irrationality' in a judicial review under UK law would appear to be much the same as a challenge of 'manifest error of assessment' under EU law.

The principles to be applied in a judicial review of decisions in market investigation cases were helpfully set out in the CAT's judgment in *BAA Ltd v Competition Commission*[30] at paragraph 20. In particular, at paragraph 20(6) of its judgment the CAT stated:

> It is well-established that, despite the specialist composition of the Tribunal, it must act in accordance with the ordinary principles of judicial review: see *IBA Health v Office of Fair Trading* [2004] EWCA Civ. 142 per Carnwarth LJ at [88]–[101]; *British Sky Broadcasting Group plc v Competition Commission* [2008] CAT 25, [56]; *Barclays Bank plc v Competition Commission* [2009] CAT 27, [27]. Accordingly, the Tribunal, like any court exercising judicial review functions, should show particular restraint in 'second guessing' the educated predictions for the future that have been made by an expert and experienced decision-maker such as the CC.

Section 179(5) of the Act provides that the CAT may dismiss the application or quash the whole or part of the decision to which it relates; and, in the latter situation, it may refer the matter back to the original decision-maker for further consideration.[31] Section 179(6) provides that an appeal may be brought before the Court of Appeal, with permission, against the CAT's decision on a point of law.[32]

It is possible to make some generalised comments about the applications for review that have been made under the market investigation

---

[29] Enterprise Act 2002, s 179(4).   [30] Case 1185/6/8/11 [2012] CAT 3.

[31] Ibid., s 179(5)(b), on which, see the ruling on relief in Case 1104/6/8/08 *Tesco plc v Competition Commission* [2009] CAT 9.

[32] Enterprise Act 2002, s 179(6) and (7).

provisions. First, three applications to the CAT challenged a decision *not* to make a market investigation reference: one case was successful,[33] one was unsuccessful[34] and one did not proceed to judgment.[35]

Secondly, as one would expect, the CAT requires that the CMA must act fairly;[36] where there is a defect in this respect the CAT will be prepared to quash the decision in question. In *BMI Healthcare v Competition Commission*,[37] one of the parties investigated successfully persuaded the CAT that the Competition Commission's decision to use a 'disclosure room' during the *Private healthcare* investigation should be annulled due to procedural irregularities on the Commission's part. In a subsequent appeal in relation to the same investigation, *HCA International v CMA*,[38] the CMA accepted that it had erred in its final report in *Private healthcare* and that fairness required that the parties be given an opportunity to comment on its revised 'insured prices analysis'.[39] The CAT quashed the CMA's decisions that there was an AEC in relation to insured patients and that HCA should divest itself of two hospitals in central London and referred the matter back to the CMA.[40] The CMA subsequently reaffirmed its AEC decision on insured patients but considered that divestment was no longer proportionate.[41]

Thirdly, in two appeals there have been challenges to the CMA's decision *not* to find an AEC: both were unsuccessful. In *AXA PPA Healthcare Ltd v CMA*,[42] the CAT held that the CMA had rationally concluded that the formation of anaesthetist groups did not give rise to an AEC in *Private healthcare*; there was insufficient evidence to support the theory of harm that anaesthetist groups have market power arising from the joint setting of prices. In *Federation of Independent*

---

[33] Case 1052/6/1/05 *Association of Convenience Stores v OFT* [2005] CAT 36.
[34] Case 1191/6/1/12 *Association of Convenience Stores v OFT* [2012] CAT 27.
[35] Case 1148/6/1/09 *CAMRA v OFT*, order of 7 February 2011.
[36] See Section 5.5.10 on the obligation of the CMA to inform firms under investigation of the 'gist' of the case.
[37] Case 1218/6/8/13 [2013] CAT 24.
[38] Case 1229/6/12/14 *HCA International Ltd v CMA* [2014] CAT 23.
[39] Ibid., at paragraph 13. At paragraph 55 the CAT said that the CMA's concession and decision to look at the matter afresh was 'the responsible thing for it to do in the circumstances'.
[40] www.competitionandmarkets.blog.gov.uk.
[41] Final Remittal Report of 5 September 2016.
[42] Case 1228/6/12/14 [2015] CAT 5.

Practitioner Organisations v CMA,[43] the Court of Appeal unanimously upheld the CMA's decision that there was no AEC resulting from insurers' buyer power in relation to consultants and the restrictions placed on consultants' fees.

Fourthly, several applications challenged the decisions to impose certain remedies; this happened in five investigations: *Groceries*, *Payment protection insurance*, *BAA airports*, *Private healthcare* and *Aggregates*. Aspects of the remedies imposed in two investigations – *Groceries* and *Payment protection insurance* – were successfully challenged before the CAT. In *Tesco v Competition Commission*[44] and *Barclays v Competition Commission*[45] the CAT was critical of the approach of the Competition Commission (the predecessor of the CMA) to evaluating the likely costs and benefits of its remedies. On reconsideration of the matters referred back to the Commission, it conducted further analysis and adopted partially modified remedies. As noted, in *Private healthcare*, the appeal by HCA International led to the CMA's decision in relation to insurance patients and the related divestment remedy being quashed and remitted to the CMA.[46]

Lastly, in the *BAA Airports*[47] investigation the Competition Commission required significant divestments by BAA of airports in the region of London and in Scotland. BAA applied for judicial review: the CAT concluded that the Commission's decision was a proportionate one but set aside its finding because there was an appearance of bias in the proceedings;[48] on appeal, the Court of Appeal reversed the decision on apparent bias and upheld the findings of the Commission.[49] An appeal against a subsequent decision of the Competition Commission not to alter its decision in the light of changed circumstances also failed.[50]

---

[43] [2016] EWCA Civ 777, dismissing an appeal against a majority CAT decision, Case 1230/6/12/14 [2015] CAT 8.

[44] Case 1104/6/8/09 [2009] CAT 6.   [45] Case 1109/6/8/09 [2009] CAT 27.

[46] Case 1229/6/12/14 *HCA International Ltd v CMA* [2014] CAT 23.

[47] Final Report of 19 March 2009.

[48] Case 1110/6/8/09 *BAA Ltd v Competition Commission* [2009] CAT 35.

[49] *Competition Commission v BAA Ltd* [2010] EWCA Civ 1097.

[50] Case 1185/6/8/11 *BAA Ltd v Competition Commission* [2012] CAT 3.

5.5 Market Investigations in the UK: Procedure

This section will explain the procedures of the CMA when conducting market investigations. The CMA has published a number of documents of relevance to its procedures. Of particular importance are the following:

- *Transparency and disclosure: statement of the CMA's policy and approach*[51]
- *CMA Rules of Procedure for Merger, Market and Special Reference Groups 2014*[52]
- *Market investigation guidelines*[53]
- *Supplemental guidance on the CMA's approach.*[54]

The major stages of an investigation are set out in paragraphs 3.36–3.64 of the CMA's *Supplemental guidance*:

- handover between a market study and a market investigation;
- information gathering;
- issues statement;
- hearings;
- assessment;
- 'put-back';
- provisional decision report;
- response hearings;
- final report.

Where the CMA finds an AEC, it is required to consider whether remedies are appropriate; if so, there will be a 'remedies implementation stage'. The implementation of remedies is discussed in paragraphs 4.1–4.25 of the *Supplemental guidance*.

Each market investigation has its own home page on the CMA's website, and it is a simple matter to follow the progress of an investigation by referring to it. This accords with the CMA's commitment to be open and transparent in its working, as set out in its *Statement on transparency and disclosure*. The home page sets out the core

---

[51] CMA 6, January 2014.
[52] CMA 17, March 2014; subject to these rules, each market investigation group can determine its own procedure: ERRA, Sch 4, paragraph 51(5).
[53] CC3, January 2014, revised July 2017, available at www.gov.uk/cma.
[54] CMA3, January 2014, revised July 2017, available at www.gov.uk/cma.

documents of an inquiry; contains the CMA's announcements, for example, on its provisional findings and final report; and makes available the written submissions and the evidence provided to the CMA, as well as summaries of hearings held. The home page may also contain surveys and working papers of relevance to the investigation and an account of roundtable discussions. For example, in *Groceries*,[55] economic roundtables were held on local competition and on buyer power; in *Local buses*,[56] researchers were appointed for a study on distinguishing exclusionary conduct, tacit coordination and competition; and in *Payday lending*, a market research agency was instructed to carry out a customer survey.[57]

A criticism of market investigations in the period after the Enterprise Act came into force in 2003 was their length. The investigation itself could take up to two years; and the remedies phase fell outside the statutory period within which the investigation must be completed, sometimes leading to protracted delay in bringing a case to a conclusion. The ERRA 2013 shortened the period of market investigations by amending the Enterprise Act and introducing time limits for the implementation of remedies.

Section 137(1) of the amended Enterprise Act now requires the CMA to complete its investigation within 18 months of the date of the reference. Section 137(2A) provides that the 18-month period may be extended by no more than six months where there are 'special reasons' for doing so;[58] only one such extension is possible. The CMA has stated that it may extend the inquiry period in complex cases, where, for example, there are multiple parties, issues or markets.[59] The time limits in section 137 may be reduced by the Secretary of State.[60]

Paragraphs 3.28 and 3.29 of the *Supplemental guidance on the CMA's approach* discuss the timescales of investigations. Each inquiry group will decide the timescales for its investigation on a case-by-case basis, but paragraph 3.29 of the *Supplemental guidance* sets out a typical timetable for a case (Figure 5.1).

---

[55] Final Report of 30 April 2008.   [56] Final Report of 20 December 2011.
[57] Final Report of 24 February 2015.   [58] Enterprise Act 2002, s 137(2A).
[59] See the CMA's *Supplemental guidance*, paragraph 3.7.
[60] Enterprise Act 2002, s 137(3).

Stage of process	Timing within 18-month investigation
Reference	Pre-reference sharing of appropriate information with the CMA by the CMA market study team/the referring body
'First day letter'/initial information requests	Months 1–2
Publication of initial Issues Statement (setting out theories of harm and inviting views on possible remedies)	
Initial submissions from main and third parties	
Site visits and hearings	Month 3
Further interaction with parties and consultation on analysis: eg roundtables, confidentiality rings, disclosure rooms, working papers	Months 2–11
Final deadline for all parties' submissions before the Provisional Decision Report	Month 11
Publication of Provisional Decision Report on the AEC and remedies (if needed)	**Month 12**
Consideration of responses to Provisional Decision Report	Months 12–16
Response hearings with parties	
Final deadline for all parties' submissions before Final Report	Month 16
Publication of Final Report	**Month 18**

Figure 5.1 CMA's Supplemental Guidance, para. 3.29: A typical timetable for a case

The ERRA introduced time limits for the implementation of remedies. Section 138A of the amended Enterprise Act provides that the CMA must discharge its duty under section 138(2), that is to say, it must accept undertakings or make an order within six months of the date of the publication of its final report under section 136. The six-month period may be extended by no more than four months where there are 'special reasons' for doing so. The CMA has said that it may extend the remedies timetable where, for example, it does 'consumer testing' of the implementation of its remedies or it has to grapple with complex practical issues.[61]

After any undertakings have been taken or an order has been made, there may be a further period during which the parties actually implement the remedies: for example, a period may be allowed for the disclosure of information required to be disclosed or for the divestiture of assets required to be divested. The period permitted for implementation must be proportionate, taking into account the impact of the remedies on the firms required to give them and the detriment to customers caused by an adverse effect on competition.

In the case of *Investment consultants*, the CMA commenced the investigation on 14 September 2017 and issued its Final Report on 12 December 2018; this was therefore the start date of the period within which remedies had to be determined. The CMA then initiated a consultation on its draft Consultancy and Fiduciary Management Market Investigation Order 2019 order on 11 February, requiring comments by 13 March 2019. The CMA received 21 responses. The actual order was made on 10 June 2019.

The CMA may use its investigatory powers for the purpose of implementing its remedies;[62] furthermore, it may 'stop the clock' if a person fails to comply with a requirement of a notice under section 174 and that failure prevents the CMA from properly discharging its duty under section 138(2).[63] This power has never been used in the context of the setting of remedies.

Paragraph 88 of the *Market investigation guidelines* explains that, once undertakings have been accepted or an order has been made, the inquiry group will normally be disbanded. Responsibility for any further work on remedies will generally then be transferred to the staff of the CMA; it is also possible to appoint a specific group of members of the CMA Panel where appropriate.

Sections 5.5.1–5.5.9 discuss the various stages of a market investigation, based on the CMA's *Market investigation guidelines* and its *Supplemental guidance*.

---

[61] See the CMA's *Supplemental guidance*, paragraph 4.7.
[62] Ibid., paragraph 4.8. See Enterprise Act 2002, s 174(1)(b).
[63] *Supplemental guidance*, paragraph 4.8. See Enterprise Act 2002, s 138A(3).

5.5.1 Handover between a Market Study
and a Market Investigation

Paragraphs 3.37–3.40 of the *Supplemental guidance* explain the process where the CMA initiates a market investigation reference. In order to ensure an efficient handover to the inquiry group, the team that worked on the initial study will begin preparatory work on a reference on a contingency basis prior to the final decision to make a reference. This will include consideration of the further information gathering and analysis that is likely to be required in the investigation. A preparatory investigation team of staff and the panel members will be established and they will be briefed on the case to date and the concerns underpinning any reference; for reasons of operational efficiency, some staff who worked on the initial study may be transferred to the market investigation itself. As noted in Section 5.4.3, the Board of the CMA may issue an advisory steer to the inquiry group; however, the group's investigation will be fully independent of the Board. Where one of the sectoral regulators makes the reference, the CMA will seek to engage with the referring body to enable it to prepare for the investigation; similar engagement would take place with the relevant Government department in the event of a reference by the Secretary of State.

5.5.2 Information Gathering

Paragraphs 3.41–3.45 of the *Supplemental guidance* explain how the CMA gathers information. At an early stage in the investigation, there will be informal meetings between the case team and the main parties to discuss the information that may be needed; 'data meetings' may be held. In due course, a detailed market and financial questionnaire will be sent; the CMA may also decide to conduct one or more surveys: the relevant parties will be consulted on the design and content of such surveys. The CMA may decide to hold site meetings. Further guidance on the type of information that the CMA will look for is provided in paragraphs 35–41 of its *Market investigation guidelines.*

Section 174 of the Enterprise Act gives the CMA powers to require information for the purpose of market investigations: these powers may be exercised during the investigation and for the purpose of implementing any remedies. The CMA can impose a penalty on a person who, without reasonable excuse, fails to comply with a notice given under section 174 or who intentionally obstructs or delays a person who is trying to copy documents required to be produced. It is a criminal offence for a person intentionally to alter, suppress or destroy any document that he or she has been required to produce under section 174: a person guilty of this offence could be fined or imprisoned for a maximum of two years. There is a right of appeal to the CAT against decisions of the CMA to impose monetary penalties: the CAT may quash the penalty or substitute a different amount or different dates of payment.[64] One of Lord Tyrie's proposals to the Secretary of State in February 2019 was that the enforcement powers under Part 4 of the Enterprise Act should be strengthened.

5.5.3 Issues Statement

At an early stage in the investigation, the CMA will publish an issues statement which will identify the theories of harm that it will be looking at. The parties will be invited to respond to this statement, including on any possible remedies that it may contain.

5.5.4 Hearings

Paragraphs 3.47–3.49 of the *Supplemental guidance* discuss the hearings that the CMA holds at an early stage of an investigation (at a later stage, it holds 'response hearings' after the publication of its provisional decision; see Section 5.5.8).

5.5.5 Assessment

Paragraphs 3.50–3.54 of the *Supplemental guidance* explain that the staff team and the inquiry group, working together, will at this stage work on the competition assessment, leading in due course to the provisional decision report; they will consider possible remedies at the same time as forming the group's competition assessment.

5.5.6 'Put-Back'

Paragraphs 3.55–3.56 of the *Supplemental guidance* describe the 'put-back' process, whereby the CMA may send text to the parties

---

[64] Enterprise Act 2002, s 174D(10) and s 114.

to enable them to verify the factual correctness of certain content and to identify confidential material. Put-back is an example of the CMA's commitment to transparency and disclosure (see further Section 5.5.10).

5.5.7 Provisional Decision Report

Paragraphs 3.57–3.59 of the *Supplemental guidance* discuss the inquiry group's provisional decision report in which it identifies any features of the market(s) that may give rise to an AEC. Where an AEC has been identified, the provisional decision report will also contain the group's provisional decision on remedies. There will then be a public consultation of not less than 21 days.

5.5.8 Response Hearings

Paragraphs 3.60–3.62 of the *Supplemental guidance* explain that 'response hearings' will then be held; this may be followed by further consultation.

5.5.9 Final Report

The inquiry group will then publish its final report. As noted in Section 5.4.4. This may then be followed by an appeal to the CAT.

5.5.10 Transparency and Disclosure

The procedure for market investigations does not involve access to the file of the kind that occurs in antitrust cases conducted by DG COMP under Articles 101 and 102 TFEU and by the CMA under the Competition Act. In antitrust cases, undertakings are accused of infringing the law: the European Commission or the CMA sets out its case in a statement of objections, and undertakings then have access to the file, as part of their rights of defence, in order to be able to understand the case and the evidence against them. Penalties may be imposed at the conclusion of cases under the Competition Act and, for the purposes of the Human Rights Act 1998, the proceedings are characterised as criminal and therefore Article 6 of the European Convention on Human Rights is engaged.

Market investigations take place under a separate regime from antitrust cases. Investigations under the Enterprise Act examine features of the market that may have adverse effects on competition, a quite different exercise from identifying wrongdoing on the part of undertakings. Antitrust cases are adversarial in nature; the market investigation process is an inquisitorial one.

The CMA has a general policy of being transparent in its dealings with stakeholders. Its position is set out in *Transparency and disclosure: statement of the CMA's policy and approach*, which applies to all CMA cases under both the Competition Act and the Enterprise Act. After an introduction, section 2 of the *Statement on transparency and disclosure* provides an explanation of the CMA's aims in respect of transparency, information requests and the handling of information. Section 3 discusses transparency in the course of a case and section 4 looks at the obtaining and use of information. Section 5 deals with complaints and accountability. Later sections deal with disclosure to UK public authorities, cooperation with overseas authorities and freedom of information and data protection. The market investigation system is characterised by considerable transparency, in particular as a result of the extensive consultation that takes place throughout investigations. As noted above, extensive materials can be found on the CMA's website in any particular case.

Section 169 of the Enterprise Act imposes a duty on the CMA, when making any decision in a market investigation case that may have a substantial impact on the interests of a person, to consult with that person before making that decision. Section 169(4) of the Act provides that, when deciding what is practicable when consulting, the CMA must have regard to timetabling constraints that the Act imposes on it and any need to protect confidentiality.

The fairness of the CMA's procedures has been considered in various judicial reviews of both market investigation and merger cases under the Enterprise Act. As noted in Section 5.4.4, the CAT found that there had been one procedural irregularity in the CMA's investigation into *Private healthcare*. In its judgment in that case, *BMI Healthcare v Competition Commission*, the CAT cited *R v Home Secretary, ex parte Doody*,[65] in which the House of Lords (at the time the top appellate court in the United Kingdom) had said that natural

___
[65] [1994] 1 AC 531, at 560.

justice required that, in administrative proceedings, 'since the person affected usually cannot make worthwhile representations without knowing what factors may weigh against his interests *fairness will very often require that he is informed of the gist of the case which he has to answer*' (emphasis added).

In the *BMI* case, the CAT recognised that what constitutes the 'gist' of the case may vary from one context to another:

Finally, whilst Lord Mustill's sixth proposition refers to a person affected by a decision being informed of the 'gist' of the case which he has to answer, what constitutes the 'gist' of a case is acutely context-sensitive. Indeed, 'gist' is a peculiarly vague term. Competition cases are redolent with technical and complex issues, which can only be understood, and so challenged or responded to, when the detail is revealed. Whilst it is obviously, in the first instance, for the Commission to decide how much to reveal when consulting, we have little doubt disclosing the 'gist' of the Commission's reasoning will often involve a high level of specificity. Indeed, this can be seen in the Commission's practice, described in paragraph 7.1 of the CC7 Guidance, of disclosing its provisional findings as part of its consultation process.[66]

In subsequent cases dealing with the fairness of merger reviews as opposed to market investigations, the CAT has applied the 'gist' test to the fairness of the CMA's proceedings and has acknowledged that it is a vague term and that it is acutely context sensitive. For example, at paragraph 225 of its judgment in *Groupe Eurotunnel SA v Competition Commission*,[67] it cited with approval paragraph 8 of its earlier ruling on confidentiality in *Ryanair Holdings plc v Competition Commission*:[68]

We agree that you do have to look at the facts of each case. At one end of the spectrum there may be a case where numbers are involved and you need to see the relevant numbers or data in order to understand the gist of what is being put. In other cases, more like the present, you need to know what the general position is.

5.5.11 Remedies Implementation Stage

The ERRA 2013 introduced statutory time limits for the implementation of remedies in market investigation cases. Paragraphs 4.1–4.25

---

[66] Case 1218/6/8/13 *BMI Healthcare v Competition Commission* [2013] CAT 24, at paragraph 39(7).
[67] Cases 1216/4/8/13 and 1217/4/8/13 [2013] CAT 30.
[68] Case 1219/4/8/13 [2013] CAT 25.

of the *Supplemental guidance* explain the changes made to this phase of market investigations by the ERRA.

Section 138A of the Enterprise Act requires the CMA to make a final order, or to accept undertakings, within six months of the date of publication of its final report: this includes a period of formal public consultation. One extension, of up to four months, is permitted where there are special reasons for doing so. The CMA has formal investigatory powers during this period, and may 'stop the clock' if any person has failed to comply with any requirement of a notice that it has issued.

The inquiry group will decide on a case-by-case basis whether to make a final order or to accept undertakings. The CMA has power, following the publication of its final report but before the investigation is finally determined, to take interim measures to prevent pre-emptive measures that might impede the final action to be taken in the case.

5.5.12 Review of Enforcement Undertakings and Orders

Section 162 of the Act requires the CMA to keep enforcement undertakings and enforcement orders under review and to ensure that they are complied with; it is also required to consider whether, by reason of a change of circumstances, there is a case for release, variation, supersession or revocation. Section 167 provides that there is a duty to comply with orders and undertakings; this duty is owed to anyone who may be affected by a breach of that duty. Any breach of the duty is actionable if such a person sustains loss or damage, unless the subject of the undertaking or order took all reasonable steps and exercised all due diligence to avoid a breach of the order or undertaking. Compliance with an order or undertaking is also enforceable by civil proceedings brought by the CMA for an injunction.

5.6 The Market Investigation Provisions in Practice

By 31 December 2020 a total of 20 market investigation references had been completed.[69] A number of points can be made about the market investigations that have so far been completed.

---

[69] A table of all the investigations to have been completed between 20 June 2003 and 31 December 2020 will be found as an Annex to this chapter (see Section 5.9).

5.6.1 Meaning of 'Adverse Effect on Competition'

Section 134(2) of the Enterprise Act 2002 says that an AEC exists where features of a market are found to prevent, restrict or distort competition. As noted in Section 5.3, these features may either be structural or they may relate to conduct on both the supply- and the demand-side of the market. The CMA uses economic thinking to facilitate its analysis of competition in the market under investigation. The CMA has not laid down a definitive test of what constitutes an AEC, but its guidelines and reports indicate that it sees the issue in terms of a realistic comparison between 'a well-functioning market' and the competitive conditions observed in practice.[70] In recent reports, the CMA has not gone into detail on what a well-functioning market would look like but has instead focused on identifying proportionate remedies to problems identified and the magnitude of their harm to consumers. The text that follows will briefly examine the approach that has been taken to identifying an AEC.

5.6.2 Market Definition

In its reports, the CMA identifies relevant markets in which there may be consumer harm and, in doing so, considers those products or services that currently constrain the prices of those under investigation.[71] Market definition provides a helpful framework for evidence gathering and economic analysis; the goods or services specified in the reference may or may not correspond to the relevant market. However, it is important to note that the CMA will not define relevant markets with the same particularity that it would do, for example, in an abuse of dominance case under the Chapter II prohibition, where market definition is a legal requirement. The Competition Commission under-took considerable econometric analysis and modelling to inform its

---

[70] See, e.g., the market investigations in *Home credit*, Final Report of 30 November 2006, paragraph 8.4; *Groceries*, Final Report of 30 April 2008, paragraph 10.7; *Rolling stock leasing*, Final Report of 7 April 2009, paragraphs 8.4–8.6 and 8.20; *Private motor insurance*, Final Report of 24 September 2014, paragraphs 6.4, 6.22, 6.56 and 6.108–6.109. See also *Market investigation guidelines*, paragraphs 30 and 320.

[71] This is consistent with the *Market investigation guidelines*, part 3, section 2.

market definition in *Groceries*.[72] In *Private healthcare*, the CMA took into account the results of its patient survey as a useful source of information about the relevant market.[73] The CMA also used a customer survey to help it to determine the degree of substitutability between payday loans and other credit products in *Payday lending*.[74]

5.6.3 Counterfactual

The CMA may seek to try to identify an appropriate 'counterfactual' against which to determine whether any feature or features of the market lead to an AEC.[75] This would normally be the market under investigation in the absence of the features that appear to be producing an AEC. Identification of a counterfactual is not a legal requirement in market investigation cases; rather, it is an analytical tool that may be helpful in determining the problems that exist in a market.

5.6.4 Theories of Harm

The CMA uses economics to frame its analysis of a particular market and considers various 'theories of harm' which may arise from one or more 'features' of the market. A theory of harm is a hypothesis of how harmful effects might arise in a market and adversely affect customers.[76] The *Market investigation guidelines* explain that competitive harm can flow from five main sources:[77]

- unilateral market power;
- barriers to entry and expansion;
- coordinated conduct;
- vertical relationships;
- weak customer response.

It would be reasonable to add that these *Guidelines* are not definitive or exhaustive and that the CMA may identify other theories of

---

[72] See the Final Report of 30 April 2008, paragraphs 4.13–4.14.
[73] Final Report of 2 April 2014, paragraphs 5.13–5.14 and fn. 187.
[74] Final Report of 24 February 2015, paragraphs 5.20–5.24.
[75] See, e.g., *Aggregates*, Final Report of 14 January 2014, paragraphs 5.78, 8.4–8.6, 8.40–8.41, 8.56, 8.228, 8.417, 8.484 and 8.494.
[76] See *Market investigations guidelines*, paragraph 163.
[77] Ibid., at paragraph 170.

harm, depending on the characteristics of the market under investigation. As pointed out in Section 5.6.6, in several reports government policy and economic regulation have been identified as problematic.

The *Market investigation guidelines* provide guidance on each source of competitive harm as well as the CMA's assessment of competition and include consideration of issues such as switching costs and barriers to entry; they also discuss market imperfections such as informational asymmetries. In *Federation of Independent Practitioner Organisations v CMA*,[78] the Court of Appeal said that the existence or absence of detrimental effects on customers is 'plainly a material indication' of whether there is an AEC.

Different theories of harm have been examined in different market investigations. In *Northern Ireland personal banking*,[79] the features of the market harming competition were that banks had unduly complex charging structures and practices, that they did not fully or sufficiently explain them and that customers generally did not actively search for alternative suppliers.[80] In *BAA airports*,[81] the theory of harm was different: it was that BAA's common ownership of many airports in the United Kingdom meant that there was a lack of competition between them, resulting in problems such as limited responsiveness to the interests of airlines and passengers. This feature of the airports market could have an AEC in more than one market: for example, if there were inadequate investment at an airport caused by lack of competition between airports that may adversely affect competition between airlines[82]. In *Local buses*,[83] the combination of high levels of concentration in the relevant market, the presence of barriers to entry and expansion and customer conduct led to an AEC. In *Energy*[84] and *Retail banking*,[85] a weak customer response to differences in price and quality gave suppliers a position of unilateral market power over their existing customers, which led to AECs.

---

[78] [2016] EWCA Civ 777, paragraph 39.   [79] Final Report of 15 May 2007.
[80] Ibid., at paragraph 5.9.   [81] Final Report of 19 March 2009, paragraph 8.2.
[82] Ibid., at paragraph 8.2.
[83] Final Report of 20 December 2011, paragraph 11.28.
[84] Final Report of 24 June 2016, section 9.
[85] Final Report of 9 August 2016, section 11.

5.6.5 Performance and Prices

In most cases, the CMA analyses pricing behaviour and relevant financial data. Profitability analysis can be a useful tool in identifying consumer detriment. In some cases, the level of prices and profitability have been considered as factors indicating the lack of competitive pressure in a market.[86] In *Home credit*,[87] the Competition Commission concluded that the fact that excessive profits were being earned was not in itself an AEC, although it was indicative of features of the market, such as an incumbency advantage and a lack of customer switching, that did produce an AEC. In *Payday lending*,[88] the CMA found that the largest lenders had earned profits significantly above their cost of capital from 2008 to 2013, which was consistent with a lack of effective price competition. On other occasions, a number of conceptual and practical difficulties have constrained the ability to conduct informative profitability analysis.[89]

5.6.6 Findings of Adverse Effects on Competition

In all but one of its reports, the Competition Commission or the CMA have found one or more AECs;[90] no adverse finding was made in *Movies on pay TV* owing to the emergence of new 'video on demand' services.[91] A few comments may be helpful about the adverse findings to date.

First, a number of references have involved oligopolistic markets where competition between suppliers was weak.[92] For example, in

---

[86] See, e.g., *Store card credit services*, Final Report of 7 March 2006, paragraphs 8.11 and 8.82; *Groceries*, Final Report of 30 April 2008, paragraph 6.76; *Classified directory advertising services*, Final Report of 21 December 2006, section 7.

[87] Final Report of 30 November 2006, paragraphs 3.61–3.143.

[88] Final Report of 24 February 2015, paragraph 6.8.

[89] See, e.g., the Final Reports in *Liquefied petroleum gas*, paragraph 5.16 (profitability analysis was inconclusive) and *Rolling stock leasing*, paragraph 8.18 (profitability analysis was not practicable).

[90] Note that ERRA 2013, Sch 4, paragraphs 55 and 57, provide that a finding of an AEC requires at least a two-thirds majority of the CMA group. On this point, see *Private healthcare*, Final Report of 2 April 2014, paragraphs 10.4–10.6.

[91] Final Report of 2 August 2012.

[92] See, e.g., *Northern Ireland personal banking*, Final Report of 15 May 2007, paragraphs 4.306–4.307; *Groceries*, Final Report of 30 April 2008, paragraph

Aggregates,[93] a combination of structural and conduct features of the cement markets in Great Britain were found to give rise to an overarching feature: coordination among the three largest cement producers: Cemex, Hanson and Lafarge. In *Energy*,[94] the CMA found that each of the six large energy suppliers had unilateral market power over its customer base and was able to charge standard variable tariffs materially above any level justified by the costs of an efficient domestic retail supply.

Secondly, a recurrent theme has been problems for consumers who did not have access to clear and effective information about the products or services on offer, and where there appeared to be impediments to switching on their part, whether for reasons of inertia or because of technical and practical difficulties.[95] This was an important issue in both *Energy*[96] and *Retail banking*[97] and several other market investigations.[98]

A third point is that the impact of government policy and economic regulation has been a concern in several investigations, including *Classified directory advertising services*,[99] *Rolling stock leasing*[100] and *BAA airports*.[101] In *Energy*,[102] the CMA found that some of OFGEM's regulatory measures were restricting the behaviour of

---

8.40; *Statutory audit services*, Final Report of 15 October 2013, paragraphs 12.1–12.3; and *Local buses*, Final Report of 20 December 2011, paragraphs 8.242–8.243.

[93] Final Report of 14 January 2014, paragraphs 12.3–12.6.

[94] Final Report of 24 June 2016, paragraph 9.283.

[95] See, e.g., *Private healthcare*, Final Report of 2 April 2014, paragraphs 10.8–10.9.

[96] Final Report of 24 June 2016, section 9 and paragraphs 20.5–20.11.

[97] Final Report of 9 August 2016, paragraphs 11.3–11.6 (personal current accounts), 11.9–11.11 (business current accounts) and 11.14–11.16 (SME lending).

[98] See, e.g., *Store card credit services*, Final Report of 7 March 2006, paragraphs 8.159 and 8.165; *Home credit*, Final Report of 30 November 2006, paragraphs 7.14–7.15; *Northern Ireland personal banking*, Final Report of 15 May 2007, paragraphs 4.222–4.228; and *Payment protection insurance*, Final Report of 29 January 2009, paragraph 9.2.

[99] Final Report of 21 December 2006, paragraphs 8.25–8.26. Yell's successor was released from the undertakings in light of the effects on classified directories of internet usage by consumers and advertisers: Final Decision of 15 March 2013.

[100] Final Report of 7 April 2009, paragraphs 6.212–6.226.

[101] Final Report of 19 March 2009, paragraphs 6.60–6.88.

[102] Final Report of 24 June 2016, paragraphs 9.478–9.513.

suppliers and constraining the choices of consumers in ways that reduced consumer welfare.[103]

5.6.7 Remedies

If the CMA concludes that there is an AEC, it must remedy the position as fully and effectively as possible. The *Market investigation guidelines* discuss different types of remedies and the principles relevant to selecting and implementing them[104]. As noted in Section 5.4.4, in some cases remedies were the subject of judicial reviews.

In two investigations – *BAA airports*[105] and *Aggregates*[106] – compulsory divestiture was ordered to remedy competition problems resulting from structural features of the relevant markets[107].

In *Private motor insurance*, the CMA identified various AECs and was able to remedy most of them by making an order which, for example, banned the use of parity clauses whereby price comparison websites prevented car insurers from offering their products more cheaply on other platforms; consumers were also given more information about the costs and benefits of no-claims bonus protection. However, unusually, the Competition Commission was unable to remedy the inefficiencies arising from the fact that the insurer liable for a non-fault driver's claim is often not the party controlling the costs: it concluded that none of the available remedies provided an effective and proportionate solution[108].

In *Private healthcare*,[109] the CMA originally ordered the divestiture of two hospitals to remedy the AECs for the provision of insured and self-pay private healthcare services in central London. Following a successful appeal by HCA,[110] the owner of the two hospitals, the

---

[103] Ibid., paragraphs 9.478–9.513.

[104] *Market investigation guidelines*, paragraphs 322–393. See also *CMA's Supplemental guidance*, paragraph 4.14.

[105] Final Report of 19 March 2009, section 10; the CMA evaluated the remedies in *BAA airports*: see the Report of 16 May 2016.

[106] Final Report of 14 January 2014, paragraphs 13.7–13.138.

[107] The requirements for the design and implementation of divestiture remedies are set out in paragraphs 3–30 of Annex B to the *Market investigation guidelines*.

[108] Final Report of 24 September 2014, paragraphs 26–40 (summary).

[109] Final Report of 2 April 2014, paragraphs 11.9–11.244.

[110] Case 1228/6/12/14 *HCA International Ltd v CMA* [2014] CAT 23.

CMA reinvestigated and decided, by a majority, that divestment was no longer proportionate, since there was insufficient certainty that the benefits of a structural remedy would outweigh its costs.[111] In *Energy*[112] and *Retail banking*,[113] the CMA chose a 'package' of measures to remedy the AECs and their respective detrimental effects on customers;[114] in the latter case, the remedies included the creation of a new organisation – Open Banking – to be funded by the largest banks and which would help to encourage fintech innovation as well as a temporary price cap for prepayment meter customers.

5.7 Analogous Market Investigation Provisions in Other Jurisdictions

Very few systems of competition law contain provisions similar to the market investigation powers contained in the UK Enterprise Act. All systems of competition law contain antitrust provisions, forbidding anti-competitive agreements and certain abusive forms of unilateral behaviour by firms with significant market power. Most systems of competition law also contain some form of merger control. It is also common for competition authorities to conduct market studies as a way of informing themselves about the competitive conditions in markets: at the end of a market study, the authority has to decide what to do next. For example, a competition authority may take enforcement action under its competition law powers to address problems identified during the market study that fall within that system's antitrust rules. Alternatively, the competition authority may possess consumer protection tools that could address those problems; or it could recommend that some other agency with such powers should take action. Market studies may also lead to recommendations to Government or sectoral regulators to take appropriate action.

However, as was explained above, the distinctive feature of the UK market investigation regime is that, if the CMA discovers during a market investigation that features of a market give rise to an AEC, remedial action can be taken, irrespective of any wrongdoing on the part of the firms investigated. The powers of the CMA to impose

---

[111] Final Remittal Report of 5 September 2016, paragraphs 12.314–12.321.
[112] Final Report of 24 June 2016, paragraphs 20.22–20.31.
[113] Final Report of 9 August 2016, section 19.
[114] See generally, *Market investigation guidelines*, paragraph 328.

remedies are far-ranging and include the possibility of imposing behavioural and/or structural remedies, including ordering the divestiture of assets.

The purpose of this section is to provide an outline of four systems of law that do contain provisions analogous to the market investigation powers established by the Enterprise Act. These are to be found in Greece, Iceland, Mexico and South Africa. Each of these systems will be reviewed in the same way that the UK law was presented above: first, the substantive provisions of the law will be described; this will be followed by an explanation of the relevant institutional regime and the possibility of judicial review; the procedure to be followed in market investigation cases will then be discussed. In each country report, there will be a brief review of whether these provisions have been applied in practice. Article 26(g) of the Romanian Competition Act of 1996 as amended contains a provision analogous to the UK market investigation provisions but it has yet to be applied in practice.

5.7.1 Greece

Greece's competition law is contained in Law 3959 of 2011 on the Protection of Free Competition. Apart from antitrust provisions and merger control, Article 11 of the Act permits the examination of specific sectors of the Greek economy: under this provision remedial measures can be taken to create effective competition in the sector in question. A similar power had existed in Article 5 of the Greek Competition Act of 1977. Greek competition law is enforced by the Hellenic Competition Commission. There are no specific guidelines on the market investigation provisions.

5.7.1.1 Substance
Article 11 of the Greek Competition Act provides for 'Regulation of sectors of the economy'. Specifically, Article 11(1) of the Act states:

The Competition Commission shall examine specific sectors of the Greek economy pertaining to its responsibility, at the request of the Minister of Economic Affairs, Competitiveness and Shipping or ex officio, and, if it finds that conditions of effective competition do not exist in that sector and that the application of Articles 1, 2 and 5 to 10 alone cannot create conditions of effective competition, it may issue a reasoned decision requiring any necessary measures to be taken to create conditions of effective competition in the sector of the economy in question.

Article 11(5) of the Competition Act provides that, at the end of the market investigation procedure, if the Competition Commission has found that conditions of effective competition do not exist, it may issue a decision imposing the specific measures which it deems strictly necessary, suitable and proportionate for creating such conditions. If the lack of effective competition is attributable to legislative acts, Article 11(6) provides that the Commission can issue an opinion that they be repealed or amended. This opinion is submitted to the minister with jurisdiction and copied to the Minister of Economic Affairs, Competitiveness and Shipping.

Article 11(6) of the Competition Act provides that economic sectors subject to decisions under Article 11(5) should be reviewed within two years in order to ascertain whether effective competition has been restored and to decide whether more or less severe measures are required.

Article 11(1) (see above) specifically states that a market investigation can be carried out only where 'Articles 1, 2 and 5–10 alone cannot create conditions of effective competition'. Articles 1 and 2 replicate Articles 101 and 102 TFEU; Articles 5–10 contain the provisions on Greek merger control. It follows that a market investigation can be conducted only where the conventional tools of competition law are insufficient to address the lack of effective competition in a market.

The Competition Act applies to all sectors of the economy. In the telecommunications and postal sectors, the competition rules are applied exclusively by the Hellenic Post and Telecommunications Commission rather than by the Competition Commission. Article 24 of the Competition Act provides for cooperation with the sectoral regulators in the application of competition law.

5.7.1.2 Institutions and Judicial Review

The Competition Commission conducts market investigations under Article 11 of the Competition Act. The Commission must adopt decisions in a plenary session. Decisions made under Articles 11(5) and 11(6) of the Act may be challenged by a party with a legitimate interest in an application for annulment before the Council of State.

5.7.1.3 Procedure

Article 11(2) of the Competition Act requires the Competition Commission within 90 days of the beginning of its procedure to provide a reasoned opinion of whether effective conditions of competition exist in the sector under review and why effective competition cannot be achieved through the conventional tools on antitrust and merger control. There must then be a public consultation of at least 30 days. If, after the public consultation, the Commission is of the opinion that effective competition does not exist, Article 11(3) of the Act provides that it must announce the specific measures that it deems to be strictly necessary, suitable and proportionate for the purpose of creating effective competition. There follows a further public consultation. Thereafter, Article 11(5) enables the Commission to impose the measures it considers to be necessary and to issue an opinion to the relevant minister if the problem is attributable to legislative acts.

Fines can be imposed on firms that fail to comply with decisions pursuant to Article 11(5) and 11(6). These can be up to 20 per cent of the firm's total turnover in the preceding financial year.

5.7.1.4 The Provisions in Practice

The market investigation provisions in Greek law have been used in one sector, the *Greek gasoline sector*. The Competition Commission has adopted two decisions, Decision 334/V/2007 and Decision 418/V/2008, under the previous law of 1977; it has since issued a Formal Opinion on 24 October 2012, Decision 29/2012, adopted under the law of 2011, in which it updated its position. In the Opinion of 2012, the Competition Commission identified a number of structural weaknesses and regulatory restraints affecting the conditions of competition at all levels of the fuel sector in Greece (refining, wholesale and retail). Numerous recommendations were made to improve the conditions of competition in this sector in Greece, most of which were adopted by the Greek State.

5.7.2 Iceland

The main provisions of Iceland's competition law are contained in Competition Law 44 of 2005. The law is enforced by the Competition Authority. There was no legal basis in the Act of 2005 for remedial action following a market investigation. However, an amendment was made to the Act of 2005 by Act 14/2011 that does provide such powers. The Authority has adopted *Rules on the market investigations carried out by the Competition Authority (Rules on market investigations)*, which are available on its website.[115]

5.7.2.1 Substance

Article 16 of Iceland's Competition Act of 2005 enabled the Competition Authority to take enforcement measures in antitrust cases and against public entities to the extent that they may have detrimental effects on competition, provided that no special legislation contains any specific provisions regarding authorisation or obligations for such acts.

Act 14 of 2011 added an important provision to Article 16(1). As amended, Article 16(1)(c) provides that the Competition Authority is able to take action against

circumstances or conduct which prevents, limits or affects competition to the detriment of the public interest. Circumstances means, among other things, factors connected to the attributes of the market concerned, including the organisation or development of companies that operate in it. Conduct means all forms of behaviour, including failure to act, that are in some way detrimental to market competition without being in violation of the Act's ban provisions.

Act 14 of 2011 also amended Article 16(2) of the Competition Act. Article 16(2) now provides that

[t]he actions of the Competition Authority may include any measure that is necessary to enhance competition, put an end to violations or respond to actions of public entities that may adversely affect competition. The Competition Authority can apply necessary remedies to amend conduct or structure relating to the issues specified in the first paragraph that are proportionate to the violation that has been committed or to the circumstances or conduct concerned.

Article 2 of the *Rules on market investigations* sets out the object of such investigations:

The object of market investigation is to identify possible competitive restrictions and improve the competitive environment in markets where there is reason to expect that circumstances or conduct are present which prevent, limit or have harmful effects on competition to the detriment of the public interest. Such circumstances or conduct that limit the efficiency of markets may include extensive concentrations in the market in question, considerable hindrances on the ability of new competitors being able to begin operations or small competitors strengthening

---

[115] www.ensamkeppni.is.

their position. This also includes the actions or failure to act by companies or public bodies which reduce the efficiency of markets.

Indications of such circumstances or conduct as described in the first paragraph and other aspects that give rise to an investigation may include the following:

a. Activity or organisation in a market that appears to facilitate the harmful tacit collusion of companies in an oligopolistic market.
b. The price, services, quality and other competitive aspects that provide an indication of the limited function of the market.
c. The development and organisation of a company with an extremely strong position in a market that may significantly limit the competitive controls that competitors can provide.
d. Disruption to competition that seems to be due to ownership and management ties between companies.
e. Anti-competitive discrimination of competitors by public authorities.
f. Fees and other costs that may limit customer options of transferring their business from one company to another.
g. Lack of information or unclear terms that may work against customers transferring their business from one company to another.
h. Insufficient access for companies to facilities that are necessary to enable them to compete efficiently in the market in question.

The legislation does not contain any specific rules on whether the Competition Authority should proceed in an individual case on the basis of the antitrust rules or the provisions on market investigations. This is decided on a case-by-case basis. Nor does the legislation contain any provisions on the relationship between the competition legislation and sectoral regulation. The Competition Authority has jurisdiction to apply the competition rules to all sectors of the economy. Sectoral regulators do not have concurrent jurisdiction to apply competition law.

5.7.2.2 Institutions and Judicial Review
The Competition Authority conducts market investigations in Iceland. Its decisions can be appealed on the merits to the Competition Appeals Committee and to the district courts in Iceland.

5.7.2.3 Procedure

The *Rules on market investigations* explain the procedure that the Competition Authority will follow.

Article 3 explains how market investigations originate and the criteria that the Authority will take into account when deciding whether to originate market research, including the importance of the market in question for consumers and the economic sector, the estimated cost of the investigation, its prioritisation principles and the funding allocated to market investigations.

Article 4 says that the Competition Authority will adopt an investigation schedule. According to Article 5, this schedule will be considered by the Board of Directors of the Authority. The Board's confirmation of the investigation schedule commences the investigation. The Board may appoint a consultative committee for each investigation consisting of at least two outside parties. The Director General of the Authority manages the execution of the investigation and is the responsible party in relation to external relations.

Section III of the *Rules on market investigations* contains detailed rules on procedure. Article 6 deals with notification to relevant parties of the beginning of the case study and on the Authority's website.

Article 7 provides that the parties under investigation enjoy all the rights that they would have in antitrust proceedings. Article 8 provides that, when the team conducting the market investigation has collected the information it requires and assessed the relevant data, it must adopt an initial assessment report which will be sent to the parties against whom it is directed. They will be given a reasonable period to respond in writing. The report will be published. This will be followed by an open meeting where stakeholders and others will have an opportunity to submit their views. This meeting must be announced in advance. In the event that the Authority contemplates the adoption of an onerous decision, it must issue a statement of objections in connection with the initial assessment report. The statement of objections is subject to the same rules as in antitrust cases.

Section IV of the *Rules on market investigations* explains what happens at the end of an investigation.

Article 9 provides that the Competition Authority must decide how to end the market investigation. Its decision may involve one of various solutions:

- to use the powers in Article 16 of the Act to change the conduct or organisation of a party that has been investigated;
- to use the powers in Article 16 of the Act against the competitively restrictive practices of public entities;
- to conduct a special investigation of possible violations of the antitrust provisions in the Competition Act;
- a statement that no further action is required.

5.7.2.4 The Provisions in Practice

The Competition Authority has been conducting a market investigation into *Fossil fuels*. Preliminary findings were published in December 2015. This investigation is ongoing at the time of writing of this chapter.

5.7.3 Mexico

Mexican competition law is contained in the Federal Economic Competition Law of 2014. The law is enforced by the Federal Economic Competition Commission, (COFECE). The substantive antitrust rules and the provisions on merger control are contained in 'Book Two' of the Competition Act, entitled 'Anticompetitive Conduct' (Articles 52–65). Titles I–III of Book Three of the Act explain the procedures to be followed by COFECE in antitrust and merger cases. Title IV of Book Three of the Act is entitled 'Special Procedures'. Chapter 1 of Title IV makes provision for 'Investigations to Determine Essential Facilities or Barriers to Competition': the relevant provisions are Articles 94 and 95 of the Act. Remedial powers, including the possibility of divestiture, are available at the end of a market investigation: they are determined by the Board of Commissioners of COFECE. There are no specific guidelines on Mexican market investigations. A helpful document in understanding the competition law system in Mexico is the OECD's 2016 manual *Market Examinations in Mexico*.[116]

5.7.3.1 Substance

Article 94 of the Mexican Competition Act[117] enables COFECE, either on its own initiative or if requested to do so by the Federal Executive

[116] Available at www.oecd.org.
[117] Note: the extracts of the Mexican Competition Act contained in English in this Report are taken from COFECE's website.

Branch, to investigate whether 'there are elements suggesting there are no effective competition conditions in a market and aiming to determine the existence of barriers to competition and free market access or of essential facilities that could generate anticompetitive effects'.

This test asks whether there are elements to suggest there are no effective competition conditions in a market and, if so, whether this is due to (a) the existence of barriers to competition and free market access or (b) essential facilities or a combination of both.

Article 3(IV) of the Competition Act provides a definition of *barriers to competition and free market access*:

Any structural market characteristic, act or deed performed by [firms] with the purpose or effect of impeding access to competitors or limiting their ability to compete in the markets; which impedes or distorts the process of competition and free market access, as well as any legal provision issued by any level of government that unduly impedes or distorts the process of competition and free market access.

Article 60 of the Competition Act provides guidance on the meaning of an essential facility:

To determine the existence of an essential facility, the Commission shall consider:

I. If the facility is controlled by one, or several [firms] with substantial market power or that have been found to be preponderant by the Federal Telecommunications Institute;

II. If the facility cannot feasibly be replicated by another [firm] due to technical, legal or economic conditions;

III. If the facility is indispensable for the provision of goods or services in one or more markets, and has no close substitutes;

IV. The circumstances under which the [firm] came to control the facility, and

V. Other criteria which, if the case may be, are provided for in the Regulatory Provisions.[118] The legislation does not contain any specific rules on whether COFECE should proceed in an individual case on the basis of the antitrust rules or the provisions on market investigations. This is decided on a case-by-case basis.

---

[118] Article 10 of the Regulatory Provisions requires the Investigative Authority to evaluate whether access to an essential facility would increase efficiency in the market.

In the event that COFECE investigates a possible case of abuse of dominance contrary to Article 54 of the Competition Act in the form of denial of or discriminatory access to an essential facility, Article 56 of the Act establishes that it does *not* have to make use of the special procedure set out in Articles 94 and 95.

When a market investigation has been completed, a preliminary report will be published by the Investigative Authority. Article 94 (VII) of the Competition Act provides that the Board of Commissioners of COFECE must then issue a final resolution within 60 days of the report. The Board of Commissioner's resolution may include the following:

- recommendations to public authorities; these may, for example, determine that legal provisions unduly impede or distort free market access; the competent authorities will then act accordingly pursuant to their scope of jurisdiction and under the procedures provided for in the laws in force;
- an order to a firm that has been investigated that it should eliminate a barrier to entry that unduly affects free market access and the process of competition;
- a determination as to the existence of essential facilities and guidelines to regulate access, prices or rates and technical and quality conditions;
- divestiture of a firm's assets, rights, partnership interest or stock, in the necessary proportions to eliminate the anticompetitive effects.

In the case of a finding of an essential facility, Article 94 specifically provides that, if the owner of the facility considers that it is no longer essential in the sense of Article 60 of the Act, it may request COFECE to review whether the requirements of that provision are still being met.

Whenever COFECE proposes measures under Article 94 of the Competition Act to address the problem of a market in which there is no effective competition, it is required, by the final paragraph of that Article, to verify that the measures that it proposes will generate efficiencies. The test for COFECE is as follows:

In all cases, the Commission shall verify that the proposed measures will generate efficiency gains in the markets, consequently these measures shall not be imposed when the Economic Agent with legal standing in the procedure demonstrates, in due course, that the barriers to competition and essential facilities generate efficiency gains and have a favorable impact on the economic competition process and free market access, thus overcoming their possible anticompetitive effects, and resulting in an increased consumer welfare. Among the gains in efficiency for consideration are those which result from innovation in the production, distribution, and marketing of goods and services.

5.7.3.2 Institutions and Judicial Review

COFECE is the institution that conducts market investigations in Mexico, except in relation to the radiobroadcasting and telecommunications sectors (see below).

Within COFECE, the Investigative Authority initiates the investigation, and when the investigation has ended it produces a preliminary report within 60 days. Thereafter, the case is conducted by the Commission, and it is the Board of Commissioners that makes the final decision in a case. There is an appeal to courts that specialise in competition and/or telecommunications cases.

Article 5 of the Mexican Competition Act provides that the Federal Telecommunications Institute (FTI) is the competent authority for competition matters in the radio broadcasting and telecommunications sectors and has exclusive powers to apply competition law in those sectors. Article 5 makes provision for jurisdictional issues between the FTI and COFECE to be resolved.

As far as other sectors are concerned, Article 94(III) provides that, where the Investigative Authority of COFECE decides in its preliminary report that corrective measures are necessary, it may request a non-binding opinion from the sector's coordinating public entity or the corresponding public authority on the proposed measures.

Article 95 of the Competition Act requires that resolutions determining the existence of barriers to competition and free market access, or essential facilities, shall be notified to the relevant sectoral regulator for it to determine, within the scope of its jurisdiction and according to the procedures in prevailing legislation, what actions should be taken to achieve competitive conditions.

5.7.3.3 Procedure

COFECE's procedure in market investigations is set out in Article 94 of the Competition Act. When the Investigative Authority initiates an investigation, it must publish the fact in the Federal Official Gazette, identifying the market subject to the investigation. Its investigation shall last not less than 30 days and not more than 120. The Commission may extend this period two times.

The Investigative Authority has the same powers in a market investigation that it would have in an antitrust case.

At the end of its investigation, the Investigative Authority must issue its preliminary report within 60 days. If the Authority finds no competition problems, it will propose to the Board of Commissioners that the case should be closed.

If the Investigative Authority does identify competition problems, it must notify the firms under investigation. Precise time limits are set out in Article 94(IV) to 94(VII) as to the next steps. At this stage, there is a trial-like procedure, as would happen in an antitrust case; however, unlike in an antitrust case, the Investigative Authority is not a formal party to the procedure in market cases. The firm or firms under investigation may offer 'suitable and economically feasible measures to eliminate the competition problems at any moment until the file is complete'. Such a proposal can be made only once. If the Board of Commissioners decide to reject these proposals, it must justify its decision. Assuming that the remedies proposed are not accepted, the Board of Commissioners will then complete the case, and can exercise the powers described in paragraph 5.7.3.1 above.

5.7.3.4 The Provisions in Practice
COFECE has carried out seven market investigations under Article 94 of the Competition Act:

– Case IEBC-001-2015 Slot allocation at Mexican airports;[119]
– Case IEBC-002-2015 Local cargo transportation in Sinaloa;[120]
– Case IEBC-001-2016 Barley production and distribution for beer factories;[121]
– Case IEBC-002-2016 Port services and transportation for bulk grains in Puerto Progreso Yucatan;[122]

---

[119] See Press Release COFECE-030-2019, available at www.cofece.mx/wp-content/uploads/2019/05/COFECE-030-2019-English.pdf.
[120] See Press Release COFECE-041-2016, available at www.cofece.mx/la-autoridad-investigadora-de-la-cofece-dictamino-la-existencia-de-barreras-a-la-competencia-en-el-marco-normativo-del-servicio-publico-de-transporte-de-carga-en-sinaloa/ (in Spanish). See also Press Release COFECE 032-2017, available at www.cofece.mx/wp-content/uploads/2018/02/COFECE-032-2017.pdf#pdf.
[121] See Press Release COFECE-003-2016, available at www.cofece.mx/inicia-cofece-investigacion-por-probables-barreras-a-la-competencia-en-mercado-de-semilla-y-grano-de-cebada-maltera-par-la-produccion-de-cerveza/ (in Spanish).
[122] See Press Release COFECE-60-2016, available at www.cofece.mx/investiga-cofece-posibles-barreras-a-la-competencia-en-los-servicios-portuarios-y-de-transporte-en-puerto-progreso/ (in Spanish).

– Case IEBC-002-2017 Distribution and transportation of unprocessed milk in Chihuahua;[123]
– Case IEBC-003-2017 Norms and standards for conformity assessment;[124]
– Case IEBC-005-2018 Card Payment Systems.[125]

5.7.4 South Africa

The main provisions of South African competition law are contained in the Competition Act, No. 89 of 1998, which contains antitrust provisions and provides for merger control. The 1998 Act did not provide an explicit legal basis for the Competition Commission of South Africa (CCSA) to conduct market inquiries; however, in 2006 it conducted a market inquiry into the banking sector, invoking section 21 of the Competition Act, which provides that one of the functions of the CCSA is to 'implement measures to increase market transparency'. An explicit basis for the conduct of market inquiries was contained in amendments made to the Competition Act in 2013, but this did not provide for any remedial powers at the end of the inquiry. The position was changed by the Competition Amendment Act, No. 18 of 2018. This Act amended the South African competition legislation in numerous ways. Specifically, sections 23 to 26 of the Amendment Act inserted new provisions, sections 43A to 43G, into the Competition Act 1998; remedial powers, including the possibility of divestiture, are available at the end of a market inquiry. As will be seen, the South African provisions closely resemble the market investigation provisions in the United Kingdom. There are no specific guidelines on South African market inquiries.

5.7.4.1 Substance
Section 43A(1) of the Competition Act 1998 as amended sets out the circumstances in which a market inquiry may be conducted. It provides for the conduct of a market inquiry into 'the general state of competition, the levels of concentration in and structure of a market for

---

[123] See Press Release COFECE-050-2017, available at www.cofece.mx/wp-content/uploads/2018/02/COFECE-050-2017.pdf#pdf. Also see Press Release COFECE-056-2018, available at www.cofece.mx/wp-content/uploads/2018/12/COFECE-056-2018-English.pdf.
[124] See Press Release COFECE-052-2017, available at www.cofece.mx/wp-content/uploads/2018/02/COFECE-052-2017.pdf#pdf.
[125] See Press Release COFECE-047-2018, available at www.cofece.mx/wp-content/uploads/2018/11/COFECE-047-2018-English-.pdf.

particular goods or services, without necessarily referring to the conduct or activities of any particular named firm'.

Section 43A(2) of the 1998 Act as amended provides that '[a]n adverse effect on competition is established if any feature, or combination of features, of a market for goods or services impedes, restricts or distorts competition in that market'.

Section 43A(3) of the Act provides that features of a market include:

a. the structure of that market or any aspect of that structure, including:
   (i) the level and trends of concentration and ownership in the market;
   (ii) the barriers to entry in the market, the regulation of the market, including the instruments in place to foster transformation in the market and past or current advantage that is not due to the respondent's own commercial efforts or investment, such as direct or indirect state support for a firm or firms in the market;
b. the outcomes observed in the market, including –
   (i) levels of concentration and ownership;
   (ii) prices, customer choice, the quality of goods or services and innovation;
   (iii) employment;
   (iv) entry into and exit from the market;
   (v) the ability of national industries to compete in international markets;
c. conduct, whether in or outside the market which is the subject of the inquiry, by a firm or firms that supply or acquire goods or services in the market concerned;
d. conscious parallel or co-ordinated conduct by two or more firms in a concentrated market without the firms having an agreement between or among themselves; or
e. conduct relating to the market which is the subject of the inquiry of any customers of firms who supply or acquire goods or services.

Section 43C of the amended Competition Act 1998 sets out the matters to be decided in a market inquiry; specifically, the CCSA must decide whether any features of a market impede, restrict or distort competition, having regard to the impact of any adverse effect on competition on small and medium businesses, or firms controlled or owned by historically disadvantaged persons. If the CCSA does find there to be an adverse effect on competition, it must decide what action should be taken. It is required to have regard to the need to achieve as comprehensive solution as is reasonable and practicable.

Section 43D of the Act provides that the CCSA may take action to remedy, mitigate or prevent any adverse effect on competition that it has identified. In so far as it considers that it is appropriate that there should be a divestiture of assets, it must make a recommendation to this effect to the Competition Tribunal and the latter institution may make an order to that effect.

The legislation does not contain any specific rules on whether the Competition Authority should proceed in an individual case on the basis of the antitrust rules or the provisions on market investigations. This is decided on a case-by-case basis.

5.7.4.2 Institutions and Judicial Review

Market inquiries under South African competition law are conducted by the CCSA. The CCSA may initiate an inquiry on its own initiative or if required to do so by the Minister. When determining whether to initiate a market inquiry on its own initiative, the CCSA will be guided by its *Prioritisation Framework*; its prioritisation criteria include impact on consumers, especially the poor, alignment with the Government's economic growth and development objectives and the prevalence of anti-competitive conduct in the economy.

Section 3(1A) of the amended Competition Act provides that the CCSA is able to exercise its jurisdiction under the Competition Act notwithstanding that the sector in question may be subject also to a sector-specific regulator. Provision is made for the CCSA to negotiate agreements with any regulatory authority to coordinate and harmonise the exercise of jurisdiction over competition matters within the relevant industry or sector and to ensure the consistent application of the principles of the Competition Act. Memoranda of Understanding have been concluded between the CCSA and 13 sectoral regulators.[126]

Section 43B(2B) of the amended Competition Act 1998 provides that a Deputy Commissioner of the CCSA will be appointed to chair the market inquiry. The inquiry panel may be undertaken solely by staff of the CCSA; however, external experts may also be utilised.

Section 43F provides that various persons, as set out in section 43G(1), may appeal to the Competition Tribunal against the CCSA's decision. The Tribunal may confirm the CCSA's determination, amend it or set it aside or make any determination or order that it (the Tribunal) considers appropriate. There is a further appeal to the Competition Appeal Court.

As noted above, the CCSA cannot order a divestiture but can make a recommendation to this effect to the Competition Tribunal; the Tribunal can make such an order if it considers it appropriate to do so.

---

[126] See www.compcom.co.uk/mou-with-sector-regulators-in-south-africa.

5.7.4.3 Procedure

Section 43B(2) of the amended Competition Act requires that, at least 20 days before commencing a market inquiry, the CCSA must publish a notice in the Gazette, setting out its terms of reference and inviting members of the public to provide written representations. If the market inquiry will investigate a sector over which a regulatory authority has jurisdiction, the CCSA must notify and consult with that authority before publishing the notice in the Gazette. The notice must explain the scope of the inquiry and its duration, which may not be more than 18 months.

Section 43G(1) of the amended Act specifies the persons who may participate in a market inquiry. These include firms in the market that is the subject of the inquiry; trades unions; officials and staff of the CCSA and witnesses who are able to substantially assist with the inquiry; any relevant regulatory authority; any Minister with responsibility for the sector under investigation and any other person with a material interest in the market inquiry or who may be able to assist its work.

Provision is made for the protection of confidential information. Determinations of the CCSA as to confidentiality may be appealed to the Competition Tribunal.

5.7.4.4 The Provisions in Practice

There have been no market inquiries under the Competition Act as amended in 2018. Details of market inquiries prior to the 2018 amendments can be found on the website of the CCSA.[127] The CCSA has completed five market inquiries under the law as it stood before the 2018 amendments:[128]

- Banking Inquiry, June 2008;
- Liquified Petroleum Gas Market Inquiry, March 2017;
- Private Healthcare Market Study, September 2019;
- Data Services Market Inquiry, November 2019;
- Grocery Retail Market Inquiry, December 2019.

There is an ongoing market inquiry into *Public Passenger Transportation*. This was initiated under the pre-2018 law.

---

[127] www.compcom.co.za.

[128] For details on the Data Services Market Inquiry and the Grocery Retail Market Inquiry, see Bonakele/das Nair/Robert, Chapter 6.

5.8 Conclusions

The market investigation provisions contained in the UK Enterprise Act are an important complement to the antitrust provisions in the Competition Act.[129] Although it may be possible that conduct that infringes the Chapter I and II prohibitions might be investigated under the Enterprise Act, in practice this is not what happens. The market investigation systems focus on detriments to competition that occur across a market and aim at remedying them, whereas Competition Act cases focus on the past or ongoing behaviour of a firm or firms and aims to stop such behaviour, punish it and deter it in the future. Market investigation cases typically focus on issues that cannot be adequately addressed under the Competition Act. Furthermore, whereas remedies in antitrust cases are designed to prevent the unlawful behaviour from occurring again, remedies in market investigation cases are focused on improving the way that competition functions in the market going forward. The range of remedies available to the CMA is very extensive.

Market investigations look at the structure of markets, but they are not limited to structural issues. The CMA also looks at conduct on the market, including conduct on the demand side as well as the supply side of the market. For example, obstacles to switching or switching inertia on the part of consumers can (and have been) investigated under Part 4 of the Enterprise Act.

There are relatively few countries with legislation that resembles the market investigation provisions in the Enterprise Act. However, the competition laws of Greece, Iceland, Mexico and South Africa are similar in numerous respects. The South African legislation is the one that is most like UK law. These provisions are for the most part fairly new, and to date there is not a lot of decisional practice on the part of the relevant competition authorities.

Market investigations in the United Kingdom are typified by a great degree of transparency and consultation, and extensive information will be found on the relevant page of the CMA in relation to any particular case.

The outcome of market investigations in the United Kingdom are subject to judicial review, though not an appeal on the merits, to the CAT.

---

[129] See also Fletcher, Chapter 8.

5.9 Annex

Table of market investigation references

	Title of report	Date of reference	Date of report	AEC?	Outcome
1	*Store card credit services*	18 March 2004	7 March 2006	Yes	Adverse effect on competition in relation to the supply of consumer credit through store cards and associated insurance in the UK; in particular, most store card holders pay higher prices for their credit than would be expected in a competitive market The *Store Cards Market Investigation Order 2006* requires full information to be made available to store card users and the provision of payment protection insurance as a separate product Slight variation to the *Store Cards Order* in 2011 to take into account the EU Consumer Credit Directive
2	*Domestic bulk liquefied petroleum gas ('LPG')*	7 July 2004	29 June 2006	Yes	Adverse effect on competition in relation to the supply of domestic bulk LPG in the UK; in particular, there was little switching by customers between suppliers for a variety of reasons leading to higher prices for the large majority of customers

| 3 | *Home credit*
This reference followed a super-complaint from the National Consumer Council | 20 December 2004 | 30 November 2006 | Yes | *See the Domestic Bulk Liquefied Petroleum Gas Market Investigation Order 2008 and the Domestic Bulk Liquefied Petroleum Market Investigation (Metered Estates) Order 2009*

Adverse effect on competition in relation to the supply of home credit; in particular, the weakness of price competition led to higher prices than could be expected in a competitive market

The *Home Credit Market Investigation Order 2007* requires home credit lenders to share customer repayment data with other potential lenders, to publish information about the loans they offer and to provide, at most every three months, an account statement, free of charge, when any of their borrowers ask for one

The Order was slightly varied in 2011 to take into account the EU Consumer Credit Directive |

(*cont.*)

	Title of report	Date of reference	Date of report	AEC?	Outcome
4	*Classified directory advertising services*	5 April 2005	21 December 2006	Yes	Adverse effect on competition in relation to classified directory advertising services; Yell's prices for advertising in Yellow Pages would be higher than in a well-functioning market if it were not for the fact that it was already subject to price control as a result of an earlier investigation under the (now repealed) Fair Trading Act 1973 On 3 April 2007, the Competition Commission accepted final undertakings from Yell capping its advertising prices; undertakings were also given in relation to other matters such as tying and bundling On 15 March 2013, Hibu (formerly Yell) was released from its undertakings as attitudes to, and demand for, classified directory advertising services had changed

5	*Northern Ireland personal banking* This followed a super-complaint from Which? in conjunction with the General Consumer Council for Northern Ireland	26 May 2005	15 May 2007	Yes	Adverse effect on competition in relation to personal current accounts in Northern Ireland; competition limited by banks' unduly complex charging structures and practices, their failure adequately to explain them and customers' reluctance to switch to another bank The *Northern Ireland PCA Banking Market Investigation Order 2008* requires Northern Irish banks to ensure that certain types of communications with customers are easy to understand and to inform customers that they can switch The Order was varied in 2011 to take into account EU Directives on consumer credit and payment services
6	*Groceries*	9 May 2006	30 April 2008	Yes	Grocery markets in many respects provide a good deal for consumers; however, action was needed to improve competition in local markets and to address relationships between retailers and their suppliers A recommendation that a 'competition test' be inserted into UK planning legislation was successfully challenged before the CAT; on remittal, the Competition

(cont.)

Title of report	Date of reference	Date of report	AEC?	Outcome
				Commission conducted further analysis and amended the scope of its recommendation to allow for small extensions to stores to be excluded from the competition test The *Groceries Supply Code of Practice* entered into force on 4 February 2010; the Groceries Code Adjudicator Act 2013 entered into force on 25 June 2013 and created an Adjudicator to enforce the Code The *Groceries Market Investigation (Controlled Land) Order 2010* addresses the issue of exclusive agreements and restrictive covenants
7 *Payment protection insurance (PPI) This followed a super-complaint from Citizens Advice*	7 February 2007	29 January 2009	Yes	Serious competition problems in the PPI market; various remedies adopted, including a ban on the sale of PPI during the sale of the credit product and for seven days afterwards; also informational remedies

					The ban on the sale of PPI at the point of sale was successfully challenged before the CAT; on remittal, the Competition Commission made essentially the same recommendation, which led to the *Payment Protection Insurance Market Investigation Order 2011*
8	*BAA airports*	29 March 2007	19 March 2009	Yes	Serious competition problems arising from BAA's common ownership of seven airports in the United Kingdom; the Competition Commission concluded that BAA must sell three airports, including Gatwick and Stansted (to different purchasers) and one of Glasgow or Edinburgh airports. BAA sold Gatwick in November 2009
					On 19 July 2011, the Competition Commission concluded that there was no material change of circumstances following BAA's first appeal that would require it to amend its remedies
					On 23 April 2012, the Commission approved the sale of Edinburgh airport
					On 21 January 2013, the Commission approved the sale of Stansted airport

(*cont.*)

	Title of report	Date of reference	Date of report	AEC?	Outcome
9	*Rolling stock leasing market investigation* Reference by the Office of the Rail Regulator (now the Office of Rail and Road)	26 April 2007	7 April 2009	Yes	Competition in the market for rolling stock is restricted by the limited number of alternative fleets available to train operating companies; various recommendations made See the *Rolling Stock Leasing Market Investigation Order 2009*
10	*Local bus services*	7 January 2010	20 December 2011	Yes	A number of features of the market were found to restrict entry into local areas by rivals and otherwise stifle competition; the Competition Commission made recommendations, in particular to the Department for Transport, the OFT and Local Transport Authorities to make the market more competitive See also the *Local Bus Services Market Investigation (Access to Bus Stations) Order 2012*
11	*Movies on pay TV* Reference by OFCOM	4 August 2010	2 August 2012	No	No adverse effect on competition was found in the market for the supply and acquisition of certain major studio movie

| 12 | Statutory audit for large companies | 21 October 2011 | 15 October 2013 | Yes | rights or in the market for the wholesale supply and acquisition of packages including Sky Movies; no remedial action was therefore necessary

Adverse effect on competition in relation to the supply of statutory audit services to large companies in the UK; in particular, there were barriers to switching, barriers to entry and expansion by mid-tier audit firms and an information asymmetry between shareholders and auditors

The Competition Commission proposed remedies to open up the UK audit market to greater competition and to ensure that audits would better serve the needs of shareholders

See the *Statutory Audit Services for Large Companies Market Investigation (Mandatory Use of Competitive Tender Processes and Audit Committee Responsibilities) Order 2014*

This Order took into account reforms to statutory audits that had been made at EU level |

	Title of report	Date of reference	Date of report	AEC?	Outcome
13	*Aggregates, cement and ready-mix concrete*	18 January 2012	14 January 2014	Yes	Adverse effect on competition in the British cement markets but no adverse effect in aggregates or ready-mix concrete markets In order to remedy the competition problems identified, the Competition Commission required a divestiture by Lafarge Tarmac to facilitate the entry of a new producer; it also accepted an undertaking by Hanson to divest itself of a blast furnace slag facility; the Commission also proposed to introduce measures to limit the flow of information and data concerning cement production and price announcements Subsequently, the European Commission approved a merger between Holcim and Lafarge (Case M. 7252, decision of 15 December 2014), subject to the same divestiture required by the Competition Commission: the European Commission approved the proposed purchaser, CRH of Ireland, on 24 April 2015

14	_Private healthcare_	4 April 2012	2 April 2014	Yes	Adverse effect on competition in relation to privately funded health care; in particular, many private hospitals face little competition in local areas across the United Kingdom and there are high barriers to entry; this leads to higher prices for self-pay patients in local areas and for both self-pay patients and insured patients in London
					The CMA required a series of remedies, including provision of greater information for patients about private hospitals' standards of performance, a crackdown on incentives offered to referring clinicians and the divestiture of certain hospitals by HCA Healthcare; subsequently, the CMA abandoned the requirement to divest
					An Order was made on 1 October 2014, the _Private Healthcare Market Investigation Order 2014_

	Title of report	Date of reference	Date of report	AEC?	Outcome
15	*Private motor insurance*	28 September 2012	24 September 2014	Yes	Adverse effect on competition in relation to private motor insurance; in particular, there were some price parity clauses in contracts between price comparison websites and motor insurers that prohibit insurers from making their products available more cheaply on other online platforms
					The CMA recommended measures to increase competition in the car insurance market and to reduce the cost of premiums for drivers
					See the *Private Motor Insurance Market Investigation Order 2015* requiring insurers to provide better information for consumers on the costs and benefits of no-claim bonus protection and banning certain price parity clauses
					The CMA also recommended that the Financial Conduct Authority look into the provision of information in the sale of motor insurance add-on products that would make it easier for consumers to compare these products
					The CMA could not identify an appropriate and proportionate remedy to address the

| 16 | *Payday lending* | 27 June 2013 | 24 February 2015 | Yes | Adverse effect on competition in relation to payday lending
Various measures proposed to increase price competition between payday lenders and to help borrowers to get a better deal |
| 17 | *Energy*
Reference by the Office of Gas and Electricity Management (OFGEM) | 26 June 2014 | 24 June 2016 | Yes | Adverse effect on competition at the retail level of energy supply but not at the wholesale level; a core concern was that many individual customers and microbusinesses were still on default tariffs
Various measures proposed to encourage and enable consumers to switch to cheaper energy suppliers
The CMA also suggested a transitional price cap for customers on prepayment meters until the introduction of smart meters enables them to access better supply offers
Numerous orders were made, and undertakings given, in 2016; the Government responded to the findings in the market investigation in February 2018 |

	Title of report	Date of reference	Date of report	AEC?	Outcome
18	*Retail banking*	6 November 2014	9 August 2016	Yes	Adverse effect on competition in retail banking; in particular, established banks do not have to compete hard enough to win and/or retain individual customers and new and smaller market entrants face expansion barriers; consumers pay supra-competitive prices for retail banking services without benefiting from new technology
					See the *Retail Banking Market Investigation Order 2017*; it was varied in 2019
19	*Investment consultancy and fiduciary management services* Reference by the Financial Conduct Authority	14 September 2017	12 December 2018	Yes	Pension trustees receive advice from investment consultants; some trustees delegate investment decisions to fiduciary managers
					The CMA identified competition problems in relation both to investment consultancy and, in particular, fiduciary management
					A specific problem arises where investment consultants also provide fiduciary management services and steer customers towards their own services

The CMA was also concerned that pension trustees may not have sufficient information on the fees or quality of investment consultancy and fiduciary management to make sensible decisions

The CMA required some competitive tendering for the provision of fiduciary management services and greater transparency on fees

The CMA also recommended that the regulatory scope of the Pensions Regulator and the Financial Conduct Authority should be expanded to ensure greater oversight of the sector in the future

See *The Investment Consultancy and Fiduciary Management Market Investigation Order 2019*

	Title of report	Date of reference	Date of report	AEC?	Outcome
20	*Funerals market*	28 March 2019	18 December 2020	Yes	Numerous remedies proposed including that all funeral directors and crematorium operators should disclose prices in a manner that will help customers to make more informed decisions
					Certain practices – for example, payments which may incentivise hospitals, care homes or hospices to refer customers to a particular funeral director – to be prohibited
					The CMA recommended that government should establish an independent inspection and registration scheme to monitor the quality of funeral director services
					The CMA will continue to monitor the sector and may consider a further market investigation in the future

6 | Market Inquiries in South Africa
Meeting Big Expectations?

TEMBINKOSI BONAKELE, REENA DAS NAIR
AND SIMON ROBERTS

6.1 Market Inquiries in South Africa: A Major Area of the Competition Commission's Work

Market inquiries, as market investigations are known in South Africa, have been an important and growing area of the competition regime established under South Africa's Competition Act of 1998. From early on, the Competition Commission responded to calls for broader engagements with market developments that went beyond its mergers and enforcement mandates.[1] It undertook studies on food prices and important intermediate industrial products as part of research activities and then, from 2006 to 2009, the Commission undertook the first market inquiry into banking.[2] These studies and the banking inquiry relied on general provisions relating to the Commission's functions including measures to improve the workings of markets in line with the Act's objectives.

With the learnings from the first market inquiry, as well as a growing recognition of the limitations of enforcement actions to rein in oligopolies in a highly concentrated emerging market economy, South Africa decided to complement competition enforcement with the versatile market inquiry tool. In the Competition Amendment Act of 2009, a market inquiry chapter was inserted (Chapter 4A) which came into effect in 2013.

In some ways, South Africa anticipated the growing expectations placed on competition authorities around the world to address the apparent problems of poorly working markets and high levels of

---

[1] The Competition Commission is responsible for investigating mergers and complaints. It makes decisions on intermediate mergers (above a defined threshold) and refers large mergers and cases of anti-competitive conduct to the Competition Tribunal for adjudication.

[2] See also Whish, Chapter 5, on invoking section 21 of the Competition Act to undertake the banking inquiry. Section 21 provides for the CCSA to 'implement measures to increase market transparency'.

concentration. The objectives of the South African competition law are broad and reflected the priorities of the first democratically elected government in 1994, led by the African Nation Congress (ANC).[3] These objectives include expanding opportunities for small and medium enterprises, widening ownership by historically disadvantaged persons in South Africa and the international competitiveness of South African businesses.

In addition to responding to the expectations of the competition regime, the issues tackled in market inquiries have also reflected the challenges experienced with unilateral conduct enforcement. Abuse of dominance cases have been highly litigious, time consuming and expensive. Market inquiries held a prospect of a more inquisitorial system, to mitigate against the highly adversarial procedures adopted in abuse of dominance cases.[4] In a number of instances, the market inquiries have succeeded in identifying and addressing problems in highly concentrated markets.

Under the 2013 amendments, the Commission could conduct a formal inquiry relating to the general state of competition in a market on its own initiative or in response to a request from the Minister of the Department of Trade, Industry and Competition (DTIC) if it has reason to believe that features of a market prevent, distort or restrict competition in that market or to achieve the purpose of the Act.[5] The Competition Commission is administratively accountable to the DTIC. The terms of reference must be published in the Government Gazette. Unlike market investigations in the United Kingdom, for example, the South African Competition Commission could not directly impose remedies under the market inquiries provision as framed in the 2013 amendments. The outcome of an inquiry was the publication of a

---

[3] Lewis, *Thieves at the Dinner Table: Enforcing the Competition Act: A Personal Account*, 2012; Klaaren, Laying the table: The role of business in establishing competition law and policy in South Africa, (2019) 33 *International Review of Applied Economics*, 119; Roberts, Competition policy, competitive rivalry and a developmental state in South Africa, in: Edigheji (ed.), *Constructing a Democratic Developmental State in South Africa: Potentials and Challenges*, 2010, at Chap. 11; Bonakele, The nature and use of economic evidence in competition enforcement (with special emphasis to the case of South Africa), in: Jenny/Katsoulacos (eds.), *Competition Law Enforcement in the BRICS and in Developing Countries*, 2016, p. 187–205.

[4] See Motta/Peitz, Chapter 2

[5] See Whish, Chapter 5, for a summary of the legal provisions for the Market Inquiries provision in the South African Competition Act.

report which could include recommendations for regulatory changes or policies, while the Commission can also initiate a complaint for further investigation under the enforcement provisions of the Act based on the inquiry.

Further amendments (in the Competition Amendment Act, No. 18 of 2018) signed into law in February 2019 broadened the scope of issues which market inquiries can consider to explicitly include the adverse effects of market features or conduct on small and medium businesses or firms controlled or owned by historically disadvantaged persons. It also gave the Commission powers to remedy, mitigate or prevent the adverse effects on competition, including to recommend divestiture to the Tribunal, where warranted. The amendments provided for the findings from an inquiry to be binding.

In this chapter, we assess the South African record with market inquiries and draw insights for the more expansive role being taken on by some competition authorities with regard to issues of concentration, market power and market outcomes.[6] We find that inquiries have played a very valuable role in South Africa in bringing evidence and analysis to bear on concerns with how markets work in a highly concentrated economy. The chapter provides an overview of market inquiries in South Africa in Section 6.2, mapping out their evolution as the competition regime developed. We then focus on two inquiries in Section 6.3, one broader (the Grocery Retail Market Inquiry) and one narrower in scope (the Digital Services Market Inquiry), in order to examine the framing, scope, process and outcomes. Section 6.4 draws out comparative lessons from the two inquiries and broader lessons from the South African experiences. Section 6.5 concludes.

We note that this is a (self)critical review in that we have all been employed by the Competition Commission at different times. In particular, as Deputy Commissioner and then Commissioner, Tembinkosi Bonakele has had overall responsibility for the inquiries. The risk of ex post justification of decisions which may not have turned out as expected can be weighed against the benefits of the first-hand insights on which we can draw in this chapter.

---

[6] See also Fletcher, Chapter 8

6.2 An Overview of Market Inquiries in South Africa

To understand the South African experience with market inquiries, it is important to map out how they have evolved, including alongside the development of the competition regime more broadly. The design and processes followed have differed over time in a number of important regards, including whether to have an independent panel conducting the investigation or whether the Commission conducted it with its own internal team. As discussed above, the law has also been amended twice in a relatively short period of time.

The first inquiry into banking was ambitious. At the time, the Commission did not have powers to compel participation or the provision of information. Moreover, the inquiry examined issues of the national payment system and banking charges which fell under the purview of the South Africa Reserve Bank (the central bank) and the National Treasury, which were naturally sensitive to issues which might be raised. However, it followed recommendations by a task team established by the National Treasury and subsequent studies on the South African banking industry which had identified competition concerns. The inquiry also followed inquiries into banking that had been conducted in other parts of the world, especially the United Kingdom.

As there had never been an inquiry of this nature before and the competition institutions were less than a decade old, it was important to build trust in the process on the part of the government and central bank, and the banks themselves. The inquiry was preceded by extensive consultations including with the South Africa Reserve Bank and National Treasury. The Commission decided that the inquiry would be conducted by an independent panel of four, constituted of a retired Judge of the High Court as chairperson, a businesswoman, a senior advocate and a civil society nominee. The design of the panel was carefully crafted to ensure the independence, credibility and legitimacy of the process. The panel was assisted by the Commission's internal and external experts. Although initially not all of the large banks agreed to participate, the process ensured that they did all come on board in due course.

The Panel published guidelines for participation in the inquiry, including information gathering processes and the conduct of public hearings.[7] The outcome was an extensive Panel Report submitted to the Competition Commission which had a set of recommendations largely focused on regulatory changes under the purview of the National Treasury and central bank.[8] The Report contained a disclaimer that the views expressed did not reflect those of the Competition Commission or Government, and that it was compiled independently. The Commission and Government formulated their responses to the Report and it led to consideration of various regulatory changes and contributed to incremental processes of opening up markets to greater rivalry.[9]

The 2009 Amendment Act meant that all of the subsequent inquiries have been undertaken under the provision explicitly providing for market inquiries to be conducted by the Commission. There have been inquiries into private healthcare, grocery retail, liquefied petroleum gas (LPG) and data services. As of the end of 2020, an inquiry into public passenger transport was still underway. In most of these sectors, competition issues overlap with regulatory regimes, a theme to which we return below.

The inquiries have been quite different in terms of their scope and framing.

---

[7] Competition Commission South Africa, Banking Market Inquiry (Chapter 1: The Enquiry Process (2008), available at http://www.compcom.co.za/wp-content/uploads/2017/11/1-Enquiry-Process_non-confidential1.pdf.

[8] For a comprehensive review of the inquiry, see Hawthorne/Goga/Sihin/Robb, Review of the Competition Commission Banking Enquiry (2014). V3.5. Centre for Competition, Regulation and Economic Development working paper, available at https://static1.squarespace.com/static/52246331e4b0a46e5f1b8ce5/t/589064096a496349b23c84ce/1485857808151/1400407_EDD-UJ_RECBP_Project%2BReport_App13_Case%2BStudy%2B-%2BBanking%2BEnquiry_Final.pdf.

[9] See, for example, National Treasury, A safer financial sector to serve South Africa better, 2011. National Treasury Policy Document, available at http://www.treasury.gov.za/twinpeaks/20131211%20-%20Item%202%20A%20safer%20financial%20sector%20to%20serve%20South%20Africa%20better.pdf; the Intergovernmental Fintech Working Group (IFWG), Fintech Workshops Report, 2019, available at https://www.fic.gov.za/Documents/IFWG_2019WorkshopsReport_v1.0.pdf; National Treasury, Review of the National Payment System Act 78 of 1998, Policy paper, September 2018, available at http://www.treasury.gov.za/publications/other/NPS%20Act%20Review%20Policy%20Paper%20-%20final%20version%20-%2013%20September%202018.pdf.

As with banking, the inquiry into healthcare (the Healthcare Market Inquiry, HMI)[10] was also very broad. Unlike banking, however, it was undertaken at the explicit request of the Minister of Health. It led to extensive recommendations which mainly related to regulations and policies for the sector. Competition-related recommendations included that the Commission review its approach to creeping mergers and provide guidance to practitioner associations on what would constitute anti-competitive conduct.

The private healthcare market in South Africa had historically been governed by collective negotiations between healthcare providers (hospital groups, practitioners, etc.) and funders (medical insurance providers). This system was dismantled when the competition institutions found that it constituted per se cartelisation of the markets. Following this intervention, there were attempts to set up a regulatory framework for prices, a process that was challenged by industry and never reached conclusion. At the same time, there were widespread concerns over rising costs, with the Minister of Health being critical of the private healthcare providers. Previous interventions by government in the private healthcare sector had been met with extensive litigation and resistance. The result of this was mistrust between the policy maker, namely, the Ministry, and the sector. As a result, government found it increasingly difficult to push through regulatory interventions and had lost major cases in court while attempting to do so.[11]

Although the Commission had powers to conduct the inquiry itself and to compel the provision of information, the example of the banking inquiry and the antagonistic climate between key stakeholders led the Commission to again decide on an independent panel and the holding of public hearings. The panel was chaired by a retired Chief Justice and included two medical experts, a health economist and an international competition economics expert. The constitution of the panel was designed to provide expertise to examine the issues objectively and to give confidence to the parties involved. The panel was

[10] Competition Commission of South Africa, Health Market Inquiry, 2019, Final Findings and Recommendations Report, available at http://www.compcom.co.za/wp-content/uploads/2020/01/Final-Findings-and-recommendations-report-Health-Market-Inquiry.pdf.

[11] Minister of Health and Another vs. New Clicks South Africa (Pty) Ltd and Others (CCT 59/2004) [2005] ZACC 14; 2006 (2) SA 311 (CC); 2006 (1) BCLR 1 (CC) (30 September 2005)

supported by a technical team led by the Commission staff and involving some external experts. The panel issued guidelines, which outlined the inquiry process and participation rights. These included extensive rights of access to data but also anonymisation and confidentiality of patient data. The process was challenged in court without success, but the challenge did delay the inquiry which took seven years to complete. This reflected the very broad scope and complex nature of the issues in what was a 'one-off' inquiry. The HMI has been criticised for the time and resources it took and we agree that the HMI experience certainly provides a caution regarding the complex nature of the issues in healthcare and such a broad framing of an inquiry. On the other side of the scales, the analysis in the HMI has been widely welcomed in the context of the process of designing a National Health Insurance scheme which will include payments for services from the private sector.

The inquiries into grocery retail, LPG and data services were focused on a narrower set of markets and saw the Commission seeking to establish a model which differed from the particular experiences in banking and healthcare. The Commission sought to recalibrate and took more control of the inquires than had been the case with both banking and healthcare. The LPG inquiry was the first to be undertaken after the amendments of the Act providing the Commission with powers to conduct an inquiry. It took three years to complete, from the terms of reference to the publication of the final report of findings and recommendations. Unlike the independent panel model of the other inquiries, the LPG inquiry was run completely internally.[12] The grocery retail inquiry was initiated by the Commission and took four years to complete. It was led by a panel, but unlike in the banking and healthcare panels, the panel and the Commission's internal team were integrated and worked together to produce the report. The data services inquiry was initiated in response to a request from the Minister of the former Economic Development Department and took a little more than two years to complete. We assess the latter two inquiries in greater detail in Section 6.3. The conclusion of market inquiries

---

[12] Competition Commission of South Africa, Market Inquiry into the LPG Sector (2017). Final Report (Non-Confidential), available at http://www.compcom.co .za/wp-content/uploads/2018/11/LPG-FINAL-NON-CONFIDENTIAL-VERSION.pdf.

undertaken by the Commission (other than the HMI) generally took less time than enforcement cases would, as we discuss below.

6.3 The Grocery Retail and Data Services Market Inquiries

6.3.1 The Grocery Retail Market Inquiry (GRMI)[13]

In 2015, the Commission announced the establishment of the Grocery Retail Market Inquiry (GRMI) following concerns of rising concentration levels and conduct that potentially distorted or restricted competition, as a handful of supermarket chains extended within urban and non-urban areas.[14]

6.3.1.1 Framing and Process of the Inquiry

The inquiry followed a number of complaints of abuse of dominance relating to the practice of exclusive leases that the large supermarket chains entered into with property developers of shopping malls and centres. The long-running exclusive leases meant that landlords or property managers could not let retail space in a given shopping mall to rivals of the main supermarket in the mall, including to specialist outlets such as butchers and bakeries. These leases sometimes spanned up to 40 years. However, after investigation, the complaints were not referred by the Competition Commission for adjudication to the Competition Tribunal given the high threshold of proof required under the enforcement provisions of the Act to demonstrate unilateral dominance and harm.[15] Cases pursued independently were embroiled in prolonged litigation. The inquiry into the sector provided an appropriate tool to consider the wider effects of exclusive leases in terms of preventing, distorting or restricting competition under the market

---

[13] Competition Commission of South Africa, Grocery Retail Market Inquiry (2019). Final Report (Non-Confidential), available at http://www.compcom.co .za/wp-content/uploads/2019/12/GRMI-Non-Confidential-Report.pdf.

[14] das Nair, The 'supermarket revolution' in the South, in: Crush/Frayne/Haysom (eds.), *Urban Food Security in the Global South*, 2020, p. 113–144; das Nair, The spread and internationalisation of South African retail chains and the implications of market power, (2019) 33 *International Review of Applied Economics*, 1.

[15] Competition Commission South Africa, Commission non-refers supermarkets investigation, 2014, Media Release, available at http://www.compcom.co.za/ wp-content/uploads/2014/09/Commission-non-refers-supermarkets-investigation.pdf.

inquiry provision which have lower evidentiary burdens than the 'substantial lessening of competition' test under the enforcement provisions. The inquiry also paved the way for voluntary changes in behaviour and provided a stronger foundation to initiate enforcement proceedings.

A second set of what we term 'competition-plus' concerns were examined relating to prevailing practices that affected participation of suppliers to the grocery retail sector. These related to the buyer power of the supermarkets and was included in the Terms of Reference following public comments. A buyer power provision was subsequently introduced to the Competition Act as part of the amendments in 2019.[16] Separate from the inquiry, the government had already introduced amendments out of concerns for high levels of concentration and low levels of inclusivity in many markets in terms of wider participation of small- and medium-sized enterprises. Amongst other things, these amendments included regulating monopsony power. The GRMI ventilated pervasive practices that could amount to such exploitation before the amendment of the Act came into effect legally, again paving the way for stronger future enforcement cases against the abuse of buyer power.

The third area that the inquiry assessed can be viewed as public policy issues including factors that affect the participation and competitiveness of smaller retailers. Under this, the inquiry investigated various barriers to entry and participation that smaller formal and informal retailers face outside of anti-competitive conduct. This included regulations and the role of local government in facilitating a diversity of retail models. Factors and business models that appear to make foreign-owned small grocery retail business more competitive than local ones were also explored.

The framing of the inquiry therefore allowed for the investigation and exposure of a wider set of factors that affect competition, participation *and* competitiveness in grocery value chains, as discussed in Section 6.3.1.2. Unlike enforcement action, which focuses on much narrower and specific competition issues, the inquiry shed light on key problems that affect overall competitiveness in the sector, in addition

---

[16] Competition Commission South Africa, Buyer Power Enforcement Guidelines, 2020, available at https://www.gov.za/sites/default/files/gcis_document/202002/43018gon168.pdf.

to specific competition problems, and made recommendations to address all three aspects.

The GRMI involved extensive engagements, consultations, site visits, focus groups and public hearings throughout the country, with evidence and submissions from different players along relevant value chains.

6.3.1.2 Outcomes

The inquiry found that the top five grocery retailers accounted for 64 per cent of the grocery retail market at a national level and that a combination of features in the sector possibly prevented, distorted or restricted competition. It recommended remedial action in three main areas:

(i) long-term exclusive lease agreements and buyer power;
(ii) competitiveness of small and independent retailers; and
(iii) the regulatory landscape.

Of these, the most successful outcomes were arguably in the first, narrowly defined, area of exclusive leases. The panel found that 'exclusive leases have substantially hindered the emergence of challenger retail chains and prevents economic participation by small independent retailers, including specialist retailers',[17] and that the defences put forward by the supermarkets for them were not credible. The practice was found to maintain high levels of concentration and to entrench the incumbency of the national supermarket chains, raising barriers to entry for small and independent retailers and ultimately restricting consumer choice.

The inquiry's recommendations included ceasing the enforcement of exclusive lease clauses immediately with respect to small- and medium-sized enterprises (SMMEs), speciality stores and other grocery retailers (and emerging challenger retailers) in shopping centres located in non-urban areas; stopping new leases from containing these clauses; and the phasing out within five years from the inquiry report's publication of existing leases with these provisions in other, including urban, areas. A period of six months was given for voluntary compliance of these recommendations, failing which, legislation, in the form of a statute, regulations or a code of practice would be considered.

---

[17] Grocery Retail Market Inquiry Final Report (fn. 7), at p. 7

Within six months of the release of the inquiry findings, in May 2020, the large supermarket chain Pick n Pay announced its decision to cease exclusive leases in line with the recommendations. This was swiftly followed by a similar decision by Shoprite Holdings, the largest supermarket chain in South Africa. Both entered into consent agreements with the Commission[18] which were confirmed by the Tribunal. While the enforcement cases against individual supermarket chains on the same matter that were initiated well before the GRMI continued to be tied up in prolonged litigation, the inquiry triggered quicker and far less litigious responses from the two largest chains, although, as of 28 February 2021, the third chain, Spar, did not agree to end their exclusive leases.

Buyer power was assessed in the inquiry in the context of the unequal bargaining framework between the national supermarket chains and Fast-Moving Consumer Goods (FMCG) suppliers, which in turn impacted the bargaining dynamics between suppliers and independent retailers including through buyer groups. The recommendations in this respect included requirements that FMCG suppliers ensured uniform trading terms to different buyers and that trading terms must have objective justifications based on cost savings, supply chain efficiencies, efficient risk-sharing or sales promotion. The inquiry stated that if voluntary compliance by these suppliers on the recommendations was not reached, government should introduce a legislative framework in the form of a code of good practice. This recommendation therefore was not targeted at the supermarket chains but rather at larger suppliers that supplied both the main supermarkets chains and independent retailers to ensure their equal treatment.

With respect to concerns of buyer power abuses against smaller suppliers, the inquiry recommended the confirmation of the amendments to the Competition Act relating to buyer power. This subsequently occurred, with buyer power regulations and guidelines released in 2020, illustrating the feedback from inquiries into market-shaping rule-making. The Amendment Act in subsection 4(a) under the

---

[18] Competition Commission South Africa, The Competition Commission refers consent agreement with Pick n Pay to the Competition Tribunal for confirmation, 20 October 2020, available at http://www.compcom.co.za/wp-content/uploads/2020/10/THE-COMPETITION-COMMISSION-REFERS-CONSENT-AGREEMENT-WITH-PICK-N-PAY-TO-THE-COMPETITION-TRIBUNAL-FOR-CONFIRMATION.pdf.

abuse of dominance provisions of section 8 prohibits a dominant firm as a buyer in designated sectors to require from or impose unfair prices or trading conditions on small and medium businesses or firms controlled or owned by historically disadvantaged persons. The amendments allow for the Minister in the Department of Trade, Industry and Competition to designate certain sectors in which this provision is applicable. The sector designated in 2020 included agro-processing, grocery wholesale and retail and the e-commerce and online services sectors. The Competition Commission began enforcement investigations under the buyer power provisions in food markets in 2020 which are still underway at the time of writing.

Other recommendations were made by the inquiry relating to policies on the competitiveness of small suppliers in food value chains. For instance, recommendations were made that the enterprise or supplier development programmes of supermarket chains be formalised and strengthened to develop small and historically disadvantaged suppliers, with binding targets on the amounts of support for them. As of February 2021, the Department of Trade, Industry and Competition is considering this in the ongoing development of the Agriculture and Agro-processing Master Plan as part of a wider industrial policy intervention. Such recommendations go beyond pure competition interventions and seek to improve competitiveness of supply chains more broadly.

The inquiry also made recommendations around how government could facilitate building capabilities and support for independent retailers and wholesalers, including through investments in infrastructure and seed finance for innovative business models in peri- and non-urban areas. Similarly, there were recommendations on the regulatory landscape, including on the need for greater coordination between local, provincial and national government to lower regulatory barriers for small businesses and to better deal with the sale of illegal counterfeit goods and lack of competitiveness of small, local independent retailers vis-à-vis foreign retailers. The inquiry only exposed the tip of the iceberg in these areas, and progress on these recommendations has been slower given their wider ambit and the need for coordination by multiple government departments and other stakeholders.

How do the interventions in the grocery retail sector in South Africa compare to interventions internationally? Interventions internationally have also included market inquiries, the outcomes of which focus on regulating supermarket conduct towards suppliers, in addition to other potential anti-competitive conduct. In the United Kingdom, a market inquiry by the former Office of Fair Trading led to the mandatory UK Groceries Supply Code of Practice in 2009, with an independent Grocery Code Adjudicator (GCA)[19] overseeing functioning and adherence of the code.

The Australian Competition and Consumer Commission (ACCC) instituted a voluntary code of conduct for which some of the supermarket chains and wholesalers signed up. Certain improvements in conduct have been reported, particularly around charging of fees, other payments and conduct towards suppliers. However, in 2018, the ACCC made recommendations for the code to be made mandatory in a review process,[20] suggesting that the voluntary nature of the initial code was insufficient to obtain the desired outcomes.

These are stronger responses than in South Africa, where the inquiry did not directly recommend a mandatory code of conduct.

The response in Namibia to concerns of growing buyer power of supermarkets is a unique one, with the Namibian government – not through the competition authority, but through the Namibia Trade Forum as part of the Ministry of Industrialisation, Trade and SME Development – creating the Namibian Retail Charter in 2016. This voluntary charter encourages supermarket signatories to support local suppliers in several ways, including actively investing in their development, giving them preferential shelf space and promoting local procurement. In addition, the charter encourages transparency and fairness in supermarket procurement and trading terms. It also commits government to invest in and provide a supporting environment to boost local suppliers. As such, the charter covers both voluntary code of conduct elements and supplier development initiatives.

---

[19] GCA Website: https://www.gov.uk/government/organisations/groceries-code-adjudicator.

[20] Australian Competition and Consumer Commission, Submission to the Food and Grocery Code of Conduct Review, 2018, available at https://www.accc.gov.au/system/files/ACCC%20submission%20to%20the%20Food%20and%20Grocery%20Code%20of%20Conduct%20Review%20-%2011%20May%20.

6.3.2 The Data Services Market Inquiry (DSMI)[21]

The Data Services Market Inquiry (DSMI) was initiated in 2017 in response to a request from the Minister of Economic Development and following widespread calls to address what were perceived to be high prices for data being charged by the telecommunications companies when compared with other countries. Within six months of the final report being published, consent agreements with Vodacom and MTN to lower data prices were confirmed by the Competition Tribunal in March and June 2020.

6.3.2.1 Framing and Process of the Inquiry

The purpose of the DSMI was set out in the terms of reference as to 'understand what factors or features of the market(s) and value chain may cause or lead to high prices for data services'.[22] The DSMI was asked to make recommendations as to how prices could be reduced, assuming that they were confirmed to be higher than appropriate benchmarks.

The objectives of the DSMI were therefore relatively focused due to the scope of the services and issues being analysed. While the terms of reference specified that it covered 'all relevant players in the value chain who contribute to or influence prices of data services in South Africa',[23] in effect, it was narrowed to prioritise mobile data services provided by the four mobile network operators. This was because fixed broadband prices were not highlighted in submissions to nearly the same extent and the services are not available in lower income areas with which the Inquiry was particularly concerned. The Inquiry did address fixed broadband to a limited extent, including questions of roll-out and the provision of free public Wi-Fi.

International comparisons undertaken using different data sources indicated that mobile prepaid data prices in South Africa were relatively high. In particular, the prices of the two main mobile operators were substantially higher (by multiples of three or more for some

---

[21] Competition Commission of South Africa, Data Services Market Inquiry Final Report, Non-Confidential, 2019, available at http://www.compcom.co.za/wp-content/uploads/2019/12/DSMI-Non-Confidential-Report-002.pdf.

[22] Data Services Market Inquiry Terms of Reference, Government Gazette. No. 41054, 18 August 2017, at p. 5.

[23] Ibid., at p. 3.

bundles) in South Africa than these companies charged in other countries (including Angola, Egypt, Ghana, Nigeria, Rwanda, Uganda and Zambia). Consumers buying small pre-paid bundles, including presumably most lower income consumers, were charged the highest prices. This was deemed to be 'anti-poor' pricing and of even greater concern given that most would not have alternatives. Wealthier consumers, by comparison, were more likely to be able to use mobile data services alongside fixed broadband lines and have Wi-Fi at work. Low-income users were also judged to be vulnerable to a lack of transparency as to rates being charged including paying for higher out-of-bundle rates.

The inquiry was an alternative route to investigating and addressing supra-competitive prices as being potentially excessive or the result of coordinated conduct. Without substantial market power, either unilateral or through some form of coordination, presumably such pricing power could not exist.

The DSMI illustrates the value of the inquiry route as it was possible for the Commission to obtain information and assess the market outcomes in a nuanced manner. In South Africa, the lessons of the first 20 years of the Competition Act point to challenges with excessive pricing cases due to the contestation around the appropriate tests and evidence, which were subject to very extensive appeals, precisely because of the possible penalties.[24] The DSMI was able to evaluate the justifications for prices charged and the underlying reasons for the market workings such as spectrum allocation, along with access to infrastructure, which can enable greater competitive challenge to the major incumbents. It was also able to focus on consumer segments which were especially vulnerable to the exertion of market power (through discriminatory or differential treatment) and consider the wider context as to why this may be the case, something which the Competition and Markets Authority (CMA) has also addressed in its focus on vulnerable consumers.

The DSMI is a good example of the value of the powers to gather information and evaluate market workings placing an onus on parties,

---

[24] Mncube/Ngobese, Working out the standards for excessive pricing in South Africa, in: Jenny/Katsoulacos (eds.), *Excessive Pricing and Competition Law Enforcement*, 2018, p. 159–172; Roberts, Assessing the record on competition law enforcement for opening-up the economy, in: Vilakazi/Goga/Roberts (eds.), *Opening the South African Economy? Barriers to Entry, Regulation and Competition*, 2020, ch. 11.

where relevant, to justify conduct which appears to exploit market power in ways which may harm competition and consumers. The DSMI set out prices and benchmarks; noted indicators of substantial market power; was able to identify consumers who were most affected, with the particular impact on low-income consumers buying pre-paid smaller bundles; and provided the opportunity for the two largest mobile network operators (MNOs), Vodacom and MTN, to justify their pricing.

The justifications given by Vodacom and MTN were critically examined by the DSMI, including through further information requests, and found not to explain the conduct. The DSMI examined differential pricing and found that pre-paid, lower income consumers were most likely to pay the highest prices, which were the prices for smaller bundles. This was not explained by costs and instead reflected the likely exploitation of behavioural biases, lack of transparency and poor alternatives of these consumers. The ability to sustain such prices is also indicative of the MNOs' market power.

The other major area to which the DSMI was able to bring evidence and analysis was in examining the role of policies and regulations. This included examination of spectrum, roaming agreements and rights of access to facilities and how these impacted on competition. The telecommunications sector has been subject to extensive contestation, lobbying and litigation as might have been expected given the financial sums at stake from decisions over rights and regulations.[25] The inquiry was able to explain the implications of decisions (and non-decisions) made in this regard, including the holding up of spectrum allocation and the delays to amendments required to the Electronic Communications Act.

6.3.2.2 Outcomes
The DSMI found that durable first-mover positions were held by Vodacom and MTN and that there were demonstrable obstacles to smaller rivals in making a competitive impact. Taking into account the mark-ups for data and voice, along with the prices for pre-paid plans, especially for smaller bundles, the DSMI observed high mark-ups (including after accounting for a fair return on capital) which

---

[25] Makhaya/Roberts, Expectations and outcomes: Considering competition and corporate power in South Africa under democracy, (2013) 40 (138) *Review of African Political Economy*, 556.

established a prima facie case of excessive pricing by Vodacom, and which was indicative of market power in the case of MTN. Moreover, the two firms (and Vodacom, in particular) were found to have resilient dominant positions.[26]

As mentioned above, the pricing took advantage of the behavioural biases of less well-informed consumers and was consistent with 'exploitative price discrimination and partitioning strategies in order to push up margins and prices'[27] and working against the poor. These strategies allowed the MNOs to respond to the offerings of rivals with lower pricing to post-paid customers without reducing the prices of lower volume usage to pre-paid consumers in areas where high speed offerings and fixed broadband were not available.

The DSMI's recommendations included 'Immediate relief on data pricing' through Vodacom and MTN reaching agreement with the Commission within two months of the final report on substantial tariff reductions in pre-paid monthly bundles. In the event, the Competition Tribunal confirmed consent agreements between the Commission and Vodacom and MTN on 25 March 2020 and 24 June 2020, respectively. These covered reductions in the prices of 30-day pre-paid bundles across all channels, and zero rating of services to various public institutions as well as lifeline data services to those in low-income communities.

There were substantial benefits to consumers with, for example, Vodacom reducing prices for the 1GB bundle by one third to 99 Rands (around EUR 5.50)[28] in April 2020, with MTN having already made price reductions. Enforcement, including by the

---

[26] According to the South African Competition Act, a firm is dominant in a market if (a) it has at least 45 per cent of that market; (b) it has at least 35 per cent, but less than 45 per cent, of that market, unless it can show that it does not have market power; or (c) it has less than 35 per cent of that market but has market power. Vodacom's share in mobile services was found to clearly exceed the thresholds in the Competition Act for dominance, while MTN's share was found to 'skirt around the threshold level where there is a rebuttable presumption of dominance'. The DSMI further found that both their shares had not changed over time and that they collectively held at least 70 per cent of data revenue and 80 per cent of total subscriber service revenue (Competition Commission of South Africa, Data Services Market Inquiry Final Report, at p. 21, para. 20).

[27] Competition Commission of South Africa, Data Services Market Inquiry Final Report, at p. 20.

[28] Bloomberg exchange rate of 17.83 Rand to the Euro on 11 March 2021.

regulator, had been unable to adequately deal with these competition issues for many years.

There were a range of other recommendations relating to competition and regulation, some of which can be considered 'competition-plus' recommendations aimed at opening up markets. These included measures to improve wholesale competition, roaming on fair terms, spectrum assignment, facilities leasing and the addressing of the gaps in the fixed-line network in lower income areas. Functional and accounting separation was also recommended for the larger vertically integrated networks with respect to their wholesale network infrastructure to guard against exclusionary conduct. These actions largely relied on steps being taken by the regulator and relevant government department. Here there has been much less success. For example, an auction of spectrum was announced in 2020; however, legal challenges at the end of the year held it up once again.

6.4 Comparative Lessons

The inquiries led to a much deeper understanding of markets, yielding substantial data and insights on prevailing competition issues, including the historical evolution of markets and market structure, contestability and barriers to entry. They have also given a better understanding of the issues impacting on inclusivity or otherwise. The inquiries have had important impacts – often leading to a much quicker, voluntary resolution of key issues (ceasing exclusive leases, lowering data cost). They have also helped set the agenda for ongoing reforms, creating a knock-on effect. What lessons can be learnt about achieving effective outcomes?

The first set of issues we consider is how the inquiries have been framed. These are naturally related to the markets involved. Some inquiries have taken on very broad questions, while others have been relatively narrow in scope. The second set of considerations we address is the design and processes of the inquiries, to foster information gathering and engagements relating to identified market issues rather than the conduct of an individual firm. Closely related are the issues of the interface of market workings with the role of regulators in many of the inquiries, which is the third topic we address. Finally, we offer a consideration of remedies, changes agreed with companies and recommendations for actions by other bodies.

6.4.1 Framing and Issues

We identify three broad tiers of issues which inquiries have tackled.

The first tier comprises relatively narrow competition issues. These include arrangements which undermine competition due to their exclusionary nature (such as exclusive leases) and pricing which exploits groups of consumers, possibly unfairly (such as mobile data prices) and direct regulatory restrictions on rivalry.

The second tier relates to what can be thought of as 'competition-plus' issues, where markets are not working well due to arrangements which raise barriers to entry, obstacles to the participation of smaller firms which may need assistance to become effective competitors and related policy and/or regulatory issues.[29] These issues impact on the ability to participate on fair terms, especially with regard to small and medium enterprises and black businesses.

The third tier relates to broad questions of public policy. While an inquiry might uncover useful information on how markets have worked, the answers may lie in sector-specific policies (such as those relating to healthcare policy and the expansion of foreign-owned stores in the informal retail sector).

The South African experience points to the value of market inquiries in addressing questions which could be the subject of competition cases, especially abuse of dominance. The exclusive leases in the GRMI and data prices in the DSMI both point to the benefits of a route where firms are put on the spot to justify arrangements which appear on the face of things to be problematic under competition law and the avenue is open to rectify the situation without an adverse competition finding. The competition cases under abuse of dominance, by comparison, would take many years to be finalised and would turn on technical questions of market definition, market power and the quantification of harm to competition.

In the case of exclusive leases, proving unilateral dominance turned on a narrow definition of the market, while at the same time it was readily apparent through the inquiry that the main chains had adopted common terms without necessarily coordinating between themselves.

[29] See also Fletcher, Chapter 8, on market investigations being able to look into 'cross-market issues', including 'factors such as economies of scale and scope, network effects, regulatory and structural barriers, and consumer behavioural factors'.

These terms undermined rivalry from smaller and single-line retailers even while there was rivalry between the main chains. Competition (including non-price dimensions) was distorted by the lease agreements and their duration was not justified. However, it was not clear that there was a substantial lessening of competition in terms of a quantifiable harm to consumer welfare in terms of higher prices which would be required under the traditional enforcement provisions.

Similarly, with data prices, the much higher effective prices charged to the typically lower-income consumer who bought smaller pre-paid data bundles was set out by the inquiry and the companies were invited to justify the huge differentials. At the time, exploitative price discrimination which did not also undermine competition was not an abuse of dominance under the competition law. The conduct would therefore have had to be addressed under the excessive pricing provision. Excessive pricing cases in South Africa have had a particularly challenging history, with prolonged litigation.

In terms of issues which fall under a 'competition-plus' heading, these may be thought to be the natural arena for market inquiries; however, the record is more mixed. In the GRMI, the issues were framed in a fairly broad manner, allowing for the exploration of barriers to entry and expansion from various perspectives. In addition to the long-term exclusive leases, the issues of buyer power and supplier development were identified where retailers are an indispensable platform. As discussed, these are issues which had been considered in inquiries in other countries, such as in the United Kingdom, where it led to a code of conduct enforced by the Groceries Code Adjudicator. The inquiry, by design, extended beyond traditional competition issues to deal with issues of participation and inclusion; however, in practice, the Commission addressed the more traditional competition issue of exclusionary conduct and referred the issues around supplier development and support to small and medium enterprises to the relevant government departments to address.

In the DSMI, there was a range of issues relating to infrastructure which could have changed the extent of rivalry from smaller market participants. Again, the wider issues were set out in the report for ongoing attention, while the Commission focused in the short term on obtaining changes from the two major firms.

With regard to the third tier, consisting of a broad basket of public policy questions relating to markets, these are naturally highly context dependent. There is a question of whether inquiries should be used in regulated markets. The HMI is perhaps the best example of this tier as the inquiry grappled with the intersections between various levels of the health value provision that were significant in understanding the overall cost drivers. It was clear from the beginning that interventions may include regulation in a sector where price determination is not straightforward. On the other hand, the inquiry could have been able to deal with a segment of the market, for example, hospitals, if it had been more narrowly framed. This could have enabled more focused recommendations with considerably less time and lower costs. But it is not clear that addressing hospitalisation would be sufficient without addressing the perverse incentives to specialists leading to over-utilisation. The inquiry set out to undertake a holistic assessment, in order to provide a detailed evidence-based set of broad recommendations which relied upon government actions to be taken forwards.

Such an approach can be criticised as an inappropriate framing for a competition inquiry. However, it reflects the challenges of finding a legitimate tool for addressing the dysfunctionality of markets with possible regulatory failures that need an outside impetus for their resolution. The banking inquiry was similarly broad and reliant on policy changes and regulations. It did lead to improvements over time, with government creating a Financial Sector Conduct Authority with an extensive consumer protection mandate. The separation of consumer protection from a prudential regulator gave consumer protection the attention it required in a market that was found to have limited competition and prevalence of consumer exploitation. Government is also considering a range of interventions to open up the banking sector, including taking into account the role of fintech.[30]

6.4.2 Design and Processes

The main design issue in South Africa has been whether an inquiry is conducted by the competition authority internally, using its staff, or it appoints an independent panel to conduct an inquiry. Of course, in both situations, the competition authority takes overall responsibility for the inquiry including allocation of resources and determining the timelines.

---

[30] See fn. 3.

Independent panels have been important to engender trust in the market inquiries. In the case of banking, undertaken before formal inquiry powers existed in the law, authorities who were mostly orientated to prudential regulation to ensure the integrity and stability of the financial sector were sensitive to any interventions that could potentially undermine it. In the private healthcare market, there was a history of litigation between the sector and the Ministry of Health. On both occasions, independent panels headed by a judge generated confidence in the process and helped get cooperation of the participants. When there were attempts to challenge the health inquiry in courts, these attempts were unsuccessful, as courts took comfort in the Commission's assurances that an independent panel was running the process.

Differences of approach to issues sometimes occur between the panel and the competition authority. Once the panel is established as independent, these differences can be difficult to navigate. The panel members have particular expertise but this is often not in competition law, implying differences in approach which may be difficult to reconcile. In addition, as issues often take longer to consider and may be more complex than initially anticipated, there can be tensions over resourcing and timelines.

The LPG market inquiry demonstrated that a market inquiry can be more focused and informal. There was no panel involved and there were no public hearings. The inquiry was completed within a short space of time and still enjoyed widespread acceptance.

The latest (2019) changes to the law provide for a more direct leadership of market inquiries by the Commission, providing that a deputy Commissioner must lead an inquiry. This does not preclude the existence of the panel, working with a deputy Commissioner.

6.4.3 Regulated Sector Challenges

All but one of the market inquiries in South Africa were in regulated sectors, which posed a challenge of managing relationships with sector regulators. In the majority of the cases, there was explicit (although rare) or an implicit (common) objection from the sector regulators to having the competition authority conducting an inquiry into its sector. But the market inquiry interventions were in areas where the sector regulator had not intervened and often there was a public outcry about the lack or failure of competition. In sectors such as telecommunications and health, it was the government ministers responsible who asked the competition authorities to intervene.

A lesson emanating from the South African experience is the need to invest time in getting the competition problem appreciated by the sector regulators and to involve them as much as possible in the process of the inquiry including the design of the remedies. A lack of consensus about competition problems can lead to resistance in implementing the recommendations. The recommendations should also carve out as much as possible a role for the sector regulator, which must have been canvassed with them prior to the recommendations.

In the banking inquiry, most recommendations were directed at sector regulators. Where they were directed at firms, such as preventing consumer exploitation, regulators were still required to take action in the event of the failure of the market. Similarly, both the DSMI and the LPG inquiries contained recommendations to the regulators.

6.4.4 Remedies

The attraction of market inquiries across the world is the ability to deeply understand competition problems in markets and to recommend or impose remedies.[31] There are no fines or retribution of any sort, and the intervention is proactive and forward looking. There is also flexibility in the design of the remedies. All this is in the control of the competition authority, not a tribunal or the courts (except for divestitures which must be referred by the Commission to the Tribunal). This flexibility has, for example, enabled the Competition Commission of South Africa, in the DSMI, to keep some details of the price reduction glide path confidential, thereby preventing the potential chilling effect of the settlement agreement on competition in the future by keeping competitors guessing how much the price reductions will be.

Broadly speaking, a distinction can be made between remedies where the market participants make specific commitments to address a competition issue and those where a change in regulation or govern-

---

[31] See Motta/Peitz, Chapter 2

ment policy is the best path. If particular anti-competitive behaviour has been identified, as with the data pricing in the DSMI, then the competition authority may have a credible threat of a prosecution to push for an agreement to change the conduct. In the DSMI, the two largest operators who were found to enjoy market power settled the possible excessive pricing complaint which emanated from the inquiry. In the case of the GRMI, the inquiry made a compelling case that the long-term exclusive lease agreements, some of which went up to 40 years with landlords (as highlighted in Section 6.3.1.1), served to exclude independent retailers and specialty stores such as fresh produce retailers and butcheries. The two largest retail groups entered into consent agreements eliminating the use of long-term exclusive lease agreements. No doubt the success of the remedy is aided by considerations of reputational harm should a market inquiry evidence be aired again in an adversarial prosecution. And, once one or two of the large players settle the matter, the other firms do not normally hold out.

In the case of regulatory remedies, the inquiry findings have not been binding on the policy makers or sector regulators. In effect, these changes depend on advocacy and they can be ignored by regulators and government. It takes time to persuade the relevant bodies of the merits of the proposed actions and results often do not match the effort involved. While advocacy is an inevitable outcome of most market inquiries, and can sometimes be the only solution, the best levers are where there is evidence of competition harm which could be taken further by the Commission, and which sees the companies seeking an alternative resolution including through appropriate regulations. The widening of competition provisions which relate to harmful conduct under abuse of dominance could also, by opening up avenues for possible competition cases, make lead parties to be more likely to accept regulatory solutions.

Remedies can also address issues that are important even though they may not have been winnable in an enforcement case. In the case of South Africa, some public interest issues can be part of the terms of reference of a market inquiry, such as issues of participation of SMMEs and employment. The remedies can involve recommendations to open up markets, which was the case in LPG, where ending long-standing exclusive arrangements of the largest producers with the largest wholesalers explicitly also provided for small enterprise participation.

6.5 Conclusions

The experience of market inquiries in South Africa has been closely linked with the evolution of the wider competition regime and the expectations on it. The record suggests that inquiries are an important tool even for a relatively young authority and that they can be used to address issues in concentrated sectors which would be extremely difficult for investigations to tackle. The inquiries can make a major contribution to understanding market outcomes and achieve changes through a less adversarial and potentially less time-consuming route. Of course, the inquiries cannot meet unrealistic expectations and most obviously have an impact where there are clearly identified competition issues.

In the context of South Africa's extremely high and persisting levels of concentration of ownership and control,[32] the inquiries have been an essential part of examining the implications of this concentration, understood in narrow and broad terms. In this sense, the international recognition of high levels of concentration have been catching up with South Africa.[33] There is a very important role for inquiries in considering what we term 'competition-plus' issues such as lower barriers to entry and improving regulations and policies to shape more inclusive markets. In our assessment, the inquiries in South Africa have played an important role in framing the issues with regard to entrenched market structures and firms controlling bottlenecks which, over time, have influenced changes in legislation and regulation. This includes amendment to the competition law to place a greater onus on dominant firms not to undermine participation by smaller businesses or discriminate against vulnerable consumers.

---

[32] Buthelezi/Mtani/Mncube, The extent of market concentration in South Africa's product markets, (2019) 7(3) *Journal of Antitrust Enforcement*, 352.

[33] See Crawford/Rey/Schnitzer, Chapter 7. See also Akcigit/Chen/Díez/Duval/ Engler/Fan/Maggi/Tavares/Schwarz/Shibata/ Villegas-Sánchez (2021), Rising corporate market power: emerging policy issues, IMF Staff Discussion Note, SDN/21/01; De Loecker/Eeckhout, Global market power (June 2018), NBER Working Paper No. w24768, available at SSRN: https://ssrn.com/abstract= 3206443; Rosenboom, Increased market power: A global problem that needs solving? (2019), Oxera, Agenda: Advancing economics in business, available at https://www.oxera.com/agenda/increased-market-power-a-global-problem-that-needs-solving/.

Inquiries are a latecomer amongst the tools of a competition authority which have been carefully implemented to result in a more inquisitorial system driven by the authority itself. The role for lawyers has
been much more limited than in the lengthy hearings which character-
ise abuse of dominance cases before the Competition Tribunal, with
extensive cross-examination of factual and expert witnesses.[34] This has
generally led to more efficient running of inquiries and allowed for an
environment where people are freer to submit information.

The flexibility to adopt different procedures for each inquiry has
allowed for learnings to be taken into account more quickly than in
enforcement cases where there are set standard rules. Rules are also
designed for each market's requirements. For example, in the HMI the
requirement of patient confidentiality required more stringent rules of
access to, and anonymisation of, patients' data.

Similarly, the experience with independent panels was an important
part of the learning curve, even while it led to the Commission being
in full control of the process, with inquiries now being led by a
deputy Commissioner.

6.5.1 Competition Issues

In terms of narrow competition issues, inquiries have often been more
effective in addressing both exploitative and exclusionary abuses than
enforcement. This is especially the case in tight oligopolies with two or
three large firms where neither unilateral dominance nor coordination
is obvious but where the conduct and impact can be widely observed
and brought to light through the inquiry. The firms have been provided
an opportunity to justify the observed outcomes in the inquisitorial
framework. The structure has allowed for changes to be agreed with
the main parties, with the alternative of investigations available to the
Commission. Where clear evidence of a competition contravention
comes to light during an inquiry, the Commission can and has
launched an investigation before the inquiry concludes, as was the case
in LPG where indications of collusive conduct came to light.[35]

---

[34] Bonakele (fn. 3), at p. 187–205.
[35] Competition Commission South Africa, Liquefied Petroleum Gas companies to
be prosecuted for price fixing (2018). Media Release, available at http://www
.compcom.co.za/wp-content/uploads/2019/03/LPG-Cylinder-Press-Release.pdf.

The process of the inquiry thus enabled shedding light on the nature and extent of pricing and other market outcomes, the arrangements which underpin these outcomes and those which have been most affected. They have been good examples of what Judge Louis Brandeis observed when he wrote that '[s]unlight is said to be the best of disinfectants' with reference to practices in banking and the 'Money Trust' in the United States.[36]

The agreements with companies can be reached without any admission of a contravention and are subject, as undertakings, to a transparent process of confirmation by the Competition Tribunal. The companies are incentivised to take a longer-term perspective, considering the reputation effects and the costs of lengthy investigation and possible litigation against undertakings that can be made. However, it is the case that some firms may agree to the changes and others will not, such as is the case in the main supermarket groups and exclusive leases where Spar, the third largest grocery chain, has declined to terminate exclusive leases while Shoprite and Pick n Pay have made this undertaking.

6.5.2 'Competition-Plus' Issues and Public Policy Questions

What we have categorised as 'competition-plus' issues cover a broad range from consumer protection concerns to arrangements which raise barriers to the entry and growth of rivals and those which impact on competition at different levels of value chains. There has been mixed success here, from which we draw out an agenda on which to build.

A number of inquiries have identified and addressed concerns cutting across the boundary of competition and consumer protection. Firms have been open to making changes to address concerns about consumers being unfairly treated, sometimes in conjunction with improved regulation (for example, in the Banking Inquiry regarding both penalty charges and bank switching). This is consistent with incumbents' incentive to protect their reputations with consumers. Firms have generally been much less open to measures which would open up markets to greater rivalry (notwithstanding the agreements following the GRMI with two major chains on exclusive leases).

[36] Brandeis, *Other People's Money and How the Bankers Use It*, 1914.

It can be argued that such changes are more properly the purview of sector regulators. However, the regulators do not have competition concerns high on their mandate and understandably are not as alive to the harm to competition which not tackling obstacles can cause. By their nature, it is also not clear in advance what benefits rivals with different business models and offerings will bring. However, in hindsight, the value of the Banking Inquiry, in putting issues of dynamic competition on the agenda, has become evident in contradiction to the criticisms levelled at the inquiry for encroaching on the terrain of banking regulation. The National Treasury and the Reserve Bank have taken up open-banking, recognising the value of rivalry from other business models made possible by digitalisation.[37]

While inquiries in South Africa have laid the basis for more incremental changes to be made, the question is whether these changes adequately meet the need to address the entrenched power of gatekeeper firms in many sectors of the economy in light of the challenges of inequality, exclusion and a stagnant economy. A more dynamic competitive rivalry requires market-shaping decisions; setting rules in order to ensure incentives for investment and innovation.[38] The potential for inquiries to be part of changing the rules governing markets for healthier competition is in line with the code of conduct to govern the imposition of charges on suppliers by large supermarket chains, as enforced in the United Kingdom following an inquiry and the establishment of the Groceries Code Adjudicator.[39] In South Africa, this route was not taken up, although these concerns are reflected in the provisions under the amended Act on buyer power with agroprocessing and grocery retail as designated sectors. Instead, South Africa has followed a different policy response to the GRMI recommendations. Through the gazetting of the National Small Enterprise Amendment Bill 2020 in December 2020, the Department of Small Business Development aims to implement an economy-wide intervention that would see the introduction of a small business ombudsman who will facilitate the resolution of disputes, including around unfair

---

[37] Intergovernmental Fintech Working Group (IFWG), at fn. 5.

[38] Mondliwa/Goga/Roberts, Competition, productive capabilities and structural transformation in South Africa, (2021) 33 *European Journal of Development Research*, 253.

[39] GCA website: https://www.gov.uk/government/organisations/groceries-code-adjudicator.

trading practices, between small businesses in all sectors and their trading partners.[40]

Lastly, some inquiries in South Africa have been framed to examine evidence on broad issues of public policy. This is most notable in the case of the HMI which took around seven years, from the initial notice to the final report and had a very substantial cost. The inquiry itself recognised that the issues in private healthcare extended beyond markets and competition to the wider policy framework for healthcare overall. A competition inquiry is clearly not a substitute for facing up to the essential policy choices.

---

[40] South African Government News Agency, Bill paves way for legal service for small enterprises, 11 December 2020, available at https://www.sanews.gov.za/south-africa/bill-paves-way-legal-service-small-enterprises.

7 | An Economic Evaluation of the EC's Proposed "New Competition Tool"[*]

GREGORY S. CRAWFORD, PATRICK REY,
AND MONIKA SCHNITZER

7.1 Introduction

On June 2, 2020, the European Commission (EC) announced an initiative to consider the development and introduction of a "New Competition Tool" (NCT) at the European level to "address structural competition problems in a timely and effective manner."[1] Commentators have drawn analogies between the NCT and the United Kingdom's "markets regime," which empowers the UK competition regulator, the Competition and Markets Authority (CMA), to initiate market studies and investigations to "[ensure] that competition and markets work well for consumers."[2]

As members of the Economic Advisory Group on Competition Policy (EAGCP) of the EC's DG Competition, in June 2020 we were asked by the Chief Economist to assess the economic merits of the proposed NCT. While our mandate was unrestricted, we were encouraged to review the United Kingdom's markets regime and assess the economic foundations of the theories of harm investigated across a range of cases and whether they could apply in markets and/or sectors other than those specifically considered in a given case.

---

[*] We would like to thank Julie Bon, Adam Land, and Chris Warner at the CMA for helpful conversations about the United Kingdom's markets regime.

[1] See https://ec.europa.eu/commission/presscorner/detail/en/ip_20_977 for the press release announcing the initiative and https://ec.europa.eu/info/law/better-regulation/have-your-say/initiatives/12416-New-competition-tool for further details.

[2] Crafts/Hirst, Comment: New EU antitrust power to tackle "structural" problems eyes algorithms, tacit collusion, 2020, MLex, available at https://mlexmarketinsight.com/news-hub/editors-picks/area-of-expertise/antitrust/new-eu-antitrust-power-to-tackle-structural-problems-eyes-algorithms-tacit-collusion; CMA, Market Studies and Market Investigations: Supplemental guidance on the CMA's approach, 2014, updated version (last revised: July 5, 2017), available at https://assets.publishing.service.gov.uk/government/uploads/system/uploads/attachment_data/file/624706/cma3-markets-supplemental-guidance-updated-june-2017.pdf (hereafter CMA3).

This is what we have done.[3] In Section 7.2, we briefly review the "Inception Impact Assessment" describing the EC's motivation for the NCT. In Section 7.3, we describe the United Kingdom's markets regime and survey some of the competition concerns the regime is intended to address. In Section 7.4, we provide a selective review of UK market studies and investigations to illustrate some of the ways these concerns have been explored. We also describe the remedies imposed or proposed (in the case of market studies or ongoing investigations).

Finally, in Section 7.5, we provide a critical evaluation of the functioning of the United Kingdom's markets regime in light of this evidence and offer seven recommendations regarding the merits and design of a New Competition Tool:

— For markets where harm has "already affected the market":

We see a strong case for the introduction of a New Competition Tool (Rec1) with a broad scope both within and across sectors (Rec2) to address factors like those covered by the United Kingdom's markets regime that prevent effective competition in markets. Such a NCT should strongly consider including a consumer protection mandate (Rec3).

— For markets where harm is "about to affect the market":

We agree that there are economic characteristics of markets that foster concentration in the long run. It is therefore important to identify markets with such characteristics, maintain a high level of awareness about their evolution (Rec4), and have a lower threshold for investigating whether they are functioning well and whether they are likely to function well in the near future (Rec5).

If such markets have not yet achieved high levels of concentration and an investigation has found features that are impeding competitive outcomes, fostering competition "in the market" requires remedying limitations on multi-homing and on

---

[3] Readers interested in this topic may also wish to see Fletcher, Chapter 8, as well as the CMA's own filing in this matter: CMA, The CMA's response to the European Commission's consultations in relation to the Digital Services Act package and New Competition Tool, 2020, available at https://assets.publishing .service.gov.uk/government/uploads/system/uploads/attachment_data/file/ 917455/CMA-response_to_DSA_and_NCT_consultations.pdf.

customer and/or supplier switching behavior as well as remedying "offensive" leveraging of firms with market power in an adjacent market into the market exhibiting factors that encourage long-run concentration (Rec6a).

If such markets have already achieved high levels of concentration and an investigation has found features that are impeding competitive outcomes, fostering competition "for the market" requires remedying limitations by dominant incumbent(s) on multi-homing and on customer/supplier switching as well as remedying "defensive" leveraging of firms with market power in the concentrated market into any adjacent market (often) providing complementary goods or services; new entrants and challengers may instead be exempted from these remedies (Rec6b).

– The implementation of a New Competition Tool requires a careful design of its governance structure to safeguard appropriate checks and balances (Rec7)

Our assessment was submitted to the Chief Economist of DG Competition in October 2020 and published on the EU Commission's website, along with other expert reports gathered in this volume.[4] In December 2020, the European Commission published its proposal for the Digital Markets Act (DMA). The proposal is limited to digital markets and focusses on ex ante rules for gatekeeper platforms. It includes provisions for the use of market investigations for three purposes: to examine whether a provider of core platform services should be designated as a gatekeeper (Article 15), to establish whether a gatekeeper has systematically infringed the regulations of the DMA (Article 16), and to investigate whether new core platform services or new practices that may limit contestability should be considered (Article 17).

The EU Commission has not, however, pursued the idea of implementing the New Competition Tool as a complementary tool for the structural competition problems that current EU competition law under Articles 101 and 102 of the Treaty on the Functioning of the European Union (TFEU) and the proposed ex ante regulation of digital platforms through the DMA cannot address or cannot address well.

---

[4] The expert reports on the New Competition Tool are available at https://ec .europa.eu/competition-policy/public-consultations/2020-new-comp-tool_en.

As we argue in this chapter, we see a strong case for the introduction of a New Competition Tool to address factors that prevent effective competition in markets, and we see no benefit to limiting it to specific sectors and to dominant firms. Thus, we strongly encourage to follow up on designing such a policy tool for the European Union in due course.

7.2 The Mandate for the NCT

The EC's Inception Impact Assessment and accompanying press release provide the context and mandate for the proposed New Competition Tool, enumerate alternative policy options for its scope, and describe likely impacts (among other things). In this section, we summarize the salient elements of this proposal for evaluating the economic foundations of the tool.

The NCT seeks to "[address] gaps in the current EU competition rules and [allow] for timely and effective intervention against structural competition problems across markets." In particular, the EC highlights "three pillars for the fair functioning of markets": enforcing current EU competition law under Articles 101 and 102 TFEU, potential ex ante regulation of digital platforms, especially those that play a "gate-keeper" role, and the NCT for structural competition problems that either of the first two pillars cannot address or cannot address well.[5]

The impact assessment emphasizes two types of structural competition problems. The first is where harm has already affected the market due to a "structural lack of competition" that prevents such markets from delivering competitive outcomes (e.g., due to its underlying economic structure or the conduct of firms in the market). Specific examples provided include markets with extreme concentration, entry barriers, consumer lock-in, lack of access to an essential input (e.g., data), and oligopoly markets with increased risk for tacit collusion, particularly those featuring increased transparency due to pricing and related strategies based on algorithmic decision-making.

The second type of structural competition problem identified is where harm "is about to affect the market," that is, where there are "structural risks for competition" such that the economic structure and/or conduct of firms in the market create a threat to competitive

---

[5] See Motta/Peitz, Chapter 2 and Schweitzer, Chapter 3.

outcomes (e.g., "tipping markets" where the economic fundamentals favor winner-take-most outcomes). Specific examples include markets with extreme economies of scale and/or scope, strong network effects, multi-sidedness, lack of multi-homing, and lock-in effects, where "the risks for competition can arise through the creation of powerful market players with an entrenched market and/or gatekeeper position, the emergence of which could be prevented by early intervention." The EC also notes that "while these characteristics are typical of digital markets, they can also be found in non-digital markets" and that "with the increasing digitalization of the economy, more and more markets will exhibit these characteristics."

The EC proposes four policy options for the limits of the proposed tool depending on two characteristics: (a) whether it would apply to all sectors of the economy versus just those sectors in which the structural factors identified above would be most prevalent ("horizontal scope" versus "limited scope") and (b) whether it would apply to dominant firms versus all firms ("dominance-based" versus "market structure-based").

Proposed remedies would be limited to what is necessary to ensure the proper functioning of the market and could include both behavioral and structural ones. Furthermore, remedies would be imposed without the finding of an infringement by any firm; hence, no fines would arise nor would there be the possibility of follow-on damages claims against firms in the affected sector. Rights of defense and judicial review would be respected, although no details were provided.

7.3 The UK's "Markets Regime"

7.3.1 Introduction

Parts of the proposed New Competition Tool resemble closely the United Kingdom's regime for market studies and market investigations (together the United Kingdom's "markets regime"). As we will show in what follows, the first type of structural competition problem proposed by the EC, where harm has "already affected the market," maps well to the United Kingdom's markets regime once one allows for the potential addition of algorithmic collusion. In what follows, we briefly describe the mandate for the United Kingdom's markets regime and the competition concerns the regime is intended to address.

7.3.2 Motivation for and Structure of the UK's Markets Regime

The United Kingdom's markets regime was created by the Enterprise Act 2002.[6] The regime was then amended by the general reform of UK competition law embodied in the Enterprise and Regulatory Reform Act 2013, which combined the separate responsibilities of the Competition Commission (CC) and Office of Fair Trading (OFT) into the newly created Competition and Markets Authority (CMA). The CMA offers guidance for stakeholders in the markets regime via policy documents that we briefly summarize here.[7]

The CMA's goal is to "[ensure] that competition and markets work well for consumers."[8] It seeks to achieve this by "promoting and protecting consumer interests throughout the UK, while ensuring that businesses are fair and competitive" (OFT519). To facilitate this goal, the CMA has the power to initiate market studies and, subject to various criteria being met, market investigations. Market studies and investigations were previously conducted by the OFT and CC, respectively, and within the combined CMA there are different decision-makers and governance structures for market studies and any subsequent market investigation.

Market studies "are examinations into the causes of why particular markets are not working well for consumers, leading to proposals as to how they might be made to work better" (OFT519). They are "one of a number of tools at the [CMA's] disposal to address competition or consumer protection problems, alongside its enforcement and advocacy activities." What distinguishes market studies from these other tools is that it "can look beyond individual abuses of dominance, agreements that reduce competition, or breaches of specific consumer protection legislation, and consider all aspects of market structure and conduct .... Looking at the whole market also provides the

---

[6] See Whish, Chapter 5.

[7] We have relied primarily on three UK markets regime guidance documents: CMA3 (fn. 3), at p. 1; OFT, Market studies: Guidance on the OFT approach, 2010, available at https://assets.publishing.service.gov.uk/government/uploads/system/uploads/attachment_data/file/284421/oft519.pdf (hereafter OFT519); and OFT, Market investigation references: Guidance about the making of references under Part 4 of the Enterprise Act, 2014, available at https://assets.publishing.service.gov.uk/government/uploads/system/uploads/attachment_data/file/284399/oft511.pdf (hereafter OFT511).

[8] See Fletcher, Chapter 8.

opportunity to address factors that may affect productivity which are beyond the scope of enforcement tools."[9]

The CMA Board initiates market studies based on a range of sources, including complaints from consumers and/or businesses, enforcement actions, referrals from other government departments, including regulatory bodies, and their own research. The process of a market study is transparent with significant stakeholder engagement, clear milestones, and a statutory time limit (12 months). The CMA has formal investigative powers to conduct such studies. A range of outcomes are possible, from a clean bill of health to consumer-focused actions, recommendations to businesses or the government, individual enforcement actions, or a market investigation reference. If the CMA Board decides a market investigation reference is to be made, it refers the matter to the CMA Chair, who constitutes the "market reference group" that will ultimately decide on the results of the investigation (with individuals different from those that made the decision to refer it for investigation). There are three types of market investigation references: "cross-market references" (where a specific feature or combination of features existing in more than one market can be investigated without the need to investigate the whole of each market concerned), "public interest references" (where the Secretary of State refers a matter to the CMA for investigation of competition issues while it investigates public interest issues for the same matter), and "ordinary references" (where neither of the previous two considerations apply).

The CMA Board may make a market investigation reference where "it has reasonable grounds for suspecting that any feature, or combination of features, of a market in the United Kingdom for goods or services prevents, restricts, or distorts competition in connection with the supply or acquisition of any goods or services in the UK or a part of the UK" (OFT511). Such a feature or combination of features constitutes an "adverse effect on competition" (AEC).

Market investigations are more detailed investigations into whether there is an AEC in the market(s) for the goods or services referred. If AECs are found, they also enable the CMA to impose remedies.[10]

---

[9] For further discussion of the role of the United Kingdom's market studies relative to these other tools, see OFT519 (fn. 5), at p. 3, at paras. 2.13–2.19.

[10] Note that while a market investigation is usually preceded by a market study, it may also be initiated upon receipt of a "super-complaint" by a designated consumer rights organization (CMA3 [fn. 3], at p. 1, at para. 1.12).

Market features are broadly defined and include (1) the economic structure of the market, (2) the conduct of sellers in a market, and/or (importantly) (3) the conduct of customers in a market. The CMA notes that "market investigation references are ... likely to focus on competition problems arising from uncoordinated parallel conduct by several firms or industry-wide features of a market in cases where the [CMA] does not have reasonable grounds to suspect the existence of anti-competitive agreements or dominance."[11]

As for market studies, the process of a market investigation is transparent with significant stakeholder engagement, clear milestones, a statutory time limit (18 months, extendible to 24), and comes with formal investigative powers. If the investigation finds an AEC, the CMA is obligated to consider how to "remedy, mitigate, or prevent" the AEC and either take action itself or recommend others (e.g., government) to take action. If it chooses to take action itself, it can accept "undertakings" (remedies) or issue an order. There are again formal procedures for the remedy stage of a market investigation, including a statutory time limit (6 months, extendible to 10) and duration and effectiveness considerations. The CMA may also impose interim measures but only after the publication of the final market investigation report.

Parties may lodge an appeal of the findings of a market investigation within two months of the publication of the final report. This is done before the Competition Appeal Tribunal (CAT), a specialist "court" created at the same time as the markets regime for the purpose of hearing appeals of various CMA decisions (among other responsibilities).[12] Appeals may only be made on grounds of "Judicial Review," that is, whether the CMA followed appropriate procedures in taking a decision, not on the merits of the facts and arguments on which the original decision was based.[13] Further appeals against CAT judgments can, if permitted, go to the Court of Appeal and ultimately to the UK Supreme Court.

---

[11] For further discussion of the role of the United Kingdom's market investigations relative to these other tools, see OFT511 (fn. 5), at p. 3, at paras. 2.2–2.8; and its (pre-Brexit) role relative to EC competition law, see OFT511 (fn. 5), at p. 3, para. 2.9–2.18.

[12] CMA3 (fn. 3), at p. 1, at para. 3.63–3.64.

[13] See https://www.regulation.org.uk/competition-regime.html and Fletcher, Chapter 8.

7.3.3 Market Characteristics of Concern

As described in Section 7.3.2, market investigations are initiated when the CMA has grounds to believe that characteristics of a market may cause an adverse effect on competition. These characteristics can be of three types: those arising from structural (economic) features of a market, those arising from firms' conduct in that market, and those arising from customers' (often consumers') conduct.[14] We briefly summarize the most empirically salient of these characteristics here; see OFT511, chapters 5–7, for further details. In Section 7.3.4, we survey a range of market studies and investigations that illustrate the economic harms that may arise from these characteristics and discuss the remedies imposed to address those harms.

Structural features of a market that may cause concerns about the effectiveness of competition in the market include high and stable market concentration (e.g., monopoly and oligopoly markets), the extent of vertical integration in the market; conditions of entry, exit, and market expansion; government regulations; and the extent of informational asymmetries between consumers and firms.

Aspects of firm conduct in a market that may cause such concerns include oligopoly conduct, especially but not exclusively tacit collusion, so-called facilitating practices (i.e., business practices such as price announcements that might facilitate reaching tacit understandings among competitors), the "custom and practice" of firms in a market (e.g., a norm of all firms charging the same fee for underwriting or estate agency), and networks of vertical agreements (e.g., selective purchasing or distribution agreements or MFN clauses).

The UK markets regime's focus on competition and markets "working well" means that it *also* looks at aspects of consumer behavior that may inhibit good outcomes. Aspects of consumer conduct in a market that may cause concerns that it is not working well include consumers' inability to act, for example, due to search or switching costs, consumers' susceptibility to "behavioral biases," and/or that the

---

[14] The first two of these categories may remind academics of the Structure-Conduct-Performance paradigm that governed Industrial Organization (IO) research through the 1980s. The markets regime does not presume that the chain of causality goes from structure to conduct to performance; rather, it argues that all of structure, conduct, and performance may be factors that inform an investigation into the functioning of competition in a market.

costs of consumers obtaining the information necessary to make informed choices may exceed likely future benefits (e.g., for learning about firms' privacy policies).

We close this section with two comments on the scope of the UK markets regime. First, we note that while harms from many of these market characteristics or conduct surveyed above would often fall under the purview of a competition authority, others would often be considered under consumer protection rules. The United Kingdom's combination of competition and consumer protection responsibilities in the CMA is therefore an important underlying foundation of this markets regime. Second, we note that, for those topics that indeed are related to competition, these market characteristics and/or conduct would not be likely to trigger investigations on the grounds of abuse of dominance or anti-competitive agreements. We return to both of these points in Section 7.5, when we make recommendations for the EC's NCT based on the UK experience.

7.4 Economic Harms in Theory and Practice: A Selective Review of UK Market Studies and Investigations

In this section, we illustrate how a selection of the market characteristics, firm conduct, and consumer conduct surveyed in Section 7.3 have been investigated in specific UK product markets and describe the remedies adopted to address any adverse effects on competition.[15]

7.4.1 Tacit Collusion

Tacit collusion is the practice of firms in an oligopoly coordinating their actions despite not having an explicit cartel agreement. Economic research has shown that if firms are patient, they can raise prices and profits above competitive levels using a range of dynamic strategies. Article 101 of the TFEU can deal with explicit collusion and associated facilitating practices but cannot address purely tacit collusion.

In its 2014 market investigation of aggregates, cement, and ready-mix concrete, the Competition Commission found evidence that the cement industry was prone to tacit collusion: there were structural

---

[15] All of the market studies and investigations cited here are available from the CMA's "Markets" page at https://www.gov.uk/topic/competition/markets.

factors facilitating tacit collusion (high market concentration), unilateral conduct enhancing market transparency (generic price announcements), indirect evidence of tacitly collusive behavior (supracompetitive return on capital and stable or increasing margins despite decreasing demand), and direct evidence of collusive strategies (tit-for-tat strategies and cross-selling).

To address this issue, the Competition Commission imposed two types of remedies. First, to reduce the concentration, it imposed the divestiture of production capacity to a new competitor. Second, to reduce market transparency, it imposed a ban on generic price announcements: firms were required to stop addressing uniform letters to customers and negotiate instead on a bilateral basis. The 2011 market investigation into local bus services also found that the conditions existed for tacit collusion.

7.4.2 Demand-Side Problems (Asymmetric Info/Behavioral Issues)

The UK markets regime is empowered to look not only at the structure of economic markets and firms' conduct in those markets but also consumer behavior and its impact on achieving competitive market outcomes. Many market studies and investigations have found informational asymmetries between consumers and firms that plausibly increase search costs, as well as "behavior frictions" such as default bias and contextual factors that limit consumer engagement, plausibly increasing switching costs. Search and switching costs, in turn, limit the substitutability of demand between alternative suppliers of products and services, raising prices relative to what they would be in their absence.

In its investigation of retail banking services started in 2014, the CMA concluded that the market was dominated by a small number of high street banks. While the investigation found no conclusive evidence that market concentration had an effect on competitive behavior, the CMA concluded that new entrants had a positive effect on the market by introducing new business models and innovative products. Yet, new entrants and smaller banks gained market share only slowly because customers switched very little even though switching would have provided them with significant savings. The investigation found that current (checking) accounts for both personal and business customers had complicated and opaque fee structures that made it difficult for customers to judge service quality and the true costs of an account and for businesses to find out the best lender.

To reduce this lack of transparency and overcome behavioral biases, the CMA imposed a number of disclosure and behavioral remedies. For example, banks were required to send occasional reminders to customers to review their banking situation; to develop and implement an open API (Application Programming Interface) standard to permit authorized intermediaries to access information about bank services, prices, and service quality; and to provide better information by publishing core indicators of service quality. This "Open Banking" initiative allowed banking customers to share their current account data with trusted third parties using this secure, standardized API, and permitted digital comparison tools to make customized pricing offers based on a secure and accurate view of a customer's existing accounts and recent financial activity.

To avoid customers paying overly high overdraft charges, banks were required to alert customers, when going into unarranged overdrafts, to grant a grace period when such events occurred and to set a ceiling on unarranged overdraft charges in the form of a maximum monthly charge. To improve information for small businesses, the largest banks were required to develop online tools allowing small businesses to receive tailored information on eligibility and pricing for lending products.

The large number of market studies and investigations involving demand-side considerations has permitted the CMA to assess the effectiveness of remedies seeking to address these concerns. Published jointly with the Financial Conduct Authority (FCA) and using examples from a host of market investigations, FCA and CMA (2018) found that the effectiveness of disclosure remedies to address demand-side problems in markets is mixed, with some improving consumer engagement while others being ineffective. Disclosure alone was found to not always be enough to influence consumers' decisions.[16] A concluding chapter usefully summarizes a set of

---

[16] FCA and CMA, Helping people get a better deal: Learning lessons about consumer facing remedies, 2018, available at https://assets.publishing.service .gov.uk/government/uploads/system/uploads/attachment_data/file/744521/ UKCN_consumer_remedies_project_-_lessons_learned_report.pdf. See also Fletcher, The role of demand-side remedies in driving effective competition:

high-level principles about the selection, design, and testing of consumer-facing remedies to maximize their effectiveness.

7.4.3 High and Stable Concentration and Barriers to Entry and Expansion

One of the primary principles in economics is that concentrated markets typically result in prices in excess of those that would arise in competitive markets. In such settings, the competitive process provides incentives for rival firms to enter the market, expanding their business by undercutting existing incumbents and improving outcomes for consumers. When this does not occur, it suggests the possibility that potential new entrants face barriers to entry and expansion. High and stable concentration with limited entry and expansion is therefore a natural competition concern.

As described in Section 7.4.2, the CMA concluded in its investigation of retail banking services that new entrants and smaller banks gained market share only slowly because customers switched very little. While there was already a Current Account Switch Service (CASS) in place, customers were not always aware of it or did not have enough confidence in it, so that its introduction only marginally increased switching.[17] The CMA's remedies, in particular its introduction of the Open Banking standard, was designed to further facilitate switching by requiring banks to provide transparent information on their charges and service quality (see Section 7.4.2), by allowing their customers to share their own bank data securely with third parties using this standard and by extending the period during which payments are redirected in case of switching. There are now over 150 new providers of banking services active in the market (largely account information and payment services) and a similar number seeking to enter. These services are already being used by 2 million consumers

---

A review for Which?, 2016, available at https://www.staticwhich.co.uk/documents/pdf/the-role-of-demand-side-remedies-in-driving-effective-competition-456067.pdf.

[17] FCA, Making current account switching easier: The effectiveness of the Current Account Switching Service (CASS) and evidence on account number portability, 2015, available at https://www.fca.org.uk/publication/research/making-current-account-switching-easier.pdf.

and small/medium businesses, with the number doubling every six months.[18]

In its 2009 investigation of the BAA airports, the CC found that BAA's airports controlled 81 percent of London's runway capacity and serviced 62 percent of UK passengers and concluded that there was no competition between the seven airports owned by the BAA. Based on this conclusion, the CC was concerned that BAA was investing too little and providing poor service at their London airports. To improve the situation, it required BAA to sell its London-area Gatwick and Stansted airports as well as Edinburgh airport, with the expectation that this would give the airport owners greater incentives to respond to customers' needs.

In 2015/2016, the CMA carried out an ex post evaluation of the remedies imposed.[19] The evaluation found downward pressure on prices and an improvement in customer service. The fact that post-divestment traffic increased more in divested airports than in other UK airports, controlling for long-term trends, was seen as evidence that consumers benefited from the structural remedies in the form of improved connectivity and choice.

7.4.4 Restrictive Contract Terms

Article 101 of the TFEU addresses anti-competitive provisions in inter-firm agreements, and Article 102 deals with restrictive terms imposed by dominant firms to their customers, including final consumers; by contrast, restrictions imposed by nondominant firms on final consumers fall outside the scope of these Articles, even though they can significantly alter the functioning of a market.

In its 2006 market investigation of liquefied petroleum gas (LPG), the Competition Commission found that switching between suppliers was low, despite price differences among them and price discrimination by suppliers against their long-term consumers. Among the key impediments to customer switching identified by the CC were

---

[18] See https://www.openbanking.org.uk/.

[19] CMA, BAA Airports: Evaluation of the Competition Commission's 2009 market investigation remedies, 2015, updated version (last revised: May 16, 2016), available at https://assets.publishing.service.gov.uk/media/ 57399d43ed915d152d00000b/evaluation_of_baa__market_investigation_ remedies.pdf.

contractual tank replacement provisions requiring the physical replacement of tanks when a customer switched supplier and contractual restrictions on switching.

A first set of simple remedies, aimed at forbidding or limiting some of most restrictive provisions, imposed changes to customer contracts (e.g., limiting notice periods to no more than 42 days and exclusivity periods to no more than two years). A more complex set of remedies was adopted to deal with the tank replacement practice. These included granting customers the right to request a tank transfer (of ownership) and giving incoming suppliers the right to buy the existing tank from an outgoing supplier, at a price negotiated by the supplier on behalf of the consumer, subject to an obligation on the outgoing supplier to sell for a maximum 'backstop price' determined by a specified methodology.

Market investigations have also found and sought to remedy significant contractual restrictions in the markets for groceries (restrictive covenants and exclusivity arrangements for land use), audit services (provisions in loan agreements restricting a company's choice of auditor), and motor insurance (wide price parity clauses). The last investigation involved four large price comparison websites that each had wide MFN clauses in their contracts, terms which were banned as a consequence of the investigation. This is interesting not only because it involved a restriction that is popular among online platforms but also because it illustrated the use of the United Kingdom's markets regime where the cumulative effects of strategies undertaken by non-dominant firms can be important.

7.4.5 *Complementary Goods and Vertical Relationships*

Markets for complementary goods and/or vertical relationships introduce the possibility that market conditions in one market may "spill over" into other "adjacent" markets. For example, the economic literature has found that tying and/or bundling of (esp. complementary) goods can exclude efficient entrants, particularly if there are increasing returns to scale in the potentially competitive market.[20] Similarly, the

---

[20] See, e.g., Whinston, Tying, foreclosure, and exclusion, (1990) 80 *American Economic Review*, 837; Carlton/Waldman, The strategic use of tying to preserve and create market power in evolving industries, (2002) 33 *Rand Journal of*

economic literature has found that vertical linkages can provide incentives for firms with market power at one level of a supply chain to profitably raise rivals' costs or refuse them supply or access, causing consumer harm.[21]

The 2009 Payment Protection Insurance (PPI) investigations dealt with (arguably) complementary goods. PPI is insurance that covers payments on credit purchased by consumers for a variety of credit products (e.g., credit cards, personal loans, and/or first or second mortgages) in the case of an adverse life event for the borrower (e.g., an accident or illness). PPI sales were often made at the point of sale of the credit product, with the credit distributor receiving a commission. There was concern over the size of these commissions (ranging from 40 to 80 percent of the gross premium paid by consumers), causing consumers in many cases to face a combined (credit + PPI) annual percentage rate of interest between 1.3 and 2.9 times as large as that on credit alone.

The investigation found that distributors were not actively competing for customers, that customers were limited in their ability to obtain the information necessary to compare PPI costs across providers, and that there were barriers to switching. Remedies included significantly greater information provision, including a personal quote that incorporated PPI costs, recommendations to the FCA, and unbundling to foster greater consumer choice and competition. In particular, PPI could no longer be offered at the credit point of sale or within seven days of the credit purchase.

The 2014 Private Healthcare investigation also included concerns about vertical issues and the potential conflicts of interest it can induce. The investigation focused on the provision of privately funded healthcare services provided by hospitals, particularly those in central London. It found high barriers to entry and expansion and weak competitive constraints, causing higher prices than would otherwise

---

Economics, 194; and Choi/Stefanadis, Tying, investment, and the dynamic leverage theory, (2001) 32(1) *Rand Journal of Economics*, 52.

[21] See, e.g., Hart/Tirole, Vertical integration and market foreclosure, (1990) *Brookings Papers on Economic Activity (Microeconomics)*, 205; Ordover/Saloner/Salop, Equilibrium market foreclosure, (1990) 80 *American Economic Review*, 127; and Allain/Chambolle/Rey, Vertical integration as a source of holdup, (2016) 83(1) *The Review of Economic Studies*, 1.

have arisen for both inpatient and some outpatient procedures.[22] It also investigated the incentives provided by private hospitals to referring clinicians, finding that the value of some direct benefits in exchange for patient referrals (cash payments early in the period, equity interests later) and their lack of transparency were likely to adversely affect competition between hospitals. As a remedy, it imposed a range of bans and restrictions seeking to prevent there being any incentive for a clinician to refer patients to the sponsoring hospitals' facilities for tests or treatments.

7.4.6 Essential Inputs

Access to an essential input is a specific example of the type of vertical concern articulated above (i.e., a firm may choose to limit access to an essential input to impact competition in downstream markets). Article 102 of the TFEU can deal with access to an "essential facility" owned or controlled by a dominant firm, and Article 101 can deal with specific inter-firm agreements restricting competition by limiting access to key resources. However, these Articles are less well suited to address access issues resulting from the interaction of multiple agreements and market-wide practices.

In its 2014 market investigation of aggregates, cement, and ready-mix concrete, introduced in Section 7.4.1, the Competition Commission also found that two firms had monopolized one market segment (GGBS, a component for a particular type of cement obtained as a by-product of steel production). Lafarge Tarmac had secured exclusivity for the raw input (BS) from all British steel producers and transformed into granulates (GBS), whereas Hanson had secured exclusivity for these granulates, which it ground to produce GGBS. As a result, Hanson was the sole supplier of GGBS in Great Britain.

To remedy this situation, the Competition Commission required both the divestiture by Hanson of one of its three active GGBS production facilities and that Lafarge Tarmac provide the acquirer with access to GBS on a secure and cost-effective basis, in such a way as to enable the acquirer to participate in any future expansion of the GGBS market.

---

[22] The basis for this decision was revisited in a 2016 Remittal Private Healthcare investigation when the CAT found that the foundation for the conclusion regarding higher prices had been based on an analysis that had an error.

The 2011 buses market investigation also touched on access to essential inputs. While there were many local bus operators, 69 percent of services were provided by one of five large operators and local bus markets were frequently monopoly or duopoly markets. Among other AECs, the CMA found barriers to entry and expansion; customer conduct, particularly their purchase and use of single-operator multi-journey tickets; and operator conduct, including exclusionary behavior and tacit coordination, were factors limiting good consumer outcomes in the market. Remedies included recommendations to Local Transport Authorities and the OFT to design and implement multi-operator ticketing schemes (a form of interoperability) and requirements that operators provide access to bus stations to rival operators on fair, reasonable, and non-discriminatory ("FRAND") terms.

7.4.7 Omnibus Case: Online Platforms and Digital Advertising

The most recent CMA market study on online platforms and digital advertising is particularly useful as it incorporates almost all of the competition concerns summarized in Sections 7.4.1–7.4.6. It also is unique among the United Kingdom's market studies and investigations in that it analyzes digital markets characterized by significant economies of scale and network effects, key characteristics in the proposed design of the New Competition Tool. For both of these reasons, we survey it in some detail.

The digital advertising market study found that Google and Facebook have market power in search and social media, that consumers do not have adequate control over the use of their data by online platforms, and that a lack of transparency, conflicts of interest, and the leveraging of market power undermine competition in the market. It concluded that, as a result, consumers have been harmed due to reduced innovation, higher prices for goods and services passed on from higher advertising prices, inadequate compensation for their attention and use of their data, insufficient control over how their personal data were used, and that there have been wider social, political, and cultural harm via its negative impact on authoritative and reliable news media.

The study found that six characteristics of these markets "inhibit entry and expansion by rivals and undermine effective competition."[23] The first, *network effects and economies of scale*, is an important factor producing extreme concentration (see concern raised in Section 7.4.3): Google benefits from significantly greater scale in the "click-and-query" data used to train search algorithms and Facebook benefits from significant direct and indirect network effects within and between users and developers.

The second characteristic is the *nature of consumer decision-making and the power of defaults* in this market (see concern raised in Section 7.4.2). The study found that defaults impact both consumers' initial choice of search engines as well as the ability of Google and Facebook to collect data about their users, concluding that these platforms' "choice architecture" (i.e., the design of the ways in which consumers make decisions on their platforms) and use of defaults inhibits consumers' ability to make informed choices.

The third characteristic is *unequal access to consumer data*. The study concluded that user data is highly valuable for targeting digital advertising, making it (in our words) an essential input (see concern raised in Section 7.4.6). This data includes user demographics and interests, as well as the ability to track user actions both online (using analytical tools such as ad and click tags) and offline (using consumers' locations). The study concluded that the inability of smaller platforms and publishers to access user data creates a significant barrier to entry (see concern raised in Section 7.4.3).

The fourth characteristic is *lack of transparency*. Given the complexity of real-time online advertising decision-making, the study found that both publishers and advertisers find it difficult to understand how decisions are made and to exercise choice effectively. The study concluded that this lack of transparency can create or exacerbate competition problems, for example, letting these platforms overstate quality, limit the ability of publishers to evaluate the effectiveness of their advertising, and undermine the ability of market participants to make informed choices (a guiding principle of the concern raised in Section 7.4.2).

[23] CMA, Online platforms and digital advertising market study, 2019, updated version (last revised: July 1, 2020), para. 21, available at https://assets.publishing.service.gov.uk/media/5fa557668fa8f5788db46efc/Final_report_Digital_ALT_TEXT.pdf.

The final two characteristics are *the importance of "ecosystems" of complementary products and services* and *vertical integration and conflicts of interests*. When platforms with market power own complementary services in potentially competitive adjacent markets, they have an incentive and ability to leverage their market power into these markets (see concern raised in Section 7.4.5), and the study concluded that Google has done so in both the market for (advertiser) demand-side platform services and throughout the "ad tech stack" (the online advertising supply chain).

Despite finding significant adverse effects on competition, the CMA chose *not* to initiate a market investigation, preferring instead to recommend to the UK government that they create a "pro-competition ex ante regulatory regime" through the creation of a digital regulator, the Digital Markets Unit (DMU).[24] That being said, the market study described in detail proposed remedies that it concluded would be appropriate to address the AECs it found.

The recommended remedies consisted of an *enforceable code of conduct* and a range of pro-competitive interventions. The code of conduct was based around three high-level objectives: fair trading, open choices, and trust and transparency. Each objective further articulated principles of platform behavior that would apply under that objective, including obligations for fair and reasonable contract terms, non-discrimination requirements, and platform design and communication strategies to enhance transparency and consumer choice.[25]

The recommended pro-competitive interventions included (1) increasing consumer control over their data (by requiring platforms give consumers the choice not to share their data and placing a duty for "Fairness by Design"), (2) mandating interoperability (for Facebook/ social networks), (3) mandating third-party access to data (for Google/ search engines and in online advertising markets), (4) lowering data barriers to entry (by mandating data separation/data silos, introducing user and transaction IDs, and enhancing data mobility), (5) restricting

---

[24] This was also the recommendation of the report of the Digital Competition Expert Panel sponsored by the UK government and released in March 2019 titled "Unlocking Digital Competition," available at https://assets.publishing.service.gov.uk/government/uploads/system/uploads/attachment_data/file/785547/unlocking_digital_competition_furman_review_web.pdf.

[25] See CMA (fn. 20), at p. 11, para. 7.74–7.89, for further details.

these platforms' ability to obtain default positions and introducing consumer choice screens, and (6) requiring separation (either operational or divestiture) to address foreclosure and conflicts of interest concerns.

With the publishing of its final report, the market study stage of the CMA's interest in the online advertising market is finished. In partnership with the Information Commissioner's Office, the United Kingdom's data protection authority, and Ofcom, the United Kingdom's communications regulator, the CMA is now considering further details about the design and implementation of the DMU via a Digital Markets Taskforce, which will provide specific recommendations to the UK government before the end of 2020.

7.5 Recommendations

In this section, we provide recommendations regarding the merits and design of the EC's proposed New Competition Tool based on a critical review of the UK experience summarized in Sections 7.3 and 7.4. We divide our recommendations into three parts: (1) for markets where harm has already affected the market due to a "structural lack of competition," (2) for markets where harm has not yet occurred, but there are "structural risks for competition" due to economic factors that favor long-run concentration, and (3) procedural recommendations.

7.5.1 A Critical Review of the Selected Case Studies

In our view, the case studies summarized in Section 7.4 present convincing evidence of the merits of the United Kingdom's markets regime. The competition concerns highlighted in each of the sections are both credible and outside of the scope of existing enforcement tools. Furthermore, the care and quality of the market studies and investigations provided evidence establishing that these concerns are not purely theoretical but have caused harm to competition and consumers in the surveyed markets.

While there is limited ex post evidence on the effectiveness of the remedies imposed to address these competition concerns outside those addressing consumer-facing harms summarized in Section 7.4.2 (and here the evidence is mixed), we see considerable merit in the remedies imposed to address structural factors limiting competitive outcomes in the aggregates and airports investigations summarized in Sections 7.4.1 and 7.4.3, as well as the limitations on contractual restrictions, vertical conflicts of interest, and essential inputs described in the market studies and investigations covering the LPG, private healthcare, aggregates, and digital advertising sections summarized in Sections 7.4.4–7.4.6. They are well-supported by economic reasoning, well-targeted to address the specified concerns, and proportionate. This review of the UK experience suggests several recommendations for the New Competition Tool, which we present in the next sections.

7.5.2 Recommendations for Markets Where Harm Has "Already Affected the Market"

We focus first on markets where, in the language of the EC Inception Impact Assessment (IIA), harm has already affected the market due to a "structural lack of competition."

Recommendation 1: We see a strong case for the introduction of a New Competition Tool to address factors like those covered by the United Kingdom's markets regime that prevent effective competition in markets. Having reviewed both the theory and practice of the UK markets regime, it is clear that there are sometimes factors that prevent markets from yielding competitive outcomes for consumers and that existing antitrust, regulatory, and consumer protection tools are too narrow in their scope to address all such factors. Antitrust enforcement under Articles 101 and 102 of the TFEU forbids anti-competitive agreements and the abuse of a dominant position, but many of the practices surveyed in Section 7.4 would not be addressable by these tools. For instance, this would be the case for tacit coordination due to high concentration and market transparency (Section 7.4.1), demand-side problems (Section 7.4.2), restrictive provisions in customer contracts (Section 7.4.4), and the bundling of complementary goods (Section 7.4.5). Furthermore, while some of these practices (e.g., restrictive contract terms) may in principle be monitored by consumer protection agencies, the objective of these agencies often fails to account for the impact of the practices on competition. A New Competition Tool would fill an important gap.

Recommendation 2: We see a strong case for a New Competition Tool with a broad scope within and across sectors ("Policy Option 3").

As summarized in Section 7.2, the EC is considering four policy options for an NCT that vary in their sectoral coverage ("limited"/ narrow vs. "horizontal"/wide) and the types of firms considered ("dominance-based"/narrow vs. "market structure-based"/wide). As discussed in Recommendation 1, one of the benefits of the New Competition Tool lies in its ability to address the conduct and practices of nondominant firms; hence, we see no benefit to limiting its applicability to dominant firms. Furthermore, as market features like those surveyed in Section 7.3 could in principle apply in any sector of the economy, we similarly see no benefit to limiting its applicability across sectors. The presence of sectoral regulators in specific industries does not make the New Competition Tool superfluous. In the United Kingdom, the CMA may investigate markets where there exist sectoral regulators (e.g., energy, banking); indeed, one reason to commence a market study or investigation is via referrals from sectoral regulators (who may not have capabilities comparable to those of a competition authority for evaluating and addressing competition issues within their sector).

Recommendation 3: We see a strong case for including a consumer protection mandate in the New Competition Tool. The CMA is both the competition and consumer protection authority in the United Kingdom and that naturally influences the scope and powers of their markets regime. We see a strong complementarity in the combination of competition and consumer protection mandates. A combined mandate allows market studies and investigations to focus not only on the economic structure of markets and the conduct of firms but whether aspects of consumer behavior (e.g., asymmetric information and/or "behavioral" issues like default bias) are preventing effective competition in a market. It furthermore allows remedies to target both consumer protection and competition problems that may be complementary and would not be effectively addressed with separate and uncoordinated responsibilities. We acknowledge that including such powers in an NCT must be coordinated with the EC's existing and proposed new consumer protection powers, as well as those of the Member States, a point we discuss further in Section 7.5.3.

The EC's Impact Assessment speaks generally about the challenges facing competition policy due to increased digitalization and specifically about how algorithm-based technological solutions may facilitate coordinated strategies between firms even in relatively unconcentrated markets. There is recent academic evidence suggesting that such "algorithmic (tacit) collusion" is possible and that its price effects can be consequential.[26] As such, it is important that competition authorities have tools to address the consequence of higher prices from such innovations if they were to arise. Given our understanding of existing EU competition law, we do not see how this would be possible with its current toolkit. As a natural extension of harms arising from tacit collusion more generally (see Section 7.4.1), however, it could be handled by a New Competition Tool along the lines we recommend here.

7.5.3 Recommendations for Markets Where Harm Is "About to Affect the Market"

For the EC's second category of potential harms, those representing "structural risks for competition" where harm "is about to affect" the market, we are on softer ground when it comes to making recommendations. In particular, this category falls outside the scope of the UK markets regime, where the focus is very much on harms in markets as constituted at the time of a market study/investigation. Furthermore, the market study of online platforms and digital advertising, surveyed in Section 7.4.7, is the only one we are aware of in which the market had features such as those highlighted as being of concern (network effects, extreme economies of scale, consumer lock-in, vertical integration, and conflicts of interest). Furthermore, this market study recommended a regulatory solution, not a market investigation with remedies like that anticipated by the NCT.

That being said, the possibility of harms in markets characterized by features that the EC has highlighted are real and there is precedent beyond the UK markets regime. In particular, there is long-standing experience within regulatory economics to foster competition in markets where structural features encourage extreme concentration (so-called natural monopoly markets), as well as practical experience implementing these ideas in communications markets (e.g., via

---

[26] Calvano/Calzolari/Denicolo/Pastorello, Artificial Intelligence, Algorithmic Pricing, and Collusion, (2020) *American Economic Review*, 110(10), 3267; Assad/Clark/Ershov/Xu, Algorithmic Pricing and Competition: Empirical Evidence from the German Retail Gasoline Market, (2020) CESifo Working Paper 8521 (pre-print on cesifo.org).

wholesale access regulation for telephone and broadband services).[27] Furthermore, the remedies suggested in the digital advertising market study, while meant to be passed to a digital platforms regulator, identify strategies well-suited in our view to applications in other settings where a market features winner-take-most characteristics.

As such, we agree with the Commission's concern about markets whose structural economic features foster concentrated outcomes in the long run and support the suitability of the NCT to address concerns in such markets. Where we are uncertain is whether a competition authority can credibly estimate *when* such markets may "tip"; furthermore, we feel that knowing this is inessential to the design of such a tool.

In forming our recommendations for markets whose economic fundamentals suggest possible future competition concerns, we adopt as an organizing principle the goal of ensuring that such markets are *contestable*, not only for existing competitors currently operating in the market but also for future competitors who could displace whoever is the winner, particularly if the economics of the existing market suggest that there will necessarily be a "winner-take-most" outcome in the long run.[28]

In fostering this goal of contestability, we focus on the merits of investigations, and potentially interventions, under the New Competition Tool that focus on two key principles of such markets: (1) facilitating customer choice and (2) preventing the entrenchment of market power. This leads to the following three recommendations.

Recommendation 4: We concur with the EC's impact assessment that there are economic characteristics of markets that foster concentration in the long run. These include (but need not be limited to) economies of scale and scope, network effects, strong consumer lock-in effects (and switching costs more generally), multi-sidedness, and binding non-negativity price constraints (i.e., "no prices below zero"). It is therefore important to identify markets with such characteristics and maintain a high level of awareness about their evolution. This

---

[27] See, e.g., Viscusi/Vernon/Harrington, *Economics of Regulation and Antitrust*, 2018, 5th ed., Chap. 14.

[28] The same point is made in the EC's expert report on shaping competition policy in the era of digitalization of Crémer/Montjoye/Schweitzer, Competition policy for the digital era, 2019, available at https://ec.europa.eu/competition/publications/reports/kd0419345enn.pdf.

awareness could be fostered by a reporting system allowing firms, customers, or suppliers in markets that are concerned about increased concentration to register these concerns with the EC.

Recommendation 5: For markets identified as having characteristics that may foster concentration in the long run, a lower threshold should be used for investigating whether the market is functioning well for consumers and suppliers and whether it is likely to continue to function well in the near future. These investigations should consider both *consumer conduct* and *firm conduct* in such markets, as well as in adjacent markets providing complementary services for the functioning of the market under consideration (including "ecosystems" if the set of such markets is large).

If the outcome of any such investigation indicates features that are impeding competitive outcomes, we offer two recommendations based on the competitive conditions in the market subject to factors that encourage long-run concentration. To fix ideas, let Market A indicate the market subject to factors that encourage long-run concentration and let Market(s) B indicate an "adjacent" market (or set of markets) (often) providing complementary services.[29]

Recommendation 6a: If the market subject to factors that encourage long-run concentration (Market A) has not yet achieved high levels of concentration and an investigation has found features that are impeding competitive outcomes, fostering competition "in the market" requires remedying limitations on multi-homing – on all sides of the market – and on customer and/or supplier switching behavior. Examples of such limitations include (but are not limited to) asymmetric information, a lack of transparency, and contractual, behavioral, or design factors that increase search and/or switching costs. Examples of remedies to these features of the affected market include (but are not limited to) "data portability" and various types of "interoperability" between the firms offering services in Market A.[30] It also requires

---

[29] In the balance of this section, we refer to Market B as a single market, but it should be understood that there could be multiple adjacent markets that provide services complementary to Market A and that all these markets should receive consideration in an investigation into the status of competition and outcomes in Market A.

[30] For example, see the remedies adopted in the Banking market investigation summarized in Section 7.4.2 and remedies proposed for the digital markets regulator in the Online platforms and digital advertising market study summarized in Section 7.5.2. Crémer/Montjoye/Schweitzer (fn. 25), at p. 14,

remedying "offensive" leveraging of firms with market power in an adjacent market (Market B) into the market exhibiting factors that encourage long-run concentration (Market A). Leveraging strategies from adjacent markets into Market A are likely to be particularly powerful when Market A is subject to factors that encourage long-run concentration, as short-run advantages provided by foreclosure strategies are likely to turn into long-run advantages due to the economic fundamentals of such markets (e.g., economies of scale, network effects, etc.). It may also make it harder to enter either market. Examples of strategies firms with market power in Market B can take to impact competition in Market A include (but are not limited to) exclusive access to inputs, customers, or suppliers, tying and/or bundling (possibly combined with, or facilitated by, acquisitions in market A), and/or product incompatibility involving Market A products, Market B products, or combinations of them. Examples of remedies to these features of the affected market include (but are not limited to) interoperability, unbundled access, and mandated offerings on fair and non-discriminatory terms and conditions.[31]

Recommendation 6b: If the market subject to factors that encourage long-run concentration (Market A) has already achieved these high levels of concentration and an investigation has found features that are impeding competitive outcomes, fostering competition "for the market" requires again remedying limitations by the dominant incumbent(s) on multi-homing and on customer / supplier switching; new entrants and challengers may instead be exempted from these remedies.[32] Fostering this competition "for the market" also requires remedying "defensive"

Chap. 4, discuss various types of interoperability that might be considered depending on the structure of the market and the findings of the market investigation.

[31] For example, see the interoperability remedies adopted in the Banking and Buses market investigation summarized in Sections 7.4.2 and 7.4.6, the limits on bundling adopted in the PPI market investigation summarized in Section 7.4.5 and recommended in the Digital advertising market study summarized in Section 7.4.7, and the FRAND terms adopted in the Aggregates and Buses market investigations summarized in Section 7.4.6.

[32] A similar asymmetric treatment can be found in regulatory regimes. For example, telecom regulators have allowed higher termination charges for new entrants. Lee (2013) shows that banning exclusivity and/or vertical integration in video game platforms would have increased both consumer surplus and sales but primarily for the incumbent; exclusivity permitted entrant platforms to better compete with incumbents. See Lee, Vertical integration and exclusivity in platform and two-sided markets, (2013) 103(7) *American Economic Review*, 2960.

leveraging of firms with market power in the concentrated market (Market A) into an adjacent market (often) providing complementary goods or services (Market B). Examples of strategies firms can take with respect to both of these factors are the same as in Recommendation 6a above, as are potential remedies to them. We note that competition for markets with factors that encourage long-run concentration (Market A) often come from adjacent layers of the supply chain in which Market A is a part and/or from complementary products that are combined with Market A's products. Furthermore, if a firm dominant in Market A is able to extend its dominance into complementary products, this can encourage a "domino effect" of its using dominance in both products to achieve dominance in further products. This is particularly a concern where a firm dominant in Market A offers an "ecosystem" consisting of a potentially large number of complementary products. As such, an NCT should particularly seek to prevent the leveraging of the market power of a firm or firms in Market A into these adjacent layers.

As is well-known, there is often a tension between encouraging competition "for the market," which calls for encouraging entry and may lead to grant a more favorable treatment to new entrants and challengers, and competition "in the market," which calls instead for a level-playing field. For this reason, the asymmetry should fade if/when the market becomes less concentrated.

Further Considerations
We acknowledge that empowering a competition authority with such tools gives it a quasi-regulatory role but think that this is appropriate. The EC's proposed regulation of digital markets, if implemented, will only cover "gatekeeper" digital platforms and may not pick up problems in markets that are either (1) still competitive even if subject to factors that foster concentration in the long run and/or (2) exhibit concentration in the present market configuration, but for which there could remain active competition *for* the market. We see regulation as being reserved for "natural monopoly" environments where there is high *and durable* market concentration.

Furthermore, we see an advantage of the NCT in that, if properly designed, it can seek to remedy competition issues in markets more quickly than a regulator could. This could be particularly important in markets subject to factors that encourage long-run concentration. To this end, we see a strong case for empowering the NCT with the ability to impose Interim Measures based on relatively low procedural hurdles.[33] While we recognize the costs this may place on affected firms, we perceive these costs to be significantly lower than those that may arise to disadvantaged firms and, ultimately, consumers if, in the absence of early intervention, the factors that favor concentration, partnered with consumer and/or firm conducts that merit investigation, indeed cause this concentration.

That being said, the NCT should have strict safeguards ensuring that it is applied in a competitively and technologically neutral way; competition authorities should avoid picking winners and losers in markets subject to these factors, especially including digital markets. Furthermore, the scope of the intervention should balance carefully the magnitude of the potential harm and the costs to firms of its imposition. For example, interventions that foster consumer switching are likely to be less invasive than are requirements for data standards, data sharing, and interoperability, which are in turn likely to be less invasive than requirements for unbundled access.

7.5.4 Procedural/Governance Issues

Our final recommendation focuses on governance issues of a New Competition Tool.

Recommendation 7: While we see a strong case for the New Competition Tool, its implementation requires a careful design of its governance structure to safeguard appropriate checks and balances. In particular, the following concerns need to be addressed:

– Firms want legal certainty, that is, they want to be able to predict what to expect from competition authorities. A tool such as the NCT, which by design is not restricted to address well-specified behavior (e.g., abuse of a dominant market position) but intended

---

[33] Note that the United Kingdom's markets regime only has the ability to impose interim measures *after* the conclusion of a market investigation but that the CMA (1) has recommended enhancing these powers to move earlier in the process (Letter from Andrew Tyrie to the Secretary of State for Business, Energy, and Industrial Strategy, 2019, available at https://www.gov.uk/government/publications/letter-from-andrew-tyrie-to-the-secretary-of-state-for-business-energy-and-industrial-strategy) and (2) has recommended in this proceeding that the EC adopt such a structure (CMA [fn. 4], at p. 1).

to address a broad range of issues, makes it more difficult for firms to know what to expect.

- A broad definition of the mandate of the NCT may give more role to the courts for its interpretation. Given the time court proceedings are known to take, this could introduce an unintended consequence of the tool. In order to limit these concerns, the mandate for the NCT could specify examples of the types of competition concerns that would call for a study or investigation, as well as examples of potential remedies that might be imposed to address those competition concerns. This would also help address firms' concerns about legal certainty. Any or all of the competition concerns surveyed in Sections 7.3 and 7.4 could be included.

- The governance structure of the NCT will have to specify on whose initiative the opening of a case is considered and who decides whether the case should go forward. In the United Kingdom, cases may begin at the suggestion of the United Kingdom's sector regulators or the CMA itself; similar initiation and referral powers should perhaps be given to EU and national competition and regulatory authorities.

- Procedures should also be specified allowing for learning across countries and time. For example, where markets are geographically distinct but share similar underlying characteristics, similar competition problems may be likely to arise across countries, albeit not as quickly in some as in others. Thus, evidence in one country (e.g., via reports of a national competition authority and/or national sector regulator) of competition problems that are likely to be shared elsewhere should serve as a normal referral channel for the initiation of a multi-country investigation. Similarly, if the market characteristics under consideration are those that encourage long-run concentration and this has already happened in one or more countries, investigations into those markets in countries where concentration has not yet arisen should naturally rely on potential evidence of harm from those where it has taken hold.

- Learning across countries and time may also arise in the application of remedies. For example, to the extent market characteristics that were found to cause harm to consumers or the competitive process in one or more countries at a given time are or become present in other countries at other times, then the procedures should (1) allow for demonstration that the market characteristics of concern are materially similar in these new countries and, if so, (2) allow for the adoption of remedies from the original investigation to the extent they can address the relevant concerns (as seems likely, but which would need to be motivated).

– We further encourage such procedures to allow for differences in the application of such remedies according to the market structures in the new countries. For example, if an investigation found that a market has already achieved high levels of concentration and imposed certain remedies upon *incumbents* in that market (as in Recommendation 6b above) but that the same characteristics in another country has not yet yielded high levels of concentration, then such remedies might instead be applied to *all firms* in the market of the new country (as in Recommendation 6a above), with similar analogies drawn according to the structure of the market(s) under consideration in the original investigation(s) relative to those for the same product or service in other countries. We also note that remedies should be country- and firm-specific; thus, a firm dominant in one (e.g., its home) market and subject to remedies there need not be subject to the same remedies in other (e.g., geographically adjacent) markets where it has not achieved a significant market position.

– In comments submitted in response to the proposed NCT, the CMA has also offered valuable suggestions about how to improve the design of its market studies and investigations regime, with implications for the design of an NCT.[34] In addition to the introduction of interim measures, already recommended above, these include ensuring strong information-gathering and enforcement powers supported by meaningful fines and penalties for non-compliance, allowing for "undertakings" (remedies) to address a subset of issues while referring remaining issues for an investigation, and having the ability to review, adjust, or change remedies where they have been found not to be effective and competition issues remain. These elements should also be included in the establishment of the NCT.

– The hybrid nature of the NCT, which potentially combines elements of competition enforcement, consumer protection, and regulation, may make it difficult for the authorities to decide and for firms to predict whether a potential case is dealt with by DG Comp in the

---

[34] See CMA (fn. 4), at p. 1, 22–23.

context of Art 101/102, by DG Connect in the context of regulation, or by DG Comp in the context of the NCT. Thus, clear rules need to be established about how such decisions are taken and by whom.

– Moreover, the guiding principles of the NCT need to be specified. Is the aim of the NCT to maximize consumer welfare, as is the case in antitrust, or are other principles to be considered as well?

– As part of a strong system of checks and balances, firms need to have access to a legal review of NCT decisions that addresses not just judicial considerations, as is the case for the UK markets regime, but also the factual foundations and economic merits of the case.

– Another issue is to select an appropriate statutory time limit for cases considered under the NCT. The United Kingdom allows a time period of 18 months for market studies, an additional 18 months for a follow-up market investigation, and six months (extendible to ten) for the implementation of remedies. The time period chosen by the EU for the New Competition Tool should account for the fact that an investigation in an EU-wide context may be more time demanding. At the same time, for a case in the fast-moving digital economy, the time period chosen should not be overly long.

8 Market Investigations for Digital Platforms

Panacea or Complement?[*]

AMELIA FLETCHER

8.1 Introduction

Over the past couple of years, there has been a fast-growing international consensus that standard competition law, while valuable, is inadequate for addressing the panoply of competition problems arising in digital platform markets. In 2019 alone, there were a wide array of policy reports published, across many different jurisdictions, all identifying concerns with existing powers in this area and the need for reform.[1] A number of jurisdictions are already introducing legislative changes to address these issues, with Germany amending its competition law to play a more regulatory role,[2] while Europe, the United

[*] This chapter is based on an earlier article published by the author in the Journal of European Competition Law & Practice, available at https://doi.org/10.1093/jeclap/lpaa078. The work was supported by the Economic and Social Research Council [grant number ES/P008976/1]. The author is a Non-Executive Board Member at the Competition Markets Authority, and was a member of the UK Government–commissioned Digital Competition Expert Panel which published *Unlocking Digital Competition* in March 2019. The author would like to thank Martin Cave, Steve Davies, Alexandre De Streel, Paul Dobson, Richard Feasey, Adam Land, Liza Lovdahl Gormson, Bruce Lyons, Philip Marsden and Massimo Motta for useful comments. However, all views expressed here are her own.
[1] The three most prominent reports are those from the EC: Crémer/Montjoye/Schweitzer, Competition Policy for the Digital Era, 2019, available at https://ec.europa.eu/competition/publications/reports/kd0419345enn.pdf; from the UK: Furman/Coyle/Fletcher/McAuley/Marsden, Unlocking Digital Competition, 2019, available at https://www.gov.uk/government/publications/unlocking-digital-competition-report-of-the-digital-competition-expert-panel; from the US: Scott Morton/Bouvier/Ezrachi/Jullien/Katz/Kimmelman/Melamed/Morgenstern, Committee for the Study of Digital Platforms, Market Structure and Antitrust Subcommittee, Stigler Center for the Study of the Economy and the State (2019), available at https://www.publicknowledge.org/wp-content/uploads/2019/09/Stigler-Committee-on-Digital-Platforms-Final-Report.pdf.
[2] Section 19a of new German Competition Act. See Franck/Peitz, Taming Big Tech: What Can We Expect From Germany's New Antitrust Tool, Promarket, 2021,

Kingdom, Australia and Japan are introducing forms of pro-competitive ex ante regulation.[3]

In its own quest to address these concerns, the European Commission was initially considering two distinct new legal powers: a 'New Competition Tool'[4] and an 'ex ante regulatory instrument for large online platforms'.[5] A menu of different variants of both were offered up for comment.

One of the most discussed variants of a 'New Competition Tool' (Option 3) appeared to be broadly modelled on the United Kingdom's market investigation power under the Enterprise Act 2002. This tool enables the UK Competition and Markets Authority (CMA) to carry out inquiries into markets and to impose remedies if it identifies that

---

available at https://promarket.org/2021/02/07/germany-antitrust-bundeskartellamt-19a-dma-big-tech/.

[3] Europe: European Commission, Proposal for a Regulation of the European Parliament and of The Council on Contestable and Fair Markets in the Digital Sector (Digital Markets Act), 2020, available at https://www.europarl.europa.eu/meetdocs/2014_2019/documents/envi/dv/mrv_/mrv_en.pdf; UK: Digital Markets Taskforce, A New Pro-Competition Regime for Digital Markets, 2020, available at https://assets.publishing.service.gov.uk/media/5fce7567e90e07562f98286c/Digital_Taskforce_-_Advice.pdf; Australia: Government Response and Implementation Roadmap for the Digital Platforms Inquiry, 2019, available at https://treasury.gov.au/publication/p2019–41708; and for Japan, an English language description of Government proposals can be found at White/Case, The Japan Cabinet proposed Direction of Bill for Digital Platform Transparency Act, 2020, available at https://www.whitecase.com/sites/default/files/2020-01/the-japan-cabinet-proposed-direction-of-bill-for-digital-platform-transparency-act.pdf.

[4] European Commission, Antitrust: Commission consults stakeholders on a possible new competition tool, Press release, 2020, available at https://ec.europa.eu/commission/presscorner/detail/en/ip_20_977.

[5] European Commission, (2020) Inception Impact Assessment. Digital Services Act package: Ex ante regulatory instrument for large online platforms with significant network effects acting as gate-keepers in the European Union's internal market, 2020, available at https://ec.europa.eu/info/law/better-regulation/have-your-say/initiatives/12418-Digital-Services-Act-package-ex-ante-regulatory-instrument-of-very-large-online-platforms-acting-as-gatekeepers. The most relevant option is Option 3: 'Adopt a new and flexible ex ante regulatory framework for large online platforms acting as gatekeepers.' This includes two sub-options: '3a. Prohibition or restriction of certain unfair trading practices by large online platforms acting as gatekeepers ("blacklisted" practices)' and '3b. Adoption of tailor-made remedies addressed to large online platforms acting as gatekeepers on a case-by-case basis where necessary and justified.'

there are 'features of a market' that create an 'adverse effect on competition'.[6]

In practice, the Commission has chosen to focus on introducing the ex ante regulatory tool.[7] While the current proposals for a new Digital Markets Act incorporate a form of market investigation, its scope is far more limited than that of the United Kingdom's market investigation powers. The new European variant is designed only to facilitate additions to regulatory scope over time and also to investigate (and impose remedies for) systematic non-compliance.

Was this a missed opportunity? What might the European Commission have expected to gain from the introduction of a market investigation tool in this context? Would it have been a valuable complement to the Commission's existing competition powers? Would it have been a panacea for digital competition concerns? Is there a more general argument for introducing this tool at the EU level beyond digital markets?

This chapter reflects on these questions, based on recent UK experience of market investigations. As discussed in Section 8.2, the tool has major positives and would be a valuable addition to the Commission's toolkit in addressing issues in digital markets.

However, as discussed in Section 8.3, the market investigation tool also has limitations. In particular, although it has huge flexibility in designing and implementing remedies, the process of monitoring, enforcing and revisiting these remedies over time has some important limitations.

The 2019 UK *Unlocking Digital Competition* report specifically considered the potential to address digital platform issues and concluded that it should not be viewed as providing a complete potential solution. Rather, there was a role for the ex ante regulation of digital markets, as a complement to market investigations. Section 8.4 considers the complementary nature of these tools in digital markets, taking interoperability as an example where they could valuably be used alongside each other.

In focusing on the UK situation, this chapter does not endeavour to consider the complexities of introducing a fully-fledged market investigation tool at the EC level. Nevertheless, certain aspects of the UK system may well be relevant to its effectiveness. The fact that the CMA

---

[6] See Whish, Chapter 5.   [7] European Commission, (fn. 3).

has both competition and consumer powers is valuable, since many market studies effectively address issues that would otherwise 'fall through the cracks' between these two areas of law. The United Kingdom's system of concurrency between the CMA and sector regulators is also important, at least for the monitoring and enforcement of market investigation remedies in these sectors.

The statutory requirements around governance within the UK process are also relevant, specifically the need for separation between the decision-makers who decide to commence a market investigation following an initial market study and those who reach findings at the end of a market investigation. Finally, the international context for intervention may of course be different at the EC level than for the CMA as a UK-focused authority.

8.2 Positives of the Market Investigation Tool

In the United Kingdom, market investigations are used as a complementary instrument alongside other competition powers, and this would also be the case at the European level. So what advantages does this tool have in this context? What can it do that existing EC competition law cannot? The remarks below consider some key benefits in relation to scope, remedies and procedure.

8.2.1 Scope

While standard competition powers and market investigations are both focused on improving competition, there are number of subtle but important differences between them in terms of scope.

8.2.1.1 A Proactive Role in Promoting Competition

Most competition law provisions are primarily focused on preventing competition from becoming worsened, for example, through mergers, collusion or abuse of dominance. A valuable contribution of market investigations is that they can play a more proactive role in promoting increased competition. So, for example, they can introduce market opening measures that are intended to shift the whole nature of competition. The Open Banking measures which arose from the UK *retail banking* market investigation are a good example, in that they were designed to open up the potential for disruptive and innovative competition from new technologies and business models.

8.2.1.2 A Broader and More Holistic Approach, Looking at Cross-Market Issues

Standard competition law is primarily focused on the conduct of firms, albeit this conduct is considered within its market context and thus wider market characteristics can play a role. By contrast, market investigations are designed more broadly to tackle any and all 'features' of markets which are found to adversely affect competition. While such features can include firm conduct, they can also comprise factors such as economies of scale and scope, network effects, regulatory and structural barriers, and consumer behavioural factors. Remedies are frequently targeted at addressing these other factors, as opposed to restricting anti-competitive conduct by firms.

Market investigations also allow for the investigation of a far wider set of competition concerns than the abuse of dominance and explicit collusion that are a core target of standard competition law. Indeed, neither dominance nor explicit collusion have been found to be concerns in the CMA's most recent market investigations.[8]

On the supply side, for example, they can examine subtle complexities in the nature of strategic interdependence between firms, including the potential for tacit coordination. Indeed, the ability to examine 'tight oligopolies' is a key benefit of the regime. The 2014 *aggregates, cement and ready-mix concrete* market investigation is a good example. The Competition Commission (the CMA's precursor) identified a combination of structural and conduct features that were leading to coordination and higher prices. These were addressed through clear structural measures (divestment and market transparency reduction), rather than via more direct, but arguably harder to police, behavioural requirements on firms to cease colluding. Market investigations can also consider the implications for firm incentives of factors such as vertical integration, principal-agent issues or regulatory barriers.

On the demand side, meanwhile, market investigations can consider firm conduct that might dampen or distort competition through

---

[8] These have examined *Energy* (final report, 2016), *Retail Banking* (2016), *Investment Consultants* (2018) and *Funerals* (2020). For a list of all CMA Markets work, including its market investigations, see: https://www.gov.uk/cma-cases?case_type%5B%5D=markets.

making consumer decision-making difficult. Examples might include failing to provide clear and comparable information, refusing to deal with price comparison website services, or including contractual terms that make switching costly or making the process of switching cumbersome. Firms can be required to make changes to their conduct in these areas. While such factors may seem to have more in common with consumer law than competition law, they are not typically covered by consumer law and can have very significant implications for competition, even in relatively non-concentrated markets.

Market investigations are especially well designed to carry out the holistic analysis of markets where problems are market-wide and there are a variety of interwoven factors – structural and behavioural – creating competition concerns. By contrast, in standard competition cases, authorities tend to be funnelled into focusing more narrowly on one issue and (in abuse cases) one firm.

Market investigations can also address markets which have become 'stuck' in bad equilibria, which are good for neither firms nor society, but where some form of intervention is required to make the shift to a better equilibrium. For example, it may not be in the interest of any individual energy company to make it easier for their own consumers to switch suppliers, even if the whole market would work more effectively and consumer trust would be increased if switching was generally easier.

8.2.1.3 No Role for Culpability or Intent

Even to the extent that firm conduct is relevant, the focus of market investigations is firmly on anti-competitive effects. It is not relevant for market investigations whether conduct is deliberately anti-competitive or whether firms are otherwise culpable for the harm. Indeed, even if the conduct in question creates efficiency benefits for consumers over the short term, and thus may well reflect a short-run pro-consumer focus on the part of firms, it could still be found to create an adverse effect on competition if there is likely to be a consequent loss of competition that would harm consumers over the medium to long term. By contrast, while the role of intent in abuse of dominance cases is somewhat ill-defined, it is typically considered hard to sanction a firm that can show it is acting in its own short-run interest, with no strategic anti-competitive intent or at least a finding of culpability.

8.2.1.4 No Need to Fit within Antitrust Precedent or Policy

The targeted market-specific nature of market investigation analysis
and remedies, and the lack of any need to show culpability, means that
only limited consideration is given to wider deterrence and precedence.
This could be seen as a negative, given the important role that wider
deterrence plays in competition law generally and in providing legal
certainty for firms. However, it does provide for more freedom to carry
out economic analysis without being unduly constrained by the policy
approaches and precedent from past cases.

For example, while the market investigation process does involve a
market definition exercise, this is not given the same weight as it is in
abuse of dominance cases. The focus is quite properly on the analysis
of competitive constraints. (This should of course also be the case in
competition law more widely but in practice is not.)

It also means that market investigations are better able than standard competition law to consider the wider context and, in particular,
the complex interplay between competition and other policy areas such
as privacy, consumer policy and fairness and environmental issues. The
CMA is especially alert to these links, given its dual role as a competition and consumer authority and the UK system of concurrency with
sector regulators.

8.2.1.5 Implications for Digital Markets

This ability to look at a panoply of interrelated issues across a market,
or markets,[9] without any need to demonstrate culpability, is likely to
be especially useful in digital platform markets. As was highlighted in
the 2019 UK *Unlocking Digital Competition* report: 'The challenges to
effective competition in digital markets do not come about solely
because of platforms' anti-competitive behaviour and acquisition
strategies.'[10]

In these markets, adverse effects on competition frequently arise
from a complex combination of firm conduct, consumer behaviour,
economic characteristics, technological factors and various aspects of
regulation. Promoting competition in this sector can therefore not be

---

[9] The scope of market investigation powers was extended to allow the
investigation of cross-market practices (as opposed to specific defined markets)
by the Enterprise and Regulatory Reform Act 2013. This wider scope has,
however, not yet been used.
[10] Furman/Coyle/Fletcher/McAuley/Marsden (fn. 1), at p. 8

purely about limiting anti-competitive conduct, important as that is. It will also require more proactive measures.

Moreover, while many of the issues in digital platform markets are associated with the strong market position of one particular firm, there may well be important cross-market issues, for example, around standards-setting or consumer choice architecture. The ability to consider carefully the synergies and tensions between interrelated policy objectives is likely to be important in digital markets, for example, given the importance of consumer data and thus the relevance of privacy policy.

The reduced reliance on formal market definition in market investigations may also be valuable in digital markets, given the complexities involved in a formal market definition process in this context. These largely arise from the wide spectrum of organisational types and relations we observe. We know that digital players can compete even where some have closed ecosystems, while others have open; even where some act only on one side of a market, while others are multi-sided; even where some are integrated into interface activities, while others are stand-alone.

These factors are important to examine carefully when assessing competition, but it is unhelpful to unduly constrain this analysis by forcing it into a narrow market definition exercise. Indeed, it could be argued that a weakness of competition law – and especially abuse of dominance provisions – is that the legal framework requires the boundaries of firms and markets to be defined in unrealistically black-and-white terms.

The proposed European Digital Markets Act addresses the need for proactive action that goes beyond standard competition law, including not requiring that firms be shown to have acted with anti-competitive intent. It also addresses the concerns raised around market definition in digital markets by referring to categories of services and avoiding conditioning designation on 'market power'.

However, while there are proposed market investigation powers within the Act, they are primarily designed to allow its scope to be extended to new services and obligations or to address systematic non-compliance. They do not provide for any powers to investigate and intervene in respect of cross-market issues.

This arguably leaves a gap. The Commission's Inception Impact Assessment for its then-proposed 'New Competition Tool' highlighted the potential to use the tool in relation to (i) markets displaying systemic failures going beyond the conduct of a particular company with market power or (ii) oligopolistic market structures with an increased risk for tacit collusion. Both of these objectives fit well with past experience of the market investigation regime.

The Commission's Impact Assessment also emphasised the potential use of the tool to intervene early to prevent markets from tipping, an issue of particular relevance in markets that exhibit strong network effects, such as digital platform markets. Such interventions may be difficult to make under standard competition law, given the absence of existing single firm dominance.

8.2.2 Remedies

The discussion above focused on comparing market investigations with standard competition law. However, the European Commission is of course already able to carry out Sector Inquiries, which have significant similarities with market investigations. So what incremental benefits do market investigations bring?

Traditionally, an important aspect of the UK market investigation regime was that it included powerful information-gathering powers, which could be used to 'shine a light' into markets in order to under-stand the barriers to competition that may exist. Since 2014, however, the CMA now has the same powers in respect to its market studies. Market studies can precede a market investigation, as a form of first stage review, but they can also be stand-alone reviews. As such, they are similar to the European Commission's own Sector Inquiries, albeit the Commission has the additional ability to carry out dawn raids, a power which is not available to the CMA for either market studies or market investigations. Like EC Sector inquiries, UK market studies can also be useful for generating recommendations for legislation, advo-cacy or enforcement.

As such, the primary additional benefits of market investigations – over both UK market studies and EC Sector Inquiries – derive from its formal remedy-making powers.

8.2.2.1 A Broad Remedy Toolkit

If an adverse effect on competition is identified, the CMA is required to achieve as comprehensive a solution as is reasonable and practicable.

The toolkit of potential market investigation remedies is extremely broad, so long as they are effective and proportionate to the identified concerns.[11] The main limitations are the requirement to target Orders at identified firms, which limits the potential to introduce non-firm-specific horizontal regulation,[12] and (to date at least) the need to respect EC modernisation and EC maximum harmonisation provisions.[13]

This breadth of opportunity could be viewed negatively, as allowing excessive scope for intervention. Indeed, the sorts of interventions imposed through market investigations can be similar to those more typically imposed in other jurisdictions though legislation but without any process of parliamentary review.[14] This reflects a wider UK focus on enabling competition-focused interventions, free of political consideration, but is also partly why there are tight checks and balances within the market investigation process.

However, the breadth of potential remedies also brings clear benefits. While standard competition law remedies tend to be narrow and backward-looking, market investigation remedies can be forward-looking and market-wide, with remedies frequently applying across the market, irrespective of individual firm market power. A package of remedies may be used to address different aspects of market failure. Supply-side measures may be utilised to reduce market power directly or to limit the potential for its exploitation, for example, through tacit collusion or exclusionary behaviour. Demand-side remedies are

---

[11] Remedies can be agreed with by firms through undertakings or imposed on firms through Orders. While the provisions that can be imposed through Orders are formally constrained by legislation, the wording is sufficiently broad to allow most options. (See UK Enterprise Act, 2002, Schedule 8). There is no constraint on what can be imposed through undertakings.

[12] Although note that market investigations can also lead to recommendations to Government to introduce such regulation.

[13] EC Modernisation provisions limit the ability of the CMA to impose remedies in relation to agreements which would be exempt from EC competition law, most relevantly vertical restraints which fall under the vertical restraints block exemption. EC maximum harmonisation provisions, such as within consumer protection or financial services regulations, may limit the ability of the CMA to impose more intrusive remedies than already required by law in some areas.

[14] Some market investigations have in fact been followed by domestic and/or EU legislation that supersedes the original remedies, and the CMA has an ongoing programme of reviewing and sometimes revoking old Orders, partly for this reason. See: https://www.gov.uk/cma-cases?case_type%5B%5D=review-of-orders-and-undertakings.

designed to enhance consumer engagement and decision-making through improved disclosure requirements and facilitating consumer search and switching or to protect consumers against unfair treatment.

Market investigation remedies can potentially also extend beyond a specific example of an issue that has been analysed, so long as this can be justified through the economic analysis. Again, this is potentially relevant to digital platforms. At the completion of the Google Shopping case, DG Competition was only able to impose a remedy relating to Google Shopping. It could not extrapolate from its findings and impose rules relating to analogous behaviour by Google in other vertical search markets such as job search, hotel search or local search. It is true that follow-on cases are easier to bring once an initial decision has been reached, but each case still needs to be assessed and proven individually. By contrast, a market investigation in this area might potentially have led to Orders which restricted Google from engaging in this sort of behaviour more generally, beyond the specific example of Google Shopping, so long as it could be shown that the same conclusions were likely to apply.

Table 8.1, setting out a non-exhaustive selection of market investigation remedies, provides a flavour of the range of different remedies that may be utilised in market investigations.

It is worth noting that where the Orders arising from market investigations are behavioural, they effectively constitute a form of ex ante regulation in that they govern future firms' behaviour. This is true for both supply-side remedies such a transparency reduction requirements and demand-side remedies such as disclosure requirements.

This ability to introduce small-scale ex ante regulation can be especially valuable in markets which require intervention in order to work more effectively but which are not covered by a sector regulator. It can also be a valuable complementary tool in regulated markets, where the issue in question is not within the scope of the regulation or where the regulator does not otherwise have the requisite powers to address it.

Finally, while interventions are typically designed to enhance competition, they can also be used to protect consumers from the harm arising from limited competition. For example, the CMA introduced a safeguard price cap for pre-payment energy customers following the market investigation into the energy market. These customers were found to be frequently vulnerable, relatively unlikely to switch provider and at risk of exploitation.

Table 8.1. *A selection of market investigation remedies, 2003–2016*

Regulatory remedies	Changes to regulatory framework	Airports, groceries, local buses, audit, energy
	Improved info for regulators	Airports
	Price regulation	Classified Directories, Energy (pre-payment customers)
Demand-side remedies	Disclosure requirements	Liquified Petroleum Gas (LPG), Home credit, Store Cards, Private Healthcare, Motor Insurance, Banking
	Measures to facilitate/ enhance search	Home credit, Payment Protection Insurance (PPI), Audit, Payday, Extended warranties, Banking
	Measures to improve consumer engagement or switching	LPG, Extended Warranties. Home Credit, Banking, Energy
	Fair terms for consumers	Home Credit, Extended Warranties, Store Cards, Banking
	Point-of-sale prohibition	PPI
	Data portability	Banking (Open Banking)
Supply-side remedies	Access to key inputs	Local buses
	Transparency reduction	Aggregates
	Unbundling	PPI, Store Cards, LPG
	Limits on restrictions in agreements	Groceries, Audit, Motor Insurance
	Limits on referral incentives	Private Healthcare
Structural remedies	Divestment	Airports, Aggregates
	Market share/expansion limits	Classified Directories, Groceries
	Market redesign	Energy (settlement market)

8.2.2.2 Structural Remedies: A Brief Comment

As is clear in Table 8.1, the UK market investigation regime also allows for structural remedies to market problems. This power is much touted, but it is utilised rarely in practice. It can be difficult to demonstrate that such an interventionist remedy is required, as the CMA found to its cost in 2016 when it was forced to abandon its attempts to require hospital divestments, following an appeal and remittal in relation to its private healthcare market investigation.

Divestment is arguably most likely to be required in situations where firms have effectively found to be single-firm dominant (albeit that terminology is not used), such that it might have been feasible to extract similar remedies under existing EC competition law. However, it can be applied where a lack of competition is harming consumers, even if there is no clear abuse. An example might be the divestiture of London and Scottish airports which resulted from the *BAA airports* market investigation. Here, the concerns related to weak investment and poor user-responsiveness, resulting from very high market shares and barriers to entry alongside inadequacies in the regulatory system. It is far from clear whether this would constitute abuse under Article 102.

That said, structural remedies can potentially be imposed in a wider set of circumstances, following a market investigation, if existing market structure is found to be contributing to an adverse effect on competition. The 2014 report requiring structural remedies in the UK aggregates sector was based on a careful economic analysis of the complex vertical oligopoly situation in the United Kingdom. It is not obvious that single-firm dominance would have been found.

However, it is important that the existence of market investigations is not viewed as a rationale for weakening (or even not strengthening) the merger regime. While it is theoretically true that a market investigation could be used to unwind an anti-competitive merger, this would be bad public policy given the high costs involved in 'unscrambling' mergers post-integration. In a different but analogous context, this is shown by the difficulties experienced in trying to address breaches of state aid law in the UK banking sector through structural remedies.

8.2.2.3 Implications for Digital Markets
There are limitations to the use of market investigations in a digital context, as will be discussed further below in this section. As such, the 2019 *Unlocking Digital Competition* report argued for the introduction of pro-competitive digital platform regulation rather than relying purely on the market investigation tool. The alternative – addressing concerns through a series of market investigations – would lead to a series of behavioural remedies that would require ongoing monitoring

and thus effectively turn the CMA into a mini-regulator by default anyway, but with the risk that such regulation would take a somewhat piecemeal and imperfect form.[15]

However, even with the introduction of pro-competitive digital platform regulation in the United Kingdom, it remains likely that market investigations will still have an important role to play in digital markets.

In the United Kingdom – as in Europe – it is proposed that the regulation should be limited to designated platforms, which will typically be the few largest online ecosystem firms. Market investigations open up the possibility of intervening, on a well-evidenced and proportionate basis, in relation to a wider set of firms or even across markets.

This can be important. For example, data portability provisions may well be so valuable for facilitating competition and innovation that they are justified even in markets where there are several firms active. An example would be the CMA's Open Banking remedy, which was imposed on the nine largest UK banks, in a context where the CMA identified the presence of factors limiting competition and innovation but made no finding of single firm market power.

Market investigations also allow for a breadth of potential remedy types and ability to develop a package of remedies, which are likely to be valuable given the complex set of drivers underpinning the issues arising in many digital markets.

In this context, it is worth noting two important differences between the regulatory proposals in the United Kingdom and Europe. First, the United Kingdom's Code of Conduct will be bespoke for each designated platform. Second, the UK regulator would separately have the power to impose Pro-competitive Interventions. This latter tool is essentially intended to function as a short and highly targeted market investigation, albeit with remedy-making powers only available in relation to designated platforms.

Each of these elements provide the UK Regulator with significant flexibility to design and implement packages of interventions that are well targeted at the problems identified. As the UK Digital Markets

---

[15] There are also funding implications. In the United Kingdom, sector regulators are typically funded by industry participants, so a specialist digital regulator would likely be funded by levies on designated firms. By contrast, the CMA is funded by UK taxpayers, with no powers to levy firms to fund its work in monitoring and enforcing remedies.

Taskforce Report sets out, these pro-competitive interventions could include data-related interventions, interoperability and common standards requirements, consumer choice and defaults interventions, obligations to provide access and separation remedies.[16]

By contrast, the EU proposals comprise a set of prohibitions and obligations, albeit with the potential for further specification of some of these, and the potential for additions to the set of obligations over time. As a result, the Digital Markets Act is seeking to achieve similar sorts of interventions but in a rather more prescriptive form and with a very tight timetable provided for any further 'specification'. In doing so, there is a serious risk that the provisions are either ineffective or have unintended consequences.

An example is the requirement that designated platforms provide effective data portability for end users.[17] Data portability has the potential to be highly pro-competitive, but this framing of the requirement carries several risks:

- *The data portability obligation could be ineffective*: The obligation rightly requires that such data portability be continuous and real-time, since this is likely to be required for many potential innovative use cases associated with data portability. However, many such use cases also require that the data is provided in an agreed format, through open and stable APIs, such that it is accessible by third parties, without having to be downloaded and re-uploaded by end users. Without this, the provision may well be ineffective.

- *The data portability obligation could create consumer detriment*: At the same time, without a clear system for checking that active consumer consent has been provided (and continues to be provided) for the data to be ported, and without any form of accreditation for third party 'porters' of the data, there are risks to consumers arising from the potential for data portability. It is also unclear where liability for any resulting consumer harm would lie or how redress might be sought.

- *The data portability obligation could be unduly costly*: There are all sorts of ways that data portability could be provided, since data can be sliced and diced in many different ways. For data portability to be truly effective, it is important to consider what sorts of data are

[16] Digital Markets Taskforce (fn. 3), at p. 43.
[17] European Commission (fn. 3), at Article 6(1)(h).

likely to be useful for third parties and in what format. If firms are required to provide data portability in every possible format, it is likely that the vast majority of these will never be utilised, and this may thus involve unnecessary cost. It could also unduly constrain the platform from changing the way in which it collects data over time.

It remains to be seen how the Digital Markets Act will address these sorts of issues, but it would seem that they are more easily addressed by the UK proposals, given their greater potential for evidence-based flexibility and the continuing availability of full market investigations.

The demand side is also very important in digital markets. As such, there may also be potential for remedies that improve consumer decision-making. For example, in its recent market study into *Online Platforms and Digital Advertising*, the CMA identified a number of possible remedies designed to give consumers greater control over their own data, including requiring the major platforms funded by digital advertising to be more transparent with consumers about the data they are providing, requiring that consumers are given a real choice (not simply 'take or leave it') and to ensure that the associated choice architecture really acts to facilitate informed choice.[18] One could also envisage more general remedies limiting the unfair use of choice architecture on platforms or the unfair design of algorithms.

In principle, such demand-side requirements could be included within the obligations imposed on designated platforms. Indeed, the proposed Digital Markets Act already imposes a prohibition on designated platforms favouring their own products and services within their own ranking services.

However, demand-side issues in these markets run wider than ranking services and also wider than the very largest digital ecosystem providers. To some extent, they may be captured by general consumer law, but there may well be a need for special provisions for digital platforms, at least if consumer choice is ever to play a significant role in driving competition in digital markets. Market investigations could play a key role in the design and implementation of such interventions.

---

[18] Competition and Markets Authority, Online Platforms and Digital Advertising: Market Study Final Report, 2020, available at https://www.gov.uk/cma-cases/online-platforms-and-digital-advertising-market-study.

8.2.3 Procedure

8.2.3.1 Two-Stage Process with Separate Decision-Making

The independence and robustness of market investigations is bolstered by the associated governance. There is a clear split of decision-making between the decision to refer a market for investigation, which is taken by the CMA Board, and the final market investigation decision, which are made by a Group of independent decision-makers, drawn from the CMA Panel. CMA Panel members are all highly experienced, non-political and bring a diversity of expertise and viewpoints. They are not CMA staff. The Group members for each market investigation are named publicly.

Market investigations effectively constitute the second phase of a two-stage process. The first stage, which takes the form of a twelve-month market study, carries out initial market analysis and considers whether a market investigation 'reference' is warranted.[19] Prior to the creation of the CMA, the two phases occurred in two separate bodies; the market study and referral decision were taken by the Office of Fair Trading and the investigation was carried out by the Competition Commission. To limit the risk of confirmation bias within the CMA, post-merger, rules require that there is no overlap of people between the Board members who take the reference decision and the Group members making the final market investigation decision.

As well as limiting confirmation bias, this two-stage process is also valuable for avoiding the market investigation process becoming a depository for unpopular political issues that no one else wants to tackle. These will typically be considered through a market study instead. This affords the CMA the same investigatory powers as a market investigation but none of the formal remedial powers.

The two-stage process can also be utilised to extract formal undertakings from parties at the end of a market study in lieu of a market investigation Reference. For example, the UK telecoms regulator has utilised this process to extract undertakings from telecoms infrastructure provider, Openreach. Like the European Commission's own Sector Inquiries, market studies can also lead to recommendations to

[19] Market investigations are sometimes known as MIRs (or Market Investigation References) for this reason.

Government or sector regulators, advocacy, guidance or enforcement action, without any market investigation reference being made.

8.2.3.2 Transparency

An important positive of market investigations is that the overall procedure is very transparent. During the process, the CMA will publish an initial issues statement, working papers and an annotated issues statement, provisional findings and possible remedies notice (if relevant), a provisional decision on remedies (if relevant) and a final report. Any interested party can comment on the intermediate documents. While confidential information will be redacted, sufficient information will typically be made public to allow effective consideration of the issues. Responses from parties are typically also published. There are hearings with parties at key stages, attended by the full decision-making Group.

8.2.3.3 A More Participative Approach

This level of transparency is substantially greater than that in standard competition law and allows for a robust and participative approach. Indeed, while market investigations clearly need to be well-evidenced and robust and issues are hard-fought, the engagement between the CMA and parties nevertheless tends to be more open, less adversarial and less legalistic in market investigations than in standard competition law cases relating to abuse of dominance or anti-competitive agreements.

As well as transparency, this less adversarial approach may reflect the economic focus of the analysis, the very limited role played by legal precedent and also the fact that market investigations can end up anywhere – including a finding of no adverse effect on competition – so parties have much to gain from engaging openly with the process. Remedies can even turn out to be unexpectedly positive for firms. The early (1993) requirement on British Gas to divest its distribution business is a case in point. The combined valuation of the two separate companies quickly exceeded that of the original vertically integrated incumbent. Moreover, good remedies can make the market work better, and firms will understand this even if they don't necessarily like it.

Market investigations also seem to be less subject to appeal than standard competition law cases. This difference of approach may partly reflect the different appeal standard in the United Kingdom; market investigation findings can be appealed on a Judicial Review (JR) basis only, while Competition Act 1998 cases receive a Full Merits review. In the context of such a JR, the high levels of transparency and other procedural safeguards could also play a role. Certainly, appellants have rarely been successful in challenging market investigation decisions; and from the authority's successes, it is clear that the CMA has a wide margin of appreciation with its diagnosis of problems and judgement as to which remedies are effective and proportionate.

Another relevant factor is that there are no fines and thus no quantum of penalty to be challenged on appeal. Perhaps less positively, an alternative explanation for the low number of appeals is that, with several companies involved, each one faces a free-rider problem in choosing whether to appeal; the appeal costs fall to the individual firm while the benefits of any appeal success would typically go to all.

8.3 Limitations of the Market Investigation tool

The above discussion, while focused on the UK experience, clearly suggests that a market investigation regime could also have merit at the EU level. However, it is also important to highlight some important limitations of the tool, not least because these might be useful when determining its precise design.

8.3.1 Timetables and Remedy Testing

Market investigations must be completed within eighteen months, albeit with the potential for extension by another six months. The final report, at the end of this period, must include not only the substantive findings but also any remedies to be imposed, together with the underlying evidence for both.

There are some positives from a tight timeline. It helps to engage minds; early intervention can reduce the extent of consumer detriment; and it can be especially important to intervene quickly if competition concerns are worsening over time, for example, because a market is quickly – but avoidably – tipping towards monopoly. It has also proven to be possible to complete a reasonably robust analysis of the substantive market issues within this time frame, greatly aided by the initial market analysis that is carried out at the market study phase of the process which can take up to a year and occurs prior to reference.

What has proven harder is to carry out effective remedy design on such a tight timetable. In the past, this issue was exacerbated by a policy approach which determined that remedies should not be considered until adverse findings had been identified. While such an approach might appear reasonable, it is simply impracticable. Remedy design is complex, and it is easy to get it wrong. As such, potential remedies are now considered from the start of the process and sometimes even (informally) before the formal market investigation launch.

While this is a positive change, the available time is still frequently insufficient for designing complex remedies or properly piloting remedies, for example, through the use of randomised controlled trials. That said, creative solutions may be available. For the consumer engagement remedies arising in the recent energy and banking market investigations, the final remedy design, testing and implementation was left to the relevant sector regulators, who could take the required time to do this properly. The CMA imposed on the parties a requirement to engage with such trials. Likewise, due to the complexity and likely time and resources involved in its Open Banking remedy, the CMA required that a new entity be set up and tasked with the detailed design and implementation of the remedy.

8.3.2 Limited Flexibility to Revisit Remedies

A more serious problem with the market investigation regime is that remedies cannot be revisited, if they are found to be imperfectly designed or ineffective, once they have been formally imposed. There is only a provision for parties to request that remedies be altered or removed if they can demonstrate that there has been a 'material change in circumstances' since they were imposed.

In considering the impact of this inability to alter a remedy package, it is interesting to note the parallel experience of market studies carried out by the UK Financial Conduct Authority. These can also give rise to remedies, but because this is done through changes to regulatory rules, there is flexibility to use trial remedies and revisit them. In some cases, the FCA has completely abandoned specific remedy proposals, following testing, and the remedy package has been (or is being) substantially revised to make it more effective.

Such flexibility is arguably in the interest of both firms and consumers; no one gains from costly, ineffective regulation. The CMA recently highlighted that there may be value in a change in its powers which would enable it, within a fixed period of time, to revisit its remedy package while continuing to rely on its substantive findings on competition.[20]

The inability to flex remedies may be especially problematic in dynamic markets which are subject to significant change. In such markets, the identified concerns may be fairly persistent (although this is not a given), but the appropriate remedies may well require flexing as the markets and technologies change.

8.3.3 *Limitations to Remedy Enforcement*

Since the majority of market investigation remedies are behavioural and quasi-regulatory, there needs to be some process for monitoring and enforcing them. In markets which are overseen by sector regulators, this task can potentially be passed to them, to be carried out alongside other monitoring and enforcement activity.

In other markets, the CMA has an experienced and expert remedy monitoring team to manage this process. The ability to impose reporting requirements as part of a remedy can be valuable for facilitating this process and maximising the impact of the CMA resources involved. In a number of instances, the CMA has also used a third-party implementation or monitoring body, funded by the companies involved. For example, the Open Banking Implementation Entity was funded by the nine major UK banks and was able to draw in technical expertise on standard-setting and implementation of APIs.

However, the resources and expertise required to carry out quasi-regulatory remedies monitoring in a complex environment should not be understated. In a digital context, with the potential for market interventions relating to highly complex areas such as interoperability, standard-setting and algorithmic design, the required monitoring could quickly start to look more like that carried out by the telecoms and financial regulators, rather than that typically done within the CMA's remedies team. This was another reason why the *Unlocking Digital Competition* report took the view that market investigations, while potentially useful, required an ex ante regulator.

[20] See Lord Andrew Tyrie (then CMA Chair): Letter to then Secretary of State Greg Clark, 21 February 2019, fn. 27, available at https://assets.publishing.service .gov.uk/government/uploads/system/uploads/attachment_data/file/781151/ Letter_from_Andrew_Tyrie_to_the_Secretary_of_State_BEIS.pdf.

A further limitation of the CMA's enforcement powers is that it has no direct ability to impose sanctions for breach. It can only go to court to obtain a court order, breach of which could then be penalised. Even then the penalties are typically low. This is unlikely to provide an effective enforcement mechanism for breaches, especially for large firms such as the major digital platforms. The (then) Chair of the CMA has recommended to Government that this situation be changed.[21]

A final challenge arises where parties' assets are located outside the United Kingdom or integrated into other parts of their global business. While the CMA can always impose Orders where they are relevant to the UK market, the monitoring and enforcement of compliance in such circumstances may be complex and entail legal proceedings in another jurisdiction. This may well be a relevant issue in digital markets, especially if different authorities take conflicting approaches to the same issues, creating a clear need for discussion and collaboration with international counterparties. In this regard, activity at the European level – through a new competition tool – may prove rather easier than national-level interventions.

8.3.4 Unduly High Public Expectations

A final negative of market investigation is arguably more political than substantive. It is the corollary of one of the major positives: the ability to impose very significant remedies. Unless expectations are very carefully managed, this can lead to the build-up of unduly high expectations around market investigations, which can in turn generate intense dissatisfaction with the CMA's performance when it concludes that only moderate remedies are justified. The CMA faced substantial criticism of this sort in 2016 at the conclusion of two major market investigations into retail banking and energy.

There can also be a need to manage expectations about the likely speed and scale of impact for market investigation remedies. In some markets, while remedies can reduce the extent of competition problems, they may not be able to overcome them entirely. Meanwhile, some remedies – indeed, often the better remedies such as Open Banking – can take some time to be effective.

---

[21] Ibid.

8.3.5 *Implications for Digital Markets*

The limitations outlined above led the *Unlocking Digital Competition* report to conclude that market investigations, while potentially useful in digital markets and more widely, were unlikely to provide a complete solution in digital platform markets. Especially important to the authors in reaching this conclusion were concerns relating to flexibility of remedy design, the resources likely to be taken up in monitoring remedies, limited enforcement powers and complexities associated with the global nature of the major digital tech companies and their assets

8.4 Digital: A Complementary Role for Market Investigations and Ex Ante Regulation

Recognising the limitations of market investigations, the UK *Unlocking Digital Competition* report proposed ex ante regulation for the major digital platforms to act alongside the market investigation regime. The CMA has since taken a similar stance. At the conclusion of its market study in *Online Platforms and Digital Advertising*, the CMA decided not to commence a formal market investigation.[22] It did so on the basis that the UK Government was planning to introduce ex ante regulation in this area and that it would be preferable to intervene via that route so far as possible. The UK Digital Markets Taskforce, led by the CMA, has since published more detailed advice to the UK Government, and the process of developing legislation is underway, while the CMA has been given funding to set up a Digital Markets Unit, from April 2021.[23]

It is therefore to be welcomed that the European Commission is also proposing ex ante regulation for the largest digital gatekeeper platforms, through the Digital Markets Act. But this leaves a residual question. Would there have been merit in the EU also introducing its 'New Competition Tool' as a complement to such ex ante regulation? What is it potentially missing in not doing so?

8.4.1 *Market Investigations in the Context of Regulation*

The Digital Markets Act proposals take the form of series of obligations and prohibitions for the largest online digital gatekeepers.

[22] Competition and Markets Authority (fn. 18).
[23] Digital Markets Taskforce (fn. 3).

There is potential within the Act for some (but not all) of these obligations and prohibitions to be further specified for each particular firm, given its specific circumstances. There is also the potential to utilise market investigations (as defined within the Act) to designate firms, add core services and obligations, and also to impose remedies (including structural remedies) to address systematic non-compliance.

However, there are at least three substantive areas where there is a potential gap in the Commission's proposals for ex ante regulation, and which could the New Competition Tool could usefully have filled.

The first gap relates to the power to impose structural remedies to address inherent conflicts of interest.

The proposed Digital Markets Act proposes that structural remedies should be an option to address non-compliance. While this is helpful, it is not obvious that non-compliance is the only situation in which structural remedies are justified. While structural remedies are imposed only rarely in market investigations, they are most usually considered where there is an inherent and serious conflict of interest. Such conflicts of interest may well be a problem even if there are no specific behavioural obligations that are being broken.

In this context, it is noteworthy that the CMA's market study into *Online Platforms and Digital Advertising* identified a serious conflict of interest associated with Google's strong position at various levels in the advertising intermediation value chain, including both on the buy-side and the sell-side of the market. To address such issues, the UK Digital Markets Taskforce has recommended that the UK Digital Markets Unit should have powers to impose operational or functional separation. While it stopped short of recommending regulatory powers to impose full ownership separation, it noted the potential to achieve this in the United Kingdom through the existing market investigations regime.

The proposed Digital Markets Act includes two main obligations to address the advertising intermediation value chain, but both relate to transparency.[24] While these are helpful, perfect compliance by Google with these obligations would nonetheless not address the inherent conflict of interest identified by the CMA.

---

[24] Proposed Digital Markets Act, European Commission (fn. 3), at Articles 5(g) and 6(1)(g).

The second gap relates to the possibility that a digital platform market is at significant risk of tipping and so creating market power for a particular firm, but has not yet done so, such that the firm does not currently meet the criteria for ex ante regulation. The proposed Digital Markets Act does provide for such a possibility by including within its potential designation criteria any firm for which 'it is foreseeable that it will enjoy such a position (i.e., an entrenched an durable market position) in the near future'.[25] However, where a firm is designated on this basis, only a subset of the obligations within the regulation will apply.[26]

Again, while useful, it is not obvious how often firms will in practice be delegated on this 'near future' basis, nor is it clear that the obligations which would most ideally be required of such a firm likely be those which are identified as potentially applicable within the proposed Digital Markets Act as it stands. In the United Kingdom, by comparison, a market investigation could be used to identify the specific factors underpinning the risk of market tipping and interventions developed which are designed to address these in a bespoke and proportionate way.

The third gap relates to the need for market-wide interventions to promote competition. It is possible in principle to impose certain ex ante regulation symmetrically to all market participants, as indeed occurs under the EU Regulatory Framework for communications. However, the ex ante regulation instrument that is currently proposed for digital gatekeepers allows requirements to be placed only on the largest digital platforms. Where interventions would be best applied to all firms across a market, a market investigation tool could have a valuable role.

Market-wide interventions can be important even where there is a single firm with a dominant position. Consider the simple example of telephone number portability. This is now a standard element of telecommunications regulation, but it was first imposed in the United Kingdom in 1995, following a market investigation–like review. Making this a market-wide requirement, rather than simply imposing it on the incumbent supplier British Telecom, was important for giving consumers confidence that they could keep their phone number not only if they switched away from the incumbent but also if they later switched back.

[25] Ibid., at Article 3(1)(c).   [26] Ibid., at Article 15(4).

This was a situation where a market-wide intervention was required in order to open up competition to a strong incumbent supplier. However, as the discussion above highlights, market-wide interventions can also be valuable for enhancing competition when there are multiple players in a market. Indeed, number portability is itself today required in mobile telephone markets, where there are typically multiple players. It is important for facilitating the switching required for effective competition and it has been shown to have a substantial impact in reducing prices.[27] The majority of the market investigation interventions in Table 8.1 were applied to multiple firms across the market and were designed to enhance competition generally, rather than specifically to open up monopolised markets.

Market-wide interventions can also be valuable in preventing markets from tipping. Again, the telecommunications sector offers a useful example, with the rules around interconnection being valuable in ensuring a level playing field for competition that overcomes the tendency towards concentration that would otherwise exist. Consider an alternative world in which there were no ability to interconnect across mobile telephone networks. In that world, the natural consumer desire to access as wide a network of contacts as possible would likely result in the market tipping to monopoly.

While the United Kingdom is in a position to introduce such market-wide interventions through its market investigations regime, this option would appear now to be closed to the European Commission, unless carried out through separate legislation (outside the aegis of the proposed Digital Markets Act).

8.4.2 Thought Experiment: The Case of Interoperability

In the United Kingdom, the proposed Digital Markets Unit will be able to impose both a Code of Conduct and bespoke Pro-competitive Interventions on designated platforms. In addition, the CMA remains in a position to utilise its wider market investigation powers.

This raises some interesting questions: Why does the United Kingdom need so many types of instruments? Are these really complementary, not substitutes? If so, which sorts of intervention might we expect to see arising under each?

[27] Park, The economic impact of wireless number portability, (2011) 59 Journal of Industrial Economics, 714. doi:10.1111/j.1467-6451.2011.00471.x.

This section addresses this question through a thought experiment on the thorny issue of interoperability. Like number (and also data) portability, interoperability can be valuable both in opening up a monopolised market to competition and also in facilitating effective competition within a non-monopolised market. In the former case, it may potentially be sufficient to impose interoperability only on the monopoly firm; but in either case, it may also be valuable to impose it more widely.

Interoperability can also work to prevent currently non-monopolised digital markets from 'tipping' to monopoly, for much the same reasons as interconnectivity in telecoms. This has an important implication: it may be valuable to impose interoperability at an early stage in the development of a market.[28] A current example might be the market for self-driving cars, where such a requirement may be important for generating effective competition and indeed maximising safety.

Given these competition benefits of interoperability, there have been many demands that the digital platforms should make their systems interoperable. But what does this really mean? It presumably cannot mean that every element of their systems is made fully interoperable; this would not necessarily be justified by the competition concerns, even if made sense as a concept.

One could, however, imagine the following three-pronged regulatory approach being taken to interoperability in the United Kingdom:

(1) Under the Code of Conduct: Blacklisted practices for designated major platforms such as:
   – where a designated digital platform has previously provided interoperability to a third party, later withholding, withdrawing or deprecating this, where doing so would have an adverse effect on platform users;
   – where a designated digital platform offers interoperability to one or more third parties, failing to offer the same functionality to all other third parties or doing so on a discriminatory basis; or
   – where the core technologies of a designated digital platform interoperate with its own ancillary services, failing to offer the same functionality with their party providers of ancillary services.

---

[28] Absent interoperability, multi-homing by users can have a similar effect, and it can equally be important to protect or promote that.

(2) Under Pro-Competitive Interventions: Specific requirements on designated platforms to provide interoperability in relation to particular areas, designed to open up competition. An example might be a requirement on a designated social media platform to enable cross-posting, as proposed by the CMA in its *Online Platforms and Digital Advertising* market study.[29]

(3) Under market investigations: Requirements for cross-market interoperability, which apply to all market participants, not just designated digital platforms. This may also require cross-industry coordination on standards and protocols, a process which can itself raise competition concerns and which may benefit from careful oversight.

In theory, all of these interventions could be achieved through market investigations. However, the issues of flexibility and monitoring described above mean that the design and enforcement of the first and second are likely to be better suited to the application of an ex ante regulatory framework.

By contrast, the EU Proposals would be constrained to addressed both the first and second categories through its core obligations, while the third would be impossible absent separate legislation. A key question to ask is then: Does this matter? If we think it does, then we can conclude that the EU is missing out by not introducing wider market investigation powers.

8.5 A Final Word

In 2002, the United Kingdom sent a delegation[30] to DG Competition to present and promote the UK market investigation regime. They failed to convince their hosts of the advantage of this tool relative to standard competition law, not least because the UK powers were themselves relatively untested at this time.

In the intervening 19 years, we have learned a lot. The potential of market investigations has been more thoroughly tested, while the limitations of standard competition law, and especially abuse of dominance provisions, have become more apparent. As has been discussed

---

[29] Competition and Markets Authority (fn. 18).
[30] The delegation included the author in her then role as Chief Economist at the Office of Fair Trading.

above, market investigations have the potential to be hugely valuable, both in the digital sphere and more widely.

Of course, there are lessons to be drawn from the UK experience of market investigations for the implementation of such a regime at the EU level. For example, because the tool is potentially so powerful and flexible, it merits strong procedural checks and balances to guard against confirmation bias or politicisation. At the same time, there is significant room for improvement within the current UK regime in relation to the powers around remedy flexibility and enforcement.

There are also some inherent limitations within the market investigation tool which mean that it would not have provided the ideal complete solution to the issues raised by digital platforms. Nonetheless, in the United Kingdom, it remains a valuable complementary tool to be utilised alongside new ex ante regulation.

It is a pity that Europe has not chosen to take this potential tool further at this time.[31] The UK experience suggests that there would be merit in Europe revisiting this decision in the future – outside the specific context and urgency of digital regulation.

---

[31] This echoes Motta/Peitz, Chapter 2, and Crawford/Rey/Schnitzer, Chapter 7.

Index